MILLER'S
Collectors

PRICE GUIDE

ⱻBROOKS

WORLD LEADERS
IN THE SALE OF
COLLECTORS CARS
AND AUTOMOBILIA

BROOKS CELEBRATED SALES HAVE INCLUDED THE MODENA COLLECTION,
THE AUTOCAR ARCHIVES, THE COLLECTIONS *of* THE LATE PETER HAMPTON
and MILLFORD FARM, THE SOCIAL HISTORY COLLECTION, THE COLLECTION
of the late ANTHONY MAYMAN, THE HISTORY *of* JAGUAR MUSEUM, THE PATRICK
COLLECTION, THE ALBERT OBRIST COLLECTION *of* RACING CAR SPARES
and THE GRIFFITHS/WOODLEY COLLECTION.

—

Brooks offers you the services of a formidable but wholly approachable team of specialists whether buying
or selling historic collectors cars, motorcycles or automobilia. We also offer a valuation service
for insurance, probate and family division.

—

To discuss any of Brooks services please call Malcolm Barber, Stewart Skilbeck,
James Knight or Peter Card (Automobilia) on 0171 228 8000
or Michael Worthington-Williams on 01559 370928.

81 WESTSIDE, LONDON, SW4 9AY

TEL: 0171 228 8000. FAX: 0171 585 0830

ⱻBROOKS
SPECIALIST AUCTIONEERS AND VALUERS

MILLER'S
Collectors
Cars
PRICE GUIDE

1997-98

Volume VI

Consultant: Judith Miller

General Editor: Robert Murfin

Foreword by John Surtees

Flux Insurance Department, Adrian S
London Road, King's Lynn, Norfolk PE30 5E3

MILLER'S COLLECTORS CARS PRICE GUIDE 1997-98

Created and designed by
Miller's Publications
The Cellars, High Street
Tenterden, Kent TN30 6BN
Telephone: 01580 766411

Consultants: Judith Miller

General Editor: Robert Murfin
Editorial and Production Co-ordinator: Sue Boyd
Editorial Assistants: Gillian Judd, Marion Rickman, Jo Wood
Artwork: Kari Reeves, Matthew Leppard, Shirley Reeves
Advertising Executive: Melinda Williams
Material Collator: Gillian Charles
Additional Photographers: Ian Booth, Simon Clay, National Motor Museum, Geoffrey Goddard, Guy Griffiths,
Robert Howarth, Roger McDonald, Bob Masters, G. Pauman, Robin Saker
Index compiled by: Hilary Bird, Goudhurst, Kent

First published in 1996
by Miller's
an imprint of Reed Consumer Books Limited
Michelin House, 81 Fulham Road, London SW3 6RB
and Auckland, Melbourne, Singapore and Toronto

Copyright © 1996 Reed International Books Limited

A CIP catalogue record for this book is
available from the British Library

ISBN 1-85732-820-5

Bromide output by Perfect Image, Hurst Green, E. Sussex
Illustrations by G. H. Graphics, St. Leonard's-on-Sea, E. Sussex
Colour origination by Scantrans, Singapore
Printed and bound in England by William Clowes Ltd,
Beccles and London

Miller's is a trademark of
Reed International Books Limited

Front cover illustrations:

1949 Chrysler Town and Country Convertible. **£55,000-58,000** *CNY*
A porcupine mascot by Bizette Lindet, 1920s, 3¾in (9.5cm) high. **£400–450** *S*
1973 Ferrari Dino 246 GTS. **Est. £45,000–50,000** *COYS*
A British Dominions Empire Motor Policy enamel advertising sign, 60 x 40in (152 x 102cm). **£1,700–2,000** *S*
1956 Pontiac Star Chief 2 Door Convertible. **£9,000–9,500** *BKS*

ACKNOWLEDGEMENTS

**The publishers would like to acknowledge the great assistance given
by our consultants**

Chris Alford   Newland Cottage, Hassocks, West Sussex BN6 8NU
                          Tel: 01273 845966
Malcolm Barber   Tel: 01883 626553
Peter W. Card   Tel: 01622 844429
Graham Clayton   East Sussex Minors, Stonegate, East Sussex
                          Tel: 01580 200203
Tom Falconer   Claremont Corvette, Snodland, Kent Tel: 01634 244444
Peter Hunter   Toyota Enthusiasts Club
Franco Macri   Tel: 01227 700555
Richard Saxton   Tel: 01622 844429
Mike Stanley   Wolseley Register, 1 Flashgate, Higher Ramsgreave Road,
                          Ramsgreave, Lancashire BB1 9DH

*We would like to extend our thanks to all auction houses and dealers who have
assisted us in the production of this book.*

HOW TO USE THIS BOOK

Miller's Collectors Cars Price Guide presents an overview of the collectors cars market during the past twelve months. The cars are listed alphabetically by make and then chronologically by model within each make. In the case of manufacturers renowned for producing both sports and saloon cars, for example Bentley and MG, we have grouped the sports and saloon cars together and then listed these cars chronologically.

Each illustration is fully captioned and carries a price range which reflects the dealer/auctioneer sale price. The prefix 'Est.' indicates the estimated price for the cars which did not sell at auction. Each illustration also has an identification code which allows you to locate the source of that particular picture by using the Key to Illustrations.

In the Automobilia section, objects are grouped alphabetically by type, for example clothing, garage equipment, and so on, then chronologically within each grouping. Racing cars, commercial vehicles, military vehicles, fire engines and micro cars all follow the same format. The Automobile Art section is listed alphabetically.

Also included in *Miller's Collectors Cars Price Guide* are price boxes, compiled by our team of experts, (including Malcolm Barber, a well-known car historian), car clubs and private collectors, which give the value of a particular model, dependent on condition.
Condition 1. A vehicle in top class condition but not 'concours d'élégance' standard, either fully restored or in very good original condition.

Condition 2. A good, clean roadworthy vehicle, both mechanically and bodily sound.
Condition 3. A runner, but in need of attention, probably to both bodywork and mechanics. Must have current MOT.
We have also included restoration projects, which cover vehicles that fail to make the condition 3 grading.

Remember, we do not illustrate every classic or collectors car ever produced. Our aim is to reflect the marketplace, so if, for example, there appears to be a large number of Lotus's and only a few Volvos, then this is an indication of the quantity, availability and, to an extent, the desirability of these cars in the marketplace over the last twelve months. If the car you are looking for is not featured under its alphabetical listing, do look in the colour sections and double-check the index. If a particular car is not featured this year, it may well have appeared in previous editions of *Miller's Collectors Cars Price Guide,* which provide a growing visual reference library.

Lastly, we are always keen to improve the content and accuracy of our books. If you feel that a particular make or model or other aspect of classic and collectable vehicles has not been covered in sufficient detail, if you disagree with our panel of experts, or have any other comments you would like to share with us about our book, please write and let us know.

We value feedback from the people who use *Miller's Collectors Cars Price Guide* to tell us how we can make it even better.

KEY TO ILLUSTRATIONS

Each illustration and descriptive caption is accompanied by a letter code. The source of any item may be immediately determined by referring to the following list in which Auctioneers are denoted by *, dealers by •, Advertisisers by †, and Clubs and Trusts by ‡. In no way does this constitute or imply a contract or binding offer on the part of any of our contributors to supply or sell the goods illustrated, or similar articles, at the prices stated.

If you require a valuation for an item, it is advisable to check whether the dealer or specialist will carry out this service and if there is a charge. Please mention Miller's when making an enquiry. Having found a specialist who will carry out your valuation it is best to send a photograph and description of the item to the specialist, together with a stamped addressed envelope for the reply. A valuation by telephone is not possible.

Most dealers are only too happy to help you with your enquiry, however, they are very busy people and consideration of the above points would be welcomed.

AAV	*	Academy Auctioneers & Valuers, Northcote House, Northcote Avenue, Ealing, London W5 3UR Tel: 0181 579 7466
ADT	*†	ADT Auctions Ltd, Classic & Historic Automobile Division, Blackbushe Airport, Blackwater, Camberley, Surrey GU17 9LG Tel: 01252 878555
AH	*	Andrew Hartley, Victoria Hall Salerooms, Little Lane, Ilkley, Yorkshire LS29 8EA Tel: 01943 816363
ALC	*	Alcocks, Wyeval House, 42 Bridge St, Hereford, Hereford & Worcs HR4 9DG Tel: 01432 344322
APP	•	Richard Appleyard, Sunderland House, Sunderland Street, Tickhill, Doncaster, Yorkshire D11 9QJ Tel: 01302 743782
ASR	‡	Austin Swallow Register, G L Walker, School House, Back Way, Great Haseley, Oxfordshire OX44 7JP
BC/ BCA	• •†	Beaulieu Cars Ltd, The Garage, Beaulieu, Hampshire SO42 7YE Tel: 01590 612689
BKS	*†	Robert Brooks (Auctioneers) Ltd, 81 Westside, London SW4 9AY Tel: 0171 228 8000
BLE	•†	Ivor Bleaney, PO Box 60, Salisbury, Wiltshire SP5 2DH Tel: 01794 390895
BLK	•	Blackhawk Collection, 3600 Blackhawk Plaza Circle, Danville, California, USA 94506 Tel: 510 736 3444
Bro	•	John Brown, Between Baldock & Royston, Hertfordshire SG8 0NL Tel: 01763 852200
C	*	Christie, Manson & Woods Ltd, 8 King Street, St James's, London SW1Y 6QT Tel: 0171 839 9060
CARS	•†	CARS (Classic Automobilia & Regalia Specialists), 4–4a Chapel Terrace Mews, Kemp Town, Brighton, Sussex BN2 1HU Tel: 01273 60 1960
Car	•†	Chris Alford Racing and Sportscars, Newland Cottage, Hassocks, Sussex BN6 8NU Tel: 01273 845966
CBG	•	Cropredy Bridge Garage Ltd, (Exclusively Jensen), Riverside Works, Cropredy, Banbury, Oxfordshire OX17 1PQ Tel: 01295 758444
CC	•	Collectors Cars, Drakeshill, Birmingham Road, Kenilworth, Warwickshire CV8 1PT Tel: 01926 857705
CCon	•	Canterbury Convertibles, Kent Tel: 01227 720306
CFI	•	Chequered Flag Inc, 4128 Lincoln Blvd, Marina Del Rey, Los Angeles, California, USA 90292 Tel: 001 310 827 8665
CGB	•†	Cars Gone By, Maidstone, Kent Tel: 01622 630220
CGOC	•†	Capital & General Omnibus Company Ltd, Cheshire Tel: 01260 223456
CNY		Christie Manson & Woods International Inc, 502 Park Avenue, (including Christie's East), New York, USA, NY 10022 Tel: 212 546 1000
COB	•	Cobwebs, 78 Northam Road, Southampton, Hampshire SO14 0PB Tel: 01703 227458
COR	•†	Claremont Corvette, Snodland, Kent ME6 5NA Tel: 01634 244444
COYS	*	Coys of Kensington, 2/4 Queens Gate Mews, London SW7 5QJ Tel: 0171 584 7444

CPUK	‡	Club Peugeot UK (General Secretary), 2 Sunnyside, Priors Hill, Tinsbury, Bath, Avon BA3 1HE
CSK	*	Christie's South Kensington Ltd, 85 Old Brompton Road, London SW7 3LD Tel: 0171 581 7611
CTOC	‡	Citroën Traction Owners Club, Steve Reed, 1 Terwick Cottages, Rogate, Nr Petersfield, Hampshire GU31 5EG
DAM	•	Les Damiers, 700 Domaine de la Vigne, 59910 Bondues, France Tel: 33 20 23 29 84
DB	•	David Baldock, North Road, Goudhurst, Kent TN17 1AD Tel: 01580 211326
DJR	•	DJR Services, Unit N4, Europa Trading Estate, Trader Road, Erith, Kent DA8 1QW Tel: 01322 442850
DM	•	Don Mitchell & Company, 132 Saffron Road, Wigston, Leicestershire LE18 4UP Tel: 0116 277 7669
ESM	•†	East Sussex Minors, The Workshop, Bearhurst Farm, Stonegate, Sussex TN5 7DU Tel: 01580 200203
FAL	•	Collection of CM Booth Historic Vehicles, Falstaff Antiques, 63–67 High Street, Rolvenden, Kent TN17 4LP Tel: 01580 241234
FFA	•†	Finesse Fine Art, 9 Coniston Crescent, Weymouth, Dorset DT3 5HA Tel: 01305 854286
FHD	•†	F H Douglass, 1a South Ealing Road, Ealing, London W5 4OT Tel: 0181 567 0570
FHF	•†	Foulkes-Halbard of Filching, Filching Manor, Filching, Wannock, Polegate, Sussex BN26 5QA Tel: 01323 487838
FM	•	Franco Macri, Kent Tel: 01227 700555
FYC	‡	Ford Y&C Model Register, Bob Wilkinson, Castle Farm, Main Street, Pollington, Goole, Humberside DN14 0DJ Tel: 01405 860836
GAR	•	The Guild of Automotive Restorers Inc, 18237 Woodbine Avenue, R R No 1, Sharon, Ontario, Canada LOG 1VO Tel: 905 895 0035
GEC	‡	Granada Mk II and Mk III Enthusiasts' Club, 10 Alder Grove, Halesowen, West Midlands B62 9TL Tel: 0121 426 2346 (Mobile 0860 423126)
GES	*	G E Sworder & Sons, 14 Cambridge Road, Stansted Mountfitchet, Essex CM24 8BZ Tel: 01279 817778
GPCC	‡	David Hayhoe, Grand Prix Contact Club, 26 Broom Road, Shirley, Croydon, Surrey CR0 8NE Tel: 0181 777 4835
H&H	*†	H & H Classic Auctions, 385 London Rd, Appleton, Nr Warrington, Cheshire WA4 5DN Tel: 01925 860471
HAM	*	Hamptons Antique & Fine Art Auctioneers, 93 High Street, Godalming, Surrey GU7 1AL Tel: 01483 423567
HCC	*	H C Chapman & Son, The Auction Mart, North Street, Scarborough, Yorkshire YO11 1DL Tel: 01723 372424
HOLL	*	Dreweatt Neate Holloways, 49 Parsons Street, Banbury, Oxon OX16 8PF Tel: 01295 253197
HSS/ P(HSS)	*	Henry Spencer and Sons (Phillips), 20 The Square, Retford, Notts DN22 6BX Tel: 01777 708633
KSC	•†	Kent Sports Cars, Coldharbour House, Coldharbour Lane, Bridge, Canterbury, Kent CT4 5HH Tel: 01227 832200

LF   *   Lambert & Foster, 77 Commercial Road, Paddock Wood, Kent TN12 6DR Tel: 01892 832325

LJ   •   Lee Jackson, 119 Whitehouse Avenue, Borehamwood, Hampshire WD6 1HB

M   *   Morphets of Harrogate, 4–6 Albert Street, Harrogate, Yorks HG1 1JL Tel: 01423 502282

MAN   •†   Stanley Mann, The Fruit Farm, Common Lane, Radlett, Hertfordshire WD7 8PW Tel: 01923 852505

MAW/   *   Thomas Mawer & Son, The Lincoln
TM   Saleroom, 63 Monks Road, Lincoln, Lincolnshire LN2 5HP Tel: 01522 524984

MM   •   Morgan Model Co, The Glen, Stonehouse Lane, Bulkeley, Malpas, Cheshire, SY14 8BQ Tel: 01829 72514

MOR   •   Morris Minor Centre Ltd, Avon House, Lower Bristol Road, Bath, Avon BA2 1ES Tel: 01225 315449

Mot   •   Motospot, North Kilworth, Nr Lutterworth, Leicestershire LE17 6EP Tel: 01455 552548/0850 450269

MPG   •   MotorPost Gallery, 5 Shadwell Park Court, Leeds, Yorks LS17 8TS Tel: 0113 225 3525

MR   *   Martyn Rowe, The Truro Auction Centre, Calenick Street, Truro, Cornwall TR1 2SG Tel: 01892 260020

MSMP   •   Mike Smith Motoring Past, Chiltern House, Ashendon, Aylesbury, Bucks HP18 0HB Tel: 01296 651283

N   *   Neales, 192-194 Mansfield Rd, Nottingham, Notts NG1 3HU Tel: 0115 962 4141

OCC   ‡   Octagon Car Club, 36 Queensville Avenue, Stafford, Staffordshire ST17 4LS Tel: 01785 51014

ONS   *   Onslows, Metrostore, Townmead Road, London SW6 2RZ Tel: 0171 793 0240

PC   Private Collection

PJF   •   P J Fischer Classic Automobiles, Dyers Lane, Upper Richmond Road, Putney, London SW15 6JR Tel: 0181 785 6633

PMB   •†   Pooks Motor Bookshop, Fowke Street, Rothley, Leicestershire LE7 7PJ Tel: 0116 237 6222

RCC   •†   Real Car Co, Snowdonia Business Park, Coed y Parc, Bethesda, Gwynedd LL57 4YS Tel: 01248 602649

ROR   •†   Rory Stokes Maritime Garage Ltd, Bath Road, Lymington, Hants SO41 3RW Tel: 01590 671888

S   *   Sotheby's, 34–35 New Bond Street, London W1A 2AA Tel: 0171 493 8080

S(NY)   *   Sotheby's, 1334 York Avenue, New York, USA, NY 10021 Tel: 212 606 7000

ScR   ‡   Scootacar Register, Stephen Boyd, Pamanste, 18 Holman Close, Aylsham, Norwich, Norfolk NR11 6DD Tel: 01263 733861

SJR   •   Simon J Robinson 1982 Ltd, Ketton Garage, Durham Road, Coatham Munderville, Darlington, Co Durham DL1 3LZ Tel: 01325 311232

SW   •†   Spinning Wheel Garage, Sheffield Road, Sheepbridge, Chesterfield, Derbys S41 9EH Tel: 01246 451772

TEC   ‡   Toyota Enthusiasts Club, c/o Secretary/Treasurer Billy Wells, 28 Park Road, Feltham, Middlesex TW13 6PW Tel: 0181 898 0740

UMC   •†   Unicorn Motor Company, Brian R Chant, MIMI, Station Road, Stalbridge, Dorset DT10 2RH Tel: 01963 363353

VIC   •†   Vicarys of Battle Ltd, 32 High St, Battle, Sussex TN33 0EH Tel: 01424 772425

WEC   •†   West End Classics, 130 High Street, Somersham, Cambs PE17 3EN Tel: 01487 842085

WL   *   Wintertons Ltd, Lichfield Auction Centre, Wood End Lane, Fradley, Lichfield, Staffordshire WS13 8NF Tel: 01543 263256

WOL   ‡   Wolseley Register, M Stanley, (Chairman), 1 Flashgate, Higher Ramsgreave Road, Ramsgreave, Nr Blackburn, Lancashire BB1 9DH

CONTENTS

FOREWORD

As we near the end of the twentieth century, I think it is fair to say that we live in a motoring age. The motor car does not only provide basic transport but to many it is a way of life. To illustrate this, one just has to look at the enormous worldwide audiences for Grand Prix racing or events such as the Goodwood Festival of Speed where over 100,000 people of all ages and from all walks of life mingle with the stars of yesterday and today. Events of this type have seen an enormous growth in popularity throughout the world in recent years and auctions which are now often associated with them have an enthusiastic market for the automobilia and cars of every description. It could be a bus or a Grand Prix car – it appears the hunger for ownership is insatiable.

As a collector of the machines that played an important and exciting part in my life, such as the Mercedes 300SL Gullwing, BMW 507, Porsche Carrera 356 and some of the Grand Prix cars that I built during the years with my racing team, I still watch with interest and am all the time becoming more aware of the pitfalls that confront a restorer or collector. The answer is, of course, research and knowledge, and it is here that publications like *Miller's Collectors Cars Price Guide*, and in particular its photographs, become an invaluable guide.

USING A CLASSIC CAR

Surprising as it may appear, not everyone who owns a classic car drives it. A car of any type, whether it be classic, vintage or veteran, was manufactured to be used and to be seen. It can also be a catalyst to forging new friendships. Whether it be as an observer or participant, it can also be family entertainment of undoubted benefit with an increasing number of events to attend.

Static Display

Joining one of the numerous local clubs which exist (*See Directory of Car Clubs on page 336*) can be a good way of getting started. Very often these clubs are invited to attend one of the many static undercover car shows around the country. These shows consist of well set out club and trade stands as well as a small autojumble area and, more often than not, a car corral. The stands are often supplied free of charge.

The club organisers are often looking for new and unseen material, and if invited to take part then jump at the opportunity. Have no fear or worry that your car is not pristine, I believe the public are just as interested in viewing good, clean, homely vehicles, possessing the patina that only age can afflict, as they are inspecting over-restored motor cars that are probably in better condition now than when they left the factory!

Choose a static show event that is close to home. Once you have arrived, make the car look its best by cleaning it and tidying up the back seat. Open the bonnet for the passers by to view the engine. Always follow the instructions of the show organisers and disconnect the battery as a safety measure.

Some of the established static shows to look out for include the Alexandra Palace, Classic Car Show. This annual event is very well supported by London-based clubs and individuals, but it is not unusual for cars and their owners to travel from the Midlands. Ian Green has developed several annual shows, at the very large Great Malvern showground, which are well worth supporting. However, the largest and perhaps the best supported is the Classic and Sports Car Show at the NEC on the May bank holiday weekend every year. This event attracts about 500 exhibitors and around 50,000 visitors.

Classic Car Runs

A classic car road run or rally is an ideal way of not only enjoying your car but also using it for the purpose for which it was built.

For the classic car owner who has a mobile car with an MOT and, where appropriate, car tax the annual Norwich Union Classic Run is a necessity. Eleven different starting points around the country lead over 1,600 cars to a large jamboree at the Silverstone race track in Northamptonshire. The event takes place at the end of May and the organisation is both excellent and professionally marshalled by local enthusiasts. Should you have the misfortune to break down then pick-up trucks are available to assist your efforts to get back home. The cost of this, like so many classic runs today, comes from your entry fee. This fee also pays for administration and a souvenir programme of the event.

For pre-war cars, the annual Bristol to Bournemouth Vintage Vehicle Run has gained a reputation for being a well organised and safe event. This road run is doubly interesting because light commercial vehicles and motorcyles are also eligible.

Another event that terminates in Bournemouth is the Daffodil Run, designed to take place at the appropriate time of year by the Bean Car Club. The event proved to be so popular in the past that today cars of all types and periods are attracted. The event starts, like so many road runs, early on Sunday morning outside the Seven Stars public house on the A4 near Maidenhead. The route will meander down delightful back roads and B roads of Berkshire and Hampshire. The lunch time stop is at Stockbridge, and the resulting spectacular display in the High Street attracts a large crowd. The run continues on to the seafront at Bournemouth.

Local Events

Every weekend during the summer months there are probably ten or more local events being held at numerous venues around the country. These are organised by enthusiastic volunteers who represent local car clubs and steam societies and the like. They often raise money for charity but are, nevertheless, usually run by very able organisers and administrators.

The typical format is usually that of a combination static display, road run and trade stands to include perhaps a small autojumble and fair. After displaying your car in the morning, each vehicle is invited to complete a short road run at lunch time. When the cars return, a *concours d'élégance* is judged. The cars, along with other assorted machinery, parade around the arena while a commentary takes place and awards are presented to the various competition winners.

Autojumbles

Driving to an autojumble in a classic car is today becoming very popular. For example, the largest autojumble in the UK is that organised by Montagu Ventures at the National Motor Museum at Beaulieu every September. Over the years, not only has the event grown substantially in size, but the public car park is increasingly packed with an interesting array of cars of all types and ages and, in consequence, well worth inspecting.

Peter W. Card

STATE OF THE MARKET

This past year the UK auction market has witnessed ever-increasing activity at all levels, and at present there are no signs that this situation is about to alter. Since January 1993, when the single market came into being, there have been increased sales to European buyers, and with the entry of Austria into the EU in the past twelve months, buyers from that country have also been much in evidence. Indeed, it is apparent that the market has seen, and continues to see, many new buyers at all levels from both within and outside the UK, and so far as the home market is concerned there are continued signs of increasing prosperity. In the past the collectors' car market has served as a useful and accurate barometer of the so-called 'feel good' factor, and whilst it is extremely unlikely that price levels will ever return in real terms to the excesses of the late 1980s, there has been a most definite upturn in the market. Prices, however, have not changed significantly. In the past year, with the exception of high quality cars with provenance, there is more activity and interest from buyers.

There has also been a notable shift in emphasis. It has to be said that interest in very early motor cars has not been as strong as could be expected. The trend has been towards more immediately useable cars. Cars requiring restoration, unless they are the most desirable and sought-after models, have tended to be shunned altogether or sold for very low prices. The 1931 Star Comet saloon and the 1925 Star Scorpio sold by Sotheby's for £350 and £1,000 respectively, illustrate this point. This, however, reflects the continuing high costs of restoration, which in economic terms make the restoration of any car valued at under £50,000 almost non-viable.

Provenance continues to play an important part in determining hammer prices. This is particularly true of racing and sports racing cars which are featured in the guide this year. Thus the ex-works Graham Hill 1964 BRM P261 Formula I car sold for £186,000 at Brooks Goodwood sale in June 1995, the ex-Betty Haig 1935 PB MG Midget sold in the same sale for £18,000 and a record breaking £564,324 was paid for the ex-Prince Bira 1954 Maserati 250F sold by Brooks in Monaco last year.

With cars belonging to folk heroes (or anti-heroes) film stars and similar personages, provenance also plays an important part, hence the £198,000 paid for the ex-Mussolini 1935 Alfa Romeo 6C 2300 Sport sold by Coys, the £101,165 paid for the ex-Charlie Chaplin 1931 Rolls-Royce 40/50 Phantom II at Brooks Monaco sale, and the £145,000 which Christie's achieved for the ex-Aga Khan Rolls-Royce Phantom IV. At Brooks in December 1995, the sporting provenance importance was underlined once more with the ex-Scuderia Ferrari/Hans Ruesch/Dick Seaman/Dennis Poore 1935 Alfa Romeo Tipo 8C-35 which realised another record at £859,500 with premium. The ex-Hon Brian Lewis Le Mans 1933 Alfa Romeo 8C-2300 sold with premium at £441,500. Brooks also achieved another high price with the ex-Carroll Shelby 1960 Maserati Tipo 61 Birdcage at Monaco in May 1996, achieving £464,834 with premium.

Thematic sales are also gaining in popularity. Coys' International Historic Festival is based at Silverstone in August. Christie's support the Pebble Beach Concours in the USA, Brooks are well established at the Goodwood Festival of Speed.

Newcomers to the auction scene have been few, but in Buxton H&H have established a series of successful sales in the Midlands. A significant newcomer to the UK market, however, is the American auctioneer, Kruse. Reports from the USA indicate that apart from prestige events like Pebble Beach the US collectors car market is not buoyant. The fact that Kruse feel it worthwhile to return to the UK underlines the strength of the European market.

Judging by the number of sales so far this year there is still a surplus of collectors' cars in the UK, but the boost to sales provided by the abolition of road tax on cars over 25 years old will be (and can already be seen to be) taking care of that, and the numbers of older cars now seen regularly on the roads of Britain bears witness to this.

In sales where there is a concentration of such vehicles, then totals have been impressive. The December Brooks sale was interesting, not only because it was held at the Natural History Museum in London – an auction 'first' – but also for the fact that it topped well over £3 million, the first time this had been achieved by any auction house since the heady days of the late 1980s.

Christie's appears to have had some impressive results at their Pebble Beach sales, whilst Coys continue to hold rather more sales than Christie's, maintaining a very respectable percentage of vehicles successfully sold. ADT, whilst concentrating on the lower priced vehicles, have also maintained successful sales levels. They have also tended to attract a totally different group of buyers, many of them from the trade, a trend which stems, no doubt, from their general car auction activity.

To sum up, the current UK auction scene is buoyant, with many new customers from both home and abroad. Good cars continue to command good prices, average condition and mediocre cars are still inexpensive. The nil road tax on cars over 25 year old seems to have given the whole movement a psychological boost, but this alone cannot explain the quite dramatic return of confidence we have witnessed in the past twelve months. I am most optimistic for the future.

Malcolm Barber

ABARTH

Formed by Carlo Abarth in the 1950s the
Abarth Company produced competition
engines for Alfa Romeo, Lancia and Fiat.
They went on to produce a series of
record-breaking motor cars for all types
of competitions.

c1960 Abarth Allemano 2200 Coupé,
6 cylinders, overhead valve, 2160cc, 135bhp at
6000rpm, 4 speed manual gearbox, 4 wheel disc
brakes, torsion bars and swing arms with anchor
rod front suspension, coil springs with quarter-
elliptic leaf springs rear, right-hand drive, Nardi
steering wheel, correct badges, original clear
plastic protective covers on seats, very original.
£6,000–6,500 *C*

*This car went on sale in the UK at £4,000 but
only two right-hand drive coupés were built, of
which this is the only known survivor.*

1959 Abarth 750 GT Zagato Coupé,
rebuilt engine, transmission and bodywork,
very good condition.
£12,000–12,500 *S*

Cross Reference
Restoration Projects

AC

Although AC, from Auto Carriers, had been
manufacturing vehicles since the turn of the
century, the Ace was the first car to make the
company name famous. The Ace enjoyed
international success but was best known as
being the forerunner of the AC Cobra.

Developed by the American racing driver
Carrol Shelby as a competition car to rival
Ferrari and the Chevrolet Corvette, the
prototype employed a 221cu in (3621cc) Ford
V8 engine. The production model, in June
1962, used the 260cu in (4260cc) version.
Following racing success the 1966 model 427
developed about 390bhp from the 7010cc
V8 engine. Two supercharged models were
made which could accelerate to 60mph in
3.8 seconds. A total of 1011 Cobras were
built between 1962 and 1967.

1921 AC 11.9hp Royal Tourer, 4 cylinder in line
monobloc Anzani engine, 1496cc, 3 speed gearbox
and reverse in back axle, rear expanding brakes,
quarter-elliptic leaf springs front and rear
suspension, right-hand drive, following museum
storage some attention required.
£11,500–13,500 *C*
*Thought to be the only surviving four-seater Anzani
engined example.*

1922 AC 2 Seater Boat Tailed Sports, extremely
rare in aluminium, full restoration.
£18,000–19,000 *H&H*

1924 AC Acedes with Dickey,
the fork-mounted CAV nickel
headlights are correct, sound
and original car.
£7,500–8,000 *S*

l. **1925 AC Acedes Royal Drophead
Coupé with Dickey,** 2 litre engine,
full restoration, excellent condition.
Est. £21,500–25,000 *S*

1933 AC 16/66 Boat Tailed 2 Seater, 2 litre single overhead camshaft, manual, restored, excellent condition with new bodywork.
£18,750–19,250 *Mot*

1948 AC Buckland MkI Tourer, 2 litre, 6 cylinder engine, excellent restored condition.
£8,500–9,000 *BKS*

One of only 3 'straight-sided' Buckland tourers known to the AC Buckland Register.

1955 AC Ace, 6 cylinder, 1991cc engine, complete engine rebuild, full weather equipment, substantial file of service history, extremely good original order throughout.
Est. £22,000–25,000 *COYS*

1961 AC Greyhound, good condition.
£10,000–12,000 *H&H*

1958 AC Ace Bristol 2 Seater Sports, excellent restored condition.
£44,000–46,000 *BKS*

1961 AC Greyhound, original factory specifications, good overall condition.
Est. £17,000–20,000 *S*

r. **1964 AC Cobra 289,** 8 cylinders, 4727cc, retains 385bhp competition engine, Hurst gearbox shifter, rear wing brake cooling vents, Halibrand wheels and quick-lift jacking points, meticulous and comprehensive restoration, good condition.
£105,000+ *COYS*

AC Model	ENGINE cc/cyl	DATES	CONDITION		
			1	2	3
Sociable	636/1	1907-12	£9,500	£8,000	£4,000
12/24 (Anzani)	1498/4	1919-27	£14,000	£11,500	£7,500
16/40	1991/6	1920-28	£18,000	£15,000	£11,000
16/60 Drophead/Saloon	1991/6	1937-40	£24,000	£21,000	£15,500
16/70 Sports Tourer	1991/6	1937-40	£35,000	£26,000	£18,000
16/80 Competition 2 Seater	1991/6	1937-40	£55,000	£45,000	£35,000

1964 AC Cobra 289 MkII, 8 cylinder, 4727cc engine, Holley
4 barrel carburettor system, Mallory twin point distributor, Hurst
gearshift, constant velocity joints on the rear driveshafts replace
the old Hardy-Spicer arrangement, only 73,000 miles from new.
Est. £75,000–85,000 *COYS*

*Only 560 examples were made to the original Tojeiro
chassis design and only 46 of those were made
with right-hand drive.*

r. **1966 AC Cobra 427,** standard 4 speed manual
gearbox, converted to right-hand drive, superbly
presented, fully restored.
£115,000+ *COYS*

*Once owned by Bill Cosby and restored by
Brian Angliss.*

1967 AC Cobra 427, 8 cylinders, 6998cc, bonnet scoop,
driver's roll-over hoop, side exhausts and chrome-plated
nudge bars, outstanding example.
£155,000+ *COYS*

1972 AC 428 Convertible, coachwork
by Frua, Ford V8, 7014cc engine,
overhead valve, hydraulic tappets,
345bhp at 4600rpm, 3 speed automatic
gearbox, independent suspension,
anti-dive, anti-squat front and rear
using unequal length wishbones with
semi-trailing arms to rear, coil
springs, 4 wheel disc brakes, right-
hand drive, excellent example of a
very rare model.
£31,000–32,000 *C*

AC Model	ENGINE cc/cyl	DATES	CONDITION 1	2	3
2 litre	1991/6	1947-55	£5,000	£2,500	£800
Buckland	1991/6	1949-54	£7,000	£4,500	£1,800
Ace	1991/6	1953-63	£27,000	£22,000	£15,000
Ace Bristol	1971/6	1954-63	£32,000	£28,000	£23,000
Ace 2.6	1553/6	1961-62	£35,000	£30,000	£29,000
Aceca	1991/6	1954-63	£24,000	£17,000	£12,000
Aceca Bristol	1971/6	1956-63	£28,000	£21,000	£16,000
Greyhound Bristol	1971/6	1961-63	£14,000	£10,500	£7,000
Cobra Mk II 289	4735/8	1963-64	£90,000	£80,000	£70,000
Cobra Mk III 427	6998/8	1965-67	£115,000	£100,000	£90,000
Cobra Mk IV	5340/8	1987-	£55,000	£40,000	£32,000
428 Frua	7014/8	1967-73	£19,000	£15,000	£11,000
428 Frua Convertible	7014/8	1967-73	£25,000	£20,000	£15,000
3000 ME	2994/6	1976-84	£15,000	£10,000	£8,000

Racing history for Cobra will put the price to over £100,000–120,000.

1969 AC 428 Convertible, coachwork by Frua, 7.2 litre engine, Ford Galaxie automatic gearbox, right-hand drive, to standard factory specification, exceptionally rare.
£35,000–36,000 *BKS*

1973 AC 428 Fastback Coupé, Ford V8, overhead valve, 7017cc, 345bhp at 4,600, Ford 3 speed automatic gearbox, 4 wheel disc brakes, independent all-round suspension, right-hand drive, 65,000 miles from new, well maintained and original example.
Est. £20,000–25,000 *C*

AC 428 Frua

- The 428 employed a lengthened Cobra chassis with a body designed by Frua.
- Available as a coupé or convertible.
- The 428cu in (7016cc) Ford V8 engine could accelerate from 0–60mph in 5.4 seconds.
- Introduced in 1965, there were believed to be only 58 coupés and 28 convertibles built before production ceased in 1973.

AJS

1930 AJS 2 Seater Tourer, Coventry Climax 1018cc side valve engine with Westmacot head, with 2 dickey seats and boot, aluminium body, very rare car.
Est. £5,800–6,500 *HOLL*

ALFA ROMEO

Anonima Lombarda Fabbrica Automobili acquired their world famous base at Milan in 1909. By 1910 the first Alfas had been produced, but it wasn't until Nicola Romeo bought the company in 1915 that the factory was restructured. Romeo persuaded Vittorio Jano to leave Fiat and by the early 1920s Jano was designing for Alfa Romeo some of the best sports racing cars ever seen. For over a decade Alfa dominated world motor sport including Grands Prix.

Badly damaged during the war, the factory was soon back in production with a series of good looking saloon and sports cars, including the Giulias and Giulliettas.

The Alfasud, built at a new factory at Naples, was intended to provide a low cost everyday Alfa, and although it was a well conceived design it was plagued with problems including the ability to rust very easily.

Fiat acquired Alfa Romeo in the late 1980s.

1930 Alfa Romeo 6C 1750 Supercharged Grand Sport Tourer, coachwork by James Young, 6 cylinder, twin overhead camshafts, Memini supercharger, 1750cc, 85bhp at 4500rpm, 4 speed manual gearbox, 4 wheel mechanical drum brakes, semi-elliptic suspension, right-hand drive, original components, gradual restoration commenced.
£51,000–52,000 *C*

The ex-Nuvolari 1930 TT winning car and London Motor Show exhibit.

Cross Reference
Restoration Projects

ALFA ROMEO Model	ENGINE cc/cyl	DATES	CONDITION 1	2	3
24HP	4084/4	1910-11	£21,000	£16,000	£12,000
12HP	2413/4	1910-11	£18,000	£11,000	£8,000
40-60	6028/4	1913-15	£32,000	£24,000	£14,000
RL	2916/6	1921-22	£30,000	£24,000	£14,000
RM	1944/4	1924-25	£28,000	£17,000	£13,000
6C 1500	1487/6	1927-28	£14,000	£10,000	£8,000
6C 1750	1752/6	1923-33	£85,000+	£60,000	-
6C 1900	1917/6	1933	£18,000	£15,000	£12,000
6C 2300	2309/6	1934	£22,000	£18,000	£15,000
6C 2500 SS Cabriolet/Spider	2443/6	1939-45	£100,000	£50,000	£40,000
6C 2500 SS Coupé	2443/6	1939-45	£60,000	£40,000	£30,000
8C 2300 Monza/Short Chassis	2300/8	1931-34	£1,000,000	£400,000	£200,000
8C 2900	2900/8	1935-39	£1,000,000	£500,000	£300,000

Value is very dependent on sporting history, body style and engine type.

**1931 Alfa Romeo 6C 1750
Gran Sport Zagato.**
£165,000–185,000 *BC*

1931 Alfa Romeo 6C 1750 GT, coachwork by
James Young, fully restored.
£35,000–40,000 *BC*

r. **1935–36 Alfa Romeo
Tipo 8C 35 Grand Prix
Monoposto,** 3.8 litre
engine, a very famous
motor car with an
excellent provenance.
£900,000+ *BKS*

*This car is an unspoiled
'time machine' after
40 years of nearly
undisturbed storage.*

**1933–35 2.3 Litre
Alfa Romeo 8C
2300 Berlina
Sport,** coachwork
by Carrozzeria
Viotti, a well-
known motor car in
superb condition.
£450,000+ *BKS*

1935 Alfa Romeo 6C 2300 Sport, Spider
coachwork by Touring of Milan, 6 cylinder,
2300cc engine.
£198,000–200,000 *COYS*

*Formerly the property of cavalliere Benito
Mussolini, the spider body by Touring of Milan
is believed to be the only spider that Touring
produced for the model.*

1948 Alfa Romeo 6C 2500SS 2-door Cabriolet,
coachwork by Pinin Farina, complete apart from
the seats, exciting restoration project.
£13,000–13,500 *BKS*

1948 Alfa Romeo 6C 2500 Super Sport,
6 cylinders, 2443cc, cabriolet coachwork by Pinin
Farina, right-hand drive, comprehensive restoration
carried out.
£48,000–50,000 *COYS*

*This is a highly collectable car with the most
sought-after specification. Only 474 examples of the
Super Sport were built.*

**c1951 Alfa Romeo 6C 2500 SS
2 door Sports Coupé,** Supergioello
(Super Jewel) coachwork by Ghia,
2.5 litre engine, right-hand drive,
bodywork is fair with some rust,
restoration would be straightforward.
£24,000–25,000 *BKS*

r. **1956 Alfa Romeo Giulietta Spider,** coachwork
by Pinin Farina, 4 cylinders, 1290cc, original Veloce
engine and 5 speed gearbox, 800 miles since
completion of rebuild.
£12,500–13,000 *COYS*

ALFA ROMEO Model	ENGINE cc/cyl	DATES	CONDITION 1	2	3
2000 Spider	1974/4	1958-61	£11,000	£9,000	£3,000
2600 Sprint	2584/6	1962-66	£11,000	£7,500	£4,000
2600 Spider	2584/6	1962-65	£14,000	£12,000	£5,000
Giulietta Sprint	1290/4	1955-62	£10,000	£7,000	£4,000
Giulietta Spider	1290/4	1956-62	£10,000	£6,000	£4,500
Giulia Saloon	1570/4	1962-72	£5,000	£3,000	£1,500
Giulia Sprint (rhd)	1570/4	1962-68	£10,500	£6,000	£2,000
Giulia Spider (rhd)	1570/4	1962-65	£10,000	£7,000	£4,000
Giulia SS	1570/4	1962-66	£16,000	£13,000	£10,000
GT 1300 Junior	1290/4	1966-72	£7,000	£5,500	£3,000
1300GT Junior	1290/4	1973-75	£5,000	£2,500	£1,000
Giulia Sprint GT (105)	1570/4	1962-68	£7,500	£5,000	£3,000
1600GT Junior	1570/4	1972-75	£7,000	£4,000	£2,000
1750/2000 Berlina	1779/ 1962/4	1967-77	£3,500	£2,000	£1,000
1750GTV	1779/4	1967-72	£9,000	£7,000	£3,000
2000GTV	1962/4	1971-77	£8,000	£5,500	£3,000
1600/1750 (Duetto)	1570/ 1779/4	1966-67	£9,500	£7,000	£4,500
1750/2000 Spider (Kamm)	1779/ 1962/4	1967-78	£8,000	£6,000	£4,000
Montreal	2593/8	1970-77	£10,000	£8,000	£5,000
Junior Zagato 1300	1290/4	1968-74	£10,000	£7,000	£4,000
Junior Zagato 1600	1570/4	1968-74	£11,000	£8,000	£5,000
Alfetta GT/GTV (chrome)	1962/4	1974-84	£3,500	£2,500	£1,000
Alfasud	1186/ 1490/4	1972-83	£2,000	£1,000	£500
Alfasud ti	1186/ 1490/4	1974-81	£2,500	£1,200	£900
Alfasud Sprint	1284/ 1490/4	1976-85	£3,000	£2,000	£1,000
GTV6	2492/6	1981-	£4,000	£2,000	£1,000

Alfa Romeo Giulietta

- Introduced as a long wheelbase coupé in 1954.
- Bodywork was designed by Bertone, the Spider body was designed by Pininfarina.
- The 1.3 litre engine could produce 80bhp.
- The Veloce model could produce 100bhp at 6500rpm.

r. **1957 Alfa Romeo Giulietta Ti,** with original documents, unmarked interior, outstanding condition, totally rust free and original.
£4,000–4,500 *FM*

1958 Alfa Romeo 2 Litre 2000 Sports Spider, coachwork by Carrozzeria Touring of Milan, left-hand drive, factory hard top, good overall condition.
£6,500–7,500 *BKS*

Only 3,443 Spiders were built before production of the 2000 ceased in 1961.

1961 Alfa Romeo Giulietta Spider, excellent condition.
£8,000–10,000 *ROR*

1963 Alfa Romeo 2600 Spider, coachwork by Touring, ground up restoration, outstanding condition.
Est. £12,000–14,000 *BKS*

1962 Alfa Romeo Giulia Spider, 4 cylinders, 1570cc, rebuilt engine, brakes overhauled.
£11,800–13,200 *COYS*

Giulia models appeared with 5 speed gearboxes and a 92bhp, 1570cc engine.

1964 Alfa Romeo Giulia SS, coupé coachwork by Bertone, 4 cylinders, 1570cc, maintained to high standard, generally in good condition.
£10,000–11,000 *COYS*

1964 Alfa Romeo 2600, Spider coachwork by Touring of Milan, 6 cylinders, 2584cc, right-hand drive, good condition but requiring some cosmetic attention.
£4,500–5,000 *COYS*

r. **1966 Alfa Romeo Duetto 1600 Spider,** fully restored including leather throughout.
£10,000–11,000 *BC*

1965 Alfa Romeo Giulia SS, coupé coachwork by Bertone, 4 cylinders, 1570cc, recent total restoration, in excellent condition.
£12,500–13,500 *COYS*

1967 Alfa Romeo Giulia 1300 GT Junior, fully restored to very good condition.
£4,800–5,200 *Mot*

1966 Alfa Romeo 2600 SZ, totally original and complete, in very good condition.
£36,000–38,000 *FM*

One of only 105 built in the period 1965–67.

1967 Alfa Romeo Giulia GTC 1600, convertible coachwork by Bertone/Touring, 4 cylinders, 1570cc, a very original car, well maintained, excellent example.
Est. £9,000–12,000 *COYS*

1967 Alfa Romeo Duetto Spider, totally restored, very low mileage.
£12,000–13,000 *FM*

Alfa Romeo Duetto 1750

- Introduced in 1966 at the Geneva Motor Show.
- Bodywork designed by Pininfarina.
- Same basic components as used in the Alfa Romeo Giulia.
- Immortalised by Dustin Hoffman in the film *The Graduate*.

1969 Alfa Romeo Duetto 1750 Spider, coachwork by Pininfarina, 4 cylinders, 1750cc, extensive refurbishment, complete engine overhaul.
£6,000–6,500 *COYS*

l. **1969 Alfa Romeo Spider Veloce,** 4 cylinders, 1750cc, right-hand drive, bare metal respray, excellent condition.
Est. £5,000–5,500 *ADT*

The Pininfarina styled Alfa Romeo Giulia Spider or Duetto was launched in 1966 with Alfas new 1570cc engine. A year later, with an uprated 1750cc unit, it was to be renamed the Spider Veloce.

1970 Alfa Romeo Junior 1300 Linificato, choice
of 1.3 or 2 litre engine when new with same
interior, excellent original condition throughout.
£5,000–5,500 *FM*

1971 Alfa Romeo 1750, excellent
condition throughout.
£4,000–4,500 *FM*

1971 Alfa Romeo 1300 GT Junior, 4 cylinders,
mechanical components excellent, bodywork
excellent for an unrestored car.
Est. £2,750–3,500 *ADT*

**1972 Alfa Romeo Junior Zagato 2 door
Sports Coupé,** engine and transmission
in good condition, original Campagnolo
alloy wheels, body sound, front end
extensively rebuilt.
£7,250–7,500 *BKS*

1972 Alfa Romeo Montreal Coupé,
coachwork by Bertone, left-hand drive,
mechanically good, repainted 3 years ago,
some minor attention required.
£5,700–5,900 *BKS*

1973 Alfa Romeo Montreal Sports Coupé,
coachwork by Bertone, recently imported,
very good original condition.
Est. £11,000–12,000 *BKS*

1973 Alfa Romeo 2000 GT,
some body restoration.
£1,750–2,000 *H&H*

1974 Alfa Romeo 2000 GT Veloce, coachwork
by Bertone, very good original condition.
£5,750–6,000 *BKS*

1975 Alfa Romeo 2 Litre 2000 Veloce Spider, coachwork by Pininfarina, subject of a major restoration using replacement genuine Alfa Romeo panels, replacement 5 speed gearbox, right-hand drive.
£6,000–6,500 *BKS*

1975 Alfa Romeo Alfasud 1.2, genuine 30,000 miles, bodywork rust free, generally good condition.
Est. £1,500–2,000 *ADT*

1976 Alfa Romeo 1600 GTV Junior 2 door Coupé, coachwork by Bertone, right-hand drive, approximately 1,900 miles, condition throughout is commensurate with low mileage.
£10,000–10,500 *BKS*

1977 Alfa Romeo 2000 Spider Veloce, coachwork by Pininfarina, manual transmission, right-hand drive, 2 owners from new, excellent condition.
Est. £8,000–9,000 *BKS*

1977 Alfa Romeo 2000 Spider, left-hand drive, good original condition.
£3,500–4,000 *H&H*

1978 Alfa Romeo Alfetta GTV Fixed Head Coupé, first class condition throughout.
Est. £2,500–3,500 *ALC*

1979 Alfa Romeo 2000 Spider Veloce, 4 cylinders, 1962cc, generally good original condition.
£3,500–4,000 *ADT*

l. **1966 Alfa Romeo TZ2 Autodelta,** totally restored, one of only about 12 built by Alfa Romeo.
£185,000+ *FM*

Cross Reference
Racing Cars

1982 AlfaSud 1.5 TiX Sports Coupé, 12,000 miles, one owner, very good overall condition.
£3,600–3,800 *BKS*

1983 Alfasud SC 1.3, one owner, good original condition.
£1,000–1,200 *H&H*

ALLARD

1950 Allard J2, 8 cylinders, 4727cc, right-hand drive, completely restored.
£30,000–32,000 *COYS*

Don't Forget!
If in doubt please refer to the 'How to Use' section at the beginning of this book.

ALLARD Model	ENGINE cc/cyl	DATES	CONDITION 1	2	3
K/K2/L/M/M2X	3622/8	1947-54	£17,000	£11,000	£7,500
K3	var/8	1953-54	£24,000	£15,000	£11,000
P1	3622/8	1949-52	£18,000	£12,000	£7,000
P2	3622/8	1952-54	£22,000	£18,000	£11,000
J2/J2X	var/8	1950-54	£60,000	£50,000	£35,000
Palm Beach	1508/4, 2262/6	1952-55	£10,000	£7,500	£4,500
Palm Beach II	2252/ 3442/6	1956-60	£22,500	£18,000	£11,000

ALVIS

The Alvis name was founded by Geoffrey de Freville before the first world war. It derived from the fact that he produced aluminium pistons. The name was sold to T. K. Johns who went on to produce the model 10/30 from de Freville's design.

Despite producing several well-known and sporting models, Alvis regularly appeared to be in financial trouble. By 1965 Rover had acquired Alvis and by 1967 production had switched from cars to armoured fighting vehicles.

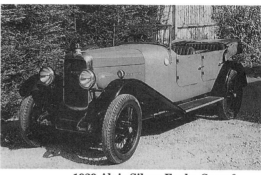

1929 Alvis Silver Eagle, Cross & Ellis style open 4 seater touring coachwork, 6 cylinder in line engine, overhead valve, Speed 20 cylinder head and block, triple SU carburettors, 2500cc, close ratio 4 speed gearbox, right-hand change, 4 wheel drum brakes, semi-elliptic front and rear suspension, re-bodied with replica body, good restored condition.
Est. £22,000–25,000 *C*

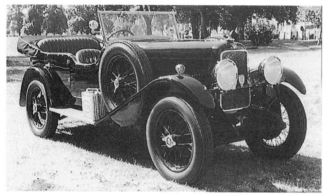

l. **1930 Alvis SA 16/95 Silver Eagle Sports Tourer,** coachwork by Cross & Ellis, 4 speed all-synchromesh gearbox from an Alvis Speed 20, rebuilt engine, very good overall condition.
Est. £25,000–30,000 *BKS*

1931 Alvis TJ 12/50 2 Seater de Luxe with Dickey, coachwork by Cross & Ellis, body and upholstery restored, hood replaced, well-documented and original example.
Est. £15,000–16,000 *S*

1932 Alvis 12/60 TL 4 Seater Open Tourer, totally restored, excellent condition.
£23,000–24,000 *S*

Alvis 12/60 TL

- Based on the well-known and very successful 12/50 model.
- The 12/60 was the last in the series of cars derived from the 4 cylinder sports cars which were introduced by Alvis in the early 1920s.
- The 4 cylinder series was replaced by the 6 cylinder series.
- The 12/60 featured a 4 cylinder, 1645cc, overhead valve engine and a 4 speed gearbox.

1933 Alvis Firefly 4 Door Tourer, remarkably original and good condition throughout.
Est. £10,000–13,000 *ALC*

l. **1934 Alvis Firefly Tourer,** needs some tidying.
£6,000–7,000 *H&H*

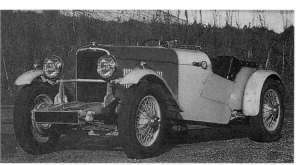

1934 Alvis 1½ Litre Firefly 2 Door Drophead Coupé, coachwork by Cross & Ellis, following museum storage requires some slight restoration. **Est. £12,000–15,000** *BKS*

1939 Alvis 12/70 2 Seater Special, 4 cylinders, 1842cc, originally saloon-bodied, fitted with special 2 seater, alloy sports coachwork in 1973, mechanical rebuild, very good condition. **£10,000–10,500** *COYS*

1939 Alvis 4.3 Litre Saloon, coachworks by Windovers, very good overall condition, has been museum stored. **£24,000–24,500** *BKS*

Introduced in August 1936, the 4.3 litre Alvis succeeded the 3.5 litre model and was claimed to be the fastest unsupercharged saloon on the British market. It was certainly one of the few pre-war saloon cars capable of 100 mph. Total production of the 4.3 litre was 198 cars of all types.

1948 Alvis TA14 Drophead Coupé, coachwork by Carbodies, comprehensive engine rebuild, generally very good condition, no known modifications from maker's original specification. **£10,000–11,000** *BKS*

1949 Alvis TA14 Saloon, coachwork by Park Ward, advanced restoration, which requires completion. **£1,250–1,500** *BKS*

> **Cross Reference**
> Restoration Projects

l. **1949 Alvis TA14,** excellent restoration. **£8,000–9,000** *H&H*

ALVIS Model	ENGINE cc/cyl	DATES	CONDITION 1	2	3
12/50	1496/4	1923-32	£20,000	£13,000	£7,000
Silver Eagle	2148	1929-37	£14,000	£10,000	£8,000
Silver Eagle DHC	2148	1929-37	£16,000	£11,000	£8,000
12/60	1645/4	1931-32	£15,000	£10,000	£7,000
Speed 20 (tourer)	2511/6	1932-36	£35,000	£28,000	£18,000
Speed 20 (closed)	2511/6	1932-36	£22,000	£15,000	£11,000
Crested Eagle	3571/6	1933-39	£10,000	£7,000	£4,000
Firefly (tourer)	1496/4	1932-34	£12,000	£10,000	£6,000
Firefly (closed)	1496/6	1932-34	£7,000	£5,000	£4,000
Firebird (tourer)	1842/4	1934-39	£13,000	£10,000	£6,000
Firebird (closed)	1842/4	1934-39	£7,000	£5,000	£4,000
Speed 25 (tourer)	3571/6	1936-40	£38,500	£30,000	£20,000
Speed 25 (closed)	3571/6	1936-40	£20,000	£15,000	£12,000
3.5 litre	3571/6	1935-36	£35,000	£25,000	£18,000
4.3 litre	4387/6	1936-40	£44,000	£30,000	£22,000
Silver Crest	2362/6	1936-40	£14,000	£10,000	£7,000
TA	3571/6	1936-39	£18,000	£12,000	£8,000
12/70	1842/4	1937-40	£14,000	£10,000	£7,000

1952 Alvis TA21 Drophead Coupé,
coachwork by Tickford, 6 cylinder engine,
2993cc, overhead valve, 93bhp at 4000rpm,
4 speed manual gearbox, Lockhead hydraulic
system, front and rear drum brakes,
independent front suspension, coil springs,
anti-roll bar, rear, rigid axle, semi-elliptic
leaf springs, considerably restored, excellent
overall condition.
£11,000–12,000 *C*

1954 Alvis TA21 Tickford Convertible,
very rare and very good condition.
£13,000–15,000 *SW*

1958 Alvis TD21 2 Door Saloon, coachwork
by Park Ward, automatic transmission, fully
restored condition throughout.
£9,250–9,500 *BKS*

1960 Alvis TD21 2 Door Saloon, coachwork
by Park Ward, mechanically in good running
order, extensively rebuilt.
£5,500–6,000 *BKS*

1960 Alvis TD21 2 Door Saloon, excellent condition
throughout, some wear to interior upholstery and trim.
£7,000–7,500 *BKS*

ALVIS Model	ENGINE cc/cyl	DATES	CONDITION 1	2	3
TA14	1892/4	1946-50	£9,000	£7,000	£4,000
TA14 DHC	1892/4	1946-50	£14,000	£12,000	£5,000
TB14 Roadster	1892/4	1949-50	£14,000	£9,000	£7,000
TB21 Roadster	2993/6	1951	£15,000	£9,000	£6,000
TA21/TC21	2993/6	1950-55	£12,000	£9,000	£5,000
TA21/TC21 DHC	2993/6	1950-55	£17,000	£13,000	£10,000
TC21/100 Grey Lady	2993/6	1953-56	£13,000	£11,000	£5,000
TC21/100 DHC	2993/6	1954-56	£18,000	£15,000	£7,000
TD21	2993/6	1956-62	£10,000	£8,000	£6,000
TD21 DHC	2993/6	1956-62	£20,000	£15,000	£10,000
TE21	2993/6	1963-67	£14,000	£10,000	£8,000
TE21 DHC	2993/6	1963-67	£22,000	£15,000	£10,000
TF21	2993/6	1966-67	£16,000	£12,000	£9,500
TF21 DHC	2993/6	1966-67	£25,000	£15,000	£11,000

1965 Alvis TE21 2 Door Saloon, disc brakes, 5 speed ZF gearbox, vertically paired headlights, original carpets, very good condition, only 2 owners from new.
£8,250–8,500 *BKS*

r. **c1947 Alvis TA14 Sports Special,** original body removed in 1980s, lightweight open body substituted.
£3,300–3,800 *ALC*

1966 Alvis TE21, 5 speed ZF gearbox, power steering, good original condition.
£16,500–17,000 *Bro*

AMERICAN LAFRANCE

1914 American LaFrance Speedster, converted to Speedster bodywork, fully restored condition.
£19,000–20,000 *COYS*

AMILCAR

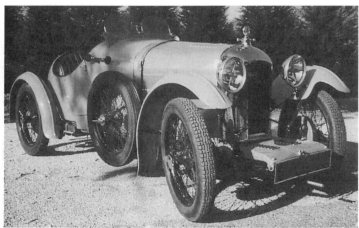

l. **1928 Amilcar CGSS Surbaisse 2 Seater Sports,** replaced side by side type body identical to the original, completely restored condition.
£16,250–16,750 *BKS*

ARIES

1910 Ariés Type V 8/10hp 4 Seater Tourer, 4 cylinder, 60 x 100mm engine, wooden artillery wheels, running board mounted acetylene generator, boa constrictor horn.
£15,000–15,500 *BKS*

Built at Courbevoie, Seine, this is the only example of the model recorded in the Veteran Car Club of Great Britain.

c1907 Ariés 4½ Litre 5 Seater Open Touring Car, 140in wheelbase, fair to good condition.
£16,000–17,000 *S*

ARMSTRONG-SIDDELEY

1947 Armstrong-Siddeley Hurricane, very rare original car.
£14,000–14,500 *SW*

1926 Armstrong-Siddeley 14hp 4 Seater Tourer, right-hand drive, older restoration, good condition throughout.
£11,000–12,000 *BKS*

Armstrong-Siddeley Sapphire

- The company was founded following an amalgamation between Sir W. G. Armstrong-Whitworth & Co Ltd and Siddeley-Deasy; Armstrong-Siddeley was located in Coventry.
- The Sapphire replaced the immediate post-war series.
- Powered by a straight six 3435cc engine and a single Stromberg carburettor which produced about 125bhp at 4800rpm.
- By the time production of all Sapphire variants had ceased in 1959 a total of 7,697 had been built.

1954 Armstrong-Siddeley Sapphire, 6 cylinders, 3435cc, manual gearbox, regularly serviced, good condition, complete with some spares.
£6,000–6,500 *COYS*

ARMSTRONG-SIDDELEY Model	ENGINE cc/cyl	DATES	CONDITION 1	2	3
Hurricane	1991/6	1945-53	£9,000	£6,000	£3,000
Typhoon	1991/6	1946-50	£7,000	£3,000	£2,000
Lancaster/Whitley	1991/ 2306/6	1945-53	£7,000	£5,000	£2,500
Sapphire 234/236	2290/4 2309/6	1955-58	£6,000	£4,000	£2,500
Sapphire 346	3440/6	1953-58	£7,000	£5,000	£3,000
Star Sapphire	3990/6	1958-60	£8,000	£6,000	£3,000

1947 Armstrong-Siddeley Hurricane Drophead Coupé,
6 cylinders, 1991cc, restored, maintained to high standard,
won many shows, only 43,000 miles from new.
£11,000–12,000 *COYS*

1952 Armstrong-Siddeley Sapphire,
good condition.
£3,000–3,500 *H&H*

ARROL-JOHNSTON

The Mo-Car Syndicate Ltd of Glasgow
was founded in 1897 by bridge builder
and civil engineer Sir William Arrol and
George Johnston.

1902 Arrol-Johnston 12hp 6 Seater Dog Cart,
original varnished wood livery, brass Powell &
Hanmer centre acetylene headlamp, Ducellier oil
sidelamps, Lucas rear oil lamp, subject of
considerable work.
£32,000–35,000 *BKS*

ASTER

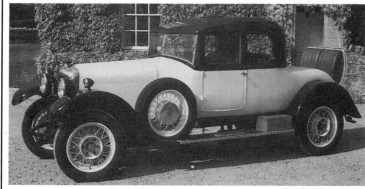

l. **1924 Aster 18/50 Fixed
Head Coupé,** with dickey
seat, one of only 2 known
to survive, generally good
condition throughout.
£15,000–16,000 *BKS*

ASA

1964 ASA Mille Spyder, coachwork by Bertone,
4 cylinders, 1032cc, carefully maintained, never
restored, good original condition throughout.
£15,500–16,000 *COYS*

1964 ASA Mille Berlinetta, coachwork by Bertone,
4 cylinders, 1032cc, excellent original example.
£18,000–18,500 *COYS*

*The ASA Mille was the first car not made by Ferrari
to have a Ferrari engine. The prototype was built in
1958, and no more than 70 ASA cars of any
description were made.*

ASTON MARTIN

The name Aston Martin, founded by Lionel Martin and Robert Bamford in 1914, is synonymous with high quality sports, grand touring cars and successful racing cars. The highly regarded Aston Martins produced between the wars led to the DB series introduced in 1942 following the company's acquisition by David (later Sir David) Brown. Competition success included a well-earned Le Mans victory in 1959. Following a series of take-overs and ownership changes, the company became part of the Ford empire in 1987.

1933 Aston Martin 1½ Litre Le Mans Sports 2/4 Seater, coachwork by Bertelli of Feltham, fully restored, excellent condition throughout. Est. £60,000–70,000 *BKS*

1937 Aston Martin 2 Litre Speed Model – the 'Black Car', 4 cylinders, 1949cc, Ulster 2 seater sports coachwork, well-known car with excellent provenance, superb condition throughout. Est. £140,000–160,000 *COYS*

1953 Aston Martin DB2, 6 cylinder engine, twin overhead camshaft, 4 speed gearbox, good restored condition. **£24,250–24,750** *DB*

1953 Aston Martin DB2 Convertible Coupé, 6 cylinders, 2580cc, excellent overall condition. **£52,000–55,000** *COYS*

Only 49 drophead coupés were made.

ASTON MARTIN Model	ENGINE cc/cyl	DATES	CONDITION 1	2	3
Lionel Martin Cars	1486/4	1921-25	£26,000	£18,000	£16,000
International	1486/4	1927-32	£28,000	£18,000	£16,000
Le Mans	1486/4	1932-33	£52,000	£38,000	£32,000
Mk II	1486/4	1934-36	£40,000	£30,000	£25,000
Ulster	1486/4	1934-36	£70,000	£50,000	
2 litre	1950/4	1936-40	£18,000	£14,000	£9,000

Value is dependent upon racing history, originality and completeness.
Add 40% if a competition winner or works team car.

l. **1954 Aston Martin DB2/4 MkI 3 Litre Drophead Coupé,** original upholstery in excellent condition, 66,000 miles, chromework refinished, bodywork restored, total engine rebuild, suspension and brakes overhauled, rewired.
£30,000–35,000 *ROR*

1955 Aston Martin DB2/4 MkI, successfully competed in 8 races, won the AMOC road going class twice, excellent condition throughout.
£18,500–19,000 *COYS*

1955 Aston Martin DB2/4 Drophead Coupé, 6 cylinders, 2922cc, good general appearance, well maintained.
£28,000–30,000 *COYS*

l. **1955 Aston Martin DB2/4 MkII Fixed Head Coupé,** coachwork by Tickford, 6 cylinders, 2922cc, very rare, *concours d'élégance* winning condition.
£23,000–25,000 *COYS*

1958 Aston Martin DB MkIII Saloon, twin SU carburettor DBA engine, excellent overall condition.
£32,000–35,000 *BKS*

1958 Aston Martin DB2/4, very original, excellent condition.
£25,000–27,000 *SW*

> *A rebuilt car is not necessarily more valuable than a car in good original condition, even if the restoration has been costly.*

r. **1960 Aston Martin DB4GT Coupé,** coachwork by Touring of Milan, comprehensive and meticulous restoration, original build sheets, comprehensive history.
£140,000+ *COYS*

Cross Reference
Competition Cars

l. **1960 Aston Martin DB4 Lightweight Coupé,** coachwork by Touring, 6 cylinders, 4200cc, very desirable racing Aston Martin, excellent race-ready condition.
Est. £38,000–45,000   *COYS*

r. **1962 Aston Martin DB4 Series IV Coupé,** coachwork by Touring of Milan, restored to 'very good' condition.
£74,000–76,000   *COYS*

1962 Aston Martin DB4 Series IV Vantage Sports Coupé, good restored condition.
£30,000–35,000   *S*

1963 Aston Martin DB4 Series V Vantage 3.7 Litre Superleggera Saloon, excellent overall condition.
£25,000–26,000   *BKS*

1964 Aston Martin DB5 Convertible, coachwork by Touring of Milan, 6 cylinders, 3995cc, excellent restored condition.
£50,000–52,000   *COYS*

Aston Martin DB5

- The Aston Martin DB5 was introduced in 1963.
- Production only lasted for 2 years.
- Immortalised as the car used by James Bond in the film *Goldfinger*.
- The DB5 cost about 3 times more than an E-Type Jaguar when new.
- Only 123 DB5 convertibles were built.

r. **1965 Aston Martin DB6 Short Chassis Volante,** concours standard throughout.
£75,000–77,000   *DJR*

1965 Aston Martin DB5, manual gearbox, recently restored, full body refurbishment.
£24,000–25,000 *H&H*

1967 Aston Martin DB6 4 Litre Sports Saloon, fitted with power steering option, good original condition.
£27,000–29,000 *BKS*

1965 Aston Martin DB5 Coupé, coachwork by Touring of Milan, concours condition.
Est. £110,000–130,000 *COYS*

For the films Goldfinger *and* Thunderball *two different DB5 models were used but only one was fitted with the innovative secret weapons devised by Q, the other car being used for most of the driving scenes. This example is unique in that it stars in the latest James Bond film,* Goldeneye.

1968 Aston Martin DB6 2 Door Saloon, with MkII flared wheel arches, power steering, sun roof and automatic transmission, engine in good condition, bodywork and upholstery excellent.
£22,000–24,000 *BKS*

Miller's is a price GUIDE not a price LIST

l. **1968 Aston Martin DB6 Coupé,** coachwork by Touring of Milan, excellent condition throughout.
£20,500–21,500 *COYS*

1969 Aston Martin DB6 MkII Vantage Volante Convertible, coachwork by Touring of Milan, manual gearbox, 46,300 miles from new, very good and original condition, minor blemishes.
Est. £75,000–85,000 *COYS*

This model, with manual gearbox is the most sought-after of all the DB series touring cars.

1971 Aston Martin DBS, good condition, needs attention.
£7,500–8,000 *ADT*

1972 Aston Martin AM V8 Saloon, automatic transmission, electric windows, power-assisted steering and air conditioning, requires respray.
Est. £9,000–11,000 *BKS*

ASTON MARTIN Model	ENGINE cc/cyl	DATES	CONDITION 1	2	3
DB1	1970/4	1948-50	£18,000	£15,000	£11,000
DB2	2580/6	1950-53	£23,000+	£17,000	£13,000
DB2 Conv	2580/6	1951-53	£32,000	£25,000	£17,000
DB2/4 Mk I/II	2580/ 2922/6	1953-57	£30,000	£18,000	£14,000
DB2/4 Mk II Conv	2580/ 2922/6	1953-57	£35,000	£20,000	£15,000
DB2/4 Mk III	2580/ 2922/6	1957-59	£32,000	£20,000	£13,000
DB2/4 Mk III Conv	2580/ 2922/6	1957-59	£35,000	£22,000	£18,000
DB Mk III Conv	2922/6	1957-59	£36,000	£24,000	£20,000
DB Mk III	2922/6	1957-59	£30,000	£19,000	£16,000
DB4	3670/6	1959-63	£30,000	£18,000	£14,000
DB4 Conv	3670/6	1961-63	£50,000	£30,000	-
DB4 GT	3670/6	1961-63	£90,000+	£70,000	-
DB5	3995/6	1964-65	£35,000	£25,000	£18,000
DB5 Conv	3995/6	1964-65	£45,000	£30,000	-
DB6	3995/6	1965-69	£22,000	£17,000	£12,000
DB6 Mk I auto	3995/6	1965-69	£20,000	£15,000	£10,000
DB6 Mk I Volante	3995/6	1965-71	£35,000	£28,000	£22,000
DB6 Mk II Volante	3995/6	1969-70	£36,000	£30,000	£24,000
DBS	3995/6	1967-72	£13,000	£10,000	£8,000
AM Vantage	3995/6	1972-73	£15,000	£11,000	£9,000

1973 Aston Martin V8 Saloon, 49,000 miles recorded, good panel work, excellent paintwork, air conditioning.
£12,000–12,500 *ADT*

1973 Aston Martin AM6 Vantage, 6 cylinder twin overhead camshaft, 3995cc, automatic gearbox, well maintained.
£10,800–11,200 *DB*

l. **1973 Aston Martin DBS V8.**
£10,500–11,500 *BLE*

1974 Aston Martin V8 Manual, fully restored condition.
£18,000–20,000 *VIC*

1974 Aston Martin V8 Drophead, very good overall condition.
£13,000–14,000 *H&H*

1977 Aston Martin V8 Sports Saloon, extensively restored to highest standards, no known modifications to original factory specifications.
Est. £22,000–24,000 *S*

1978 Aston Martin V8 Series 3 Coupé, well maintained, good original condition.
Est. £13,000–16,000 *BKS*

r. **1980 Aston Martin V8 Vantage,** good useable condition.
Est. £15,000–17,000 *ADT*

1980 Aston Martin V8 Coupé, full engine rebuild, suspension and braking system completely overhauled, Vantage spoiler, grilles, spotlights and bumpers, good restored condition.
£30,000–32,000 *BKS*

1982 Aston Martin Lagonda, 8 cylinders, 5340cc, low mileage, very good original condition.
Est. £13,500–14,000 *ADT*

1983 Aston Martin Lagonda LWB, under 5,000 miles from new, left-hand drive, colour TV with remote control to rear compartment, stereo systems front and rear, electric windows, rear picnic tables and drinks cabinet.
£27,000–29,000 *COYS*

This is one of just 3 long wheelbase Lagondas specially coachbuilt by Tickford for Aston Martin.

1989 Aston Martin V8 Vantage Volante, one of only 100 made, superb condition throughout.
£90,000–95,000 *DJR*

ATALANTA

r. **1938 Atalanta Open 2 Seater Sports,** coachwork by Abbott of Farnham, Ford flat head V8 engine, Offenhauser cylinder heads and intake manifolds, triple carburettors, 4 speed manual gearbox with overdrive, hydraulic drum brakes, independent suspension all-round, right-hand drive, major restoration, very good condition throughout.
£35,000–36,000 *C*

This car is one of only 15 Atalanta's known to have been built during the short production period between 1937-39.

AUBURN

r. **1931 Auburn Model 8/98A,** fully restored to exceptional standards, wooden artillery wheels.
Est. £15,000–20,000 *H&H*

1932 Auburn 8-125 Speedster,
8 cylinders, 4895cc, good
condition throughout.
£35,000–36,000 *COYS*

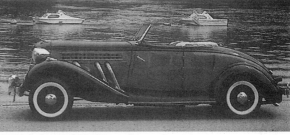

1935 Auburn 851 Supercharged,
excellent original condition.
£26,000–27,000 *COYS*

AUDI

1983 Audi Quattro, original
specification in all respects,
excellent condition throughout.
£4,250–4,750 *S*

*The all new Audi Quattro of 1980 was
developed from the off-road Volkswagen Iltis,
powered by the engine unit from the 200 Turbo,
suitably modified, and driven by the inter-axle
differential from the Volkswagen Polo.*

1994 Audi 2.3 Cabriolet,
very good low mileage condition,
unusual royal provenance.
£24,000–25,000 *S*

*Formerly the property of HRH
The Princess of Wales.*

AUSTRO-DAIMLER

r. **1925 Austro-Daimler 19/70hp,**
6 cylinder in line engine, single
overhead camshaft, monobloc, 2650cc,
4 speed and reverse, central change,
gearbox, 4 wheel cable operated
brakes, semi-elliptic front suspension,
cantilever rear, right-hand drive,
would benefit from minor attention
following period of museum storage.
£30,000–31,000 *C*

AUSTIN

Austin has always produced family cars at
affordable prices from the ubiquitous Austin
Seven, over 290,000 had been made before
production ceased in 1939, to the Issigonis
designed Mini of 1959.

The Austin A90 Atlantic was introduced in
1949. In an attempt to appeal directly to the
American market, the Atlantic was a very
stylish motor car, but not to everyone's taste.
Available in both saloon and soft top
versions, the soft top featured an hydraulic-
electrically operated hood mechanism and
both models featured the 'cyclops' third
central headlight. Despite a vigorous sales
pitch and the achievement of many records
the A90's style failed to attract sufficient
buyers on either side of the Atlantic.

1923 Austin 12 Tourer, 4 cylinders, 1661cc,
4 speed gate change gearbox, 6 volt electrics (CAV),
pram hood, buttoned leather upholstery, newly
restored to high standard and correct specification.
£16,750–17,500 *Mot*

1929 Austin 20/4 Limousine, coachbuilt by
Woodall Nicholson, 4 cylinders, 3610cc side
valve engine, plush velvet upholstery to rear,
full tasselled blinds, inlaid mahogany,
cocktail cabinet, cut glass dome lamps, very
good and original condition.
£18,750–19,500 *Mot*

1911 Austin 40hp Shooting Brake, 4 cylinder engine,
side valve, water-cooled separate cylinders, 6234cc, 3 speed
manual gearbox, rear wheel brakes only, semi-elliptic leaf
spring front suspension, fully elliptic leaf springs rear,
right-hand drive, Brevetto acetylene headlamps, Lucas
sidelamps, boa constrictor horn, Austin instrument gauges,
wooden artillery type wheels, original coachwork,
excellent condition throughout.
£30,000–35,000 *C*

1929 Austin 12hp Clifton Tourer, very good original
condition, but careful recommissioning advisable.
£11,500–12,000 *BKS*

1927 Austin 7 Chummy Tourer, good
original condition, would benefit from some
cosmetic attention.
£6,000–6,400 *BKS*

1927 Austin 7 Top Hat, good condition
throughout, interior original except for seat
squabs and carpet.
£5,400–5,800 *LF*

l. **1928 Austin 7 Chummy,**
very good condition.
£6,500–6,800 *CC*

1930 Austin 7 Chummy, 4 cylinders, 747cc, good mechanical and authentic condition, new hood.
£5,400–5,800 *ADT*

1930 Austin 7 Saloon, short scuttle body, good useable condition.
£3,300–3,600 *ADT*

1930 Austin 7 Saloon, good condition throughout, would benefit from some tidying.
Est. £4,000–4,500 *LF*

1931 Austin 7 RM Box Saloon, good condition throughout.
£4,400–4,800 *S*

1931 Austin Swallow Saloon, right-hand drive, original example from a private collection, now requires some restoration, paintwork requires attention.
£6,400–6,800 *C*

Cross Reference
SS

1932 Austin 7 Saloon, very good restored condition.
£3,400–3,600 *BKS*

1932 Austin 7 RN Series Saloon, good and unaltered from original specification, mechanically good in all respects.
£3,250–3,500 *ADT*

l. **1932 Austin 7 Box Saloon.**
£2,600–2,800 *HOLL*

1932 **Austin 7 Saloon,** bodywork good and original, engine in very good condition.
£2,600–2,800 *ADT*

1932 **Austin Box Saloon,** superb original condition, very correct restoration.
£5,000–6,000 *SW*

Austin 7

- Introduced in 1922 and was produced until the outbreak of WWII.
- Powered by a 747cc side valve engine, the Austin 7 brought motoring to the masses almost completely replacing the motorcycle combination.
- Over 290,000 were produced of all models.
- Built under licence in France (Rosengart), Germany (Dixi), Japan and America.
- Racing success came with the Ulster Variant, including a win at Brooklands.

1933 **Austin 7 Long Door Saloon,** generally tidy and complete.
Est. £3,800–4,800 *ADT*

l. 1934 **Austin 7 Saloon,** totally rebuilt, including engine, gearbox, brakes, full rewire, refurbished chassis, new tyres.
£4,100–4,400 *H&H*

1929 **Austin 7 Chummy.**
£4,250–4,750 *HOLL*

r. 1934 **Austin De Luxe Saloon,** excellent condition but some minor recommissioning required.
£5,400–5,800 *S*

AUSTIN Model	ENGINE cc/cyl	DATES	CONDITION		
			1	2	3
25/30	4900/4	1906	£35,000	£25,000	£20,000
20	3600/4	1919-27	£18,000	£12,000	£6,000
12	1661/4	1922-26	£8,000	£5,000	£2,000
7	747/4	1924-39	£7,000	£4,000	£1,500
7 Coachbuilt/Nippy/Opal etc	747/4	1924-39	£10,000	£9,000	£7,000
12/4	1861/4	1927-35	£5,500	£4,000	£2,000
16	2249/6	1928-36	£9,000	£7,000	£4,000
20/6	3400/6	1928-38	£12,500	£10,000	£8,000
12/6	1496/6	1932-37	£6,000	£4,000	£1,500
12/4	1535/4	1933-39	£5,000	£3,500	£1,500
10 and 10/4	1125/4	1932-47	£4,000	£3,000	£1,000
10 and 10/4 Conv	1125/4	1933-47	£5,000	£3,500	£1,000
18	2510/6	1934-39	£8,000	£5,000	£3,000
14	1711/6	1937-39	£6,000	£4,000	£2,000
Big Seven	900/4	1938-39	£4,000	£2,500	£1,500
8	900/4	1939-47	£3,000	£2,000	£1,000
28	4016/6	1939	£6,000	£4,000	£2,000

1934 Austin 7 Saloon, 4 cylinders, 747cc, very good condition, some minor cosmetic attention required.
Est. £4,500–5,500 *ADT*

1934 Austin 10hp 2 Seater and Dickey, original specification, very good original condition.
£5,750–6,000 *BKS*

1935 Austin 7 Open Road Tourer, 4 cylinders, 747cc, unrestored original condition throughout.
Est. £4,750–5,500 *ADT*

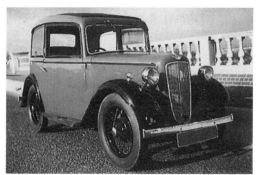

1935 Austin 7 Ruby, 4 cylinders, 747cc, restored to very good standard, mechanically good in all respects.
£4,500–4,750 *ADT*

r. **1936 Austin 7 Cabriolet,** totally rebuilt.
£6,000–7,000 *SW*

l. **1936 Austin 7 Ruby,** totally restored condition.
£5,000–6,000 *SW*

1937 Austin 7 Ruby, 4 cylinders, 747cc, good condition throughout.
£3,300–3,600 *ADT*

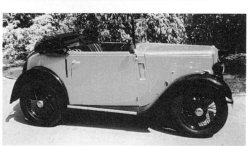

1937 Austin 7 Opal, very good condition.
£4,500–4,900 *CC*

l. **1938 Austin 7 Ruby,** completely restored within last 5 years, very good condition.
£4,500–4,750 *COYS*

1938 Austin 7 Ruby, seats original, fully rebuilt, excellent condition.
£2,750–3,250 *H&H*

1933 Austin 7 Paxton Special, professionally restored.
£4,000–4,300 *S*

1931 Austin Ulster Replica, alloy body as new.
£8,000–9,000 *SW*

1934 Austin 10/4 Cabriolet, very good condition.
£7,500–8,000 *CC*

1934 Austin 10, very good condition.
£4,000–4,500 *CC*

1935 Austin 10/4 Lichfield, 4 cylinders, 1125cc,
4 speed gearbox, restored, new leather interior,
good paintwork and mechanics.
£3,800–4,200 *Mot*

1934 Austin 7 Sports Tourer, converted into
an open tourer in late 1950s, aluminium sports
body fitted, would make excellent trials car.
£4,000–4,200 *H&H*

1927 Austin 7 Cup Open Tourer,
totally rebuilt in 1995, superb condition.
£4,600–4,800 *H&H*

1934 Austin 10/4 Lichfield, 4 cylinders, 1125cc,
major restoration, good condition throughout.
£6,250–6,500 *ADT*

1928 Austin Heavy 12/4 Fabric Saloon,
very good condition.
£10,000–10,500 *CC*

1931 Austin Light 12/6 Harley Saloon,
6 cylinder monobloc engine, 1496cc, RAC rating of
13.9hp, extensive renovation, very correct example.
£7,500–8,000 *ADT*

*The Light 12/6 in saloon form was designated
Harley, open versions being the Eton 2 seater with
dickey seat and the Open Road 4 seater tourer.*

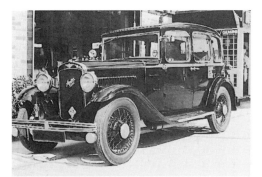

1932 Austin Harley 12/6 Saloon,
totally original condition.
£11,500–12,500 *SW*

1934 Austin 12/6 Kempton Sports Saloon,
very good condition.
£6,500–7,000 *CC*

1936 Austin 14 Goodwood, superb condition.
£6,000–7,000 *SW*

1932 Austin 16/6 Saloon, very good condition.
£7,500–8,000 *CC*

The first Austin car was marketed in 1906 by Herbert Austin, who had previously been responsible for certain products from the nearby Wolseley factory. Since that time the Austin has played a major role in the British motor industry and the 'dependable Austin', as the marque was known, was a true reflection of English social life in the 1920s and '30s. The Austin Seven was designed as a vehicle that the average working family could afford, replacing the traditional motorcycle plus combination unit.

1937 Austin 18 4 Door Saloon, good original
condition throughout.
Est. £4,500–6,500 *ALC*

1947 Austin 8 Saloon, 4 cylinders, 900cc side valve
engine, 37,000 miles, totally original condition.
£2,600–2,800 *AH*

1951 Austin A40, 4 cylinder overhead
valve engine, 4 speed gearbox, good
unrestored condition.
£900–1,000 *DB*

r. **1952 Austin A40 Somerset,**
very good condition.
£2,000–2,500 *CC*

1951 Austin A135 Princess 4 Litre 4 Door Saloon, coachwork by Vanden Plas, excellent condition throughout.
£10,750–11,000 *BKS*

The Sheerline, when introduced, used a 6 cylinder, 3460cc engine, but on the MkII Princess a more powerful engine of 3993cc was employed. A total of 760 cars were built at Kingsbury to the MkII specification.

1949 Austin A90 Atlantic Convertible,
2660cc, power-assisted hood and windows, good all-round condition, believed to have been original motor show car.
£6,300–6,800 *H&H*

1954 Austin A40 Somerset Saloon, no known modifications, good overall condition.
Est. £1,700–2,000 *S*

1958 Austin A55 Cambridge, excellent overall condition.
£2,300–2,600 *H&H*

Cross Reference
Commercial Vehicles

AUSTIN Model	ENGINE cc/cyl	DATES	CONDITION 1	2	3
16	2199/4	1945-49	£3,000	£2,000	£1,000
A40 Devon	1200/4	1947-52	£2,000	£1,200	£750
A40 Sports	1200/4	1950-53	£6,000	£4,000	£2,000
A40 Somerset	1200/4	1952-54	£2,000	£1,500	£750
A40 Somerset DHC	1200/4	1954	£5,000	£4,000	£2,500
A40 Dorset 2 door	1200/4	1947-48	£2,000	£1,500	£1,000
A70 Hampshire	2199/4	1948-50	£2,000	£1,500	£1,000
A70 Hereford	2199/4	1950-54	£2,000	£1,500	£1,000
A90 Atlantic DHC	2660/4	1949-52	£8,000	£6,000	£4,000
A90 Atlantic	2660/4	1949-52	£6,000	£4,000	£3,000
A40/A50 Cambridge	1200/4	1954-57	£1,200	£750	£500
A55 Mk I Cambridge	1489/4	1957-59	£1,000	£750	£500
A55 Mk II	1489/4	1959-61	£1,000	£750	£500
A60 Cambridge	1622/4	1961-69	£1,000	£750	£500
A90/95 Westminster	2639/6	1954-59	£2,000	£1,500	£750
A99 Westminster	2912/6	1959-61	£1,500	£1,000	£500
A105 Westminster	2639/6	1956-59	£2,000	£1,500	£750
A110 Mk I/II	2912/6	1961-68	£2,000	£1,500	£750
Nash Metropolitan	1489/4	1957-61	£2,500	£1,500	£750
Nash Metropolitan DHC	1489/4	1957-61	£4,000	£3,000	£1,500
A30	803/4	1952-56	£1,000	£500	-
A30 Countryman	803/4	1954-56	£1,500	£1,000	-
A35	948/4	1956-59	£1,000	£500	-
A35 Countryman	948/4	1956-62	£1,500	£1,000	-
A40 Farina Mk I	948/4	1958-62	£1,250	£750	£200
A40 Mk I Countryman	948/4	1959-62	£1,500	£1,000	£400
A40 Farina Mk II	1098/4	1962-67	£1,000	£750	-
A40 Mk II Countryman	1098/4	1962-67	£1,200	£750	£300
1100	1098/4	1963-73	£1,000	£750	-
1300 Mk I/II	1275/4	1967-74	£750	£500	-
1300GT	1275/4	1969-74	£1,250	£1,000	£750
1800/2200	1800/2200/4	1964-75	£1,500	£900	£600
3 litre	2912/6	1968-71	£3,000	£1,500	£500

1955 Austin A30 Saloon, interior original but worn, good original condition.
Est. **£250–500** *ALC*

1957 Austin A35, 4 cylinders, 948cc, body generally sound, bumpers require re-chroming.
£800–900 *ADT*

1957 Austin Princess DS7, 3995cc, restored.
£4,800–5,200 *DB*

1965 Austin A40 Farina Countryman, good original condition.
£900–975 *LF*

Cross Reference
Mini

1966 Austin A110 Westminster, good condition.
£1,200–1,500 *H&H*

1968 Austin A60 Cambridge Saloon, 4 cylinders, 1622cc, 61bhp at 5250rpm, 4 speed manual gearbox, front disc brakes, drum rear, independent coil springs front suspension, half elliptic leaf springs rear, right-hand drive, genuine car, requires some restoration.
£80–100 *C*

A rebuilt car is not necessarily more valuable than a car in good original condition, even if the restoration has been costly.

l. **1975 Austin Allegro Vanden Plas,** recorded mileage of 12,570, very good condition throughout.
£2,500–2,750 *ADT*

AUSTIN HEALEY

1960 Austin Healey 'Frogeye' Sprite, outstanding condition throughout.
£5,600–5,800 *H&H*

1960 Austin Healey Sprite MkI, 4 cylinders, 948cc, mechanically good order, good condition throughout.
£6,300–6,600 *ADT*

1965 Austin Healey Sprite MkIII, 4 cylinders, 1098cc, excellent condition throughout.
Est. £5,500–6,000 *ADT*

The Austin Healey Sprite and the MG Midget were identical, using the same body shell, with the exception of badging and extra chrome body strips on the Midget.

1959 Austin Healey Sprite, fibreglass bonnet, good overall condition.
£3,500–4,000 *H&H*

1953 Austin Healey 100/4 2 Seater Roadster, 4 speed gearbox with overdrive as on the BN2 cars, fully restored, superb condition throughout.
£22,000–23,000 *BKS*

l. **1954 Austin Healey 100/4,** 4 cylinders, 2660cc, excellent restored condition.
£13,400–13,800 *ADT*

1954 Austin Healey 100/4, 4 cylinders, overhead valve, twin carburettors, 2660cc, 90bhp at 4000rpm, 3 speed synchromesh gearbox with overdrive on 2nd and 3rd, front and rear drum brakes, independent front suspension, live rear axle, right-hand drive, meticulous chassis-up rebuild to highest standard.
£29,000–30,000 *C*

l. **1954 Austin Healey 100/4,** 4 cylinders, 2660cc, left-hand drive, major restoration, very good condition throughout.
£13,800–14,500 *COYS*

1955 Austin Healey 100/4 2 Seater Sports, right-hand drive, extensively restored, fully rebuilt engine, no known modifications, excellent condition. £13,800–14,500 *BKS*

1957 Austin Healey 100/6 2+2 Seater Sports, 6 cylinders, 2639cc, 102bhp at 4600rpm, 4 speed manual gearbox with overdrive, drum brakes all-round, independent coil front suspension, semi-elliptic rear, right-hand drive, originally left-hand drive, very good restored condition. £10,800–11,500 *C*

1957 Austin Healey 100/6 2 Seater Sports Roadster, genuine UK market right-hand drive, completely restored, excellent condition. £10,500–11,000 *BKS*

1958 Austin Healey 100/6, 6 cylinders, 2660cc, excellent condition in every respect, complete with FIA papers. Est. £25,000–30,000 *COYS*

Cross Reference
Racing Cars

1958 Austin Healey 100/6, 6 cylinders, 2660cc, original right-hand drive, one of 133 two seaters made for the home market, excellent condition throughout, completely restored. £20,000–21,000 *COYS*

1958 Austin Healey 100/6, left-hand drive, completely restored. £22,000–23,000 *COYS*

1959 Austin Healey 100/6, prepared to works rally specifications in early 1960s, good history, running order, requires restoration. £7,000–7,500 *CGOC*

1960 Austin Healey 3000 MkI, fitted with MkIII double carburettor engine, comprehensive restoration. Est. £13,000–15,000 *S*

1960 Austin Healey 3000 MkI BT7 2+2, 6 cylinders, 2912cc, 4 speed gearbox with overdrive, wire wheels, left-hand drive, restored, rebuilt engine. £11,800–12,200 *Mot*

1960 Austin Healey 3000 MkI Roadster, refurbished throughout, 60 spoke wire wheels, rebuilt engine, left-hand drive. £10,500–10,800 *BKS*

1961 Austin Healey 3000 MkII, right-hand drive, total restoration, concours condition in every respect.
Est. £27,000–33,000 *COYS*

1961 Austin Healey 3000 MkI BT7, left-hand drive, good restored body and interior.
£11,500–12,000 *Mot*

1961 Austin Healey 3000 MkII,
good original car.
£13,000–13,500 *CGOC*

1963 Austin Healey 3000 MkII, older restoration, original right-hand drive.
Est. £12,000–14,000 *ALC*

1963 Austin Healey 3000 MkIIa, original right-hand drive, less than 1,000 miles since complete rebuild.
£15,000–15,500 *ADT*

1964 Austin Healey 3000 MkII, new leather trim and chrome, left-hand drive, good restored condition.
£13,250–13,750 *Mot*

1964 Austin Healey 3000 MkIII, 6 cylinders, 2912cc, complete ground up restoration, repainted, chrome wire wheels.
Est. £18,000–19,000 *ADT*

1965 Austin Healey 3000 MkIII Roadster, chassis-up rebuild, converted to right-hand drive, excellent condition throughout.
Est. £17,000–20,000 *BKS*

AUSTIN HEALEY Model	ENGINE cc/cyl	DATES	CONDITION 1	2	3
100 BN 1/2	2660/4	1953-56	£20,000	£14,000	£8,000
100/6, BN4/BN6	2639/6	1956-59	£18,000	£13,500	£8,000
3000 Mk I	2912/6	1959-61	£20,000	£13,000	£8,500
3000 Mk II	2912/6	1961-62	£22,000	£15,000	£9,000
3000 Mk IIA	2912/6	1962-64	£23,000	£15,000	£11,000
3000 Mk III	2912/6	1964-68	£24,000	£17,000	£11,000
Sprite Mk I	948/4	1958-61	£5,000	£4,000	£2,000
Sprite Mk II	948/4	1961-64	£3,000	£2,000	£1,000
Sprite Mk III	1098/4	1964-66	£3,500	£2,000	£1,000
Sprite Mk IV	1275/4	1966-71	£3,500	£1,500	£1,000

1966 Austin Healey 3000 MkIII Phase II, 6 cylinders, 2912cc, total body restoration and mechanical overhaul, left-hand drive, excellent condition in every respect.
£28,000–29,000 *COYS*

1966 Austin Healey 3000 MkIII BJ8, converted to right-hand drive, good mechanics and chrome, paintwork poor, trim fair.
£12,250–12,750 *Mot*

1967 Austin Healey 3000 MkIII, originally exported to USA, converted to right-hand drive, totally renovated, excellent condition throughout.
£18,000–19,000 *COYS*

1966 Austin Healey 3000 MkIII, 6 cylinders, 2912cc, 150bhp with servo-assisted brakes, right-hand drive, no known modifications from original specification, fully restored, only 1,000 miles since restoration, excellent condition.
£20,500–22,000 *COYS*

AUSTIN METROPOLITAN

1958 Austin Metropolitan 1500 Coupé, good original condition.
£3,000–3,250 *ADT*

1957 Austin Metropolitan Convertible, 4 cylinders, 1489cc, dry stored for a number of years, good condition.
£2,000–2,250 *ADT*

BAYLISS-THOMAS

The Bayliss-Thomas was manufactured for just 7 years by the Excelsior Motor Company Ltd, who were better known for two-wheeled vehicles. They were made only in small numbers and are now extremely rare.

r. **1925 Bayliss-Thomas 4 Seater Tourer,** original condition, needs some restoration.
Est. £6,000–9,000 *ALC*

BENTLEY

1924 Bentley 3 Litre Red Label, 'The Golden Bentley', 4 cylinders, 2996cc, very well-known with excellent provenance, superb original condition.
Est. £65,000–75,000 *COYS*

1922 Bentley 3 Litre Open 4 Seater, replica coachwork in the style of Vanden Plas, 4 cylinders, 2996cc, 70bhp at 3500rpm, 4 speed manual gearbox, 4 wheel drum brakes, semi-elliptic suspension, right-hand drive, fully rebuilt to 3 litre Red Label short chassis specification with vertical SU carburettors.
Est. £50,000–60,000 *C*

The chassis frame is not original, but the Bentley Drivers' Club have allocated a chassis number.

1924 Bentley 3 Litre Speed Model.
£86,000–88,000 *MAN*

1925 Bentley 3/4½ Litre Boat-Back Convertible, coachwork by S. MacNielle of Walsall, 4 cylinders, 4398cc, 175bhp at 3500rpm, 4 speed manual gearbox, 4 wheel drum brakes, semi-elliptic suspension, right-hand drive, excellent restored condition.
Est. £85,000–95,000 *C*

1928 Bentley 4½ Litre Vanden Plas.
£110,000+ *BLE*

1926 Bentley 3/4½ Litre Original Vanden Plas.
£150,000+ *MAN*

r. **1928 Bentley Corsica Body 4½ Litre Corsica Body.**
£105,000+ *MAN*

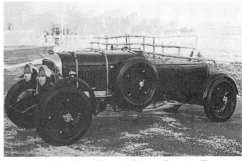

1929 Bentley 4½ Litre Sports 4 Seater Tourer, replica Vanden Plas coachwork by Robinson, originally Mulliner saloon coachwork. **Est. £90,000–120,000** *BKS*

This is one of 244 4½ litre Bentleys built during 1929. Total production of the model was 665.

1929 Bentley 4½ Litre Sports Tourer. £108,000+ *MAN*

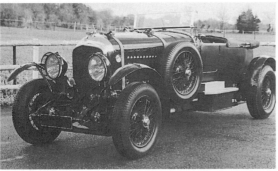

1929 Bentley 4½ Litre Open 4 Seater Tourer, coachwork by Vanden Plas, 4 cylinder in line engine, 4398cc, 110bhp at 3500rpm, 4 speed and reverse gearbox, 4 wheel drum brakes, semi-elliptic leaf spring suspension, right-hand drive, restored to highest standard. **£180,000+** *C*

1929 Bentley 4½ Litre Team Car. £750,000+ *MAN*

1929 Bentley 4½ Litre Le Mans.
£175,000+ *MAN*

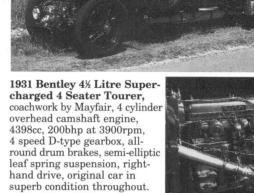

Bentley 8 Litre

- Only 100 8 litre Bentleys were built, and unlike other Bentley models they were not intended to race.
- The 8 litre Bentley was powered by a 7892cc straight-6 cylinder engine with 4 valves per cylinder which could exceed 100mph.
- It cost about £1,850 for the chassis alone, the body could cost up to another £1,000.
- It is alleged that the 8 litre was built by W. O. Bentley to dispel the reputation that Rolls-Royce was the best car in the world.

1931 Bentley 4½ Litre Supercharged 4 Seater Tourer, coachwork by Mayfair, 4 cylinder overhead camshaft engine, 4398cc, 200bhp at 3900rpm, 4 speed D-type gearbox, all-round drum brakes, semi-elliptic leaf spring suspension, right-hand drive, original car in superb condition throughout. £480,000+ *CNY*

1931 Bentley 8 Litre 4 Light Saloon, coachwork by H. J. Mulliner, highly original, very good condition. £190,000+ *COYS*

1931 Bentley 8 Litre Open Tourer, coachwork by Corsica, 6 cylinders, 7892cc, maintained to highest standards, excellent condition. £360,000+ *COYS*

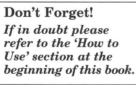

r. **1934 Bentley 3½ Litre 2 Door Saloon,** coachwork in the style of Park Ward, excellent restored condition. Est. £26,000–28,000 *S*

Don't Forget!
If in doubt please refer to the 'How to Use' section at the beginning of this book.

1934 Bentley 3½ Litre Sedanca Coupé, coachwork by Freestone & Webb, 6 cylinder in line engine, overhead valves, 3669cc, twin SU carburettors, coil ignition, 4 speed manual gearbox with synchromesh on 3rd and 4th, 4 wheel drum brakes, semi-elliptic all-round suspension, right-hand drive, older restoration, very good condition. £42,000–43,000 *C*

r. **1934 Bentley 3½ Litre 4 Door Sports Saloon,** maintained to a good standard. Est. £35,000–40,000 *BKS*

This car has the distinctive provenance of being formerly the property of Sir Malcolm Campbell.

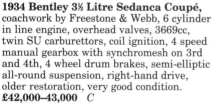

1935 Bentley 3½ Litre Close-Coupled Coupé,
coachwork by J. Gurney Nutting, 6 cylinders,
3669cc, remarkable car with excellent provenance,
concours condition.
£75,000–78,000 *COYS*

1935 Bentley 3½ Litre Park Ward,
6 cylinders, 3500cc, good restored condition.
£15,000–15,500 *DB*

1936 Bentley 4¼ Sport Low Vision Coupé,
coachwork by Gurney Nutting, 6 cylinders, 4257cc,
overhead valve, 125bhp at 4500rpm, 4 speed gearbox,
4 wheel drum brakes, semi-elliptic leaf spring
suspension, right-hand drive, full tool set in boot lid,
original fitted luggage, very good overall condition.
£30,000–35,000 *CNY*

1937 Bentley 4¼ Litre Overdrive Tourer,
'Malcolm Campbell Design' coachwork by Vanden
Plas, excellent restored condition throughout.
Est. £85,000–100,000 *COYS*

1937 Bentley 4¼ Litre Sedanca Coupé,
coachwork by J. Gurney Nutting, 6 cylinders,
4357cc, fully restored to superb condition.
£68,000–72,000 *COYS*

1937 Bentley 4¼ Litre Sports Saloon,
coachwork by Barker, 6 cylinder in line engine,
4257cc, 125bhp at 4500rpm, 4 speed manual
gearbox, 4 wheel drum brakes assisted by
mechanical servo, semi-elliptic leaf spring
suspension, right-hand drive, original engine,
good condition, running and driving well.
£16,000–17,000 *C*

1937 Bentley 4¼ Litre Close-Coupled Sports Saloon,
coachwork by Park Ward, good overall condition.
Est. £18,000–20,000 *S*

r. **1939 Bentley 4¼ Litre MX Series Drophead Coupé,**
coachwork by Vanden Plas, overall condition good,
bodywork recently restored.
Est. £60,000–65,000 *S*

BENTLEY Model	ENGINE cc/cyl	DATES	CONDITION 1	2	3
3 litre	2996/4	1920-27	£100,000	£75,000	£50,000
Speed Six	6597/6	1926-32	£400,000	£250,000	£160,000
4.5 litre	4398/4	1927-31	£175,000	£125,000	£80,000
4.5 litre Supercharged	4398/4	1929-32	£600,000	£300,000	£200,000
8 litre	7983/6	1930-32	£350,000	£250,000	£100,000
3.5 litre Saloon & DHC	3699/6	1934-37	£70,000	£30,000	£15,000
4.25 litre Saloon & DHC	4257/6	1937-39	£70,000	£35,000	£20,000
Mark V	4257/6	1939-41	£45,000	£25,000	£20,000

Prices are very dependent on engine type, body style and original extras like supercharger, gearbox
ratio, history and originality.

1939 Bentley 4¼ Litre MX Lightweight Tourer, major mechanical overhaul.
Est. £30,000–35,000 *BKS*

This car was delivered with James Young coupé coachwork, and was rebodied in post-war years. The mechanical detail remained in all major respects to original factory specification.

1939 Bentley 4¼ Litre MX Series Drophead Coupé, coachwork by Barker, 6 cylinder overhead valve engine, 4257cc, 125bhp at 4500rpm, 4 speed manual gearbox with overdrive, 4 wheel drum brakes, semi-elliptic suspension, right-hand drive, older restoration but very good overall condition.
£60,000–62,000 *C*

1948 Bentley MkVI Sports Saloon, 6 cylinders, 4257cc, complete body and chassis restoration, major mechanical overhaul.
Est. £12,000–16,000 *COYS*

1948 Bentley MkVI Standard Steel Saloon, good original condition throughout.
£8,500–9,000 *S*

> *A rebuilt car is not necessarily more valuable than a car in good original condition, even if the restoration has been costly.*

1949 Bentley MkVI Saloon, coachwork by H. J. Mulliner, shabby but chassis in sound condition.
£11,000–11,500 *RCC*

1949 Bentley MkVI 4 Door Saloon, coachwork by H. J. Mulliner, good useable condition.
Est. £10,000–12,000 *S*

1950 Bentley MkVI Saloon, good condition throughout.
Est. £6,500–7,500 *LF*

1951 Bentley MkVI Standard Steel Saloon.
£24,000–26,000 *PJF*

1951 Bentley MkVI, coachwork by
H. J. Mulliner, 6 cylinders, 4257cc,
good original condition throughout.
Est. £13,500–15,500 *ADT*

1952 Bentley MkVI Standard Steel,
6 cylinders, 4500cc, manual gearbox,
excellent unrestored condition.
£11,000–11,500 *DB*

Bentley R-Type Continental

- Introduced in 1952, the R-Type Continental
  was the world's fastest 4 seater tourer.
- It was the most expensive production car in
  the world at that time.
- The wonderfully stylish fastback coupé
  body was built by H. J. Mulliner and Co Ltd
  of Chiswick.
- Top speed was over 120mph.
- Sadly, only 207 were built.

**1952 Bentley MkVI Standard Steel
Saloon,** original interior, good
condition in all respects.
£9,000–9,500 *BKS*

**1953 Bentley R-Type Continental Fastback
Coupé,** coachwork by H. J. Mulliner, meticulously
maintained, very fine, original example.
£60,000–64,000 *COYS*

1954 Bentley R-Type Sports Saloon, coachwork
by James Young of Bromley, Kent, requires
restoration, basically sound and very original.
£4,000–4,500 *BKS*

**1954 Bentley R-Type Series D Two Door
Continental Sports Saloon,** coachwork by
H. J. Mulliner, automatic gearbox and
electric windows from new, right-hand drive,
very good condition.
Est. £70,000–80,000 *BKS*

1954 Bentley R-Type, automatic gearbox.
£14,500–15,000 *BLE*

l. **1954 Bentley Hooper Empress R-Type Sports Saloon,**
6 cylinder, in line engine, 4566cc, overhead valve, twin
carburettors, 150bhp at 4500rpm, automatic gearbox, hydraulic
front, mechanical rear servo assisted brakes, front wishbone
suspension, coil spring rear suspension, rigid axle with semi-
elliptic rear springs, right-hand drive, meticulous and complete
mechanical and cosmetic restoration to highest standards.
£64,000–66,000 *C*

BENTLEY Model	ENGINE cc/cyl	DATES	CONDITION 1	2	3
Abbreviations: HJM = H J Mulliner; PW = Park Ward; M/PW = Mulliner/Park Ward					
Mk VI Standard Steel	4257/4566/6	1946-52	£16,000	£11,000	£6,000
Mk VI Coachbuilt	4257/4566/6	1946-52	£25,000	£20,000	£12,000
Mk VI Coachbuilt DHC	4566/6	1946-52	£40,000	£30,000	£20,000
R Type Standard Steel	4566/6	1952-55	£12,000	£10,000	£7,000
R Type Coachbuilt	4566/6	1952-55	£25,000	£20,000	£15,000
R Type Coachbuilt DHC	4566/4887/6	1952-55	£50,000	£35,000	£25,000
R Type Cont (HJM)	4887/6	1952-55	£80,000	£40,000	£29,000
S1 Standard Steel	4887/6	1955-59	£15,000	£12,000	£7,000
S1 Cont 2 door (PW)	4877/6	1955-59	£30,000	£25,000	£20,000
S1 Cont Drophead	4877/6	1955-59	£80,000	£75,000	£50,000
S1 Cont F'back (HJM)	4877/6	1955-58	£45,000	£35,000	£25,000
S2 Standard Steel	6230/8	1959-62	£15,000	£9,000	£6,000
S2 Cont 2 door (HJM)	6230/8	1959-62	£60,000	£40,000	£30,000
S2 Flying Spur (HJM)	6230/8	1959-62	£45,000	£33,000	£22,000
S2 Conv (PW)	6230/8	1959-62	£60,000	£50,000	£35,000
S3 Standard Steel	6230/8	1962-65	£16,000	£11,000	£9,000
S3 Cont/Flying Spur	6230/8	1962-65	£45,000	£30,000	£25,000
S3 2 door (PW)	6230/8	1962-65	£30,000	£25,000	£18,000
S3 Conv (modern conversion - only made one original)	6230/8	1962-65	£40,000	£28,000	£20,000
T1	6230/6, 6750/8	1965-77	£10,000	£8,000	£4,000
T1 2 door (M/PW)	6230/6, 6750/8	1965-70	£15,000	£12,000	£9,000
T1 Drophead (M/PW)	6230/6, 6750/8	1965-70	£25,000	£18,000	£12,000

l. **1954 Bentley R-Type Standard Saloon,** with Harold Radford Countryman conversion, 6 cylinder, in line engine, single camshaft, 4566cc, 3 speed automatic gearbox, 4 wheel drum brakes, independent coil springs and wishbones front suspension, live axle with half-elliptic springs rear, right-hand drive, very good overall condition.
Est. £14,000–16,000 *C*

r. **1955 Bentley R-Type Continental Fastback Saloon,** coachwork by H. J. Mulliner, manual gearbox with right-hand change, very good original condition throughout.
£88,000–92,000 *BKS*

r. **1955 Bentley R-Type 4 Door Saloon,** coachwork by James Young of Bromley, 6 cylinders, 4500cc, automatic gearbox.
£7,250–7,750 *DB*

1957 Bentley S1 Continental Fastback Coupé, coachwork by H. J. Mulliner, good condition throughout.
£42,000–44,000 *COYS*

1958 Bentley S1, good overall condition.
£8,000–8,500 *ADT*

1958 Bentley S1 Continental Sports Saloon,
coachwork by Park Ward & Co Ltd, original
example, recently undergone some recommissioning.
Est. £22,000–28,000 *BKS*

1958 Bentley S1, very good overall condition.
£15,000–16,000 *SW*

**1959 Bentley S2 Four Door Standard Steel
Saloon,** mechanically excellent, coachwork
good, chassis in very good condition.
£6,800–7,200 *BKS*

1960 Bentley S2 Continental Fixed Head Coupé,
coachwork by H. J. Mulliner, 8 cylinders, 6230cc,
extensively restored, excellent condition throughout.
£36,000–38,000 *COYS*

1960 Bentley S2 Continental 2 Door Saloon, coachwork by
H. J. Mulliner, considerably refurbished, superb restored condition.
£52,000–53,000 *BKS*

1960 Bentley S2 Standard Saloon,
V8 overhead valve engine, 6230cc, 200bhp
at 5000rpm, 4 speed automatic gearbox,
4 wheel drum brakes, independent front
suspension by coil springs and wishbones,
semi-elliptic rear suspension, right-hand
drive, low mileage, very good original
condition throughout.
£17,000–19,000 *C*

1960 Bentley S2 Standard Steel Saloon,
good condition throughout.
Est. £13,000–15,000 *S*

1960 Bentley S2 Continental Drophead, coachwork by
Park Ward, 6250cc, interior and hood replaced, engine
overhauled, completely restored, excellent condition.
£34,000–36,000 *H&H*

**1961 Bentley S2 Flying Spur 4 Door
Saloon,** coachwork by Mulliner Park Ward,
bodywork in excellent condition, engine,
transmission, chassis and electrics in good
condition, 77,100 miles from new.
£33,000–35,000 *BKS*

1960 Bentley S2 Continental Convertible, coachwork by Park Ward, very good condition throughout.
Est. £39,000–42,000 *S*

r. **1962 Bentley S2 Standard Steel Saloon,** regularly serviced and maintained, no known modifications from original factory specification, excellent overall condition. £13,500–14,000 *S*

1961 Bentley S2 Standard Steel Saloon, good overall condition, no known modifications to original specification. Est. £10,000–12,000 *S*

1962 Bentley S2 Continental Flying Spur, coachwork by H. J. Mulliner. £60,000–65,000 *PJF*

1963 Bentley S3 Standard Saloon, V8 overhead valve engine, 6230cc, 4 speed automatic gearbox, independent front suspension with wishbones, semi-elliptic leaf spring rear, 4 wheel drum brakes, right-hand drive, regularly serviced, good condition. £12,000–12,500 *C*

1963 Bentley S3 Continental 4 Door Saloon, coachwork by James Young, very good original condition. Est. £27,000–30,000 *S*

1963 Bentley S3 Continental Flying Spur, coachwork by H. J. Mulliner. £62,000–65,000 *PJF*

1964 Bentley Continental Flying Spur, service details from new, excellent condition throughout. £40,000–42,000 *H&H*

1964 Bentley S3 Continental Flying Spur Saloon, coachwork by H. J. Mulliner, paintwork recently restored, good mechanical condition throughout. £24,000–25,000 *BKS*

1964 Bentley S3 Continental Fixed Head Coupé, coachwork by Mulliner Park Ward, 8 cylinders, 6225cc, very good all-round condition. £19,000–20,000 *ADT*

1965 Bentley S3, V8 engine, 6250cc, automatic gearbox, unrestored, unused for 5 years. £6,000–6,500 *DB*

1965 Bentley S2 Continental 2 Door,
coachwork by Mulliner Park Ward, V8 engine,
automatic gearbox, good restored condition.
£30,000–32,000 *DB*

1966 Bentley T-Type, good overall condition.
£5,250–5,500 *BLE*

1968 Bentley T1, very good condition.
£8,000–9,500 *SW*

1979 Bentley T2, 6750cc, completely restored,
very good condition.
£13,000–15,000 *H&H*

1989 Bentley Mulsanne S Sports Saloon,
20,000 miles from new, superb condition.
£28,000–29,000 *COYS*

r. **1949/1962 Bentley R-Type Special,** Daimler
V8 Majestic Major engine, thorough restoration,
rewired, repainted, reupholstered, engine
stripped and rebuilt, a well-known car.
Est. £18,000–25,000 *COYS*

1965 Bentley S3 Standard Steel Saloon,
long wheelbase.
£25,000–30,000 *PJF*

1966 Bentley T1 Coupé, coachwork by
Mulliner Park Ward, good original condition,
some tidying required.
Est. £9,500–10,500 *ADT*

1968 Bentley T1, 8 cylinders, 6230cc,
good original condition.
£11,500–12,500 *ADT*

1982 Bentley Turbo 2 Door Coupé, twin headlamp
conversion, coupé conversion, colour-coded bumpers,
grille surround, high level rear brake light, flying B
mascot and rear quarter badges, 15in factory alloy
wheels, original Hooper supplied picnic tables and
cocktail requisites, front centre console fitted.
Est. £40,000–45,000 *S*

BENZ

1898 Benz Comfortable 3½hp Vis-a-Vis, single cylinder, rear-mounted, horizontal automatic inlet valve engine, 1045cc, 2 speed gearbox, belt and chain final drive, rear wheel brakes, fully elliptic leaf spring suspension all-round with transverse full elliptic 'helper' front spring, right-hand tiller steering, original coachwork, generally good condition, leather upholstery possibly original, correct carriage lamps, museum storage for past 28 years, recommissioning prior to use may be necessary.
£34,000–35,000 *C*

1894 Benz Velo 1.5hp 2 Seater, single cylinder engine, transmission by belt with chain final drive from a countershaft to rear wheels, Crypto third speed probably installed at a later date, oil headlamp mounted centrally at the front, twin candle lamps at each side, twin oil lamps at rear, spoon braking, bodywork in excellent condition.
£54,000–56,000 *BKS*

BIANCHI

Bianchi produced their first single cylinder voiturette in 1899. Bianchi, like Fiat in the 1920s, catered for the mass market with a range of quality and attractively priced cars.

BITTER

1984 Bitter SC Coupé Automatic, one of only 7 coupés to be registered in UK.
£11,000–11,500 *H&H*

l. **1928 Bianchi S4 10/15hp Faux Cabriolet,** little used since restoration, recent *concours d'élégance* successes.
£7,750–8,250 *BKS*

BIZZARRINI

1968 Bizzarrini 5300 America, Berlinetta coachwork by Bertone, 8 cylinders, 5354cc, fibreglass body, independent rear suspension, subject of a 2 year restoration in Italy, prepared ready to race.
Est. £45,000–60,000 *COYS*

l. **1929 Auburn 120 Boat Tail Speedster,** restored to immaculate condition. **£98,000+** *BLK*

Founded at Auburn, Indiana, the Auburn Automobile Company was producing cars as early as 1900. The most famous Auburns were made in the late 1920s, and although over 25,000 were built in 1929, the Great Depression saw their sales plummet in 1930. Sales of these sytlish and sophisticated cars had fallen to below 500 cars in 1936, and the company closed the following year.

1927 Buick Master 6 Model, fawn interior, exterior finished in dark blue and black, in very good order throughout. **£10,000–12,000** *CGB*

1907 Cadillac 9-10hp Series M Four Seater Tonneau, original upholstery, may require minor mechanical attention, but otherwise in excellent overall condition. **£18,000–19,000** *S*

1926 Cadillac Series 314 Dual Windshield Phæton, V8 engine, 3 speed manual gearbox, 4 wheel drum brakes, semi-elliptic leaf spring suspension front and rear, excellent restored condition. **£30,000–40,000** *CNY*

1929 Cadillac Series 341B Dual Cowl Sport Phæton, coachwork by Fisher, V8 engine, 90bhp at 3000rpm, 3 speed manual gearbox, drum brakes, semi-elliptic leaf spring suspension, left-hand drive. **£112,000–120,000** *CNY*

1931 Cadillac Model 355 Sport Phæton V8, coachwork by Fleetwood, 353cu in engine, 95bhp at 3000rpm, 3 speed manual gearbox, drum brakes, semi-elliptic leaf spring suspension, left-hand drive. **£65,000–75,000** *CNY*

1933 Cadillac Model RS De Luxe Fixed Head Golfer's Coupé with Rumble Seat, imported into the UK in 1988, excellent condition. **£30,000–32,000** *S*

l. **1941 Cadillac De Luxe Convertible Coupé,** total body-off restoration, excellent overall condition. **£55,000–60,000** *BLK*

The 61 series designation was introduced in 1941 to replace the La Salle marque in the Cadillac range of automobiles.

1934 Cadillac Model 452-D V16 Convertible Sedan, extremely rare car, restored, excellent driving condition. **£150,000–160,000** *BLK*

1955 Cadillac Eldorado Special Sport Convertible, sabre wheels, fully restored to original condition. **£50,000–55,000** *BLK*

1949 Cadillac S62 4 Door Sedan, left-hand drive, generally sound condition, some light cosmetic work required. **£5,000–6,000** *CGB*

1959 Chevrolet Corvette V8, 283cu in engine, 290bhp at 6200rpm, 4 speed manual gearbox, drum brakes, independent front suspension, rear live axle, left-hand drive, very good original condition. **£18,500–22,000** *CNY*

1976 Cadillac Eldorado Bicentenial Convertible, V8 overhead valve 500cu in engine, 190bhp at 4400rpm, turbo hydramatic gearbox, front disc, rear drum brakes, independent front suspension, semi-elliptic leaf springs rear, left-hand drive, low mileage. **£21,000–23,000** *CNY*

1959 Chevrolet Corvette, 4.7 litre engine, 4 speed gearbox, fully restored condition. **£25,000–27,000** *COR*

1961 Chevrolet Corvette, 8 cylinder, 4638cc engine, 4 speed manual gearbox, excellent condition throughout. **£16,000–17,000** *COYS*

1962 Chevrolet Corvette 2 Door Sports,
V8 overhead valve engine, left-hand drive, earlier
series grille fitted, excellent condition throughout.
£17,500–18,500 *BKS*

1966 Chevrolet Corvette Convertible,
5.4 litre engine, manual gearbox, power
steering, excellent condition throughout.
£15,000–15,500 *COR*

1978 Chevrolet Corvette T-Roof Pace Car,
5.7 litre automatic, silver leather interior,
superb condition.
£14,000–14,500 *COR*

1980 Chevrolet Corvette T-Roof,
5.7 litre manual, uprated engine, stainless
steel exhaust, good overall condition.
£10,000–10,500 *COR*

1990 Chevrolet Corvette Coupé,
5.7 litre automatic, BBS wheels,
very good condition throughout.
£12,000–15,000 *COR*

1991 Chevrolet Corvette ZR-1,
5.7 litre engine, 375bhp at 175 mph,
6 speed gearbox, excellent condition.
£29,000–30,000 *COR*

1993 Chevrolet Corvette Coupé,
5.7 litre engine, 300bhp, 6 speed gearbox,
very low mileage, as new condition.
£25,000–26,000 *COR*

**1931 Chrysler Model CG Imperial Dual Cowl
Phæton,** coachwork by LeBaron, 8 cylinder, 384.84cu
in engine, 125bhp at 3200rpm, 4 speed manual gearbox,
drum brakes, left-hand drive, restored condition.
£86,000–90,000 *CNY*

1949 Chrysler Highlander Convertible,
flathead 6 cylinder engine, automatic gearbox,
very good condition throughout.
£16,500–17,500 *GAR*

**1937 Cord 812 Supercharged 2 Door 4 Seat
Phæton,** 4 speed gearbox, right-hand drive, rebuilt,
recommissioning is recommended.
£34,000–36,000 *BKS*

1935 Duesenberg S. J. Bohman & Schwartz Town Car, a one-off, original supercharged car, restored to excellent condition. **£500,000–600,000** *BLK*

1903 Ford Model A Two Passenger Roadster, 8hp, 2 cylinder opposed engine, 2 speed, forward and reverse gearbox, 2 wheel brakes, full elliptic leaf springs front and rear suspension, right-hand drive, excellent condition throughout. **£22,000–24,000** *CNY*

1904 Ford Model C Four Passenger Rear Entrance Tonneau, 2 cylinder, 10hp engine, excellent overall condition. **£31,000–33,000** *CNY*

1954 Oldsmobile F-88 Motorama Show Car, prototype, fully restored, first in class at the Chicago International *Concours d'Elégance* in 1991. **£280,000+** *BLK*

1956 Packard Caribbean Convertible, a professional ground-up restoration to concours condition. **£80,000–85,000** *BLK*

One of 276 produced in 1956.

1913 Ford Model T Runabout, 4 cylinders, 22hp, 2 speeds, late Model T engine, starter and generator, very good restored condition. **£18,000–19,000** *CNY*

1956 Ford Thunderbird 4.7 Litre Two Seater Convertible, restored, excellent. **£17,000–18,000** *BKS*

1962 Ford Thunderbird Roadster, 390cu in tri-power motor, Kelsey-Hayes wire wheels, power steering, brakes, windows and top. **£25,000–27,000** *BLK*

l. **1931 Pierce-Arrow Model 41 Coupé,** coachwork by LeBaron, straight 8 engine, 385cu in, 132bhp at 3000rpm, 4 speed manual gearbox, 4 wheel drum brakes, semi-elliptic leaf springs suspension front and rear, left-hand drive, completely restored. **£46,000–50,000** *CNY*

1963 AC Experimental V8 Drophead Coupé,
289cu in, 4727cc, Ford GT40 engine, ZF 5 speed
gearbox, fully independent suspension, original
seats replaced.
Est. £40,000–50,000 *S*

**'The Rimoldi', 1933 Alfa Romeo 8C-2300 Corto
Spyder,** coachwork by Carrozzeria Touring,
straight 8 engine, supercharged, 2600cc, 4 speed
manual gearbox, superb condition, right-hand drive.
£1,250,000+ *CNY*

1964 Alfa Romeo 2600 Two Door Sprint Coupé,
coachwork by Bertone, restored and resprayed,
excellent original condition throughout.
£7,300–7,600 *BKS*

1965 Alfa Romeo Giulia Spider Voloce, coachwork
by Pininfarina, 4 cylinders, 1570cc, 5 speed gearbox,
extensively restored, good condition throughout.
£10,750–11,500 *COYS*

r. **1988 Alfa Romeo Spider Veloce Convertible,**
coachwork by Pininfarina, left-hand drive,
European specification.
£5,500–6,000 *CARS*

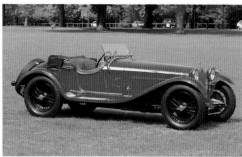

**1930 Alfa Romeo 1.75 Litre Supercharged 6C
1750 Two Seater Sports,** coachwork in the style
of Carrozzeria Zagato, by Ashton Keynes
Restorations, excellent restored condition.
£65,000–68,000 *BKS*

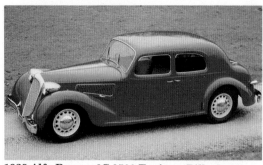

**1939 Alfa Romeo 6C 2500 Turismo Pillarless
Saloon,** 6 cylinders, 2443cc, twin overhead camshaft,
87bhp at 4600rpm, original unrestored condition.
£12,000–12,500 *COYS*
Production ended in 1943 with just 279 examples built.

1964 Alfa Romeo Giulia Sprint Speciale,
coachwork by Bertone, race-prepared by Angelini
of Rome, excellent condition throughout.
£13,500–13,750 *BKS*

1933 Alvis Speed 20 SA 3 Position Drophead Coupé, coachwork by Vanden Plas, refurbished aluminium panelling, original restored wings and running boards, excellent restored condition.
Est. £38,000–42,000 *S*

1948 Alvis TA14 Drophead, 4 cylinder, 1892cc engine, slight cosmetic attention required, otherwise very good original condition throughout.
£9,200–9,800 *ADT*
The TA14 was the pre-war 14 model with slight modifications.

1962 Alvis TD 21 Saloon, coachwork by Park Ward, good original condition.
£5,000–5,500 *ADT*

1955 Aston Martin DB 2/4 2 Door Coupé, manual gearbox, very good condition throughout.
£17,500–18,000 *BKS*

1965 Alvis TE 21 Two-Door Saloon, coachwork by Park Ward, optional power steering, 5 speed ZF gearbox, restored, good overall condition.
Est. £11,000–13,000 *BKS*

1936 Alvis Speed 25 Open 4 Seater Tourer, coachwork by Cross & Ellis, 6 cylinder, overhead valve, 3571cc engine, 106bhp at 3800rpm, triple SU carburettors, 4 speed manual gearbox, right-hand drive, well restored original car.
£45,000–46,000 *C*

1961 Alvis TD21 2 Door Saloon, coachwork by Park Ward, excellent original condition throughout.
£11,500–12,000 *BKS*

1965 Alvis TE 21 2 Door Convertible, coachwork by Park Ward, generally good condition overall.
£12,400–12,800 *BKS*

1935 Aston Martin Ulster MkII 1500cc 2 Seater Sports, rebuilt and restored, excellent condition throughout, full history
£80,000–82,000 *BKS*

1961 Aston Martin DB4 Sports Coupé,
6 cylinder in line engine, 3670cc, 240bhp at
5550rpm, 4 speed manual gearbox, 4 wheel disc
brakes, independent suspension, right-hand drive,
only 3 owners, extremely good condition.
£30,000–31,000 *C*

1963 Aston Martin DB4 Series V Vantage,
6 cylinders, 3670cc, 266bhp at 5700rpm, meticulously
maintained, good condition throughout.
Est. £27,000–32,000 *COYS*

1966 Aston Martin DB6 Coupé, coachwork by
Touring of Milan, 6 cylinders, 3995cc, 282bhp at
5550rpm, ZF 5 speed gearbox, low mileage, very
good original condition throughout.
£21,000–22,000 *COYS*

1966 Aston Martin DB6 Vantage Saloon,
6 cylinders, 3995cc, ZF manual gearbox, bare
metal respray, very good condition throughout.
£29,000–30,000 *BKS*

1967 Aston Martin DB6 Vantage Coupé,
6 cylinders, 3995cc, twin overhead camshaft,
282bhp at 5550rpm, ZF 5 speed gearbox, engine
overhauled, excellent condition throughout.
£20,000–21,000 *COYS*

1968 Aston Martin DB6 MkI Volante, ZF 5 speed
gearbox, excellent original condition.
£48,000–49,000 *BKS*

**1968 Aston Martin DB6
Two Door Saloon,**
3995cc twin overhead
camshaft engine,
automatic transmission,
excellent condition.
£21,250–21,750 *BKS*

1979 Aston Martin V8 Volante, 5.3 litres, 4 twin
choke down draught Weber carburettors, 330bhp,
0–60mph in approximately 6 seconds, top speed of
145mph, meticulously restored and maintained.
£42,000–43,000 *S*

r. 1981 Aston Martin V8 Coupé,
8 cylinders, 5340cc, good original condition.
£16,000–17,000 *COYS*

1990 Aston Martin V8 Vantage Coupé,
low mileage, excellent original condition.
Est. £55,000–58,000 *BKS*

1987 Aston Martin V8 Vantage Volante,
5.3 litre V8 engine, 400bhp at 6000rpm.
£115,000+ *S*

*This car was given by His Royal Highness to the
Prince of Wales' Charities Trust.*

1937 Austin 7 Ruby, 4 cylinder, 747cc
engine, good condition in all respects.
£2,250–2,750 *COYS*

1934 Austin 7 Ruby, very good
condition overall.
£5,500–6,500 *SW*

1954 Austin Healey 100/4 2 Seater Roadster,
3 speed gearbox, Laycock-de Normanville overdrive,
right-hand drive, good overall condition.
£10,800–11,300 *BKS*

1936 Austin Sherbourne,
excellent original condition.
£5,000–6,000 *SW*

1959 Austin Healey Sprite,
good original car with hard and
soft tops, original metal bonnet.
£3,750–4,250 *CGOC*

1955 Austin Healey 100/4,
4 cylinder, 2660cc engine,
4 speed gearbox, imported
from California, conversion
to right-hand drive, restored
including new wings, sills
and boot lid.
£12,000–13,000 *ADT*

r. **1963 Austin Healey
3000 MKIII (BJ8),** good
condition throughout.
£17,000–17,500 *CGOC*

1960 Austin Healey 3000 MkI 2+2 Sports Roadster, subject of a major restoration retaining originality in all major respects, wire wheels.
£12,750–13,500 *BKS*

1966 Austin Healey 3000 MkIII Phase II, 2912cc, twin SU carburettors, 124bhp at 4600rpm, 162lb ft torque at 2700rpm, 4 speed gearbox capable of 100mph, 116mph with overdrive, 0–60mph in 11.4 seconds, completely rebuilt, excellent condition throughout.
£15,500–16,500 *COYS*

1924 Bentley 3 Litre Speed Model Sports Tourer, coachwork by Vanden Plas, twin SU carburettors, original, with matching engine, gearbox and chassis, very good original condition.
Est. £60,000–70,000 *BKS*

1929 Bentley 4½ Litre Dual Cowl Phæton, coachwork by Vanden Plas, 4 cylinder, 4398cc overhead camshaft engine, 100bhp at 3500rpm, 4 speed and reverse gearbox, drum brakes, semi-elliptic leaf spring suspension, right-hand drive, superb original condition.
£245,000+ *CNY*

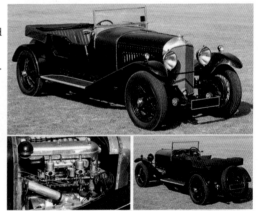

1931 Bentley 8 Litre 4 Seater Tourer, exceptional car.
£250,000+ *S*

Priced at £1,850 for the chassis only, this Bentley was the largest British car produced at the time.

1929 Bentley Sports 4½ Litre 4 Seater Tourer, replica Vanden Plas style body by Robinson, extensively restored.
Est. £90,000–120,000 *BKS*

r. **1929 Bentley 6½ Litre Barker Sports Torpedo,** body mounted on Bentley's longest wheelbase, pontoon bumpers patterned after Sir Malcolm Campbell's famous Bluebird racer, Olympia Motor Show display car, excellent restored condition.
£500,000+ *BLK*

This car was a record-setter at Daytona Beach in February 1928.

1934 Bentley 3½ Litre Drophead Coupé,
coachwork by Park Ward, considerable restoration
over a period of years, excellent condition throughout.
£52,000–55,000 *BKS*

**1937 Bentley 4¼ Litre Supercharged 2 Seater
Sports Racing Special,** coachwork by Caffyns of
Worthing, new supercharger belts.
£46,000–48,000 *BKS*

1937 Bentley 4¼ Litre Pillarless Saloon,
coachwork by Park Ward, razor edge styling,
stored for many years, restoration project.
£12,500–13,000 *RCC*

1938 Bentley 4¼ Litre Drophead Coupé,
coachwork by Vanden Plas, complete
mechanical restoration, excellent condition.
£60,000–65,000 *COYS*

1938 Bentley 4¼ Litre Drophead Coupé,
coachwork by Kellner of Paris, excellent restored
condition to original specification.
£38,000–40,000 *BKS*

1950 Bentley Mark VI 4¼ Litre Saloon, coachwork
by H. J. Mulliner & Co, excellent original condition,
complete set of original tools and inspection lamp.
£22,000–24,000 *BKS*

1951 Bentley Mark VI Drophead Coupé,
coachwork by Park Ward, 6 cylinder, 4257cc
overhead valve engine, 135bhp at 4000rpm, 4 speed
manual gearbox, drum brakes, independent front
suspencion, semi-elliptic leaf springs rear, left-hand
drive, immaculate *concours d'élégance* winner.
£53,000–55,000 *CNY*

1952 Bentley Mark VI Drophead Coupé, coachwork
by Park Ward, undergone major restoration.
£55,000–58,000 *BKS*
*Formerly owned by HM the King of Denmark, this car
was discovered partially dismantled 2 years ago.*

1953 Bentley R Type Saloon, coachwork by H. J. Mulliner, manual gearbox, correct and complete in specification, needs some recommissioning work.
£12,750–13,500 *RCC*

1954 Bentley R Type 4½ Litre 2 Door Coupé, coachwork by Abbott, 6 cylinder in line, 4566cc overhead valve, twin carburettor engine, 150bhp at 4500rpm, 4 speed manual gearbox, very good restored condition.
£21,000–23,000 *C*

1959 Bentley S1 Continental Drophead Coupé, coachwork by Park Ward, 6 cylinder, overhead inlet valves, side exhaust, 4887cc engine, 178bhp at 4000rpm, 4 speed automatic gearbox, excellent restored condition throughout.
£205,000+ *CNY*

1956 Bentley 4.9 Litre S1 Standard Steel Saloon, 6 cylinder, 'F' head engine, with overhead inlet, side exhaust valves, low mileage, good original condition.
£12,500–13,500 *BKS*

l. **1956 Bentley S1 Continental Coupé,** coachwork by Park Ward, left-hand drive, with original owners manual and tools, pristine condition.
£110,000+ *S*

1965 Bentley S3 Continental Flying Spur, coachwork by Mulliner/Park Ward, V8, 6230cc overhead valve engine, 275bhp at 4500rpm, 4 speed automatic gearbox, left-hand drive, low mileage, very good overall condition.
£53,000–55,000 *CNY*

1965 Bentley S3 Continental, coupé by Mulliner/Park Ward, excellent overall condition.
£16,000–17,000 *COYS*

1960 Bentley S2 Continental Convertible, coachwork by Park Ward, excellent restored condition throughout.
Est. £65,000–75,000 *BKS*

1990 Bentley Turbo R, long wheelbase, active ride, cocktail cabinets to rear, full Rolls-Royce service history.
£40,000–45,000 *VIC*

1926 Bugatti Type 35A 2 Litre Grand Prix 2 Seater, in race trim, starter motor, lights and wings missing, not registered for road use in the UK. **£125,000+** *BKS*

1931 Bugatti Type 51 2.3 Litre Supercharged, winner of the British Owners' Club concours. **Est. £300,000–350,000** *BKS*

l. **1927 Bugatti Type 40,** standard Molsheim coachwork, 4 cylinder 1.5 litre engine, superb overall condition. **£100,000+** *BLK*

The Bugatti Type 40 was built between 1926–32. The 4 seater roadster body was powered by an unblown 4 cylinder overhead camshaft engine.

1899 Daimler 6hp Wagonette, twin vertical cylinders, water-cooled, side valve, 1551cc, 4 speed gearbox, double chain drive, spoon brakes, semi-elliptic front and rear suspension, museum stored from 1970, requires careful recommissioning. **£45,000–48,000** *C*

1900 Daimler 4½hp Wagonette/Detachable Tonneau, still running on original 'hot tube' ignition, with rear-entrance tonneau alternative body, very good original condition throughout. **£35,000–38,000** *BKS*

1934 Bugatti Type 57 Stelvio Drophead Coupé, coachwork by Gangloff, superb condition throughout. **Est. £110,000–150,000** *BKS*

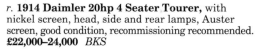

r. **1914 Daimler 20hp 4 Seater Tourer,** with nickel screen, head, side and rear lamps, Auster screen, good condition, recommissioning recommended. **£22,000–24,000** *BKS*

l. **1938 Daimler 4½ Litre Big Eight Touring Limousine,** coachwork by Rippon Brothers, electric sunroof, division window, interior lighting, pair of his and her vanities in sterling, ivory and cloisonné, central drinks cabinet. **£64,000–72,000** *S(NY)*

This car made its debut in 1938 and was awarded first prize for coach building at the Earl's Court Motor Show.

1950 Daimler DB 18 Special Sports Drophead Coupé, coachwork by Hooper, ground up restoration, original log book with first name HM George VI. **£60,000–65,000** *S*

1964 Daimler SP250 C Series, restored to very high standard. **£18,500–19,000** *CGOC*

1960 Daimler SP250, 8 cylinder, 2548cc engine, wire wheels, 5,000 miles, extremely comprehensive restoration. **£11,500–12,500** *ADT*

1904 De Dion Bouton 8hp Rear Entrance Tonneau with Canopy, **£35,000–38,000** *BKS*

1903 Darracq Type L 8hp Rear Entrance Tonneau, spare gearbox and engine, requires recommissioning. **£36,000–38,000** *BKS*

Discovered in 1943 in a scrapyard and bought for £15.

1931 Delage D8C Three Position Drophead Coupé, coachwork by Figoni et Falaschi, 4050cc engine, detachable cast-iron cylinder head and block, 2 overhead valves per cylinder, original Delage specifications. **£43,000–45,000** *S*

1937 Delahaye 135 Sports 2 Seater, 3.5 litre 6 cylinder engine, Cotal electro-magnetic gearbox, excellent condition throughout. **Est. £30,000–40,000** *BKS*

1937 Delahaye Type 135 MS Drophead Coupé, coachwork by Figoni et Falaschi, engine rebuilt, restored to concours standard. **£92,000–98,000** *BKS*

1959 Ferrari 250 GT Series II Convertible, coachwork by Carrozzeria Pininfarina, V12 engine, 240bhp at 7000rpm, 4 speed gearbox, dry stored, left-hand drive, sound and original condition.
£60,000–64,000 *BKS*

1961 Ferrari 250 GT Series II Cabriolet, coachwork by Pininfarina, new 12 cylinder engine, left-hand drive, original hard top and factory tool roll, excellent condition.
£85,000–90,000 *S*

1963 Ferrari 250 GT Berlinetta Lusso, coachwork by Scaglietti, single overhead camshaft engine, 3 twin choke Weber carburettors, top speed of 150mph, bare metal respray, mechanically sound condition.
Est. £80,000–90,000 *S*

1971 Ferrari 365 GTB/4 Daytona, V12 engine, 4 overhead camshafts, 4390cc, 355bhp at 7500rpm, 5 speed manual gearbox, 4 wheel disc brakes, independent suspension, low mileage, repainted, engine overhauled, good condition.
£52,000–54,000 *C*

1960–63-Type Ferrari 275 GT, short wheelbase Berlinetta coachwork by Piero Drogo/Carrozzeria Sports Cars, 3.3 litre V12 engine, 6 Weber 40DCN carburettors, dry-sump lubrication, 310bhp, restored, finished to high standards.
Est. £60,000–90,000 *BKS*

1964 Ferrari 330 GT 2+2 Coupé, coachwork by Pininfarina, 56,000 miles, good condition.
Est. £18,000–22,000 *BKS*

1968 Ferrari 365 GT 2+2 Coupé, coachwork by Pininfarina, right-hand drive, very good condition.
£26,000–28,000 *BKS*

1969 Ferrari 365 GT 2+2 Coupé, coachwork by Pininfarina, top speed of 152mph, totally restored, with original colour and specification.
Est. £26,000–30,000 *COYS*

l. **1972 Ferrari 365 GTC/4 Coupé,** coachwork by Pininfarina, 12 cylinders, 4390cc, excellent condition throughout.
£30,000–32,000 *COYS*
This is one of 32 right-hand drive examples built.

1972 Ferrari 246GTS Dino, Spyder coachwork by Pininfarina, 6 cylinder, 2418cc engine, left-hand drive, subject of a thorough and meticulous restoration. **£46,000–48,000** *COYS*

1972 Ferrari 246 GT Dino, Berlinetta coachwork by Pininfarina, 6 cylinder, 2418cc engine, extensively restored, engine rebuilt, good overall condition. **Est. £32,000–36,000** *COYS*

r. **1973 Ferrari 365 GTB/4 Daytona Coupé,** original, unrestored, only 188 miles recorded, wire wheels, finished in silver and black. **£230,000+** *BLK*

The Ferrari 365 GTB/4 is known as the Daytona after the company's victory at the famous race circuit in Florida.

1973 Ferrari 308 GT4 Dino, Berlinetta coachwork by Bertone, 8 cylinder, 3000cc engine, 250bhp, right-hand drive, engine overhauled, excellent original condition throughout. **£10,000–12,000** *COYS*

1979 Ferrari 308 GTB Berlinetta, coachwork by Scaglietti to a Pininfarina design, 4 cam, 3 litre, 90° V8 engine, 205bhp at 6600rpm, to original specification throughout. **£26,000–28,000** *BKS*

1980 Ferrari 308 GTS, Spyder coachwork by Pininfarina, right-hand drive, meticulously maintained, very good order. **Est. £24,000–28,000** *COYS*

1987 Ferrari Testarossa, Berlinetta coachwork by Pininfarina, very good condition throughout. **£45,000–48,000** *COYS*

l. **1986 Ferrari Testarossa,** only 2,700 miles recorded, as new condition, converted to Spyder configuration by Straman. **£85,000–95,000** *BLK*

The Ferrari Testarossas all have red cylinder heads on their engines, hence the name, literally meaning 'red head'.

1913 Fiat Tipo 3A 20/30hp Landaulette, coachwork by Vincents of Reading, outstanding original condition. **£32,000–35,000** *BKS*

1914 Fiat Type 55 42hp Raceabout, 4 cylinders, 9 litres, chassis and engine restored, 2 bucket seats. **£19,000–20,000** *S*

1973 Fiat-Abarth 695, 2 cylinders, converted from a standard 500, restored, excellent condition. **£5,000–5,600** *COYS*

1966 Ford Lotus Cortina MkI, 1600cc twin camshaft engine, highly modified suspension, restored. Est. **£7,250–8,500** *ADT*

1975 Ford Escort RS1800, close-ratio 'Rocket' competition gearbox, high-ratio steering rack, up-rated suspension, limited slip differential. **£6,000–7,000** *BKS*

1930 Frazer-Nash 2 Seater Sports, excellent provenance, good condition throughout. **£32,000–34,000** *BKS*

1934 Frazer-Nash TT Replica 2 Seater Sports, very good condition throughout. Est. **£40,000–45,000** *BKS*

The first 1660cc Blackburne engine appeared in May 1933 and 14 TT Replicas were fitted with this engine.

1934 Frazer-Nash Shelsley Open Tourer, totally renovated, rebuilt engine, excellent condition. **£44,000–46,000** *COYS*

1937 Frazer-Nash BMW 328 Sports 2 Seater, 6 cylinders, overhead valve, 1970cc, 80bhp, 4 wheel drum brakes, independent front suspension, torsion bar rear, right-hand drive, completely restored. Est. **£85,000–95,000** *C*

1954 Frazer-Nash Targa Florio MkII Open Sports, 6 cylinders, 1971cc, very good condition. Est. **£56,000–62,000** *COYS*

Frazer-Nash cars were expensive, so only 14 examples of the Targa Florio were produced.

BMW

Founded in 1917, the Bayerische Motoren
Werke company bought the Dixi Car
Company in Eisenach in East Germany, and
with it the licence to build the Austin Seven.
Fine sports cars were produced before WWII
and it was some time before BMW were able
to achieve such success.

The successor to the 2002 range was the
Three Series which, to date, has been BMW's
most popular product.

1938 BMW 327/80 Cabriolet, original
controls and dials, including a pre-war
cigar lighter and ivory ashtray,
outstanding condition, having
undergone a comprehensive rebuild.
£35,000–36,000 *BKS*

1939 BMW Typ 327/328 Cabriolet, coachwork
by Ambli-Budd, 6 cylinders, 1971cc, complete
engine rebuild.
£27,500–30,000 *COYS*

*During its production life of 1938–40, only 482
cabriolets were made, together with 86 coupés.*

1969 BMW 2000 Coupé, 4 cylinders,
1990cc, automatic gearbox, left-hand drive,
pillarless, good original condition.
£1,900–2,100 *ADT*

BMW 2000 Series

- 2000 Series first introduced in 1965.
- Initially powered by 1573cc engine
  producing 100bhp.
- 120bhp was available from the
  1990cc engine fitted in the 2000Ti.
- Only 3,000 of the 2000C (coupé)
  models were built. Other variants
  included the CS and the LUX.

1972 BMW 2000, 4 cylinders, 1990cc, only
40,000 miles and one registered owner
from new, outstanding condition.
£2,800–3,000 *ADT*

r. **1972 BMW 2000 Touring,** 4 cylinders,
1990cc, manual gearbox, good to fair condition.
£1,200–1,400 *BKS*

BMW Model	ENGINE cc/cyl	DATES	CONDITION 1	2	3
Dixi	747/4	1927-32	£7,000	£3,000	£2,000
303	1175/6	1934-36	£11,000	£8,000	£5,000
309	843/4	1933-34	£6,000	£4,000	£2,000
315	1490/6	1935-36	£9,000	£7,000	£5,000
319	1911/6	1935-37	£10,000	£9,000	£6,000
326	1971/6	1936-37	£12,000	£10,000	£8,000
320 series	1971/6	1937-38	£12,000	£10,000	£8,000
327/328	1971/6	1937-40	£30,000+	£18,000	£10,000
328	1971/6	1937-40	£60,000+	-	-

1972 BMW 2500 2.5 Litre Saloon, recorded mileage of only 44,000, very good original condition. **Est. £3,000–4,000** *BKS*

1973 BMW 3.0 CSL 3 Litre 2 door Sports Coupé, modified engine including 3 Weber 45 DCOE carburettors, gas flowed head and road/race camshaft, all original components including rare aluminium bonnet. **Est. £6,000–9,000** *BKS*

1973 BMW 3.0 CSL 3 Litre 2 Door Sports Coupé, complete, in need of remedial work, extensive restoration required. **£1,500–1,800** *BKS*

1974 BMW 3.0 CSL 'Batmobile' Sports Coupé, no known modifications from original specification, very good overall condition, excellent provenance. **£18,000–19,000** *BKS*

Perhaps the rarest of all 1970s BMWs is the 3.0 CSL (Coupé Sport Leichmetal) of which it is believed that only 39 were built and perhaps only 5 were imported into the UK. Produced only in left-hand drive form, the 'Batmobile' was effectively a homologation special for Group 2 racing.

1975 BMW 2002 Sports Cabriolet, coachwork by Baur, manual gearbox, right-hand drive, BMW factory X-spoke alloy wheels, excellent condition throughout. **Est. £5,000–7,000** *BKS*

1975 BMW 3.0 CSA, good original condition. **£3,200–3,600** *H&H*

1976 BMW 3.3 Li Saloon, coachwork by Dexter Brown, 3 litre engine, very good overall condition. **Est. £2,000–3,000** *BKS*

Don't Forget!

If in doubt please refer to the 'How to Use' section at the beginning of this book.

l. **1981 BMW 320 Cabriolet,** coachwork by Baur, 6 cylinders, 1990cc, excellent condition. **£3,600–4,000** *ADT*

BMW Model	ENGINE cc/cyl	DATES	CONDITION		
			1	2	3
501	2077/6	1952-56	£9,000	£7,000	£3,500
501 V8/502	2580,				
	3168/8	1955-63	£10,000	£8,000	£4,500
503	3168/8	1956-59	£25,000	£20,000	£15,000
507	3168/8	1956-59	£85,000	£70,000	£50,000
Isetta (4 wheels)	247/1	1955-62	£4,000	£2,000	£1,000
Isetta (3 wheels)	298/1	1958-64	£5,000	£2,000	£1,000
Isetta 600	585/2	1958-59	£1,500	£1,000	£500
1500/1800/2000	var/4	1962-68	£1,100	£700	£200
2000CS	1990/4	1966-69	£5,500	£4,000	£1,500
1500/1600/1602	1499/				
	1573/4	1966-75	£2,500	£1,500	£800
1600 Cabriolet	1573/4	1967-71	£6,000	£4,500	£2,000
2800CS	2788/6	1968-71	£5,000	£4,000	£1,500
1602	1990/4	1968-74	£2,000	£1,500	£1,000
2002	1990/4	1968-74	£3,000	£2,000	£750
2002 Tii	1990/4	1971-75	£4,500	£2,500	£800
2002 Touring	1990/4	1971-74	£3,000	£2,000	£500
2002 Cabriolet	1990/4	1971-75	£4,000	£3,000	£2,500
2002 Turbo	1990/4	1973-74	£9,000	£6,000	£4,000
3.0 CSa/CSi	2986/6	1972-75	£8,000	£6,000	£4,000
3.0 CSL	3003/				
	3153/6	1972-75	£16,000	£12,000	£9,500
MI	3500/6	1978-85	£60,000	£45,000	£35,000
633/635 CS/CSI	3210/3453/6	1976-85	£7,000	£3,000	£2,000
M535i	3453/6	1979-81	£4,500	£3,000	£2,500

r. **1981 BMW 323i Baur Cabriolet,** 2315cc engine, left-hand drive. **£2,000–2,400** *H&H*

1984 BMW Alpina, good overall condition. **Est. £3,000–4,000** *H&H*

1983 BMW Alpina B9 4 Door Saloon, 6 cylinder in line engine, overhead camshaft, water-cooled unit of 3500cc, 5 speed gearbox, black Recaro upholstery, excellent condition throughout. **Est. £5,400–5,800** *S*

l. **1988 BMW M3 Evolution Sports Coupé,** 2.3 litre, 4 cylinder, 16 valve engine, 220hp at 6750rpm, 960 miles from registration, very good condition. **£22,000–24,000** *BKS*

Of the total production of 263 only 25 M3's were allocated to Britain.

BOND

1971 Bond Bug 700ES, 4 cylinders, Reliant 700cc die-cast engine, overhead valve, 29bhp.
Est. £800–1,000 *ADT*

Traditionally painted in orange with a black interior.

1965 Bond Equipe GT4S, 1147cc Triumph Spitfire engine, built on a Triumph Herald chassis, Les Leston steering wheel as standard.
£2,000–2,500 *ScR*

There were many different versions of the Bond Equipe manufactured from around 1963, but it is believed that there are only 50 cars of this actual type remaining.

l. **1973 Bond Bug 700ES,** very good overall condition.
£1,400–1,600 *ScR*

The Bond Bug was built under Reliant management and was the last car to carry the Bond badge.

BRISTOL

Don't Forget!
If in doubt please refer to the 'How to Use' section at the beginning of this book.

l. **1948 Bristol 400,** 6 cylinders, 1971cc, subject of restoration with all working parts being renewed or refurbished, original leather interior requires work in order to complete the restoration.
£9,000–9,500 *COYS*

Bristol 400

- Powered by Bristol's own version of the BMW 328 engine.
- The engine was a very advanced 2 litre, 6 cylinder, featuring 18 pushrods operating the valves.
- The engine could produce 80bhp at 4200rpm.
- With good handling qualities the 400 was also capable of over 90 mph.
- About 700 Bristol 400's were built.

1948 Bristol 400 Saloon, in primer paint with tan leather interior, right-hand drive, unrestored classic ready for restoration, complete except for the bumpers and starter motor, poor condition throughout.
£3,000–3,400 *C*

Cross Reference
Restoration Projects

l. **1948 Bristol 400 Sports Saloon,**
6 cylinders, 1971cc, 80bhp at 4200rpm.
£10,000–11,000 *COYS*

1950 Bristol 400 Sports Saloon, very good condition throughout.
Est. £14,500–17,500 *COYS*

1950 Bristol 400 Sports Saloon, 6 cylinders, 1971cc, complete restoration, good condition and excellent running order.
£17,000–18,000 *COYS*

r. **1955 Bristol 403,** 2 litre 100B2 engine, fitted with overdrive, disc brakes, subject of a thorough rebuild.
£17,000–20,000 *PC*

1952 Bristol 401 Two Door Sports Saloon, 2 litre pushrod unit with 3 carburettors, close ratio gearbox, good throughout with minor blemishes.
£7,000–8,000 *BKS*

Bristol 405

- Introduced in 1954, it initially sold alongside the 403 and 404 models.
- Powered by the 6 cylinder, 1971cc, 100B2 engine.
- Nicknamed at the time 'the flying greenhouse'.
- The saloon version was the first Bristol to feature 4 door bodywork.

1953 Bristol 401 Sports Saloon, very good overall condition.
£8,000–9,000 *BKS*

1955 Bristol 405 Four Door Saloon, 300 miles since being rebuilt, original upholstery.
£7,000–8,000 *BKS*

1955 Bristol 405 Sports Saloon, Daimler V8 2.5 litre engine, sympathetic restoration required.
£3,000–3,500 *BKS*

BRISTOL Model	ENGINE cc/cyl	DATES	CONDITION 1	2	3
400	1971/6	1947-50	£15,000	£12,000	£8,000
401	1971/6	1949-53	£15,000	£11,000	£7,000
402	1971/6	1949-50	£20,000	£18,000	£11,000
403	1971/6	1953-55	£18,000	£12,000	£8,000
404 Coupé	1971/6	1953-57	£19,000	£14,000	£10,000
405	1971/6	1954-58	£14,000	£11,000	£9,000
405 Drophead	1971/6	1954-56	£20,000	£18,000	£14,000
406	2216/6	1958-61	£10,000	£9,000	£5,000
407	5130/8	1962-63	£9,000	£7,000	£5,000
408	5130/8	1964-65	£10,000	£9,000	£5,000
409	5211/8	1966-67	£10,500	£9,500	£5,500
410	5211/8	1969	£12,000	£10,000	£5,500
411 Mk 1-3	6277/8	1970-73	£12,000	£9,000	£6,000
411 Mk 4-5	6556/8	1974-76	£12,500	£9,500	£7,000
412	5900/ 6556/8	1975-82	£14,500	£8,500	£5,500
603	5211/ 5900/8	1976-82	£12,000	£8,000	£5,000

1959 Bristol 406 Sports Coupé, engine rebuilt, gearbox reconditioned, resprayed, carefully maintained, very good overall condition.
£14,500–15,500 *S*

1965 Bristol 408, good overall condition.
£5,600–6,000 *H&H*

1972 Bristol 411 Four Seater Coupé, 8 cylinders, 6277cc.
£8,200–9,800 *COYS*

l. **1967 Bristol 409 Two Door Sports Coupé,** extensively restored throughout, well maintained.
£12,000–14,000 *ROR*

BROWN BROTHERS

The London-based factors, Brown Brothers Ltd, offered a variety of cars under their own name between 1901 and 1911. Star of Wolverhampton also produced some vehicles for Brown.

c1905/6 Brown Brothers 18/20hp 4/5 Seater Side Entrance Tonneau, engine restored, originally mounted on a Brown Brothers' car, bodywork 90% restored and needs floor covering.
Est. £11,000–13,000 *BKS*

Most of the present body was discovered in the early 1970s.

BSA

1931 BSA Front Wheel Drive Three-Wheeler Sports, 1100cc engine, 3 speed manual gearbox, subject of restoration, bodywork in black fabric, metal bonnet, to correct original specification.
£5,000–5,500 *BKS*

1934 BSA Three-Wheeler Special Sports, 4 cylinder engine, right-hand drive, major restoration carried out, although mellowed a little, good in all respects.
£5,600–6,000 *C*

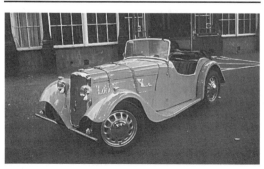

l. **1939 BSA Scout Sports,** very good overall condition.
£4,400–4,800 *H&H*

BUGATTI

Ettore Bugatti worked for a number of motor manufacturers before he set up on his own in 1909. He designed the famous Peugeot Bébé, but it was not until the 1920s that real fame was achieved on the race track.

The Bugatti Royale was the opposite of his world-beating race cars. The Royale was the largest production car of the 1920s with a 12,763cc, in line, 8 cylinder engine producing about 200bhp. Although 25 cars were promised, only 6 were ever built.

1930 Bugatti T46 Four Door Sports Saloon, coachwork by Lancefield of West London, little used since 1963, good original condition. **£75,000–80,000** *BKS*

> *A rebuilt car is not necessarily more valuable than a car in good original condition, even if the restoration has been costly.*

l. **1924 Bugatti Type 23 Brescia Three Seater Sports,** coachwork by Maurice Proux Carosserie, all original apart from a replica front axle, electric fuel pump, restored, excellent condition. **Est. £38,000–45,000** *BKS*

r. **1935 Bugatti Type 57 Four Seater Coupé,** coachwork by Gangloff, twin overhead camshaft straight 8 engine, all-round correct and original order, excellent condition. **£110,000+** *COYS*
The 4-light Ventoux 'coach' coupé body derives directly from Jean Bugatti's Coupé Profilée on the Type 50.

BUGATTI Model	ENGINE cc/cyl	DATES	1	CONDITION 2	3
13/22/23	1496/4	1919-26	£40,000	£32,000	£25,000
30	1991/8	1922-36	£45,000	£35,000	£30,000
32	1992/8	1923	£45,000	£35,000	£30,000
35	1991/8	1924-30	£110,000	£90,000	£80,500
38 (30 update)	1991/8	1926-28	£44,500	£34,000	£28,000
39	1493/8	1926-29	£120,000	£90,000	£80,000
39A Supercharged	1496/8	1926-29	£140,000+	-	-
35T	2262/8	1926-30	£140,000+	-	-
37 GP Car	1496/4	1926-30	£110,000	£90,000	£75,000
40	1496/4	1926-30	£50,000	£42,000	£35,000
38A	1991/8	1927-28	£48,000	£40,000	£35,000
35B Supercharged	2262/8	1927-30	£170,000+	-	-
35C	1991/8	1927-30	£170,000+	-	-
37A	1496/4	1927-30	£125,000+	-	-
44	2991/8	1927-30	£50,000	£40,000	£35,000
45	3801/16	1927-30	£150,000+	-	-
43/43A Tourer	2262/8	1927-31	£180,000+	-	-
35A	1991/8	1928-30	£140,000	£110,000	£90,000
46	5359/8	1929-36	£140,000	£110,000	£90,000
40A	1627/4	1930	£55,000	£45,000	£35,500
49	3257/8	1930-34	£55,000	£45,000	£35,500
57 Closed	3257/8	1934-40	£40,000	£35,000	£30,000
57 Open	3257/8	1936-38	£80,000	£60,000	£55,000
57S	3257/8	1936-38	£250,000+	-	-
57SC Supercharged	3257/8	1936-39	£250,000+	-	-
57G	3257/8	1937-40	£250,000+	-	-
57C	3257/8	1939-40	£140,000+	-	-

Bugatti continues to be popular with not much movement in prices during 1995/96.

BUICK

1907 Buick Model 10 Three Seater Touring, very original and mostly conforming to original specification.
£12,000–13,000 *S*

Cross Reference
Colour Section

1923 Buick Golfer's Coupé with Dickey, 2.2 litre, 6 cylinder engine.
£8,800–10,000 *H&H*

BUICK Model	ENGINE cc/cyl	DATES	CONDITION 1	2	3
Veteran	various	1903-09	£18,500	£12,000	£8,000
18/20	3881/6	1918-22	£12,000	£5,000	£2,000
Series 22	2587/4	1922-24	£9,000	£5,000	£3,000
Series 24/6	3393/6	1923-30	£9,000	£5,000	£3,000
Light 8	3616/8	1931	£18,000	£14,500	£11,000
Straight 8	4467/8	1931	£22,000	£18,000	£10,000
50 Series	3857/8	1931-39	£18,500	£15,000	£8,000
60 Series	5247/8	1936-39	£19,000	£15,000	£8,000
90 Series	5648/8	1934-35	£20,000	£15,500	£9,000
40 Series	4064/8	1936-39	£19,000	£14,000	£10,000
80/90	5247/8	1936-39	£25,000	£20,000	£15,000
McLaughlin	5247/8	1937-40	£22,000	£15,000	£10,000

Various chassis lengths and bodies will affect value. Buick chassis fitted with English bodies previous to 1916 were called Bedford-Buicks. Right-hand drive can have an added premium of 25%.

1936 Buick Century Sedan, coachwork by Fisher, rare in UK, as found condition, stored for many years, coachwork damaged and rusty, door trims and rear windscreen missing, in need of total restoration.
£250–300 *COYS*

Cross Reference
Restoration Projects

r. **1963 Buick Riviera,** V8, overhead valve, 401cu in engine, 325bhp at 4400rpm, 3 speed automatic gearbox, 4 wheel hydraulic drum brakes, independent front suspension, semi-elliptic leaf springs rear, left-hand drive, good original condition.
£7,200–8,200 *CNY*

1938 Buick S40 Special 4 Door Sedan, left-hand drive, owned by one family, 40,600 miles only, totally original, stored for 20 years.
£6,000–7,000 *CGB*

BUICK Model	ENGINE cu in/cyl	DATES	CONDITION 1	2	3
Special/Super 4 door	248/ 364/8	1950-59	£6,000	£4,000	£2,000
Special/Super Riviera	263/ 332/8	1950-56	£8,000	£6,000	£3,000
Special/Super convertible	263/ 332/8	1950-56	£7,500	£5,500	£3,000
Roadmaster 4 door	320/ 365/8	1950-58	£11,000	£8,000	£6,000
Roadmaster Riviera	320/ 364/8	1950-58	£9,000	£7,000	£5,000
Roadmaster convertible	320/ 364/8	1950-58	£14,500	£11,000	£7,000
Special/Super Riviera	364/8	1957-59	£10,750	£7,500	£5,000
Special/Super convertible	364/8	1957-58	£13,500	£11,000	£6,000

CADILLAC

By the end of the 1920s, Cadillac, under the direction of Alfred P. Sloan, was determined to dominate the luxury car market. The V8 engine had been developed by Cadillac and had ensured the veracity of the Company's slogan 'Standard of the World'. Packard had a V12 engine which could not be seen to be copied, therefore, the V16 was decided upon. Designed by engineer Ernest Seaholm and designer Owen Nacker, the Cadillac V16 produced 165hp from 452cu in and provided effortless, almost silent power, for some of Cadillac's finest motor cars.

1931 Cadillac Model 370A Sport Phæton, coachwork by Fleetwood, V12, 368cu in engine, 135bhp at 3400rpm, 3 speed manual gearbox, drum brakes, semi-elliptic springs front and rear suspension, left-hand drive.
£100,000+ *CNY*

A National First Prize winner with both the Classic Car Club of America and the Antique Automobile Club of America. Specialist equipment includes a full set of accessory lights and a Cadillac lowboy trunk mounted on the rear. 5,725 Series 370A V12s were sold.

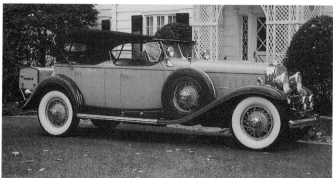

1931 Cadillac Model 452B V16 Sport Phæton, coachwork by Fleetwood, V16, 452cu in engine, 165bhp at 3400rpm, 3 speed gearbox, semi-elliptic leaf springs with hydraulic dampers front and rear suspension, left-hand drive, correct twin front and rear compartment speedometers, rear tonneau Jaeger chronometer, complete nut and bolt restoration, original bodied example.
£208,000+ *CNY*

This vehicle scored the maximim 100 points in the Classic Car Club of America.

1963 Cadillac Coupé de Ville 2 Door, hard top, left-hand drive, original car.
£8,000–9,000 *CGB*

1955 Cadillac Eldorado Convertible with 1955 Cadillac Sedan Parts Car, V8, 331cu in engine, 270bhp at 4600rpm, 4 speed hydromatic gearbox, power assisted drum brakes, independent front suspension, semi-elliptic leaf springs rear, left-hand drive, sound overall condition.
£4,200–5,000 *CNY*

The front end of this car has been damaged in a fire. Included is a 1955 Cadillac Fleetwood parts car that will be useful during the restoration.

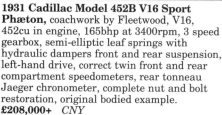

1964 Cadillac de Ville Convertible, 50,000 miles recorded, good overall condition.
Est. £5,500–6,000 *S*

CADILLAC (pre-war) Model	ENGINE cc/cyl	DATES	CONDITION		
			1	2	3
Type 57-61	5153/8	1915-23	£20,000	£14,000	£6,000
Series 314	5153/8	1926-27	£22,000	£15,000	£6,000
Type V63	5153/8	1924-27	£20,000	£13,000	£5,000
Series 341	5578/8	1928-29	£22,000	£15,000	£6,000
Series 353-5	5289/8	1930-31	£32,500	£22,000	£12,000
V16	7406/16	1931-32	£50,000	£32,000	£18,000
V12	6030/12	1932-37	£42,000+	£25,000	£15,000
V8	5790/8	1935-36	£30,000+	£15,000	£6,000
V16	7034/16	1937-40	£45,000+	£30,000	£18,000

1971 Cadillac Eldorado Convertible,
8 cylinders, 8195cc, 3 speed automatic gearbox,
only non-original feature is fog lamp of UK
specification, good order throughout.
£7,800–8,200 *ADT*

1979 Cadillac Seville, 8 cylinders, 5700cc,
good order throughout, drives superbly.
Est. £4,500–5,500 *ADT*

CADILLAC Model	ENGINE cu in/cyl	DATES	CONDITION 1	2	3
4 door sedan	331/8	1949	£8,000	£4,500	£3,000
2 door fastback	331/8	1949	£10,000	£8,000	£5,000
Convertible coupé	331/8	1949	£22,000	£12,000	£10,000
Series 62 4 door	331/365/8	1950-55	£7,000	£5,500	£3,000
Sedan de Ville	365/8	1956-58	£8,000	£6,000	£4,000
Coupé de Ville	331/365/8	1950-58	£12,500	£9,500	£3,500
Convertible coupé	331/365/8	1950-58	£25,000	£20,000	£10,000
Eldorado	331/8	1953-55	£35,000	£30,000	£18,000
Eldorado Seville	365/8	1956-58	£11,500	£9,000	£5,500
Eldorado Biarritz	365/8	1956-58	£30,000	£20,000	£15,000
Sedan de Ville	390/8	1959	£12,000	£9,500	£5,000
Coupé de Ville	390/8	1959	£15,000	£9,000	£5,500
Convertible coupé	390/8	1959	£28,000	£20,000	£10,000
Eldorado Seville	390/8	1959	£13,000	£10,000	£6,000
Eldorado Biarritz	390/8	1959	£30,000	£20,000	£14,000
Sedan de Ville	390/8	1960	£10,000	£8,000	£4,500
Convertible coupé	390/8	1960	£27,000	£14,000	£7,500
Eldorado Biarritz	390/8	1960	£25,000	£17,000	£10,000
Sedan de Ville	390/429/8	1961-64	£7,000	£5,000	£3,000
Coupé de Ville	390/429/8	1961-64	£8,000	£6,000	£4,000
Convertible coupé	390/429/8	1961-64	£15,000	£9,000	£7,000
Eldorado Biarritz	390/429/8	1961-64	£19,500	£14,000	£9,000

CATERHAM

r. **1992 Caterham
Seven 1700 Super
Sprint,** 5 speed De
Dion gearbox, HPC
alloys, competition
side-exit exhaust.
£13,000–13,500 *KSC*

l. **1987 Caterham
Seven,** high
specification, in
good condition.
£8,000–8,400 *CGOC*

1992 Caterham Seven Cosworth BDA,
5 speed De Dion gearbox, leather adjustable
seats, 3,000 miles recorded.
£17,000–17,500 *KSC*

1988 Caterham Super Seven, Lotus twin
camshaft engine, with dry sump, polished
aluminium with black wings and nose,
competition exhaust and adjustable seats.
£11,000–11,500 *KSC*

CENTURY

Ralph Jackson, a bicycle maker of Altrincham since 1885, began vehicle manufacture with the Century Tandem, a 2 seater tricar with 2¼hp single cylinder engine and wheel steering which sold for £115. Following a move to London, the company was taken over by Sydney Begbie who had earlier introduced Aster engines to England.

1902 Century Forecar, 6½hp single cylinder, water-cooled, original Aster engine, original 'push-pull' steering, 2 speed gearbox with alternate chain drive to the rear wheel, careful recommissioning prior to use necessary, rare example.
£8,250–8,750 *C*

CHEVROLET

Louis Chevrolet was a racing driver who saw a great future in the manufacture of motor cars. He teamed up with William Durant, late of General Motors, and by 1913 their famous factory at Flint, Michigan, USA, was in full production.

One of the early milestones in the company's long and distinguished history was the Chevrolet 490, called the 490 because it cost 490 dollars. Launched in 1915, to compete directly with Ford's domination of the marketplace, the 490 had sold over 150,000 units by 1920, the year that William Durant left the company.

1937 Chevrolet Master De Luxe Sport Coupé, with rumble seat, right-hand drive, very good condition.
£7,500–8,500 *CGB*

CHENARD-WALCKER

Founded in 1899, the company made pedal tricycles before the manufacture of its first car, introduced in 1901. It was a 1000cc twin cylinder with mechanically operated side valves in a T-head. The vehicles were renowned for their workmanlike construction and the variety of engines offered. The classic radiator design was introduced before the war and this distinguishing feature was carried through to the company's demise in 1946.

1926 Chenard-Walcker, 4 cylinder, 1300cc side valve, short stroke engine, magneto ignition and 3 speed gearbox, very good overall condition.
Est. £6,000–7,000 *ADT*

1926 Chevrolet Superior 4 Door Saloon, coachwork by Fisher, right-hand drive, subject of major restoration, very good condition throughout.
£10,000–11,000 *BKS*

> *A rebuilt car is not necessarily more valuable than a car in good original condition, even if the restoration has been costly.*

r. **1941 Chevrolet Special De Luxe,** 6 cylinder, 5000cc engine, 3 speed manual gearbox, low mileage, only 2 owners from new.
£5,500–5,800 *ADT*

CHEVROLET Model	ENGINE cc/cyl	DATES	CONDITION 1	2	3
H4/H490 K Series	2801/4	1914-29	£9,000	£5,000	£2,000
FA5	2699/4	1918	£8,000	£5,000	£2,000
D5	5792/8	1918-19	£10,000	£6,000	£3,000
FB50	3660/4	1919-21	£7,000	£4,000	£2,000
AA	2801/4	1928-32	£5,000	£3,000	£1,000
AB/C	3180/6	1929-36	£6,000	£4,000	£2,000
Master	3358/6	1934-37	£9,000	£5,000	£2,000
Master De Luxe	3548/6	1938-41	£9,000	£6,000	£4,000

1949 Chevrolet Fleetline Special Sedan,
6 cylinder, 3530cc engine, column-type gear
change, referred to as a 'Hand-E-gearshift',
mechanically good, electrical system could
benefit from a rewire.
Est. £5,500–6,500 *ADT*

1954 Chevrolet Bel Air Sedan, to original
factory specification, good overall condition,
minor cosmetic attention required.
£2,200–2,600 *BKS*

1957 Chevrolet Corvette Convertible 283,
manual, fully restored and correct.
£25,000–26,000 *COR*

1961 Chevrolet Corvette, 4.7 litre, 4 speed
gearbox, extensively restored.
£20,000–21,000 *COR*

1963 Chevrolet Corvette Split Window Coupé,
5.7 litre, manual, some competition history,
good overall condition.
£20,000–21,000 *COR*

**1964 Chevrolet Corvette Sting Ray Sports
Convertible,** left-hand drive, very good
original condition.
£12,000–13,000 *BKS*

l. **1966 Chevrolet Corvette Sting Ray,**
8 cylinder, 5379cc engine,
good all-round condition.
£7,000–7,500 *COYS*

CHEVROLET Model	ENGINE cu in/cyl	DATES	CONDITION 1	2	3
Stylemaster	216/6	1942-48	£8,000	£4,000	£1,000
Fleetmaster	216/6	1942-48	£8,000	£4,000	£1,000
Fleetline	216/6	1942-51	£8,000	£5,000	£2,000
Styleline	216/6	1949-52	£8,000	£6,000	£2,000
Bel Air 4 door	235/6	1953-54	£6,000	£4,000	£3,000
Bel Air sports coupé	235/6	1953-54	£7,000	£4,500	£3,500
Bel Air convertible	235/6	1953-54	£12,500	£9,500	£6,000
Bel Air 4 door	283/8	1955-57	£8,000	£4,000	£3,000
Bel Air sports coupé	283/8	1955-56	£11,000	£7,000	£4,000
Bel Air convertible	283/8	1955-56	£16,000	£11,000	£7,000
Bel Air sports coupé	283/8	1957	£11,000	£7,500	£4,500
Bel Air convertible	283/8	1957	£14,500	£10,500	£8,000
Impala sports sedan	235/6, 348/8	1958	£12,500	£9,000	£5,500
Impala convertible	235/6, 348/8	1958	£14,500	£11,000	£7,500
Impala sports sedan	235/6, 348/8	1959	£8,000	£5,000	£4,000
Impala convertible	235/6, 348/8	1959	£14,000	£10,000	£5,000
Corvette roadster	235/6	1953	£18,000	£14,000	£10,000
Corvette roadster	235/6, 283/8	1954-57	£16,500	£13,000	£9,000
Corvette roadster	283, 327/8	1958-62	£16,000	£12,000	£9,000
Corvette Sting Ray	327, 427/8	1963-67	£15,500	£12,000	£10,000
Corvette Sting Ray DHC	327, 427/8	1963-66	£22,000	£15,000	£8,000
Corvette Sting Ray DHC	427/8	1967	£16,000	£13,000	£10,000

Value will also be regulated by build options, rare coachbuilding options, and de luxe engine specifications etc.

l. **1967 Chevrolet Corvette Convertible,** 327-350cu in, manual, fully restored, genuine low mileage. **£20,000–21,000** *COR*

Make the most of Miller's

Condition is absolutely vital when assessing the value of a vehicle. Top class vehicles on the whole appreciate much more than less perfect examples. Rare, desirable cars may command higher prices even when in need of restoration.

1969 Chevrolet Corvette 427 Convertible, manual, extensively restored, all correct. **£18,000–19,000** *COR*

1970 Chevrolet Corvette Convertible, 5.7 litre manual, very good condition overall. **£16,000–16,750** *COR*

1973 Chevrolet Corvette T-Roof, 5.7 litre L-82 automatic, low mileage, very good original condition throughout.
£8,000–9,000 *COR*

1976 Chevrolet Corvette Stingray, 8 cylinder, 5700cc engine, stainless steel exhaust system, engine and gearbox excellent, good condition throughout.
£5,200–5,600 *ADT*

1976 Chevrolet Corvette Stingray.
£3,000–3,750 *H&H*

1976 Chevrolet Corvette Stingray, 8 cylinder, 350cu in engine, superb factory original specification car, original lightweight alloys, fibreglass body, excellent order.
£6,400–6,800 *ADT*

1978 Chevrolet Corvette, well maintained, good overall condition.
£8,750–9,250 *COR*

1985 Chevrolet Corvette Coupé, 5.7 litre manual, low mileage, good original condition.
£9,000–10,000 *COR*

1978 Chevrolet Corvette Stingray Targa Top, excellent overall condition.
£8,750–9,250 *BLE*

1992 Chevrolet Corvette Convertible, 5.7 litre automatic, 22,000 miles recorded, excellent condition overall.
£24,750–25,500 *COR*

1988 Chevrolet Corvette Coupé, 5.7 litre automatic, low mileage, very good original condition.
£13,750–14,250 *COR*

CHRYSLER

Having worked for several motor manufacturers, including Willys and Buick, by the time Walter Chrysler acquired Maxwell-Chalmers in 1923 he had firm ideas as to the products America required. He was responsible for organising the design and production of the Chrysler 75, which sold over 50 million dollars worth of orders within its first year of production.

Chrysler expanded rapidly, acquiring a number of famous marques, and by the outbreak of WWII they were the second largest car manufacturer in America.

1931 Chrysler Model CM Roadster, 6 cylinder in line, 217.8cu in engine, 78bhp at 3400rpm, 3 speed manual gearbox, 4 wheel hydraulic drum brakes, semi-elliptic leaf spring suspension, left-hand drive.
£19,000–21,000 *CNY*

Former National First Prize Winner of the Antique Automobile Club of America.

1930 Chrysler Model L-80 Imperial Roadster, 6 cylinder in line, 309.3cu in engine, 100bhp at 3200rpm, 3 speed manual gearbox, 4 wheel hydraulic brakes, semi-elliptic leaf spring suspension, left-hand drive, complete frame off restoration.
£53,000–55,000 *CNY*

National First Prize winner in both Antique Automobile and Classic Car Clubs of America.

r. **1931 Chrysler Model CG Imperial Town Car,** coachwork by LeBaron, straight 8, 384.84cu in engine, 125bhp at 3200rpm, 4 speed manual gearbox, 4 wheel hydraulic drum brakes, semi-elliptic leaf spring suspension, left-hand drive, superb original condition.
£110,000+ *CNY*

This car was formerly the property of Mrs Walter P. Chrysler.

CISITALIA

Conceived by Piero Dusio, a well-known racing driver, the Cisitalia company based in Turin produced a small but selective range of sports, grand touring and competition cars.

The name is derived from Compagnia Industriale Sportiva Italia, but sadly production had ceased by 1965.

1948 Cisitalia 202SMM Spyder, first class order, confirmed provenance.
£68,000–69,000 *S*

l. **1948 Cisitalia 202SC,** Spyder coachwork by Vignale, 4 cylinder, 1089cc twin carburettor Sport Competizione engine with an original Abarth manifold, completely restored.
Est. £35,000–40,000 *COYS*

CITROËN

André Citroën, one of the most famous names in the history of the motor car industry, was an engineer and designer. He invented and developed a 'double chevron' gear system which was employed in machinery and ships as well as cars. It is the stylised inverted double V that has been borne on all Citroën motor vehicles since.

Although a comparatively late entrant, the Paris based factory was not founded until 1919, Citroën became one of the most successful and famous manufacturers in the world.

1936 Citroën 11BL 4 Door Saloon, left-hand drive, extensively restored, no modifications from original specification. **£5,200–5,600** *BKS*

It is said to have been the 1936 Paris Salon car.

1924 Citroën 5CV Cloverleaf 7.5hp 3 Seater Tourer, excellent order all-round, left-hand drive. **£6,000–6,400** *S*

1952 Citroën 11BL Traction Avant, original, unrestored condition. **£1,250–1,450** *COYS*

> *A rebuilt car is not necessarily more valuable than a car in good original condition, even if the restoration has been costly.*

1939 Citroën 11B Normale Traction Avant, excellent restored condition. **£24,500–25,500** *CTOC*

1953 Citroën 11BL, for restoration. **£1,250–1,400** *DB*

CITROËN Model	ENGINE cc/cyl	DATES	CONDITION 1	2	3
A	1300/4	1919	£4,000	£2,000	£1,000
5CV	856/4	1922-26	£7,000	£4,000	£2,000
11	1453/4	1922-28	£4,000	£2,000	£1,000
12/24	1538/4	1927-29	£5,000	£3,000	£1,000
2½litre	2442/6	1929-31	£5,000	£3,000	£1,500
13/30	1628/4	1929-31	£5,000	£3,000	£1,000
Big 12	1767/4	1932-35	£7,000	£5,000	£2,000
Twenty	2650/6	1932-35	£10,000	£5,000	£3,000
Ten CV	1452/4	1933-34	£5,000	£3,000	£1,000
Ten CV	1495/4	1935-36	£6,000	£3,000	£1,000
11B/Light 15/Big 15/7CV	1911/4	1934-57	£9,000	£5,000	£2,000
Twelve	1628/4	1936-39	£5,000	£3,000	£1,000
F	1766/4	1937-38	£4,000	£2,000	£1,000
15/6 and Big Six	2866/6	1938-56	£7,000	£4,000	£2,000

CITROËN Model	ENGINE cc/cyl	DATES	CONDITION		
			1	2	3
2CV	375/2	1948-54	£1,000	£500	£250
2CV/Dyane/Bijou	425/2	1954-82	£1,000	£800	£500
DS19/ID19	1911/4	1955-69	£5,000	£3,000	£800
Sahara	900/4	1958-67	£5,000	£4,000	£3,000
2CV6	602/2	1963 on	£750	£500	£250
DS Safari	1985/4	1968-75	£5,000	£3,000	£1,000
DS21	1985/4	1969-75	£5,000	£3,000	£1,000
DS23	2347/4	1972-75	£5,000	£3,000	£1,000
SM	2670/ 2974/6	1970-75	£8,000	£6,000	£4,500

Imported (USA) SM models will be 15% less.

l. **1971 Citroën SM 2+2 Coupé,** alloy quad-camshaft V6, 2670cc engine, 170bhp at 5500rpm, 5 speed manual gearbox, disc brakes all-round.
£13,000–14,000 *COYS*

This car was launched at the 1970 Geneva Motor Show and the V6 engine is three-quarters of Maserati's proven V8.

r. **1956 Citroën 11B,** 4 cylinder, 1911cc engine, left-hand drive, traditional finish of black coachwork and red/grey interior.
£3,400–3,600 *ADT*

1956 Citroën Type 11BL Light 15 Saloon, very good condition throughout.
£7,800–8,000 *BKS*

1972 Citroën DS 23 Décapotable, cabriolet by Chapron, 4 cylinder, 2347cc engine, rare right-hand drive, good order in all respects.
£7,500–8,000 *COYS*

1972 Citroën SM 2 Door Coupé, good condition throughout.
£5,200–5,500 *S*

1973 Citroën SM Maserati 2.9 Litre 2 Door Sports Saloon, V6 dual overhead camshaft, 2965cc engine, 180bhp at 6250rpm, 5 speed manual gearbox, disc brakes, hydropneumatic front and rear suspension with anti-roll bars, left-hand drive, air conditioning, totally rebuilt, comprehensive restoration.
£12,000–12,750 *C*

1973 Citroën Maserati SM Saloon, slight rust and minor damage. **Est. £4,000–5,000** *BKS*

CLEMENT

1900 Clement 2¼hp Voiturette, De Dion engine with water-cooled cylinder head, atmospheric inlet valve and mechanical exhaust valve, displayed in a museum for many years, dated by the Veteran Car Club.
£21,000–22,000 *BKS*

CLENET

Alain J. M. Clenet, a Frenchman, emigrated to the United States in the 1970s to work for American Motors in Detroit.

1978 Clenet Roadster, Lincoln V8 overhead valve engine, 210bhp, automatic gearbox, hydraulic brakes, all independent suspension, left-hand drive.
£23,000–25,000 *CNY*
This car is number 55 of the first 250 Series I cars built, it has only 588 miles recorded from new and as such is virtually a new car.

CORD

Although the principle of front wheel drive had been discussed, designed and developed it was Erret Lobban Cord who manufactured the first front wheel drive production car, the Cord L-29. Launched in 1929, the year of the Wall Street Crash, the L-29, due to reasons beyond their control, failed to fulfil its obvious potential.

Make the most of Miller's
Condition is absolutely vital when assessing the value of a vehicle. Top class vehicles on the whole appreciate much more than less perfect examples. Rare, desirable cars may command higher prices even when in need of restoration.

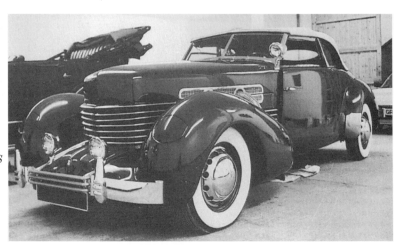

r. **1936 Cord 810 Two Door 4 Seater Phæton,** left-hand drive, no known modifications from maker's original specification, good condition throughout.
Est. £34,000–36,000 *BKS*

DAIMLER

One of the oldest and most revered names in motoring history, the Daimler company was formed in 1897. The first Daimler Double Six, Great Britain's first production 12 cylinder motor car, was made in 1926. The Double Six was designed by chief engineer Laurence Pomeroy and initially had a 7136cc power unit. By 1931 the Double Six 40–50 range was launched with a 6511cc engine.

The name Double Six was also given to the Jaguar V12 powered Sovereign launched in 1973. With its Royal patronage and unsurpassed limousines the Daimler name is still carried today on luxury Jaguar products.

1911 Daimler TG15, 4 cylinder, 2.1 litre Daimler-Knight sleeve valve engine, with an RAC rating of 15.9hp, largely original.
Est. £30,000–33,000 *ADT*

1900 Daimler 6hp 5 Seater Phæton, a 'barn discovery', substantially complete, with spare engine, a challenging restoration project.
£33,000–35,000 *BKS*

This vehicle was discovered derelict in Solihull in 1953 by a VCC member and has remained unrestored in his family ever since.

1911 Daimler 25hp Landaulette, 4 cylinder version of the Knight double sleeve valve engine, only 2 owners from new, very good condition throughout.
£42,000–45,000 *BKS*

1922 Daimler TT 20hp Doctor's Coupé with Dickey Seat, original coachwork by North of England Motor Trading, 4 cylinder sleeve valve engine, good condition throughout.
Est. £12,000–14,000 *S*

1928 Daimler Model V 20/70hp 4 Door Open Tourer, coachwork by Tony Robinson in the style of Hooper, engine running well and the car drives, bodywork framed and skinned, requires finishing, trimming and painting, no windscreen.
Est. £8,000–10,000 *BKS*

1933 Daimler 15 Drophead Coupé with Dickey Seat, coachwork by Mann-Egerton, opening front screen, side-mounted spare wheel, water outlet pipes corroded, rear brakes require attention.
£8,500–9,000 *S*

1939 Daimler ELS 24 Saloon, coachwork by Charlesworth, subject of a major restoration, excellent overall condition.
Est. £11,000–13,000 *BKS*

1949 Daimler DB18, convertible by Barker, very smart all-round condition.
£11,250–11,750 *Bro*

1951 Daimler Consort Saloon, good original condition.
£4,400–4,800 *WL*

Daimler DB18 Consort

- Introduced in 1949 the Consort cost £2,075 when new.
- The beautiful leather and walnut interior to the Mulliner designed coachwork on the Daimler DB18 chassis.
- The 2522cc 6 cylinder engine produced about 70bhp and drove through a Wilson pre-selector gearbox.

1952 Daimler DB18 Consort Saloon, coachwork by Mulliner, largely complete car, requiring restoration.
Est. £1,000–2,000 *S*

Cross Reference
Restoration Projects

1956 Daimler Conquest, 6 cylinder, 2433cc engine, low mileage, excellent original condition.
£4,200–4,600 *ADT*

1954 Daimler Conquest Century, restored.
£850–1,250 *CC*

DAIMLER Model	ENGINE cc/cyl	DATES	CONDITION		
			1	2	3
Veteran (Coventry built)	var/4	1897-1904	£75,000	£60,000	£30,000
Veteran	var/4	1905-19	£35,000	£25,000	£15,000
30hp	4962/6	1919-25	£40,000	£25,000	£18,000
45hp	7413/6	1919-25	£45,000	£30,000	£20,000
Double Six 50	7136/12	1927-34	£40,000	£30,000	£20,000
20	2687/6	1934-35	£18,000	£14,000	£12,000
Straight 8	3421/8	1936-38	£20,000	£15,000	£12,000

Value is dependent on body style, coachbuilder and condition of the sleeve valve engine.

1956 Daimler Conquest, 6 cylinder, 2433cc engine, very good condition overall.
£4,400–4,800 *ADT*

1957 Daimler Conquest Century.
£1,200–1,500 *HOLL*

1965 Daimler Majestic Major Saloon, V8, overhead valve, 4561cc engine, twin SU carburettors, 220bhp at 5500rpm, automatic gearbox, coil spring front suspension, rigid axle and semi-elliptic leaf spring rear, one owner from new, with full history, regularly serviced, very good condition overall.
£3,300–3,600 *C*

1961 Daimler Dart 2.5 Litre V8, extensively restored 4 years ago, wire wheels, good condition.
£10,000–12,000 *UMC*

1961 Daimler SP250, 8 cylinder, 2548cc engine, very good restored condition.
Est. £12,000–13,000 *ADT*

1962 Daimler SP250 B Series, hard and soft tops, good original condition.
£10,500–11,000 *CGOC*

1960 Daimler SP250 A Series, a 2½ litre car uprated to 4½ using Majestic engine, good condition.
£6,250–6,750 *CGOC*

1961 Daimler SP250, 8 cylinder, 2548cc engine, very good original condition throughout.
£6,400–6,800 *ADT*

1962 Daimler SP250 B Series, wire wheels, restored, good condition.
£13,500–14,500 *CGOC*

1963 Daimler SP250 C Series, hard and soft tops, very good condition, good history, factory extras.
£13,750–14,250 *CGOC*

r. **1964 Daimler 250 V8 Saloon,** has undergone a major rebuild, in outstanding condition.
£6,800–7,200 *H&H*

1964 Daimler 250 V8 Saloon, wire wheels, green leather interior, fully restored, outstanding condition.
£16,000–17,000   *H&H*

1967 Daimler 2.5 Litre V8 Sports Saloon, only 2,000 miles recorded since restoration, photographic record of work carried out.
£7,500–8,000   *BKS*

1967 Daimler 250 V8, 8 cylinder, 2548cc engine, paintwork fair, structure good, fair but original condition.
£3,400–3,800   *ADT*

1968 Daimler 250 V8, 8 cylinder, 2548cc engine, overhauled automatic gearbox, original trim, engine runs well, original condition.
£3,300–3,600   *ADT*

1969 Daimler 250 V8, 8 cylinder, 2548cc engine, very good condition.
£5,000–5,500   *ADT*

1969 Daimler 420 Sovereign, fully restored, in excellent order throughout.
£6,000–7,000   *H&H*

1967 Daimler Sovereign 4.2, 6 cylinder, 4235cc engine, fair to good original condition.
£2,400–2,800   *ADT*

1974 Daimler Double Six SII, 12 cylinder, 5343cc engine in superb condition, automatic gearbox, very good condition overall.
Est. £1,500–2,000   *ADT*

DAIMLER Model	ENGINE cc/cyl	DATES	CONDITION 1	2	3
DB18	2522/6	1946-49	£7,500	£4,000	£1,000
DB18 Conv S/S	2522/6	1948-53	£11,000	£6,000	£2,000
Consort	2522/6	1949-53	£5,000	£3,000	£1,000
Conquest/Con.Century	2433/6	1953-58	£4,000	£2,000	£1,000
Conquest Roadster	2433/6	1953-56	£10,000	£6,000	£3,000
Majestic 3.8	3794/6	1958-62	£5,000	£2,000	£1,000
SP250	2547/8	1959-64	£12,000	£10,000	£4,500
Majestic Major	4561/8	1961-64	£6,000	£4,000	£1,000
2.5 V8	2547/8	1962-67	£8,000	£5,250	£2,500
V8 250	2547/8	1968-69	£6,000	£4,000	£2,000
Sovereign 420	4235/6	1966-69	£5,000	£3,500	£1,500

1974 Daimler Double Six Vanden Plas, resprayed 5 years ago, good condition throughout. **£3,000–3,400** *ADT*

1975 Daimler Sovereign 4.2 Litre Coupé, good condition. **£900–1,000** *BKS*

1977 Daimler Coupé, 6 cylinder, 4235cc engine, generally good condition. **£750–3,000** *COYS*

Daimler Double Six

- Launched in 1972 the Daimler Double Six was named after the first V12 Daimler introduced in 1926.
- The Daimler Double Six featured the Jaguar 5.3 litre XJ12 engine.
- The long wheelbase version was trimmed by the famous coachbuilders, Vanden Plas.

1984 Daimler Sovereign 4.2 Saloon, 6 cylinder, double overhead camshaft, 4235cc engine, 198bhp at 5500rpm, automatic gearbox, disc brakes, all independent suspension, right-hand drive, good running order, paintwork poor, some corrosion. **£900–1,000** *C*

1975 Daimler 2 Door Coupé, good condition throughout. **Est. £4,500–5,000** *S*

1976 Daimler Double Six Vanden Plas Saloon, coachwork trimmed by Vanden Plas, in excellent condition throughout. **£3,000–3,300** *S*

1977 Daimler 4.2 Litre, good condition. **£2,000–2,500** *H&H*

1978 Daimler Double Six, 5343cc, automatic, only 41,616 miles recorded from new, one of only 307 produced, excellent condition. **£5,000–6,000** *H&H*

1985 Daimler Double Six Series III Saloon, automatic, one owner, 18,500 miles recorded, immaculate order throughout. **£8,750–9,000** *S*

l. **1973 Daimler DS 420 Limousine,** 6 cylinder, 4200cc engine, automatic gearbox, fair condition. **£2,250–2,750** *DB*

DARRACQ

1926 Darracq 20/98hp 2.9 Litre Grande Sports Type TL 4 Door Weymann Saloon, coachwork by Darracq of Acton, completely original, right-hand change 4 speed gearbox, Marchal lighting set.
£9,500–9,750 *BKS*

DATSUN

1977 Datsun, very good original condition.
£3,000–3,500 *Mot*

DATSUN Model	ENGINE cc/cyl	DATES	CONDITION		
			1	2	3
240Z	2393/6	1970-71	£6,000	£4,000	£2,000
240Z	2393/6	1971-74	£4,500	£3,250	£1,500
260Z	2565/6	1974-79	£3,000	£2,250	£1,000
260Z 2+2	2565/6	1974-79	£2,800	£1,500	£800

DE DION

1901 De Dion Engined 4½hp Rear Entrance 4 Seater Tonneau, identity of its original maker is not known, right-hand drive, single cylinder De Dion Bouton engine, well maintained, good condition throughout.
Est. £20,000–25,000 *BKS*

1905 De Dion Bouton Double Phæton with Removable Rear Seats, single cylinder, 8hp engine, 3 speed manual gearbox, right-hand drive, wooden spoked wheels, has been on display in a motoring museum for many years.
£16,000–16,500 *C*

1911 De Dion Bouton 12/14hp Side Entrance Tonneau, fitted with side entrance tonneau coachwork in the late 1980s, generator and electric lighting, full pressure lubrication system and water pump, top speed around 50mph.
£20,000–21,000 *BKS*

1918 De Dion Bouton Model HD 15CV Charabanc, 2.1 litre side valve 4 cylinder engine, 3 speed gearbox fully operative, magneto and chassis restored, in good running order.
£10,000–10,500 *BKS*

Believed to have been bodied by De Dion as a French army staff car in WWI, subsequently passing into service with the police and, when found on a French airfield in 1984, serving as a fire tender.

DELAGE

| Cross Reference |
| Restoration Projects |

l. **1923 Delage 'Gunboat' Body Tourer,** original.
£20,000–30,000 *FHF*

1925 Delage DI 4 Door 4 Seater Tourer, left-hand drive, largely restored, mechanically complete, to be finished.
Est. £10,000–11,000 *HOLL*

r. **1930 Delage D8N Coach (4 Door Saloon),** 4 litre straight 8 pushrod overhead valve engine, developing 105bhp, X-braced chassis with servo-assisted braking, perfect mechanical order, good condition.
Est. £33,000–40,000 *BKS*

1935 Delage D8-105 Coach Profilé, impeccable provenance, excellent condition.
Est. £55,000–68,000 *BKS*

1937 Delage D6-70 'Vita 70' Sports Saloon, coachwork by Coachcraft, restored but minor detailing remains to be done to bodywork, good condition overall.
Est. £14,000–18,000 *BKS*

DELAHAYE

The Delahaye factory was founded at Tours, subsequently moving to Paris, where Emile Delahaye started to make cars in 1894.

Often the market leaders in both engineering development and style, Delahaye absorbed the Delage company in 1935. The company merged with Hotchkiss in 1954 and the Delahaye name disappeared shortly afterwards.

1928 Delahaye Saloon, 4 cylinder, 2000cc engine, good sound condition.
£5,200–5,600 *ADT*

DELAUNAY-BELLEVILLE

1926 Delaunay-Belleville P4B Limousine, coachwork by Maythorn, excellent original condition, with good provenance.
£16,000–16,500 *BKS*

DELOREAN

1981 DeLorean Coupé, coachwork by Giugiaro, Peugeot 2849cc fuel injected V6 engine, 130bhp at 5500rpm, 162lb ft at 2750rpm, 5 speed gearbox, finished in brushed steel, excellent condition.
£14,500–15,000 *COYS*

Originally owned by the DeLorean factory, this car was converted to right-hand drive by the original DeLorean subcontractor.

DE SOTO

1958 De Soto Firesweep Coupé, V8 engine, 350cu in, 280bhp at 4600rpm, automatic powerflite gearbox, 4 wheel drum brakes, front independent suspension with torsion bars, semi-elliptic leaf springs rear suspension, left-hand drive, good original condition.
£6,500–7,000 *CNY*

Equipment fitted in this car includes original plastic seat covers, dual antennae on the rear fins, fender skirts, and Frigiking air conditioning installed by the dealer.

DE TOMASO

Founded by Alejandro de Tomaso, a racing driver from Argentina, the first De Tomaso, the Vallelunga, appeared in 1965. The Pantera, which was developed from the 4.7 litre Ford V8-powered Mangusta, used the 5.8 litre Ford V8 engine which produced over 330bhp. A top speed of 162mph was claimed, with acceleration to 60mph in less than six seconds.

1977 De Tomaso Pantera 5.8 Litre GTS Tipo 874 Coupé, very low mileage, good running order, left-hand drive, good condition throughout.
£13,000–13,500 *BKS*

DODGE

1928 Dodge Senior Sedan, 6 cylinders, completely refurbished, new interior.
£5,000–6,000 *GAR*

1994 Dodge Viper, 4,000 miles, excellent condition.
£30,000–35,000 *CFI*

EXCALIBUR

The Excalibur Automobile Corporation manufacture their cars in Milwaukee, Wisconsin and are described as replica SSK Mercedes-Benz. Designed by Brooks Stevens, the first engines employed were manufactured by Studebaker, but after 1974 the Chevrolet Corvette V8 6.5 litre engine was used on most models.

1977 Excalibur Roadster, 8 cylinders, 6500cc, power steering, disc brakes, air conditioning, automatic transmission and suspension control, low mileage, as new condition.
£14,500–15,000 *ADT*

FACEL VEGA

Facel Vega, founded by Jean Daninos, took the name from his engineering company 'Les Forges et Ateliers de Construction de l'Eure et Loire'. Originally making car bodies for Simca, amongst other companies, the first true Facel Vega was unveiled in 1954. Despite the manufacture of stylish top of the range grand touring cars the company failed in 1964.

Make the most of Miller's

Condition is absolutely vital when assessing the value of a vehicle. Top class vehicles on the whole appreciate much more than less perfect examples. Rare, desirable cars may command higher prices even when in need of restoration.

1960 Facel Vega HK500, 8 cylinders, 6286cc, excellent restored condition.
£20,000–21,000 *ADT*

1963 Facel Vega Facel II HK2 Coupé, excellent original condition.
£26,000–28,000 *S*

FERRARI

1949 Ferrari Tipo 166 Inter Berlinetta, coachwork by Stabilimenti Farina, present condition reflects meticulous maintenance and restoration over a long period.
£66,000–68,000 *BKS*

1957 Ferrari 250 GT Boano Coupé, coachwork by Boano/Ellena, partially dismantled, semi-restored, engine substituted by an identical unit from another 250GT Boano, straightforward project.
£30,000–32,000 *COYS*

> **Cross Reference**
> Restoration Projects

Ferrari 250 GTE

- Developed from the Ferrari 250 GT which was effectively Ferrari's first production road car.
- Designed by Pininfarina.
- The 250 GTE was introduced in 1960 and was the first real 4 seater production car.
- Production ceased in 1963 after 930 cars had been built.

1961 Ferrari 250 GTE Coupé, coachwork by Pininfarina, 12 cylinders, 2995cc, engine completely overhauled, extremely good order throughout.
£21,000–23,000 *COYS*

1962 Ferrari 250 GTE Coupé, totally original condition, recently imported from USA.
Est. £25,000–30,000 *S*

Ferrari 275 GTS

- Developed from the 250 series, the 275 GTS was designed for both road and track.
- Produced alongside the famous 275 GTB.
- The 250 series V12 engine now developed 3.3 litres producing up to 300bhp.
- Bodywork designed by Pininfarina, only 200 had been built when production ceased in 1966.

1965 Ferrari 275 GTS Spyder, coachwork by Pininfarina, good condition throughout.
£68,000–72,000 *COYS*

1967 Ferrari 330 GT 2+2 Fixed Head Coupé, excellent restored condition.
Est. £28,000–32,000 *S*

1965 Ferrari 330GT Coupé, coachwork by Pininfarina, Borrani wire wheels respoked and rechromed, good original condition.
Est. £20,000–22,000 *BKS*

1965 Ferrari 276 GTB Berlinetta, coachwork by Pininfarina, 12 cylinders, 3286cc, comprehensive rebuild, right-hand drive, superb all-round condition.
Est. £105,000–115,000 *COYS*

1968 Ferrari 365 GT 2+2 Sports Berlina,
coachwork by Carrozzeria Pininfarina,
manual gearbox, left-hand drive, very
good condition throughout.
Est. £34,000–36,000 *BKS*

1969 Ferrari 365 GT 2+2 Two Door Berlina,
coachwork by Pininfarina/Scaglietti, left-hand
drive, generally good overall condition.
£22,000–24,000 *BKS*

1972 Ferrari 365 GTC/4 Sports Coupé,
coachwork by Pininfarina, left-hand drive,
very good overall condition.
£30,000–32,000 *BKS*

1972 Ferrari 365 GTC/4 Coupé, coachwork by
Pininfarina, engine replaced by 400 series unit,
chassis renovated as necessary, extremely good
and very original condition throughout.
Est. £28,000–35,000 *COYS*

1970 Ferrari 246 GT Dino Sports Coupé,
well maintained, cast-alloy wheels, right-hand
drive, good condition.
£30,000–32,000 *BKS*

1972 Ferrari 246 GT Dino 2 Door Berlinetta,
fully restored, left-hand drive.
Est. £33,000–35,000 *S*

FERRARI Model	ENGINE cc/cyl	DATES	CONDITION 1	2	3
250 GT	2953/12	1959-63	£32,000	£22,000	£20,000
250 GT SWB (steel)	2953/12	1959-62	£235,000	£185,000	-
250 GT Lusso	2953/12	1962-64	£80,000	£65,000	£50,000
250 GT 2+2	2953/12	1961-64	£30,000	£21,000	£18,000
275 GTB	3286/12	1964-66	£100,000	£80,000	£70,000
275 GTS	3286/12	1965-67	£90,000	£70,000	£50,000
275 GTB 4-cam	3286/12	1966-68	£150,000	£110,000	£80,000
330 GT 2+2	3967/12	1964-67	£22,000	£18,000	£15,000
330 GTC	3967/12	1966-68	£55,000	£40,000	£25,000
330 GTS	3967/12	1966-68	£80,000	£70,000	£60,000
365 GT 2+2	4390/12	1967-71	£28,000	£20,000	£15,000
365 GTC	4390/12	1967-70	£40,000	£35,000	£30,000
365 GTS	4390/12	1968-69	£110,000	£80,000	£70,000
365 GTB (Daytona)	4390/12	1968-74	£90,000	£70,000	£50,000
365 GTC4	4390/12	1971-74	£45,000	£38,000	£30,000
365 GT4 2+2/400GT	4390/ 4823/12	1972-79	£20,000	£15,000	£10,000
365 BB	4390/12	1974-76	£55,000	£38,000	£30,000
512 BB/BBi	4942/12	1976-81	£50,000	£40,000	£30,000
246 GT Dino	2418/6	1969-74	£35,000	£25,000	£15,000
246 GTS Dino	2418/6	1972-74	£42,000	£28,000	£20,000
308 GT4 2+2	2926/8	1973-80	£15,000	£10,000	£8,000
308 GTB (fibreglass)	2926/8	1975-76	£25,000	£18,000	£15,000
308 GTB	2926/8	1977-81	£22,000	£16,000	£10,000
308 GTS	2926/8	1978-81	£26,000	£18,000	£11,000
308 GTBi/GTSi	2926/8	1981-82	£24,000	£17,000	£10,000
308 GTB/GTS QV	2926/6	1983-85	£21,500	£16,500	£9,500
400i manual	4823/12	1981-85	£15,000	£12,000	£10,000
400i auto	4823/12	1981-85	£13,000	£12,000	£8,000

l. **1972 Ferrari 246 Dino
2 Door Coupé,** coachwork by
Pininfarina, very low mileage,
excellent original condition.
£50,000–54,000 *BKS*

r. **1973 Ferrari 246 GT Dino Sports
Coupé,** coachwork by Pininfarina,
bare metal repaint, right-hand drive,
good condition throughout for its age.
Est. £28,000–30,000 *BKS*

Don't Forget!
*If in doubt please refer to
the 'How to Use' section at
the beginning of this book.*

1973 Ferrari 246 GTS Dino, 6 cylinder mid-engine, 2418cc, double overhead camshaft, cast iron block
and light alloy heads, 178bhp at 7000rpm, 5 speed manual gearbox, front and rear independent
suspension with unequal length A-arms, coil springs, tubular shock absorbers, 4 wheel disc brakes,
original right-hand drive Spyder, good working condition.
Est. £38,000–42,000 *C*

l. **1972 Ferrari 365 GTB/4
Daytona,** Berlinetta
coachwork by Pininfarina,
right-hand drive, only 18,000
miles, extensively rebuilt.
Est. £65,000–75,000 *COYS*

Ferrari 365 GTB/4 Daytona

- Named after the famous 24-hour
  race victory at Daytona when
  Ferrari took the first 3 places
  in 1967.
- 4390cc V12 engine developed
  355bhp and claimed a top speed
  of over 170mph.
- The last and the fastest of the
  Ferrari front-engined GT cars.
- The coupé by Pininfarina was
  introduced in 1968, and 127
  were built with Spyder bodywork
  by Scaglietti.

1973 Ferrari 365 GTB/4 Daytona, Berlinetta coachwork
by Pininfarina, 31,000 miles, body completely restored,
excellent condition throughout.
Est. £78,000–88,000 *COYS*

r. **1973 Ferrari 365 GTB/4 Daytona,** V12 engine, 4 overhead camshafts, single plug per cylinder, 4390cc, 355bhp at 7500rpm, 5 speed manual gearbox, integral with final drive, 4 wheel disc brakes, independent all-round suspension, double wishbones, coil springs, original right-hand drive, excellent condition. **Est. £77,000–82,000** *C*

1977 Ferrari Boxer 365 GTB4, only 26,000 miles, rebuilt engine. **£49,000–51,000** *KSC*

1975 Ferrari 365 GT4 Berlinetta Boxer, Berlinetta by Pininfarina, 12 cylinders, 4390cc, only 1,550 miles from new, engine fully rebuilt, superb condition throughout. **£60,000–62,000** *COYS*

Ferrari 365 GT4

- The mid-engined 365 GT4 Berlinetta Boxer was introduced in 1971.
- Bodywork designed by Pininfarina was steel monocoque over a tubular steel chassis.
- Flat 12 cylinder 4390cc alloy engine produced 360bhp and claimed a top speed in excess of 180mph.
- It could accelerate to 60mph in 5.3 seconds and 100mph in 11 seconds.
- Only 387 examples of this model were produced before it was replaced by the 512BB in 1976.

1977 Ferrari 512BB 2 Door Sports Coupé, coachwork by Carrozzeria Pininfarina, very good overall condition. **£29,000–32,000** *BKS*

> *A rebuilt car is not necessarily more valuable than a car in good original condition, even if the restoration has been costly.*

l. **1977 Ferrari 308 GT4,** coachwork by Bertone, 40,000 miles, very good condition throughout. **£14,000–18,000** *VIC*

r. **1981 Ferrari 308 GTB,** 8 cylinders, 2962cc, non-standard rear aerofoil fitted, very good condition throughout. **Est. £24,000–26,000** *ADT*

1982 Ferrari 308 GTBi, 8 cylinders, 2962cc, very good condition overall. **Est. £26,000–28,000** *ADT*

r. **1985 Ferrari Mondial QV,** 8 cylinder, 2926cc engine, good original condition. **£17,000–18,000** *ADT*

1984 Ferrari 400i Berlina, coachwork by Pininfarina, very good condition. **Est. £10,000–14,000** *BKS*

1985 Ferrari 288GTO, Berlinetta coachwork by Pininfarina, 8 cylinder, 2855cc engine, only 8,700 miles recorded, immaculate condition. **Est. £195,000–225,000** *COYS*

Less than 20 Ferrari 288GTOs were imported into the UK.

r. **1987 Ferrari 328 GTB 3.2 litre,** Berlinetta coachwork by Pininfarina, just over 41,000 miles recorded, excellent condition throughout. **£31,000–33,000** *BKS*

FIAT

Fiat, latin for 'let it be', was founded in 1899.
The name, an acronym for Fabbrica Italiana
di Automobili Torino, was adopted as FIAT
in 1906. Owned by Giovanni Agnelli with
others, Fiat was soon to become the biggest
manufacturer in Italy.

Now one of the largest multi-national
companies in the world, in all types of
industry, Fiat own Lancia and Abarth as
well as Ferrari.

**1931 Fiat 514 Four Door
Fabric Saloon,** coachwork by
Weymann, right-hand drive,
apart from a small crack in
the cylinder block in good
condition throughout.
Est. £3,000–4,000 *BKS*

l. **1925 Fiat 501 Five Seater
Open Tourer,** right-hand drive,
totally restored, original owners
manual, in show condition.
£10,000–11,000 *H&H*

> **Don't Forget!**
> *If in doubt please
> refer to the 'How to Use'
> section at the beginning
> of this book.*

r. **1935 Fiat Balilla 508S
Coppa d'Oro,** 4 cylinder
in line monobloc, 995cc
engine, 4 speed central
change gearbox with
synchromesh on
3rd and top, hydraulic
brakes, semi-elliptic
leaf springs front and
rear suspension, right-
hand drive, maintained
in perfect condition.
£18,500–19,500 *C*

*The body is original to
the car, being a period
imitation of the Italian
Coppa d'Oro design,
made by an unknown
London coachbuilder.*

1937 Fiat Topolino Tipo 500A 2 Door Coupé,
right-hand drive, imported from New Zealand, total
mechanical overhaul, will require some attention.
£5,000–5,500 *BKS*

1937 Fiat Topolino 500A, 4 cylinder, 560cc engine,
extensively restored including an engine rebuild.
£5,000–5,500 *ADT*

1937 Fiat Topolino 500A, original right-hand drive, subject of a 4 year rebuild.
£4,000–4,500 *H&H*

1939 Fiat Topolino 500, 4 cylinder water-cooled engine, unrestored condition.
£1,000–1,500 *DB*

1949 Fiat Topolino 500C 2 Door Coupé, extensively modified mechanically and bodily from earlier types, front-mounted 4 cylinder, 569cc overhead valve engine, one lady owner from new, interior is fair, partially disassembled, not in running order.
£1,800–2,200 *BKS*

1954 Fiat Topolino Cabriolet, totally rust free, unmarked interior, from a private collection.
£3,800–4,000 *Bro*

Make the most of Miller's

Condition is absolutely vital when assessing the value of a vehicle. Top class vehicles on the whole appreciate much more than less perfect examples. Rare, desirable cars may command higher prices even when in need of restoration.

1952 Fiat 8V Demon Rouge, Berlinetta coachwork by Michelotti/Vignale, V8, 1996cc engine, superb condition throughout.
£58,000–60,000 *COYS*

1962 Fiat 600 Jolly 4 Seater Convertible, generally in good original condition.
£8,000–8,500 *BKS*

FIAT Model	ENGINE cc/cyl	DATES	CONDITION 1	2	3
501	1460/4	1920-26	£6,000	£3,500	£1,500
519	4767/6	1923-29	£9,000	£7,000	£3,000
503	1473/4	1927-29	£8,000	£4,000	£2,000
507	2297/4	1927-28	£9,000	£5,500	£3,500
522/4	2516/6	1932-34	£10,000	£8,000	£3,500
508	994/4	1934-37	£5,000	£2,500	£1,500
527 Sports	2516/6	1935-36	£14,000	£8,000	£3,500
1.5 litre Balilla	1498/6	1936-39	£10,000	£7,000	£3,000
500	570/4	1937-55	£6,000	£2,500	£1,000
1100 Balilla	1089/4	1938-40	£4,500	£2,000	£1,000

1963 Fiat Fissore, 4 cylinder twin cam, 1568cc engine, light alloy cylinder head and twin Weber carburettors, 5 speed manual gearbox, good mechanical condition throughout.
£3,500–3,800 *ADT*

1967 Fiat Dino 2 Door Coupé, coachwork by Bertone, engine totally overhauled, bodywork excellent, left-hand drive, only 5,500 miles recorded.
£7,000–7,500 *BKS*

1970 Fiat Dino 2400 Spyder, Spyder coachwork by Pininfarina, 6 cylinder, 2418cc engine, an outstanding example, in excellent condition.
£22,000–24,000 *COYS*

1970 Fiat 'Shellette' 850 Spyder, good original condition.
£5,500–6,000 *BKS*

Based on the Fiat 850, this car is one of an exclusive production of personal runabouts created by Italian coachbuilder Giovanni Michelotti during the 1970s. These 'Shellette' spyders are similar in concept to the well-known Ghia Jolly vehicles of the 1960s.

1970 Fiat Dino Coupé, 6 cylinder, 1987cc engine, left-hand drive, generally very good condition.
Est. £5,000–5,500 *ADT*

1976 Fiat 'Shellette' 850 Spyder, wickerwork seats and dashboard, very low mileage.
Est. £5,000–7,000 *BKS*

1968 Fiat Gamine Roadster, coachwork by Vignale, 2 cylinder, 499cc engine, very good condition throughout.
£3,500–4,000 *COYS*

l. **1971 Fiat Gamine Roadster,** coachwork by Vignale, 2 owners only, good general condition. **£3,250–3,750** *COYS*

1977 Fiat 130 Pininfarina Coupé, stored for many years, in good order throughout. **Est. £5,500–6,500** *S*

1972 Fiat Gamine 500, only 29,000 miles recorded, good restored condition. **£3,500–4,000** *ADT*

Fiat 500

- Developed from the post WWII Topolino (little mouse), the 500 series provided enormous fun and very economical motoring.
- Although underpowered and underrated against its rivals, the French 2CV and the British Mini, it has a keen following.
- The 600 series, introduced in 1955 was slightly larger and more powerful.
- The Enid Blyton character Noddy was one of the famous customers for the 'Gamine' variant.

1972 Fiat 500, extensively restored 5 years ago, very good condition throughout. **£2,600–2,800** *COYS*

r. **1981 Fiat X1/9,** good condition overall. **£2,400–2,600** *ADT*

FIAT Model	ENGINE cc/cyl	DATES	CONDITION 1	2	3
500B Topolino	569/4	1945-55	£5,000	£2,000	£750
500C	569/4	1948-54	£4,000	£1,700	£1,000
500 Nuova	479,499/2	1957-75	£3,000	£1,500	£750
600/600D	633, 767/4	1955-70	£3,000	£2,000	£1,000
500F Giardiniera	479, 499/2	1957-75	£3,000	£1,500	£1,000
2300S	2280/6	1961-68	£3,000	£1,700	£1,000
850	843/4	1964-71	£1,000	£750	-
850 Coupé	843, 903/4	1965-73	£1,500	£1,000	-
850 Spyder	843, 903/4	1965-73	£3,000	£2,000	£1,000
128 Sport Coupé 3P	1116/ 1290/4	1971-78	£2,500	£1,800	£1,000
130 Coupé	3235/6	1971-77	£5,500	£4,000	£2,000
131 Mirafiori Sport	1995/4	1974-84	£1,500	£1,000	£500
124 Sport Coupé	1438/ 1608/4	1966-72	£3,000	£2,000	£1,000
124 Sport Spyder	1438/ 1608/4	1966-72	£4,000	£2,500	£1,500
Dino Coupé	1987/ 2418/6	1967-73	£7,500	£5,500	£2,500
Dino Spyder	1987/ 2418/6	1967-73	£10,000	£7,000	£5,000
X1/9	1290/ 1498/4	1972-89	£3,500	£1,500	£1,000

FORD

1904 Ford Model C Tourabout, older restoration.
£14,500–15,500 *GAR*

1905 Ford Model F 4 Passenger Side Entrance Tonneau, 2 cylinders, 12hp, 2 speed planetary gearbox, rear drum brakes, full elliptical suspension, right-hand drive, good overall condition.
£25,000–30,000 *CNY*

1911 Ford Model T Towncar, 4 cylinders, 176.7cu in, 22hp, planetary 2 speeds forward one reverse, 3 pedal one lever gearbox, contracting band on transmission brakes, transverse springs, front and rear suspension, left-hand drive, fully rebuilt to a very high standard.
£15,000–18,000 *CNY*

1911 Ford Model T 2 Seater Torpedo Roadster, good condition throughout.
£13,500–14,000 *S*

This model is rare and said to be the first type with operating doors.

1915 Ford Model T 4 Seater Tourer, subject of a complete rebuild including engine and gearbox.
Est. £11,000–13,000 *BKS*

1924 Ford Model T 4 Seater Tourer, fitted with a self-starter, older restoration, sound and presentable, would benefit from a little cosmetic work.
Est. £7,000–9,000 *BKS*

l. **1925 Ford Model T Doctor's Coupé,** 4 cylinders, cast iron, side valve, 2890cc, planetary 2 speed forward, one reverse gearbox, rear wheel drum brakes, front and rear transverse leaf spring suspension, left-hand drive, very good condition throughout.
£8,500–9,000 *C*

1926 Ford Model T Roadster, minor recommissioning may be required prior to road use. **Est. £8,000–9,000** *S*

1926 Ford Model T 2 Seater Roadster, left-hand drive, original condition. **£5,400–5,800** *H&H*

FORD Model	ENGINE cc/cyl	DATES	CONDITION 1	2	3
Model T	2892/4	1908-27	£10,000	£7,000	£4,000
Model A	3285/4	1928-32	£8,500	£6,000	£3,500
Models Y and 8	933/4	1933-40	£4,000	£3,000	£1,500
Model C	1172/4	1933-40	£4,000	£2,000	£1,000
Model AB	3285/4	1933-34	£10,000	£8,000	£4,500
Model ABF	2043/4	1933-34	£9,000	£6,000	£4,000
Model V8	3622/8	1932-40	£8,500	£6,000	£4,500
Model V8-60	2227/8	1936-40	£7,000	£5,000	£2,000
Model AF (UK only)	2033/4	1928-32	£9,000	£6,000	£3,500

A right hand drive vehicle will always command more interest than a left hand drive. Coachbuilt vehicles, and in particular drophead coupés, achieve a premium at auction. Veteran cars (i.e. manufactured before 1919) will often achieve a 20% premium.

l. **1929 Ford Model A Tudor,** older restoration. **£3,250–3,750** *GAR*

1930 Ford Model A Roadster De Luxe with Dickey, 24hp engine, totally rebuilt to excellent condition. **£7,200–8,400** *H&H*

c1933 Ford Model Y Saloon, very good condition. **£4,500–5,500** *SW*

1933 Ford Model Y, restored, good condition.
£2,500–2,700 *H&H*

1934 Ford Model Y 'Kerry' Tourer,
fully restored to original condition.
£8,000–10,000 *FYC*

There are only 2 known roadworthy survivors.

1935 Ford Model C 4 Door Saloon, complete and
roadworthy, requiring some work for full restoration.
£1,500–2,000 *FYC*

1936 Ford Model CX 4 Door Saloon,
very good condition.
£3,000–4,000 *FYC*

1936 Ford 8 Model Y, 4 cylinders, 933cc,
very original and good overall condition.
£2,400–2,800 *ADT*

1936 Ford Model Y 8hp Popular 2 Door Tudor,
very good condition.
£3,500–4,000 *FYC*

1936 Ford Model Y Saloon, 4 cylinders, 933cc,
24bhp at 4000rpm, 3 speed manual gearbox,
4 wheel drum brakes, transverse leaf springs front
and rear suspension, right-hand drive, meticulously
restored, excellent condition.
£6,250–6,500 *C*

1939 Ford V8 Four Door Saloon, left-hand
drive, restored over a 10 year period, very tidy
original car.
£5,000–5,250 *BKS*

1952 Ford Popular 2 Door Saloon,
part restored condition.
£1,500–1,750 *HSS*

1953 Ford Popular.
£3,000–3,500 *H&H*

1958 Ford Popular 103E, 4 cylinders, 1172cc,
good original condition.
£2,100–2,400 *ADT*

1955 Ford Popular 103E, 4 cylinders, 1172cc,
side valve, 3 speed gearbox, sound
and original condition.
£900–1,000 *DB*

1959 Ford Zephyr Convertible,
4 cylinders, 2588cc, very good
restored condition.
£5,500–5,800 *ADT*

1953 Ford Consul MkI, show condition with all period
extras, including Ekco radio.
£2,750–3,250 *Mot*

1961 Ford Zephyr Convertible, very good condition.
£6,250–7,750 *CC*

1960 Ford Consul MkII 4 Door Saloon,
good original condition.
Est. £2,000–2,500 *HOLL*

1960 Ford Popular De Luxe, 1172cc, side valve
engine, 3 speed gearbox, good original condition.
£800–1,000 *Mot*

1960 Ford Escort Van, with windows,
4 cylinders, side valve, 1172cc, 3 speed
gearbox, good condition.
£800–850 *DB*

Make the most of Miller's

*Condition is absolutely vital when
assessing the value of a vehicle. Top class
vehicles on the whole appreciate much
more than less perfect examples. Rare,
desirable cars may command higher
prices even when in need of restoration.*

Cross Reference
Commercial Vehicles

1962 Ford Anglia 105E, fair condition,
some work required.
£380–400 *CC*

l. **1960 Ford Anglia 105E,** excellent condition.
£2,000–2,500 *SW*

FORD (British built) Model	ENGINE cc/cyl	DATES	CONDITION 1	2	3
Anglia E494A	993/4	1948-53	£2,000	£850	£250
Prefect E93A	1172/4	1940-49	£3,500	£1,250	£900
Prefect E493A	1172/4	1948-53	£2,500	£1,000	£300
Popular 103E	1172/4	1953-59	£1,875	£825	£300
Anglia/Prefect 100E	1172/4	1953-59	£1,350	£625	£250
Prefect 107E	997/4	1959-62	£1,150	£600	£200
Escort/Squire 100E	1172/4	1955-61	£1,000	£850	£275
Popular 100E	1172/4	1959-62	£1,250	£600	£180
Anglia 105E	997/4	1959-67	£1,400	£500	£75
Anglia 123E	1198/4	1962-67	£1,550	£575	£150
V8 Pilot	3622/8	1947-51	£7,500	£4,000	£1,500
Consul Mk I	1508/4	1951-56	£2,250	£950	£400
Consul Mk I DHC	1508/4	1953-56	£4,750	£3,000	£1,250
Zephyr Mk I	2262/6	1951-56	£3,000	£1,250	£600
Zephyr Mk I DHC	2262/6	1953-56	£6,800	£3,250	£1,500
Zodiac Mk I	2262/6	1953-56	£3,300	£1,500	£700
Consul Mk II/Deluxe	1703/4	1956-62	£2,900	£1,500	£650
Consul Mk II DHC	1703/4	1956-62	£5,000	£3,300	£1,250
Zephyr Mk II	2553/6	1956-62	£3,800	£1,800	£750
Zephyr Mk II DHC	2553/6	1956-62	£8,000	£4,000	£1,500
Zodiac Mk II	2553/6	1956-62	£4,000	£2,250	£750
Zodiac Mk II DHC	2553/6	1956-62	£8,500	£4,250	£1,800
Zephyr 4 Mk III	1703/4	1962-66	£2,100	£1,200	£400
Zephyr 6 Mk III	2552/6	1962-66	£2,300	£1,300	£450
Zodiac Mk II	2553/6	1962-66	£2,500	£1,500	£500
Zephyr 4 Mk IV	1994/4	1966-72	£1,750	£600	£150
Zephyr 6 Mk IV	2553/6	1966-72	£1,800	£700	£150
Zodiac Mk IV	2994/6	1966-72	£2,000	£800	£150
Zodiac Mk IV Est.	2994/6	1966-72	£2,200	£950	£150
Zodiac Mk IV Exec.	2994/6	1966-72	£2,300	£950	£150
Classic 315	1340/ 1498/4	1961-63	£1,400	£800	£500
Consul Capri	1340/ 1498/4	1961-64	£2,100	£1,350	£400
Consul Capri GT	1498/4	1961-64	£2,600	£1,600	£800

1962 Ford Anglia 105E Saloon, mileage of 27,000 believed correct, totally original, good condition.
£1,700–1,900 *H&H*

1964 Ford Anglia 105E De Luxe, 1 litre engine, comprehensive bodywork restoration.
Est. £2,000–3,000 *BKS*

l. **1966 Ford-Lotus Cortina 1.6 Litre 2 Door Saloon,** rebuilt 1558cc Lotus twin-cam engine, bodywork renovated, very good condition throughout.
£7,800–8,200 *BKS*
This car is well-known in the world of vintage racing.

Cross Reference
Lotus

r. **1966 Ford Cortina GT 2 Door Saloon,** 4 cylinders, 1498cc, modifications including blueprinted engine with twin Webers, rally prepared to Works specification, extensively prepared within FIA regulations.
£4,200–4,500 *COYS*

Cross Reference
Racing Cars

1966 Ford Cortina GT MkI, fully restored body, virtually unused.
Est. £3,250–3,750 *ADT*

1966 Ford Cortina Super, as new condition.
£2,000–3,000 *SW*

Don't Forget!
If in doubt please refer to the 'How to Use' section at the beginning of this book.

l. **1966 Ford Cortina MkI 1500 Four Door Saloon,** in good condition generally.
£1,000–1,200 *ADT*

1969 Ford Lotus Cortina MkII, 4 cylinders, 1558cc, totally restored.
£3,500–3,750 *ADT*

1970 Ford Cortina 1600E, very good overall condition.
Est. £3,000–3,500 *ADT*

Ford Capri

- Launched in 1969 as 'the car you have always promised yourself', it was designed to follow the successful marketing of the Mustang in America.
- There were 26 basic models when introduced including engine sizes 1300, 1600 and 2000cc. 3 litre V6 variants followed later.
- Nearly 375,000 models of all types were produced between 1969–73.

1969 Ford Capri MkI Two Door Coupé, 1600cc engine, manual gearbox, one private owner from new, condition throughout is commensurate with careful single ownership.
£1,800–2,000 *BKS*

l. **1972 Ford Capri 1600 GT XLR,** good condition throughout.
£1,400–1,600 *ADT*

FORD (British built) Model	ENGINE cc/cyl	DATES	CONDITION		
			1	2	3
Cortina Mk I	1198/4	1963-66	£1,550	£600	£150
Cortina Crayford Mk I	1198/4	1963-66	£3,500	£1,800	£950
Cortina GT	1498/4	1963-66	£1,800	£1,000	£650
Lotus Cortina Mk I	1558/4	1963-66	£9,000	£7,500	£4,500
Cortina Mk II	1599/4	1966-70	£1,000	£500	£100
Cortina GT Mk II	1599/4	1966-70	£1,200	£650	£150
Cortina Crayford Mk II DHC	1599/4	1966-70	£4,000	£2,000	£1,500
Lotus Cortina Mk II	1558/4	1966-70	£5,500	£3,000	£1,800
Cortina 1600E	1599/4	1967-70	£2,800	£1,000	£450
Consul Corsair	1500/4	1963-65	£1,100	£500	£250
Consul Corsair GT	1500/4	1963-65	£1,200	£600	£250
Corsair V4	1664/4	1965-70	£1,150	£600	£250
Corsair V4 Est.	1664/4	1965-70	£1,400	£600	£250
Corsair V4GT	1994/4	1965-67	£1,300	£700	£250
CorsairV4GT Est.	1994/4	1965-67	£1,400	£700	£350
Corsair Convertible	1664/ 1994/4	1965-70	£4,300	£2,500	£1,000
Corsair 2000	1994/4	1967-70	£1,350	£500	£250
Corsair 2000E	1994/4	1967-70	£1,500	£800	£350
Escort 1300E	1298/4	1973-74	£1,900	£1,000	£250
Escort Twin Cam	1558/4	1968-71	£8,000	£5,000	£2,000
Escort GT	1298/4	1968-73	£3,000	£1,500	£350
Escort Sport	1298/4	1971-75	£1,750	£925	£250
Escort Mexico	1601/4	1970-74	£4,000	£2,000	£750
RS1600	1601/4	1970-74	£5,000	£2,500	£1,500
RS2000	1998/4	1973-74	£4,500	£2,200	£1,000
Escort RS Mexico	1593/4	1976-78	£3,500	£2,000	£850
Escort RS2000 Mk II	1993/4	1976-80	£6,000	£3,500	£2,000
Capri Mk I 1300/ 1600	1298/ 1599/4	1969-72	£1,500	£1,000	£550
Capri 2000/ 3000GT	1996/4 2994/6	1969-72	£2,000	£1,000	£500
Capri 3000E	2994/6	1970-72	£4,000	£2,000	£1,000
Capri RS3100	3093/6	1973-74	£6,500	£3,500	£2,000
Cortina 2000E	1993/4	1973-76	£2,500	£550	£225
Granada Ghia	1993/4 2994/6	1974-77	£4,000	£900	£350

1972 Ford Capri 3000E Manual, only 22,000 miles recorded, outstanding original condition.
£2,600–2,800 *H&H*

1973 Ford Capri 1600 GT, 4 speed manual gearbox, very good order.
£2,100–2,300 *ADT*

Ford Escort

- Replacing the Ford 105E Anglia, the Escort was launched in 1968.
- A Ford Escort won the gruelling 15,000 mile London-Mexico Rally in 1970 which led to the introduction of the Escort Mexico.
- The Mexico's 1598cc engine produced 99bhp with a top speed of about 100mph.
- Further successes followed and a new competition car, the Escort RS Cosworth, was developed.
- The 1993cc Cosworth engine produced 227bhp and a top speed of nearly 140mph.

1971 Ford Mexico 2 Door Coupé, rebuilt engine, recorded mileage 57,000 since new, full restoration, overall immaculate condition.
£6,800–7,400 *S*

1978 Ford RS2000 Custom, rebuilt and uprated engine, lowered suspension and vented front discs, Janspeed exhaust and manifold, partly restored, excellent condition.
Est. £3,500–4,500 *ADT*

1979 Ford Escort RS2000, good condition.
£2,000–2,400 *H&H*

1981 Ford Escort Ghia Saloon, no listed modifications from original factory specifications, including a sunroof, except a silver frog mascot on the bonnet, good overall condition.
£4,800–5,200 *S*

This car was formerly the property of HRH The Princess of Wales.

1979 Ford Granada 2.8 Ghia, superb condition.
£3,800–4,200 *GEC*

**Miller's is a price
GUIDE not a price LIST**

r. **1985 Ford Granada 2.8i Ghia.**
£4,400–4,600 *GEC*

1957 Ford Fairlane Retractable, V8 engine, completely restored.
£15,000–17,000 *GAR*

1962 Ford Thunderbird 2 Door Coupé, good restored condition.
£6,600–6,800 *BKS*

Ford Thunderbird

- Launched in 1954 the Thunderbird, or TBird as it became, was built at Dearborn.
- In production for over 30 years it was the 1955-57 period which achieved the cult following.
- Only about 50,000 vehicles were produced during this period.
- Powered by a Ford V8 engine of 5113cc which produced 225bhp and a top speed of 116mph.

1963 Ford Galaxie 500XL, V8, 390cu in engine, 300bhp at 4600rpm, 3 speed automatic gearbox, 4 wheel drum brakes, independent front suspension, live axle rear, left-hand drive, excellent original example.
£3,800–4,200 *C*

Cross Reference
Racing Cars

l. **1965 Ford Mustang Convertible**, Challenger V8, 289cu in engine, standard bodywork, very sound condition, excellent provenance.
£7,400–7,800 *ADT*

The Ford Mustang was available in three versions, the fastback, the 2+2 and the convertible. The power convertible top cost $54 when new as an optional extra.

FORD (American built) Model	ENGINE cu in/cyl	DATES	CONDITION 1	2	3
Thunderbird	292/ 312/8	1955-57	£18,500	£13,500	£9,000
Edsel Citation	410/8	1958	£9,000	£4,500	£2,500
Edsel Ranger	223/6- 361/8	1959	£6,000	£3,500	£2,000
Edsel Citation convertible	410/8	1958	£12,000	£6,000	£4,000
Edsel Corsair convertible	332/ 361/8	1959	£10,500	£7,000	£4,500
Fairlane 2 door	223/6- 352/8	1957-59	£8,000	£4,500	£3,000
Fairlane 500 Sunliner	223/6- 352/8	1957-59	£12,000	£8,000	£6,500
Fairlane 500 Skyliner	223/6- 352/8	1957-59	£14,000	£10,000	£8,000
Mustang 4.7 V8		1964-66	£9,000	£4,000	£2,000
Mustang GT 350		1966-67	£15,000	£10,000	£6,000
Mustang hardtop	260/6- 428/8	1967-68	£6,000	£4,000	£3,000
Mustang GT 500			£20,000	£14,000	£6,000

l. **1965 Ford Mustang GT,** rare factory engined high performance 289cu in, V8 engine, 4 speed manual gearbox, excellent condition.
£12,000–13,500 *CFI*

r. **1967 Ford Mustang Hard Top Coupé,** 5 litre engine, uprated coil springs, modified Koni adjustable shock absorbers, 11in disc brakes with Kelsey-Hayes 4 pot Mustang calipers, resprayed interior, stripped for racing, rebuilt and unused since.
£9,500–10,000 *BKS*

1973 Ford 2 Door Coupé, 9,000 miles recorded from new, condition throughout as new.
£7,500–8,000 *H&H*

This car was a Motor Show display vehicle, but these cars were not imported into the UK.

1977 Ford Granada Ghia (USA), 8 cylinders, 302cu in, excellent condition throughout, recommissioned 2 years ago.
Est. £2,750–3,500 *ADT*

l. **1978 Ford Mercury Marquis Station Wagon,** 8 cylinders, 7539cc, reconditioned engine, average condition.
£2,500–2,750 *COYS*

The Mercury Marquis range provided some of the most luxurious models produced by Ford. They were available as two door, four door and station wagons.

A rebuilt car is not necessarily more valuable than a car in good original condition, even if the restoration has been costly.

Cross Reference
Military Vehicles

r. **1944 Ford GPW Jeep,** 2.2 litre flathead 4 cylinder power unit, complete with hood, jerry can and shovel, garaged and carefully maintained.
£4,400–4,800 *BKS*

FRAZER-NASH

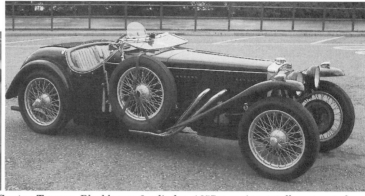

1934 Frazer-Nash Shelsey 2 Seater Tourer, Blackburne 6 cylinder, 1657cc engine, totally renovated including ash frame and chassis, correct new front wings, rebuilt engine and radiator, excellent condition. **Est. £45,000–55,000** *COYS*

l. **1937 Frazer-Nash BMW 328,** 6 cylinder, 1971cc engine, ground up restoration, excellent order throughout. **Est. £75,000–85,000** *COYS*

The first Frazer-Nash BMWs were based on the BMW type 315 1½ litre model and appeared in 1934. By 1937 the type 328 with a 1971cc engine could produce 80bhp.

1952 Frazer-Nash MkI Le Mans Replica, 6 cylinder, overhead valve, 1971cc engine, 132bhp at 5750rpm, 4 speed manual gearbox, drum brakes, transverse leaf spring and inclined telescopic shock absorbers front, torsion bars and live rear axle, located by A-bracket, right-hand drive, 31,000 miles recorded. **£135,000+** *C*

This is one of the most original and authentic of all Le Mans Replicas.

1936 Frazer-Nash BMW 319 Cabriolet, 1.9 litre engine, coackwork by Karosseriewerk Reutter & Co of Stuttgart, runs very well, good condition throughout. **£10,000–10,500** *BKS*

Don't Forget!
If in doubt please refer to the 'How to Use' section at the beginning of this book.

GARDNER

r. **1923 Gardner 'Radio Special' 5 Seater Open Tourer,** left-hand drive, restored, new double duck hood, with cover, side screens, a modern Auster screen arrangement and a complete set of tools. **£7,200–7,600** *S*

The Radio Special was intended for the Australasian market and featured special colour schemes as well as disc wheels and nickel-plated trim.

GINETTA

1992 Ginetta G32 Sports, Ford XR3i engine,
5 speed gearbox, showroom display model.
£8,000–8,800 *H&H*

1967 Ginetta G4, Ford 1600cc X-flow engine, twin
40 DCOE Weber carburettors, factory fitted hard
top, excellent restored condition.
£14,500–15,500 *KSC*

HANNOMAG

Hannomag vehicles were produced in
Hanover-Linden from 1924 to 1939. The
first private car appeared in 1924 and
was the 2/10PS 2 seater model, known
in Germany as the *Kommisbrot* or Army
Loaf, due to its unusual shape. It
catered for the small cheap mass-
market, and was advertised as 'cheaper
than a 3rd class railway ticket'! The
single overhead valve 499cc engine is
mounted in the rear, the axle being
driven by a chain.

c1925 Hannomag 2/10PS Two Seater,
right-hand drive, fully restored from the
chassis upwards, museum stored since, in
running order and extremely rare in the UK.
£6,250–6,750 *C*

HEALEY

1949 Healey Silverstone 2.4 Litre Sports 2 Seater,
good mechanical order with no major modifications to
factory specification apart from the addition of a
Kenlowe fan, excellent provenance.
£20,000–22,000 *BKS*

> **Cross Reference**
> Austin Healey

1950 Healey Silverstone 2 Seater Sports,
Riley 2.4 litre engine, trailing arm
independent front suspension.
£18,000–20,000 *BKS*

> **Cross Reference**
> Restoration Projects

1953 Healey Sports Convertible, coachwork by
Panelcraft of Birmingham, engine and transmission
fully rebuilt, reconditioned interior.
Est. £15,000–17,000 *S*

*Only 25 examples of the sports convertible, popularly
known as the Alvis-Healey, were completed.*

1953 Healey Tickford Saloon, dry barn stored
for 30 years, requires restoration.
£1,400–1,800 *BKS*

*Although the Tickford was the most common of
the Riley-engineered Healeys, only 224 were built
between 1951–54.*

HEINKEL

1958 Heinkel 175cc Bubble Car, fully restored, 300 miles since restoration.
£7,500–8,000 *BKS*

This bubble car won first prize in the National Micro Car in 1992.

Cross Reference
Micro Cars

1929 Hillman 14 Tourer, excellent condition.
£13,000–14,000 *SW*

1936 Hillman Hawk, 21hp, 3181cc, fully restored.
£15,000+ *PC*

Originally a De Luxe saloon with a half-sliding sunshine roof, the whole roof was replaced during restoration due to damage.

1957 Hillman Minx Saloon, 25,000 recorded miles, dry stored for 23 years, excellent original condition.
Est. £900–1,000 *S*

HILLMAN

1919 Hillman 11hp 'Peace' Model Type HP Doctor's Coupé, coachwork possibly by Vanden Plas, not run for some time, requires restoration.
£5,750–6,250 *BKS*

1930 Hillman 14 Saloon, very good condition throughout.
£4,750–5,500 *H&H*

1934 Hillman Minx Saloon.
£3,750–4,500 *FHF*

1954 Hillman Minx Californian, 4 cylinder in line overhead valve 1265cc engine, 43bhp at 4400rpm, 4 speed manual gearbox, Lockhead hydraulic front and rear drum brakes, independent front suspension, coil springs rear, rigid axle with semi-elliptic leaf springs rear, right-hand drive, 54,000 recorded miles, generally good and original, interior upholstery is original and in excellent condition.
£1,400–1,600 *C*

HILLMAN Model	ENGINE cc/cyl	DATES	CONDITION 1	2	3
Minx Mk I-II	1184/4	1946-48	£1,750	£800	£250
Minx Mk I-II DHC	1184/4	1946-48	£3,500	£1,500	£250
Minx Mk III-VIIIA	1184/4	1948-56	£1,750	£700	£350
Minx Mk III-VIIIA DHC	1184/4	1948-56	£3,750	£1,500	£350
Californian	1390/4	1953-56	£2,000	£750	£200
Minx SI/II	1390/4	1956-58	£1,250	£450	£200
Minx SI/II DHC	1390/4	1956-58	£3,500	£1,500	£500
Minx Ser III	1494/4	1958-59	£1,000	£500	£200
Minx Ser III DHC	1494/4	1958-59	£3,750	£1,500	£400
Minx Ser IIIA/B	1494/4	1959-61	£1,250	£500	£200
Minx Ser IIIA/B DHC	1494/4	1959-61	£3,750	£1,250	£500
Minx Ser IIIC	1592/4	1961-62	£900	£500	£200
Minx Ser IIIC DHC	1592/4	1961-62	£3,000	£1,500	£500
Minx Ser V	1592/4	1962-63	£1,250	£350	£150
Minx Ser VI	1725/4	1964-67	£1,500	£375	£100
Husky Mk I	1265/4	1954-57	£1,000	£600	£200
Husky SI/II/III	1390/4	1958-65	£1,000	£550	£150
Super Minx	1592/4	1961-66	£1,500	£500	£100
Super Minx DHC	1592/4	1962-64	£3,500	£1,250	£450
Imp	875/4	1963-73	£800	£300	£70
Husky	875/4	1966-71	£800	£450	£100
Avenger	var/4	1970-76	£550	£250	£60
Avenger GT	1500/4	1971-76	£950	£500	£100
Avenger Tiger	1600/4	1972-73	£2,000	£1,000	£500

1959 Hillman Minx De Luxe, 18,450 recorded miles, two owners from new, not used since 1978, completely original and in good condition. **£700–900** *COYS*

r. **1960 Hillman Minx Drophead.** **£1,800–2,500** *HOLL*

A rebuilt car is not necessarily more valuable than a car in good original condition, even if the restoration has been costly.

HISPANO-SUIZA

HOLDEN

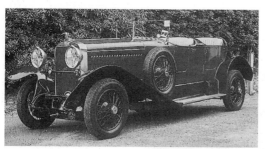

1924 Hispano-Suiza H6B Four Seater Torpedo, completely restored, excellent condition throughout. **Est. £77,000–85,000** *S*

1958 Holden Station Wagon, good condition. **£3,000–4,000** *H&H*

HOLLEY

Engineer George M. Holley set up the Holley Motor Company in Bradford, Pennsylvania, in 1900, to build runabout light cars. They were powered by a single cylinder engine and were conventional in appearance.

c1904 Holley Autobuggy High Wheeler, single cylinder Holley engine with atmospheric inlet valve with 3½in bore x 4½ in stroke, mounted in a former horse-drawn buggy with transmission by chain, candle lamps, tiller steering, cape cart hood and buttoned cloth upholstery, stored and unused for the past 10 years.
£6,000–6,500 *BKS*

HRG

HRG, of Tolworth, Surrey, was established in 1935 and took its name from the initials of its three partners, E. A. Halford, Guy H. Robins, and H. R. Godfrey. The prototype HRG was launched later that year. The HRG two seater sports car incorporated the 1½ litre Meadows 4ED engine. Excellent road holding and brisk performance provided the basis of good competition cars and many successes were gained in rallying and off-road trials.

HOTCHKISS

1938 Hotchkiss Grand Sport Coupé, in sound condition throughout, some minor cosmetic attention required.
£19,500–20,500 *BKS*

r. **1940 HRG 1500 'Square Rigger',** 4 cylinder, single overhead camshaft, 1496cc engine, 61bhp at 4800rpm, 4 speed manual gearbox, drum brakes all round, quarter-elliptic leaf springs front suspension, half-elliptic leaf springs rear, right-hand drive, condition is commensurate with an older restoration.
£15,500–16,500 *C*

HUDSON

r. **1924 Hudson Super Six Tourer,** right-hand drive, many desirable original features.
Est. £14,000–16,000 *BKS*

> **Don't Forget!**
> *If in doubt please refer to the 'How to Use' section at the beginning of this book.*

HUMBER

Humber, along with Hillman, was acquired by the Rootes brothers in 1930. Originally formed by bicycle maker Thomas Humber as early as 1868, Humber produced motor cars at Beeston and Coventry, although the Beeston-made cars were considered to be better made.

A series of good quality 6 cylinder cars were made up to and during WWII. Army staff cars, including General Montgomery's 'old faithful', were invariably Humbers.

Chrysler bought Rootes in 1964, by which time only the dated Sceptre model was in production and despite some badge engineering, the Humber name had disappeared by 1976.

1914 Humberette Cycle Car, 1000cc V-twin air-cooled engine, good condition throughout. **£7,800–8,200** *DB*

1903 Humberette 5hp 2 Seater, rebuilt over a number of years with good attention to detail to original specification, modern radiator shell, VCC dating certificate. **£15,000–16,000** *S*

1924 Humber 11.4hp 2 Seater and Dickey, extensive chassis-up restoration, front wheel brakes fitted. **£9,750–10,250** *BKS*

This car is believed to be one of only 2 genuine examples of the Humber 11.4hp two seater model to survive.

1951 Humber Super Snipe MkIII, 4086cc side valve engine, 4 speed column change, very good original condition, 78,000 recorded miles, one registered owner from new. **£3,750–4,250** *Mot*

1964 Humber Sceptre, original condition. **£650–700** *H&H*

HUMBER Model	ENGINE cc/cyl	DATES	CONDITION 1	2	3
Veteran	var	1898			
		1918	£25,000	£20,000	£14,000
10	1592/4	1919	£7,000	£5,000	£3,000
14	2474/4	1919	£8,000	£6,000	£4,000
15.9-5/40	2815/4	1920-27	£9,500	£7,000	£4,000
8	985/4	1923-25	£7,000	£5,000	£2,500
9/20-9/28	1057/4	1926	£7,000	£5,000	£4,000
14/40	2050/4	1927-28	£10,000	£8,000	£5,000
Snipe	3498/6	1930-35	£8,000	£6,000	£4,000
Pullman	3498/6	1930-35	£8,000	£6,000	£4,000
16/50	2110/6	1930-32	£9,000	£7,000	£5,000
12	1669/4	1933-37	£7,000	£5,000	£3,000
Snipe/Pullman	4086/6	1936-40	£7,000	£5,000	£3,000
16	2576/6	1938-40	£7,000	£5,000	£3,000
Pre-1905 or Brighton Run cars are very popular.					

1965 Humber Super Snipe, good original condition.
£2,800–3,000 *H&H*

1966 Humber Imperial, 6 cylinder, 2965cc engine, automatic transmission, standard Imperial features include picnic trays to the rear of the front seats, good original condition.
£500–600 *ADT*

HUMBER Model	ENGINE cc/cyl	DATES	CONDITION 1	2	3
Hawk Mk I-IV	1944/4	1945-52	£2,750	£1,500	£600
Hawk Mk V-VII	2267/4	1952-57	£2,500	£1,500	£400
Hawk Ser I-IVA	2267/4	1957-67	£2,500	£850	£325
Snipe	2731/6	1945-48	£5,000	£2,600	£850
Super Snipe Mk I-III	4086/6	1948-52	£4,700	£2,400	£600
Super Snipe Mk IV-IVA	4138/6	1952-56	£5,500	£2,300	£550
Super Snipe Ser I-II	2651/6	1958-60	£3,800	£1,800	£475
Super Snipe SIII VA	2965/6	1961-67	£3,500	£1,800	£400
Super Snipe S.III-VA Est.	2965/6	1961-67	£3,950	£1,850	£525
Pullman	4086/6	1946-51	£4,500	£2,350	£800
Pullman Mk IV	4086/6	1952-54	£6,000	£2,850	£1,200
Imperial	2965/6	1965-67	£3,900	£1,600	£450
Sceptre Mk I-II	1592/4	1963-67	£2,050	£900	£300
Sceptre Mk III	1725/4	1967-76	£1,600	£600	£200

HUPMOBILE

1914 Hupmobile Model H 32hp Tourer, full weather equipment, tonneau cover and quickly detachable wheels, VCC dating certificate, very good condition.
£13,000–14,000 *BKS*

1927 Hupmobile Coupé, 6 cylinder engine, original engine and interior, repainted in 1950s.
£5,900–6,200 *GAR*

r. **1928 Hupmobile 8,** 8 cylinder engine, completely restored to concours condition.
£14,750–15,500 *GAR*

INVICTA

Built by Noel Macklin in his garage at Cobham, Surrey, the first Invicta was sold in 1924. Larger cars with bigger engines were produced during the 1920s and competition success followed.

Invicta, like most prestige car manufacturers, suffered in the Depression of the 1930s. The company was sold and soldiered on until 1949 when what was left was bought by the AFN Group.

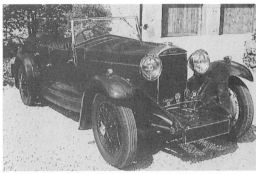

1932 Invicta Type L 12/70 Four Seater Tourer, coachwork by Carbodies of Coventry, very good restored condition.
£22,000–23,000 *BKS*

l. **1932 Invicta 12hp Sports Saloon,** coachwork by Carbodies, good original car with excellent interior.
£14,900–15,400 *CGOC*

ISO

Like other grand touring car manufacturers of the time, the Iso company produced luxuriously bodied cars, powered by American V8 engines. Giotto Bizzarrini joined the company and was responsible for the Iso Rivolta, launched in 1962. The Grifo, (Italian for griffin – a legendary creature that feeds on horses, intended as a pun insomuch as the prancing horse is the badge of Ferrari), was as first-class machine with a top speed of 150mph.

In 1969 the Lele was introduced, a stunning motor car with exceptional performance, however, the company suffered as a result of the 1970s oil crisis and had disappeared by 1974.

1965 Iso Rivolta Coupé, coachwork by Bertone, low mileage, Borrani light alloy triple laced wheels, attention to electric windows required.
£7,500–8,000 *COYS*

c1974 Iso Grifo Series II Coupé, coachwork by Bertone, 8 cylinder, 5300cc engine, very good overall condition.
£17,500–18,000 *COYS*

1966 Iso Grifo Series I, 5.4 litre, right-hand drive, manual gearbox, Holly 4BBL carburettor, restored, good condition.
£19,000–22,000 *UMC*

1975 Iso Lele Sport, Ford 5.8 litre V8 engine, 5 speed manual transmission, disc brakes, limited-slip differential, excellent original condition.
Est. 11,000–13,000 *BKS*

1976 Iso Lele Sport, 8 cylinder, 5756cc engine, automatic gearbox, original right-hand drive, full body restoration, excellent condition.
£6,400–6,800 *ADT*

JAGUAR

William Lyons built the first SS (Swallow Sidecars) in Blackpool in 1922, but soon moved to Coventry. Following WWII the initials SS were unsuitable and Jaguar became the trade name.

Jaguar became the epitome of fast saloon cars and more famously synonomous with a range of world beating sports cars. The XK series, C- and D-Types and probably the best of all the E-Type were all market leaders and highly sought after by collectors and enthusiasts today.

c1939 Jaguar SS 1½ Three Position Drophead Coupé, wonderfully preserved 'barn discovery', has remained in the same ownership from new, retaining most of its original tools.
£19,000–20,000   *S*

Cross Reference
Restoration Projects

l. **1938 Jaguar SS100 3½ Litre Open Sports,** original engine and body panels, it has never needed restoration, in excellent original condition.
£80,000–85,000   *COYS*

1947 Jaguar 1½ Litre SE, 4 cylinder, 1776cc engine, cloth covered seats, air conditioning equipment, excellent original condition.
£3,600–3,900   *COYS*

1939 Ex-Works Jaguar SS100 3½ Litre Open Sports, 6 cylinder, 3485cc engine, with excellent provenance, in impeccable condition, concours winner at Jaguar Drivers' Club meetings.
£135,000+   *COYS*

1949 Jaguar XK120 Lightweight, 6 cylinder, 3442cc engine, rare early lightweight alloy-bodied, correct in every detail, original right-hand drive, in superb restored condition.
£66,000–72,000   *COYS*

The first 57 right-hand drive, and 183 left-hand drive Jaguar XK120s were produced in lightweight aluminium alloy.

1950 Jaguar XK120 Competition Car, excellent provenance, in totally original condition.
£80,000–100,000   *COYS*

r. **1951 Jaguar XK120,** 6 cylinder, 3442cc twin overhead camshaft engine, producing 160bhp, restored, excellent condition.
£27,500–30,000   *COYS*

1952 Jaguar XK120 Roadster, left-hand drive, re-imported from the USA, in good condition. Est. £24,000–29,000 *ADT*

Jaguar XK120

- Introduced in 1948 the XK120 could exceed 130mph.
- At a cost of £1,275 more than 12,000 were produced, the bulk of which were for the American market.
- Straight 6 cylinder, overhead camshaft engine of 3442cc produced 150bhp.
- Available as a fixed head coupé, drophead coupé and roadster.

1952 Jaguar XK120 Roadster, re-imported from the USA, restored, including conversion to right-hand drive, in good order throughout. £17,000–18,000 *ADT*

1953 Jaguar XK120 Roadster, original right-hand drive, completely restored, in excellent condition. £30,000–35,000 *ROR*

1953 Jaguar XK120 Two Seater Sports Drophead Coupé, recently re-imported into the UK, retains left-hand drive, good condition throughout. £22,000–24,000 *BKS*

1954 Jaguar XK140 Fixed Head Coupé, maintained and used regularly, very original. £17,000–18,000 *COYS*

1954 Jaguar XK120 Fixed Head Coupé, genuine right-hand drive, in remarkable original condition. £36,000–38,000 *BKS*

JAGUAR Model	ENGINE cc/cyl	DATES	CONDITION		
			1	2	3
SSI	2054/6	1932-33	£20,000	£16,000	£12,000
SSI	2252/6	1932-33	£22,000	£17,000	£13,500
SSII	1052/4	1932-33	£18,000	£15,000	£11,000
SSI	2663/6	1934	£26,000	£22,000	£15,000
SSII	1608/4	1934	£18,000	£15,000	£12,000
SS90	2663/6	1935	£60,000+		
SS100 (3.4)	3485/6	1938-39	£70,000+		
SS100 (2.6)	2663/6	1936-39	£60,000+		

Very dependent on body styles, completeness and originality, particularly original chassis to body.

1955 Jaguar XK140, with Webasto sunroof, well maintained, very original.
£15,500–17,000 *COYS*

1955 Jaguar XK140SE Drophead Coupé,
6 cylinder, 3442cc engine, original right-hand drive, fully restored to a high standard.
£42,000–45,000 *COYS*

1955 Jaguar XK140, left-hand drive, restored to the highest standards.
Est. £36,000–40,000 *COYS*

1955 Jaguar XK140 3.4 Litre Fixed Head Coupé, older restoration, some recommissioning required.
£14,500–15,500 *BKS*

Jaguar XK140

- Following the XK120 the XK140 produced 190bhp developed from the straight six 3.4 litre engine.
- Improved handling as a result of the independent front suspension and semi-elliptic rear leaf springs.
- Launched in 1954, most of the 9,000 cars produced went to America.

1956 Jaguar XK140 Roadster, left-hand drive Special Equipment roadster, with wire wheels.
Est. £28,000–30,000 *S*

1956 Jaguar XK140 Drophead Coupé,
an excellent original car, many factory extras, very good condition.
£24,000–26,000 *CGOC*

1956 Jaguar XK140 Fixed Head Coupé,
right-hand drive, only 1,200 miles recorded since restoration.
Est. £30,000–35,000 *BKS*

1957 Jaguar XK140 SE Roadster, left-hand drive, Special Equipment 210bhp engine, restored, excellent condition.
£26,000–28,000 *COYS*

1958 Jaguar XK150 Drophead Coupé, UK delivered example, body renovated, interior renewed, engine completely rebuilt. **£19,500–20,500** *COYS*

1958 Jaguar XK150 SE, excellent original condition. **£20,500–21,500** *COYS*

1958 Jaguar XK150S Roadster, converted to right-hand drive, generally good throughout. **Est. £19,000–21,000** *ADT*

1959 Jaguar XK150 Fixed Head Coupé, left-hand drive, extensive restoration to as new condition. **£23,000–25,000** *S*

1959 Jaguar XK150 Drophead Coupé, fully restored to superb condition. **£26,000–27,000** *COYS*

1959 Jaguar XK150 Drophead Coupé, good overall condition. **Est. £20,000–25,000** *BKS*

l. **1960 Jaguar XK150 2+2 Drophead Coupé,** imported from USA, good condition throughout. **Est. £18,000–22,000** *S*

JAGUAR Model	ENGINE cc/cyl	DATES	CONDITION 1	2	3
XK120 roadster aluminum	3442/6	1948-49	£35,000	£20,000	£15,000
XK120 roadster	3442/6	1949-54	£22,000	£18,000	£14,000
XK120 DHC	3442/6	1953-54	£20,000	£15,000	£11,000
XK120 Coupé	3442/6	1951-55	£16,000	£10,000	£8,000
C-type	3442/6	1951	£150,000	+	
D-type	3442/6	1955-56	£400,000	+	
XKSS (original)	3442/6	1955-57	£400,000	+	
XK140 roadster	3442/6	1955-58	£28,000	£23,000	£15,500
XK140 DHC	3442/6	1955-58	£25,000	£20,500	£15,000
XK140 Coupé	3442/6	1955-58	£14,000	£9,000	£5,500
XK150 roadster	3442/6	1958-60	£24,000	£20,500	£14,000
XK150 DHC	3442/6	1957-61	£22,000	£15,000	£5,000
XK150 Coupé	3442/6	1957-60	£14,000	£9,000	£6,000
XK150S roadster	3442/ 3781/6	1958-60	£35,000	£22,000	£17,000
XK150S DHC	3442/ 3781/6	1958-60	£34,000	£22,000	£16,500
XK150S Coupé	3442/ 3781/6	1958-61	£22,000	£17,000	£11,500

1960 Jaguar XK150 Fixed Head Coupé,
bodywork needs attention, respray relatively
poor, original upholstery in poor condition,
would benefit from some remedial work
£6,000–6,500 *BKS*

1960 Jaguar MkII 3.8 Litre Saloon, very good
overall condition.
Est. £11,000–12,000 *ADT*

1960 Jaguar XK150S Fixed Head Coupé, in
original condition, bodywork good, slight rust
around the shut face pillars and rear wheel arches,
Minilite wheels fitted, original wire wheels retained.
£21,000–23,000 *BKS*

1962 Jaguar 3.4 Litre, manual gearbox,
leather interior.
£6,750–7,250 *DB*

Jaguar MkII Saloon

- Launched in 1959 the MkII saloon was
  available with a 2.4, 3.4 or 3.8 litre engine.
- Following the MkI saloon the MkII was
  luxuriously appointed inside with leather
  and walnut trim as well as fold-down picnic
  trays and twin spotlights.
- The S-Type featured hooded headlights,
  redesigned grille and a narrow bumper.
- Superseded by the 240/340 saloon in 1967.

1961 Jaguar MkII 3.8 Litre Saloon, original
right-hand drive version, excellent panelwork,
rebuilt engine, usable condition.
Est. £9,500–10,500 *ADT*

1964 Jaguar S-Type 3.8 Litre Saloon, manual
gearbox and overdrive, original body, good paintwork.
£4,400–4,800 *ADT*

1965 Jaguar S-Type, automatic, new battery
and stainless steel exhaust, spare rear axle.
£2,000–3,000 *H&H*

*l.***1965 Jaguar MkII 3.8 Litre 4 Door Saloon,**
totally retrimmed and upholstered, would benefit
from some cosmetic attention.
Est. £6,000–7,000 *BKS*

1965 Jaguar MkII 4 Door Saloon, extensively restored including a bare metal respray, retrim and full engine rebuild, chromework replaced, woodwork refurbished.
£6,400–6,800 *BKS*

1966 Jaguar MkII 2.4 Litre 4 Door Saloon, manual gearbox with overdrive, mechanically excellent, very good interior, fair bodywork.
£3,400–3,800 *BKS*

r. **1966 Jaguar S-Type 3.4 Litre 4 Door Saloon,** 6 cylinder, double overhead camshaft, 3442cc engine, 210bhp at 5500rpm, 4 speed manual gearbox with overdrive, 4 wheel disc brakes, independent suspension, right-hand drive, generally sound although areas would benefit from attention, chrome wire wheels.
£2,000–2,400 *C*

1967 Jaguar 340, 4 speed manual gearbox, power steering, sound condition.
£6,200–6,800 *ADT*

1967 Jaguar MkII 2.4 Litre, 4 speed manual gearbox with overdrive, stainless steel exhaust, sound condition.
£4,000–4,400 *ADT*

1968 Jaguar 340 Saloon, very good original condition.
£3,800–4,200 *ADT*

1968 Jaguar MkII 340, manual gearbox, completely rebuilt, concours winning condition.
£11,000–11,500 *H&H*

1968 Jaguar 340 Four Door Saloon, totally restored, very good condition throughout.
Est. £14,000–16,000 *BKS*

r. **1968 Jaguar 340,** manual gearbox with overdrive, sunroof, retrimmed in leather, restored.
£10,000–12,000 *UMC*

1968 Jaguar MkII 3.4, fully restored within the last 5 years, very good condition.
£9,500–10,000 *COYS*

1968 Jaguar 240 Four Door Saloon,
6 cylinder overhead camshaft, 2400cc engine, manual gearbox, unrestored but usable.
£4,250–4,750 *DB*

1968 Jaguar 240 Four Door Saloon, automatic transmission, subject of considerable restoration, more work is needed.
£3,500–3,900 *BKS*

1968 Jaguar 240 Four Door Saloon, 6 cylinder, twin overhead camshaft, 2483cc engine, 133bhp, 4 speed synchromesh gearbox, independent front suspension, completely renovated, in showroom condition.
£8,500–9,000 *N*

l **1968 Jaguar 340 Saloon,** 6 cylinder, in line double overhead camshaft, 3442cc engine, 210bhp at 5500rpm, 4 speed manual gearbox with overdrive, 4 wheel disc brakes, independent front suspension, live axle, semi-elliptic leaf spring rear, right-hand drive, one owner from new, just 50,000 miles recorded, good order throughout.
£5,400–5,800 *C*

JAGUAR Model	ENGINE cc/cyl	DATES	CONDITION 1	2	3
1½ Litre	1775/4	1945-49	£8,500	£5,500	£2,000
2½ Litre	2663/6	1946-49	£10,000	£7,500	£2,000
2½ Litre DHC	2663/6	1947-48	£17,000	£11,000	£8,000
3½ Litre	3485/6	1947-49	£12,000	£6,000	£4,000
3½ Litre DHC	3485/6	1947-49	£19,000	£13,500	£5,500
Mk V 2½ Litre	2663/6	1949-51	£8,000	£5,000	£1,500
Mk V 3½ Litre	3485/6	1949-51	£11,000	£7,000	£1,800
Mk V 3½ Litre DHC	3485/6	1949-51	£20,000	£17,000	£8,500
Mk VII	3442/6	1951-57	£10,000	£7,500	£2,500
Mk VIIM	3442/6	1951-57	£12,000	£8,500	£2,500
Mk VIII	3442/6	1956-59	£8,500	£5,500	£2,000
Mk IX	3781/6	1958-61	£9,000	£7,000	£2,500
Mk X 3.8/4.2	3781/6	1961-64	£7,500	£3,500	£1,500
Mk X 420G	4235/6	1964-70	£5,000	£3,000	£1,200
Mk I 2.4	2438/6	1955-59	£7,000	£5,500	£2,000
Mk I 3.4	3442/6	1957-59	£9,000	£6,000	£2,500
Mk II 2.4	2483/6	1959-67	£6,000	£5,000	£2,000
Mk II 3.4	3442/6	1959-67	£9,000	£6,500	£3,000
Mk II 3.8	3781/6	1959-67	£9,850	£6,000	£4,000
S-Type 3.4	3442/6	1963-68	£9,000	£6,500	£2,000
S-Type 3.8	3781/6	1963-68	£10,000	£6,500	£2,000
240	2438/6	1967-68	£7,000	£5,000	£2,500
340	3442/6	1967-68	£8,000	£7,000	£3,000
420	4235/6	1966-68	£6,000	£3,000	£2,000

Manual gearboxes with overdrive are at a premium.

1969 Jaguar 340 Saloon, 6 cylinder, double overhead camshaft, 3442cc engine, 210bhp at 5500rpm, 4 speed manual gearbox with overdrive, 4 wheel disc brakes, independent front suspension, semi-elliptic rear, right-hand drive, MkII style bumpers, wire wheels and leather upholstery, original example, needs some attention before being roadworthy.
£2,800–3,200 *C*

1961 Jaguar E-Type 3.8 Roadster Flat Floor, repainted to a high standard, completely rebuilt original engine.
£19,000–20,000 *ADT*

1974 Jaguar E-Type V12 Roadster, automatic, converted to right-hand drive, hard and soft tops, totally restored, superb condition.
£21,500–23,000 *H&H*

1961 Jaguar E-Type Series I 3.8 Litre Roadster, totally restored, excellent provenance and condition throughout.
Est. £40,000–50,000 *BKS*
This car was the property of Jackie Stewart.

Jaguar E-Type

- Introduced in 1961 to replace the world beating XK sports cars.
- Originally powered by a 3.8 litre straight 6 cylinder engine, producing 245bhp, it had a top speed of about 150mph.
- Launch price was about £2,100.
- A 4.2 litre engine was introduced in 1965, the second series was wider and featured a 2+2.
- In 1971 the 5.3 litre V12 engine was available and the E-Type was phased out in 1975.

1961 Jaguar E-Type Series I Flat Floor Roadster, excellent condition all round.
Est. £32,000–35,000 *S*

1961 Jaguar E-Type Series I 3.8 Litre Coupé, extensively restored, including conversion to right-hand drive, full engine, gearbox and chassis rebuild, excellent order throughout.
£17,000–18,000 *COYS*

1962 Jaguar E-Type Series I Roadster, 6 cylinder, double overhead camshaft, 3781cc engine, 265bhp at 5500rpm, 4 speed manual gearbox, disc brakes all-round, independent front suspension with torsion and anti-roll bars, independent with lower wishbones, radius arms, coil springs and anti-roll bar rear, right-hand drive, the subject of a major restoration in recent years, original engine rebuilt, excellent condition.
£23,000–25,000 *C*

1962 Jaguar E-Type 3.8 Litre Fixed Head Coupé, rear bumpers need replating otherwise very good condition.
Est. £9,500–10,500 *S*

1962 Jaguar E-Type Fixed Head Coupé, the subject of extensive restoration.
£14,000–15,000 *ADT*

1963 Jaguar E-Type Coupé, 6 cylinder, twin camshaft, 3800cc engine, unrestored.
£6,500–7,000 *DB*

1963 Jaguar E-Type Series I, re-imported from USA, restored professionally retaining left-hand drive.
£12,500–13,500 *COYS*

1964 Jaguar E-Type 3.8 Roadster, subject of a well documented and photographically-recorded restoration.
£32,000–34,000 *BKS*

1964 Jaguar E-Type 3.8 Litre Roadster, restored some years ago, drives well and has no known modifications.
£22,000–24,000 *BKS*

1966 Jaguar E-Type 4.2 Roadster, excellent restored condition.
£25,000–27,000 *ADT*

1966 Jaguar E-Type 4.2 Litre 2+2, excellent overall condition.
£14,000–15,000 *ADT*

1967 Jaguar E-Type Series I 4.2 Litre, 6 cylinder, 4235cc engine, right-hand drive, excellent condition throughout.
£16,000–17,000 *COYS*

1967 Jaguar E-Type Series I, original right-hand drive, completely resprayed, interior retrimmed, 52,881 miles from new, good original order.
£17,000–18,000 *COYS*

1968 Jaguar E-Type 4.2 Litre Roadster, extremely well restored, less than 4,000 miles since restoration.
£28,000–30,000 *BKS*

1968 Jaguar E-Type Open Sports Convertible, very good condition throughout.
£23,000–25,000 *S*

> *A rebuilt car is not necessarily more valuable than a car in good original condition, even if the restoration has been costly.*

1968 Jaguar E-Type 4.2 Litre 2+2 Coupé, original condition, good order throughout.
Est. £11,000–14,000 *BKS*

1968 Jaguar E-Type Fixed Head Coupé, well restored and in very good condition.
£11,000–12,000 *ADT*

1969 Jaguar E-Type Series II 4.2 Litre Roadster, 6 cylinder in line, double overhead camshaft, 4235cc engine, 171bhp at 5400rpm, 4 speed manual gearbox, disc brakes all-round, independent torsion bar front suspension, independent coil rear, left-hand drive, comprehensive mechanical rebuild, good condition.
£19,000–20,000 *C*

l. **1968 Jaguar E-Type 4.2 Roadster,** mechanical condition good, fully restored.
Est. £22,000–24,000 *ADT*

JAGUAR Model	ENGINE cc/cyl	DATES	CONDITION 1	2	3
E-type 3.8 flat floor roadster (RHD)		1961	£40,000	£30,000	£22,000
E-type SI 3.8 roadster	3781/6	1961-64	£28,000	£18,000	£15,000
E-type 3.8 FHC	3781/6	1961-64	£18,000	£13,000	£10,000
E-type SI 4.2 roadster	4235/6	1964-67	£22,000	£18,000	£12,000
E-type 2+2 manual FHC	4235/6	1966-67	£15,000	£10,000	£9,000
E-type SI 2+2 auto FHC	4235/6	1966-68	£13,000	£9,000	£8,000
E-type SII roadster	4235/6	1968-70	£22,000	£18,000	£12,000
E-type SII FHC	4235/6	1968-70	£18,000	£12,000	£8,000
E-type SII 2+2 manual FHC	4235/6	1968-70	£15,000	£10,000	£8,000
E-type SIII roadster	5343/12	1971-75	£35,000	£24,000	£15,000
E-type SIII 2+2 manual FHC	5343/12	1971-75	£19,000	£14,000	£10,000
E-type SIII 2+2 auto FHC	5343/12	1971-75	£17,000	£12,000	£9,000
XJ6 2.8 Ser I	2793/6	1968-73	£2,600	£1,500	£1,000
XJ6 4.2 Ser I	4235/6	1968-73	£3,000	£2,000	£1,000
XJ6 Coupé	4235/6	1974-78	£7,000	£3,000	£2,000
XJ6 Ser II	4235/6	1973-79	£3,500	£2,000	£750
XJ12 Ser I	5343/12	1972-73	£3,500	£2,250	£1,500
XJ12 Coupé	5343/12	1973-77	£8,000	£4,000	£2,000
XJ12 Ser II	5343/12	1973-79	£2,000	£1,500	-
XJS manual	5343/12	1975-78	£6,000	£4,500	£2,500
XJS auto	5343/12	1975-81	£4,000	£2,200	£1,500

1969 Jaguar E-Type Series II Fixed Head Coupé, fully documented mileage of 23,600, outstanding original car.
£21,000–22,000 *BKS*

1970 Jaguar E-Type 4.2 Litre Series 1½ Roadster, one owner from new, impressive provenance, fully restored, retaining original components.
£23,000–25,000 *BKS*

1970 Jaguar E-Type Series II Roadster, subject of much restoration, engine rebuilt, coachwork resprayed.
Est. £18,000–22,000 *COYS*

1971 Jaguar E-Type Series III V12 Roadster, good condition throughout.
Est. £25,000–27,000 *S*

*r.***1971 Jaguar E-Type Series III 2+2 Fixed Head Coupé,** good overall condition.
Est. £11,000–12,500 *ADT*

1969 Jaguar E-Type 4.2 Litre Roadster, re-upholstered in tan leatherette, stored for a time in the USA, fair to good condition, would benefit from regular use.
Est. £17,500–19,500 *S*

1970 Jaguar E-Type 4.2 Litre Coupé, very good condition.
£12,000–14,000 *H&H*

One of only 3 special rear-end-bodied cars.

1970 Jaguar E-Type 4.2 Litre 2 Seater Fixed Head Coupé, 6 cylinder, twin overhead camshaft, triple SU carburettors, 4235cc engine, 4 speed synchromesh gearbox, Dunlop servo disc brakes, independent front and rear suspension, right-hand drive, subject of a considerable amount of mechanical and bodywork attention, good condition throughout.
£13,500–14,500 *C*

1971 Jaguar E-Type V12 Roadster, subject of a comprehensive rebuild, good condition throughout.
£27,000–29,000 *S*

**1949 Healey 2.4 Litre Silverstone Sports
2 Seater**, fully rebuilt, bodywork restored, rewired, to original specification, good condition throughout.
£26,000–27,000 *BKS*

**1949 Healey Silverstone 2.4 Litre D Type
2 Seater Sports Roadster**, new hood and tonneau, stainless steel exhaust, fully restored.
£27,000–28,000 *BKS*

**1931 Invicta 4½ Litre S-Type Low Chassis
Tourer**, coachwork by Carbodies, No. 2605, excellent original condition throughout.
£160,000+ *BKS*

c1934 Hispano-Suiza T60 RLA, coachwork 7mm wood from Oregon, covered with 2mm Kume wood, over 2,000 copper rivets, fully restored to excellent overall condition.
£75,000–78,000 *S*

1951 Jaguar Mark V 3½ Litre Sports Saloon, 6 cylinders, overhead valve, 3500cc, 125bhp at 4500rpm, 4 speed manual gearbox, good original condition, very good running order.
£8,000–8,500 *C*

**1953 Jaguar 3.4 Litre C-Type Sports Racing
2 Seater**, 6 cylinder XK series engine, triple Weber twin choke carburettors, drum brakes, excellent condition throughout.
Est. £220,000–250,000 *BKS*

1954 Jaguar XK140 Roadster, 6 cylinder in line engine, twin overhead camshafts, 3442cc, 190bhp at 5500rpm, 4 speed manual gearbox, longitudinal torsion bars, hydraulic drum brakes, converted to right-hand drive, restored to highest order.
£35,000–37,000 *C*

1956 Jaguar XK140 MC Roadster, extensively restored to factory specification in all major respects.
Est. £28,000–34,000 *BKS*

r. **1955 Jaguar XK140 SE Roadster**, 6 cylinder in line engine, double overhead camshaft, 3442cc, 210bhp at 5750rpm, 4 speed manual gearbox, drum brakes, semi-elliptic suspension, original right-hand drive,
Est. £25,000–35,000 *C*

1966 Jaguar E-Type, 4.2 litre engine, totally restored condition throughout. **£16,000–17,000** *SW*

1967 Jaguar E-Type 4.2 Litre 2 Seater Sports Roadster, manual transmission, totally restored. **Est. £28,000–30,000** *BKS*

1967 Jaguar Model 420 Saloon, 6 cylinder, 4235cc, double overhead camshaft engine, automatic gearbox, power steering and factory fitted air conditioning, 40,000 miles from new, minor cosmetic attention required. **£5,400–5,700** *CNY*

1970 Jaguar E-Type Series II Roadster, chrome wire wheels, excellent overall condition. **Est. £20,000–22,000** *BKS*

The Series II was developed to meet new US safety regulations.

1971 Jaguar E-Type Series III, 12 cylinders, 5343cc engine, manual gearbox, concours condition throughout following a complete rebuild. **£18,500–19,500** *COYS*

1973 Jaguar E-Type 5.3 Litre V12 Series III 2 Seater Roadster, restored to original specifications. **£36,000–38,000** *BKS*

1972 Jaguar E-Type Fixed Head Coupé, largely original condition, requiring some cosmetic attention. **Est. £13,000–14,500** *ADT*

1974 Jaguar E-Type V12 Roadster, chrome wire wheels, 60,000 miles, original condition. **£34,000–38,000** *VIC*

1972 Jaguar E-Type 5.3 Litre V12 Series III Roadster, manual transmission, good overall condition, slight bodywork imperfections. **Est. £20,000–25,000** *BKS*

1974 Jaguar XJ12L 5.3 Litre 4 Door Saloon, former *concours d'élégance* winner, standard factory trim. **Est. £7,000–10,000** *BKS*

1957 Jaguar Mark VIII, 6 cylinders, 3442cc, automatic transmission, right-hand drive, very good condition overall.
£6,000–7,000 *ADT*

1958 Jaguar XK150S, 6 cylinders, 3442cc, left-hand drive, good condition.
£23,000–25,000 *COYS*

1958 Jaguar XK150 Drophead Coupé,
6 cylinder in line engine, twin overhead camshaft, 3442cc, 4 speed manual gearbox, 4 wheel disc brakes, original right-hand drive, bare metal respray, engine overhauled.
Est. £24,000–26,000 *C*

1958 Jaguar XK150, original left-hand drive, comprehensive body and mechanical restoration.
Est. £34,000–36,000 *ADT*

1960 Jaguar XK150S 3.8 Litre, 6 cylinder, 3781cc engine, very good condition in every respect.
£19,000–20,000 *COYS*

1961 Jaguar E-Type 3.8 Two Seater Coupé, comprehensive history, extensive restoration.
£13,000–14,000 *BKS*

1961 Jaguar E-Type Series I Two Seater Roadster, right-hand drive, extensive restoration, excellent throughout.
Est. £30,000–35,000 *BKS*

1962 Jaguar E-Type 3.8 Roadster, 6 cylinder, 3781cc engine, very good condition throughout.
Est. £22,000–24,000 *ADT*

r. **1966 Jaguar XJ13,** 30 digital fuel injected, 5.3 litre, dry sump V12 engine, 485hp, all-alloy, full monocoque structure, constructed over a 2 year period, built to original specifications, totally correct including original instruments, correct windshield from factory moulds.
£19,500–22,000 *BLK*

1956 Jensen 541 2 Door GT Coupé, subject of considerable work, very good condition throughout. **Est. £11,000–14,000** *BKS*

1968 Jensen MKI FF 6.3 Litre Sports Coupé, Ferguson type hypoid final drive to all 4 wheels, fully restored, engine and bodywork excellent, 48,000 miles from new. **£15,000–16,000** *BKS*

1974 Jensen Interceptor MkIII Convertible, coachwork by Vignale, 8 cylinders, 7212cc, excellent. **£17,000–18,000** *COYS*

1970 Jensen FF 6.3 Litre 2 Door Saloon, good condition, recommissioning recommended before use. **£11,500–12,500** *BKS*

1935 Lagonda M45 Tourer, 6 cylinders, overhead valve, 4453cc, 140bhp at 4000rpm, 4 speed manual gearbox, drum brakes, semi-elliptic suspension, very good condition, some minor attention required. **£35,000–37,000** *C*

1938 Lagonda V12 Sedanca Coupé, coachwork by James Young, excellent restored condition. **Est. £79,000–82,000** *S*

This car is one of only 2 cars designed by James Young on this chassis.

1935 Lagonda 3½ Litre 2 Door Sports Tourer, originally a saloon, later rebodied with open touring coachwork following the factory T9 body style, very good order throughout. **Est. £30,000–32,000** *BKS*

r. **1934 Lagonda M45S Roadster,** by Wylders of Kew, excellent original condition. **£185,000+** *BLK*

This car was custom built, and has been driven less than 30,000 miles since new.

1974 Lamborghini Urraco P250 Coupé, coachwork by Bertone, V8 engine, 2463cc, 220bhp. £9,000–10,000 *COYS*

1975 Lamborghini Espada, coachwork by Bertone, 12 cylinders, 3929cc, excellent condition. £11,000–12,000 *COYS*

1933 Lanchester 15/18 Saloon, coachwork by Car Bodies, 2½ litre straight 6 engine, chassis-up rebuild using original parts, rebuilt engine, refurbished interior. Est. £10,000–14,000 *COYS*

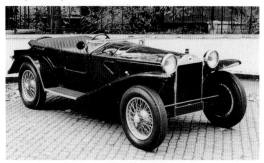

1925 Lancia Lambda Torpedo Tourer, factory coachwork, very good working condition. £23,000–24,000 *COYS*

1934 Lancia Dilambda Sports Saloon, by The Carlton Carriage Company, excellent condition throughout. £26,000–28,000 *BKS*

1951 Lancia Aurelia B10, coachwork by Vignale, 6 cylinders, 1754cc, very good condition. £15,000–16,000 *COYS*

1952 Lancia Aurelia B20 GT, exceptionally original, very good condition. £25,000–26,000 *COYS*

1953 Lancia Aurelia B20 Series II, Berlinetta coachwork by Pinin Farina, 6 cylinders, 2451cc. £20,000–21,000 *COYS*

1954 Lancia Aurelia B20 Series IV, Berlinetta coachwork by Pinin Farina, fully restored to a very high standard, incorrect bumpers. £23,000–24,000 *COYS*

1971 Lancia Fulvia 1.6 HF Series II, 4 cylinders, 1584cc, 5 speed gearbox, alloy wheels, very good restored condition. Est. £7,000–9,000 *COYS*

1959 Lotus Elite 1.3 Litre 2 Seater Sports Coupé,
4 speed MG manual gearbox, restored, including engine
rebuild, stainless steel exhaust, twin Weber carburettors,
excellent condition throughout.
£19,000–20,000 *BKS*

1971 Lotus Elan Sprint Drophead Coupé,
rebuilt engine, in gold leaf colours.
£12,500–13,500 *KSC*

1969 Lotus Europa S2, 4 cylinders, 1470cc, 82bhp at
6500rpm, 4 speed Renault transaxle, all independent
suspension, restored, very good condition.
£5,500–6,000 *COYS*

1987 Lotus Esprit Turbo HC, with leather
interior, only 15,000 miles from new.
£16,500–17,500 *KSC*

This car is one of a limited edition of only 21 built.

1964 Lotus Elan SI 26R, fast road-tuned
engine, Cosworth cams with 40DCOE31 Weber
carburettors, close ratio gearbox, racing
steering wheel, long range aluminium fuel
tank, original factory hard top and many other
original fittings, restored on a new chassis.
£39,000–41,000 *KSC*
A very early racing version of the Elan.

1969 Lotus Europa S2, early Type 54,
Renault engine, very good condition throughout.
£5,750–6,250 *KSC*

1972 Lotus Europa Twin Cam Special,
4 speed gearbox, totally rebuilt on Lotus galvanised
chassis, trimmed in non-original leather.
£10,500–11,500 *KSC*

1973 Lotus Europa Twin Cam Special,
5 speed gearbox, fully restored, in John Player
Special colours.
£14,500–15,500 *KSC*

1968 Maserati Ghibli Tipo AM 115 4.7 Litre 2 Door Convertible, styling by Ghia, completely restored, excellent condition. **Est. £35,000–40,000** *BKS*

1906 Mercedes-Simplex 75hp Rothschild Tourer, rebuilt engine. **£400,000+** *BLK*

This car has unique features including mid-passenger seats that swivel, allowing the rear passengers to face one another.

1979 Maserati Type 117 'Bora', coachwork by Ital Design, V8, 4930cc engine, 280bhp at 5500rpm, 5 speed manual gearbox, 4 wheel disc brakes, independent suspension, good overall condition. **£27,000–28,000** *C*

1935 Mercedes-Benz 500K Windovers 3 Position Drophead, recent comprehensive restoration. **£250,000+** *BLK*

1930 Mercedes-Benz 38/250 SS Tourer 7.8 Litre, coachwork by Berrisford to a Scott-Moncrieff design, based on a long wheelbase right-hand drive chassis. **£450,000–500,000** *BKS*

1927 Mercedes-Benz '26/120/180' Model S 6.7 Litre Supercharged Sports Tourer, 6 cylinder, 6789cc engine, 120bhp at 2800rpm, extensively restored by Hill & Vaughan. **£475,000+** *BKS*

Once owned by the American cartoonist Charles Addams.

1936 Mercedes-Benz 540K Cabriolet B, restored to show standards. **£370,000+** *BLK*

l. **1936 Mercedes-Benz 500K Cabriolet C,** extensively restored, excellent condition, finished in black livery, beige hood. **£440,000+** *BLK*

The 500 (5 Litre) K (for Kompressor supercharger) was introduced in 1933, and was superseded by the 540K in the mid-1930s. There was a prototype 580K displayed in 1939 but it never went into production.

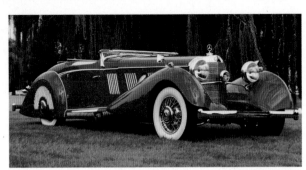

1936 Mercedes-Benz 540K Mayfair Roadster, coachwork by Mayfair of London, made entirely of aluminum, completely restored.
£1,300,000+ *BLK*

1954 Mercedes-Benz 300B, 6 cylinders, 2996cc, 4 speed manual gearbox, well maintained throughout its life.
£7,000–7,500 *COYS*

1957 Mercedes-Benz 300SL Roadster, 3 litres, 6 cylinders, left-hand drive, very good condition throughout.
£85,000–95,000 *BKS*

1937 Mercedes-Benz 540K Cabriolet, the only one known to have coachwork by Offord & Sons, superb condition throughout.
£250,000+ *BLK*

1959 Mercedes-Benz 220S Convertible, 6 cylinders, 2195cc engine, left-hand drive, 35,000 miles from new.
£33,000–35,000 *CNY*

1951 Mercedes-Benz 300 Cabriolet D, correct and extensive restoration to the smallest detail, authentic interior fabric used.
£116,000+ *BLK*

l. **1955 Mercedes-Benz 300SL Gullwing,** 34,000 miles, excellent condition throughout.
£234,000+ *BLK*

r. **1960 Mercedes-Benz 220SE Cabriolet,** one of an identical pair, excellent restored condition.
£110,000+ *BLK*

This car has been on display for some years and used for maintenance purposes only.

1960 Mercedes-Benz 190SL, 4 cylinders, 2000cc, 4 speed manual gearbox, right-hand drive, good condition.
Est. £18,000–24,000 *ADT*

1962 Mercedes-Benz 300SL Roadster, 6 cylinders, 2996cc, overhead camshaft, 240bhp at 5800rpm, 4 speed manual gearbox, disc brakes, left-hand drive, low mileage, excellent original condition.
£160,000+ *CNY*

1963 Mercedes-Benz 190SL Roadster, 4 cylinder, 1897cc, single overhead camshaft, 105bhp at 5700rpm, 4 speed manual gearbox, drum brakes, left-hand drive, only 26,400 miles, superb original example.
£32,500–35,500 *CNY*

1959 Mercedes-Benz 190SL, 4 cylinders, 1897cc, 120bhp at 5700rpm, all-round coil spring suspension, 25,104 miles from new, excellent original condition.
£25,000–26,000 *COYS*

1971 Mercedes-Benz 250CE 2 door Coupé, 2496cc straight 6 overhead camshaft engine, automatic gearbox, excellent original condition.
Est. £7,000–9,000 *BKS*

1960 Mercedes-Benz 190SL Roadster, hard top, original right-hand drive, 3 owners from new, thorough restoration, excellent overall condition.
£22,000–24,000 *BKS*

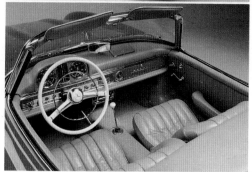

1961 Mercedes-Benz 300SL Roadster, 6 cylinder in line engine, 2996cc, 215bhp, 4 speed manual gearbox, hydraulic disc brakes all-round, left-hand drive, excellent restored condition.
£105,000+ *CNY*

1969 Mercedes-Benz 280SE 2.8 Litre Convertible, 6 cylinders, replaced seats, complete history, engine, gearbox and chassis in excellent condition.
£21,000–22,000 *BKS*

Available as saloon, fixed or drophead coupé.

1982 Mercedes 280SL, 6 cylinder, twin overhead camshaft, automatic gearbox, 73,000 miles, excellent condition.
£13,000–13,500 *Mot*

1929 MG 18/80 2.5 Litre 4 Seater Sports Tourer, coachwork by Carbodies, part restored, good condition. **Est. £25,000–30,000** *BKS*

1933 MG J2, 4 cylinders, 847cc, extensively restored with new body frame, panelling, paintwork, interior and weather equipment. **£11,000–12,000** *COYS*

1934 MG Midget PA Open Sports, 4 cylinders, 847cc, restored, very good condition. **£12,500–13,000** *COYS*

1933 MG 18/80 MkII (Speed Model) Open 4 Seater Tourer, restored, excellent condition. **Est. £30,000–35,000** *C*

1935 MG NB, 6 cylinder in line overhead camshaft engine, 56bhp at 5500rpm, 4 speed gearbox, drum brakes, excellent condition. **£18,000–19,000** *C*

1934 MG Midget PA, comprehensively restored, engine, gearbox and steering components rebuilt, new body and ash frame. **£15,000–15,500** *ADT*

1935 MG PB Midget 2 Seater Sports, original chassis and body, excellent condition. **£22,000–23,000** *BKS*

1936 MG Q-Type Replica, 4 cylinder, 939cc supercharged engine, 4 speed manual gearbox, drum brakes, excellent condition. **Est. £22,500–25,000** *C*

1937 MG SA 'Tickford' Drophead Coupé, coachwork by Salmons of Newport Pagnell, 6 cylinders, overhead valve, 2288cc, 78.5bhp at 4200rpm, 4 speed manual gearbox, drum brakes, semi-elliptic leaf springs, excellent condition. **Est. £25,000–30,000** *C*

1936 MG SA Open 4 Seater Tourer, coachwork by Charlesworth, 6 cylinder, overhead valve 2288cc engine, 78.5bhp at 4200rpm, 4 speed manual gearbox, drum brakes, semi-elliptic leaf spring suspension, very good overall condition, from a famous private collection. **£26,000–27,000** *C*

1937 MG SA Saloon, 6 cylinders, 2288cc, 78.5bhp at 4200rpm, 4 speed manual gearbox, very good original condition, from a famous private collection. **£15,500–16,500** *C*

1937 MG TA Open Sports 2 Seater, 4 cylinders, overhead valve, 1250cc, 54bhp at 5200rpm, original restored condition, from an important private collection. **£14,500–15,000** *C*

1937 MG TA Open Sports, 4 cylinders, 1298cc, overhead valve, very good and original condition throughout. **£8,500–9,000** *COYS*

1937 MG TA Open Sports, original components include the correct bronze carburettors and Luvax shock absorbers, completely restored. **£17,000–18,000** *COYS*

1952 MG TD Midget Sports 2 Seater, 4 cylinders, overhead valve, 1250cc at 5500rpm, original specification, sound and original condition. **Est. £8,000–10,000** *C*

1952 MG TD Midget, 4 cylinders, 1250cc, independent front suspension, left-hand drive, major restoration in 1989, remains unused from that date. **Est. £11,500–12,500** *ADT*

1939 MG TA 'Tickford' 2 Seater Drophead Coupé, coachwork by Salmons of Newport Pagnell, very good restored condition, from private collection. **£22,500–23,500** *C*

1939 MG VA 'Tickford' Drophead Coupé, coachwork by Salmons of Newport Pagnell, restored, very good condition, from private collection. **Est. £18,000–22,000** *C*

1954 MG TD Arnolt Coupé, coachwork by Bertone, 4 cylinders, single overhead camshaft, 1250cc, 57bhp at 5200rpm, 4 speed manual gearbox, 4 wheel drum brakes, semi-elliptic rear suspension, left-hand drive. **Est. £15,000–18,000** *C*

1956 MG TD Arnolt Drophead Coupé, coachwork by Bertone, 4 cylinders, single overhead camshaft, 1250cc, 57bhp at 5200rpm, 4 speed manual gearbox, 4 wheel drum brakes, independent front suspension, semi-elliptic rear suspension, left-hand drive. **£24,000–25,000** *C*

1960 MGA 1500 Drophead Coupé, fully restored, finished in blue. **£11,000–11,500** *BLE*

1960 MGA 1600 Roadster, 4 cylinder, 1588cc engine, imported from USA, converted to right-hand drive. **£10,500–11,000** *COYS*

1968 MGC GT, chrome wheels, good restored condition, finished in British racing green. **£6,000–8,000** *VIC*

1964 MGB Hardtop Roadster Ex-Works Competition Car, good condition, but some cosmetic attention required. **£18,500–19,000** *BKS*

1978 MGB Roadster, excellent condition, only 62,000 miles recorded. **£5,000–6,000** *VIC*

1975 Morgan 4/4, 4 cylinder, 1600cc engine, good unrestored condition. **£9,500–10,000** *DB*

1934 Morris Minor 2 Seater, 4 cylinder, 850cc side valve engine, good original condition. **£4,000–4,250** *DB*

1975 Morgan 4/4 4 Seater, 4 cylinders, 1600cc, excellent condition. **£11,000–11,500** *DB*

1935 Morris Isis Coupé, 6 cylinder, overhead camshaft, 2468cc engine, 4 speed synchromesh gearbox, 4 wheel drum brakes, original condition throughout, some recommissioning necessary. **£9,500–10,000** *C*

1935 Morris 8 2 Door Saloon, original green and red interior and sunroof, finished in black and green. **£4,000–4,500** *CGB*

1955 Morris Minor, 4 cylinders, 853cc, engine rebuilt, reupholstered, new exhaust sytem and tyres, sills renewed, traditional black paint with red interior, excellent condition.
Est. £1,200–1,800 *ADT*

1957 Morris Minor 1000 Saloon, 950cc, overhauled, only 20,000 miles from new, original condition.
£4,500–5,000 *MOR*

1956 Morris Traveller with Split Screen, originally 803cc, converted to 1098cc, completely restored.
£3,000–3,400 *ESM*

1958 Morris Minor Convertible, red interior, very good condition.
£3,250–3,750 *CCon*

1959 Morris Minor Convertible, 1098CC engine, yellow paintwork, navy blue roof, red wheels and radiators.
£1,800–2,200 *CCon*

1958 Morris Minor 1000, 4 cylinders, 948cc, new chrome headlight trim and semaphore arm, 13,800 recorded miles from new, very good original condition.
£2,400–2,800 *ADT*

1961 Morris Minor 1000 Convertible, 950cc engine, 73,000 miles, very good condition.
£6,250–6,750 *CCon*

1961 Morris Minor Million, very good condition.
£4,250–4,750 *CCon*

350 examples of the Morris Minor Million were produced, all in the same colour, to celebrate the millionth Minor made.

1963 Morris Minor 1000 Convertible, 1098cc engine, original condition, floor missing, good restoration project. **£750–950** *CCon*

1964 Morris Minor 1000 Traveller, 1100cc, 5 speed gearbox, disc brakes, restored, good condition. **£3,000–3,750** *MOR*

1967 Morris Minor 1000 Traveller, totally rebuilt, show winning condition. **£5,000–6,000** *SW*

1968 Morris Minor 1000 Traveller, 1098cc, new wood, completely rebuilt. **£6,000–7,000** *MOR*

1970 Morris Minor 1000 Saloon, 1098cc, completely rebuilt. **£5,250–5,850** *MOR*

1964 Morris Minor 1000 Convertible, 1098cc engine, well maintained, very good condition. **£3,750–4,250** *CCon*

1968 Morris Minor 1000 Convertible, 1098cc engine, fully restored, very good condition. **£7,250–7,750** *CCon*

1968 Morris Minor 1000 Convertible, disc brakes, overhauled chassis, excellent condition. **£5,250–5,750** *MOR*

1972 Morris 1000 Van, with 1100cc low compression engine, good running condition. **£2,500–3,000** *MOR*

1913 Peugeot Bébé Type BP1 Two Seater, 856cc engine, good restored condition.
Est. £12,000–15,000 *BKS*

1931 Peugeot 201 Berline, 4 cylinders, 1122cc, 3 speed gearbox, superb example, excellent condition.
£4,500–5,000 *COYS*

1973 Porsche 911T Two Door Saloon, 2 litre engine, outstanding original condition.
£10,000–10,500 *BKS*

1974 Porsche Carrera RS Grand Touring Competition Coupé, 3 litres, entered 1975 Le Mans 24 hour race, exceptional all-round condition.
Est. £40,000–70,000 *BKS*

1976 Porsche 934 Sports/Racing Coupé, 6 cylinders, 3300cc, excellent overall condition.
Est. £28,000–34,000 *COYS*

1979 Porsche 924 Carrera GT Prototype, 4 cylinders, 1984cc, one of 2 built, good condition.
Est. £10,000–14,000 *COYS*

1988 Porsche 959 Two Door Sports Coupé, very low mileage, as new condition.
Est. £180,000–200,000 *BKS*

1954 Renault 750 Saloon, 4 cylinders, 750cc, uprated to Gordini specification, meticulously restored.
£3,500–3,750 *COYS*

1930 Riley Brooklands Open Sports, body-off chassis restoration, excellent condition.
Est. £35,000–40,000 *COYS*

1934 Riley MPH 12/6 Two Seater Sports Racer, 1.5 litres, 6 cylinders, 1458cc, restored to original specification, historic car with good provenance.
Est. £80,000–90,000 *BKS*

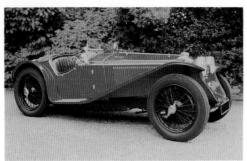

1934 Riley Imp 9hp 2 Seater Sports,
4 cylinder, modified inlet camshaft, manual
gearbox with remote control gear lever
extension, excellent restored condition.
£32,000–35,000 *BKS*

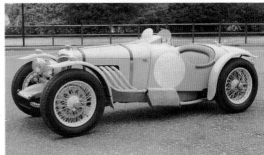

1935 Riley Imp Open Sports, 4 cylinders, 1087cc
'hemi-head' engine, restored over past 8 years, very
good condition and provenance.
Est. £30,000–35,000 *COYS*

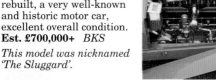

**1911 Rolls-Royce
'London–Edinburgh'
40/50hp**, overhead inlet
valve, single-seat body,
rebuilt, a very well-known
and historic motor car,
excellent overall condition.
Est. £700,000+ *BKS*

*This model was nicknamed
'The Sluggard'.*

**1914 Rolls-Royce 40/50hp Silver Ghost Open
Drive Landaulette**, coachwork by Barker,
6 cylinders, 7428cc, side valves, 48bhp at 1000rpm,
4 speed manual gearbox, 2 wheel rear drum
brakes, excellent original condition.
£145,000+ *C*

**1921 Rolls-Royce 40/50hp Silver Ghost Six-Light
Saloon**, coachwork by Moeremans of Brussels,
originally fitted with Barker touring coachwork,
interesting provenance and excellent condition.
Est. £35,000–40,000 *BKS*

**1914 Rolls-Royce Silver Ghost Alpine
Eagle 40/50hp Sports**, coachwork by John
Marston of Birmingham, 6 cylinders, 7428cc
engine, excellent overall condition and
good provenance.
Est. £250,000–300,000 *BKS*

1923 Rolls-Royce 20hp Barrel Sided Tourer,
coachwork by Barker & Co, original in all major
respects, good and useable condition.
Est. £45,000–50,000 *S*

**1923 Rolls-Royce 20hp 4 door Weymann Fabric
Type Saloon**, coachwork by R. Harrison & Sons, an
early and very original example.
Est. £28,000–30,000 *BKS*

1971 Jaguar V12 2+2, automatic, good condition.
£8,000–8,500   *H&H*

1972 Jaguar E-Type V12 Roadster,
excellent restored condition, 1,300 miles
recorded since rebuild.
£27,000–28,000   *H&H*

r. **1972 Jaguar E-Type
Series III 5.3 Litre V12
Roadster,** right-hand drive,
restored, 2,000 miles
recorded since restoration,
excellent condition.
£27,000–29,000   *BKS*

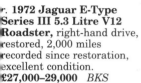

1971 Jaguar E-Type V12 Fixed Head Coupé,
good original condition.
Est. £13,000–14,000   *ADT*

**1972 Jaguar E-Type Series III 2+2 Fixed Head
Coupé,** stainless steel exhaust, sun roof, engine
rebuilt, very good condition.
£14,000–15,000   *BKS*

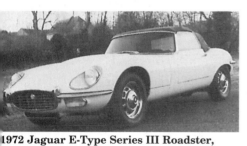

1972 Jaguar E-Type Series III Roadster,
low mileage, original.
£25,000–28,000   *ADT*

1972 Jaguar E-Type 2+2 Fixed Head Coupé.
£13,000–14,000   *ADT*

l. **1973 Jaguar E-Type Series III Fixed Head
Coupé,** automatic, imported from America in
1991, extensively restored including hand drive
conversion, bare metal respray, total engine
rebuild, excellent condition.
Est. £12,000–14,000   *ADT*

1973 Jaguar E-Type Series III Fixed Head Coupé, automatic 3 speed gearbox, mechanically sound, generally good condition.
£9,000–11,000 *ADT*

1973 Jaguar E-Type V12 2+2 Fixed Head Coupé, manual gearbox, 11,050 miles recorded from new, totally original.
£22,000–24,000 *S*

1973 Jaguar E-Type Series III, manual transmission, original right-hand drive example, good and largely original condition throughout.
Est. £12,000–15,000 *COYS*

1973 Jaguar E-Type V12 Roadster.
£18,000–20,000 *HOLL*

1974 Jaguar E-Type Series III, automatic transmission, good original order throughout.
£22,000–23,000 *COYS*

1974 Jaguar E-Type Series III, manual transmission, 4,000 miles from new, excellent condition.
£40,000–43,000 *COYS*

1974 Jaguar E-Type V12 Roadster, automatic, restored
£28,000–32,000 *VIC*

1974 Jaguar E-Type Series III.
£20,000–22,000 *COYS*

1974 Jaguar E-Type 5.3 Litre V12 Roadster, automatic.
£19,000–21,000 *BKS*

**1975 Jaguar E-Type
'Commemorative' Roadster,**
manual, concours
condition throughout.
Est. £45,000–55,000 *COYS*

1963 Jaguar MkX, automatic, very good original
order throughout.
Est. £6,000–7,500 *COYS*

1967 Jaguar 420G 4 Door Saloon, good
coachwork, original interior, rebuilt engine,
overhauled gearbox.
£6,200–6,800 *BKS*

**Miller's is a price
GUIDE not a price LIST**

r. **1967 Jaguar 420G 4 Door Saloon,** automatic.
Est. £4,000–5,000 *BKS*

1967 Jaguar 420G 4 Door Saloon, original condition, excellent order throughout.
£5,000–5,600 *S*

1967 Jaguar MkX 4 Door Saloon, 4 speed synchromesh gearbox, good condition.
£3,000–3,400 *BKS*

1968 Jaguar 420, twin SU carburettors, 245bhp at 5500rpm, restored, sound overall condition.
£6,250–6,750 *C*

1968 Jaguar XJ6 Series I 4.2 Litre Saloon, 2 owners from new, relatively low mileage, would benefit from some restoration work.
Est. £800–1,200 *BKS*

1976 Jaguar XJ 5.3 Litre Coupé, automatic, power steering, air conditioning.
£5,000–5,500 *ADT*

> *A rebuilt car is not necessarily more valuable than a car in good original condition, even if the restoration has been costly.*

1973 Jaguar XJ6 4.2 Litre, automatic, 52,000 miles recorded, air conditioning, excellent example of its type.
Est. £4,500–5,500 *ADT*

1978 Jaguar XJ V12 Coupé, excellent condition.
£4,200–4,600 *ADT*

1984 Jaguar XJS 3.6 Cabriolet, very good condition throughout.
£7,000–8,000 *H&H*

> **Don't Forget!**
> *If in doubt please refer to the 'How to Use' section at the beginning of this book.*

1978 Jaguar XJ12 C 2 Door Coupé, engine recently rebuilt, interior trim in average condition, otherwise good condition throughout.
£2,250–2,500 *BKS*

l. **1983 Jaguar HE V12 XJS Estate/Eventer,** coachwork by Lynx Engineering.
£9,000–9,500 *BKS*

1989 Jaguar XJS 3.6 Litre, automatic, 2 owners, 48,000 miles, excellent condition.
£9,500–10,500 *Mot*

1983 Lister-Jaguar XJS Coupé, conversion by Exeter-Pearce Ltd.
£5,000–5,400 *BKS*

1955 WFH Jaguar XK140 Special Boat Tail Sports Roadster, race-prepared engine from a MkII saloon.
£9,000–9,500 *BKS*

JENSEN

1961 Jensen 541S, unrestored, excellent original condition.
£10,500–11,500 *Bro*

Jensen 541

- Six cylinder in line overhead valve engine of 3993cc producing 150bhp.
- One of the first production cars to feature glass fibre bodywork.
- Launched in 1953, it was also in 1956 the first production car to have disc brakes all-round.
- Superseded by the Jensen CV8 in 1963.

1966 Jensen CV8 MkIII Saloon, excellent overall condition.
Est. £12,000–13,000 *S*

1968 Jensen FF, excellent restored condition.
£16,000–17,000 *SW*

1970 Jensen FF MkII, good condition.
£11,750–12,500 *CBG*

r. **1973 Jensen Interceptor MkIII,** 8 cylinders, 7212cc, good condition throughout.
£5,500–5,800 *ADT*

1964 Jensen CV8 MkII, good condition throughout.
£7,750–8,250 *CBG*

1965 Jensen CV8 MkIII Sports Coupé, fair to good condition throughout, interesting history.
£6,250–6,750 *BKS*

1968 Jensen MkI FF 6.3 Litre Sports Coupé, 48,000 miles from new, excellent condition.
£11,750–12,250 *BKS*

1969 Jensen Interceptor MkI, excellent condition throughout.
£9,750–10,500 *CBG*

1973 Jensen Interceptor Convertible,
converted to factory specification.
£14,750–15,500 *CBG*

1973 Jensen Interceptor, 8 cylinders, 7212cc,
good original condition, some attention required.
£3,000–3,250 *ADT*

1974 Jensen Interceptor Convertible,
20,000 miles from new, bare metal respray,
very good original condition.
£12,000–12,500 *ADT*

**1974 Jensen Interceptor Series III
Convertible,** mileage approximately 23,000,
condition reflects limited use.
Est. £14,000–16,000 *S*

**1975 Jensen Interceptor
MkIII,** very good
original condition.
£6,200–6,500 *COYS*

1975 Jensen Interceptor Convertible,
left-hand drive, fair condition overall.
£11,500–12,500 *CBG*

1976 Jensen Interceptor Convertible,
walnut dash model, superb condition.
£19,500–20,500 *CBG*

1975 Jensen Interceptor MkIII, 8 cylinders,
7212cc, reconditioned automatic gearbox and
torque converter, good condition throughout.
£9,200–9,600 *COYS*

JENSEN Model	ENGINE cc/cyl	DATES	CONDITION		
			1	2	3
541/541R/541S CV8 Mk I-III	3993/6 5916/ 6276/8	1954-63	£11,000	£6,000	£4,000
Interceptor SI-SIII	6276/8	1962-66	£12,000	£6,000	£5,000
Interceptor DHC	6276/8	1967-76	£10,000	£6,000	£5,000
Interceptor SP	6276/8	1973-76	£20,000	£12,000	£9,000
FF	7212/8	1971-76	£10,000	£8,000	£6,500
Healey	6766/8	1967-71	£13,000	£10,000	£9,000
Healey GT	1973/4	1972-76	£5,000	£3,000	£1,500
	1973/4	1975-76	£6,000	£3,000	£2,000

The Jensen CV8 and 541 are particularly sought after.

JENSEN-HEALEY

In 1968 Jensen was acquired by the bankers William Brandt, with Kjell Qvale as president and Donald Healey as chairman. In an effort to revive the company it was decided to launch a new sports car called the Jensen-Healey. Powered by a 2 litre Lotus 16 valve engine, based originally on the Vauxhall Victor engine, it produced 140bhp.

The Jensen-Healey was notably rust prone, but even so nearly 11,000 were built between 1972–76, including 473 GT hard top 2+2s.

Unfortunately the Jensen-Healey failed to revive the ailing company and it was not until the late 1980s that Jensen returned to motor car manufacture with an updated Interceptor.

1973 Jensen-Healey MkII Two Seater Sports, 5 speed gearbox, recently resprayed, engine rebuilt. **Est. £3,500–4,500** *BKS*

> **Don't Forget!**
> *If in doubt please refer to the 'How to Use' section at the beginning of this book.*

l. **1972 Jensen-Healey MkI 2 Litre,** twin cam all-alloy engine produced by Lotus, subject of major repair, good overall condition. **£2,250–2,500** *S*

The Jensen-Healey had a 92in wheelbase which was the same as on the Austin Healey 3000.

1973 Jensen-Healey, excellent condition. **£4,000–4,500** *H&H*

1974 Jensen-Healey, rebuilt 2 years ago. **£4,750–5,250** *APP*

l. **1974 Jensen-Healey II,** left-hand drive. **£5,250–5,750** *CBG*

> *A rebuilt car is not necessarily more valuable than a car in good original condition, even if the restoration has been costly.*

r. **1976 Jensen-Healey II,** 5 speed gearbox, just refurbished. **£5,250–5,750** *CBG*

JOWETT

William and Ben Jowett had built a light car as early as 1905 but continued to work for Scott motorcycles until 1910. The first Jowett saloon car appeared in 1926, and reliable, albeit old fashioned, motor vehicles were produced up to the WWII.

Jowett are probably best known for the two famous post-war marques, the Javelin and the Jupiter sports cars. Over 30,000 Javelins were built before the company ceased trading in 1954.

c1952 Jowett Jupiter Sports, believed to date from 1952 having been rebodied in 1964, good overall condition.
Est. £10,750–12,000 *ADT*

1928 Jowett 7/17 Sports, very good condition throughout.
£6,250–6,750 *H&H*

1952 Jowett Jupiter, 3 year restoration, in concours condition.
£17,500–18,000 *COYS*

KAISER-FRAZER

Founded by former Willys-Overland president Joseph W. Frazer and shipbuilder Henry J. Kaiser in 1946, Kaiser-Frazer planned to produce two series of cars in an aeroplane factory built by Henry Ford. Both models were powered by 6 cylinder Continental engines. The cars were not cheap, yet by 1948 Kaiser-Frazer was established as the USA's eighth largest manufacturer.

By 1954, however, Kaiser-Frazer had been taken over by the Willys-Overland Corporation to form Kaiser-Wil-Motors and the following year production ceased.

1954 Kaiser-Frazer 4 Door Manhattan, 6 cylinders, 3706cc, rare supercharged model, good condition.
£4,200–4,400 *COYS*

KOUGAR

Kougar
- Inspired by the Frazer-Nash Le Mans replica design.
- Built around Jaguar running gear and Jaguar donor engine.
- Conceived in 1974 and built by Rick Stevens.

c1987 Kougar Sports 4.2 Litre 2 Seater Roadster, Jaguar 420 running gear and engine, twin 2in SU carburettors, double wishbone front suspension, Spax adjustable shock absorbers, excellent condition throughout.
£12,250–12,750 *BKS*

Cross Reference
Replica Cars

l. **1966/77 Kougar Sports 4.2 Litre 2 Seater Roadster,** 14,000 miles recorded, excellent condition throughout.
Est. £8,000–11,000 *BKS*

LAGONDA

Wilbur Gunn from Ohio came to England at the turn of the century. His first products were motorcycles which were named Lagonda after the Indian name for the river near where he had been brought up. Early cars were exported from the Staines factory and were not sold in England until 1912. Competition success followed, including a famous Le Mans victory.

Wilbur Gunn died in 1930, and in 1935 the company was bought by Alan Ford who employed W. O. Bentley as the Technical Director. Superbly engineered and extremely stylish Lagonda cars were of the highest standard. After WWII David Brown bought Lagonda to enable him to fit the Lagonda engine to his Aston Martin sports cars.

1930 Lagonda Low Chassis 2 Litre Speed Model, 4 cylinders, 1954cc, meticulously and precisely maintained, comprehensive documented history. **£26,000–28,000** *COYS*

1933 Lagonda M45 T7 Open Tourer, 6 cylinders, 4497cc, engine changed to LG6 Sanction 4 unit, spare wheel mounted to the side of scuttle, black weather equipment, fully restored. **Est. £45,000–55,000** *COYS*

1931 Lagonda 14/60 Low Chassis 2 Litre Tourer, used regularly and maintained. **£28,000–30,000** *BKS*

Lagonda 16/80

- The 16/80 model was launched in 1932.
- Pushrod operated overhead valve engine of 1991cc enabled the 16/80 to accelerate to 60mph in 19 seconds.
- Averaging 25mpg the 16/80 cost £595 when new and had a top speed of about 80mph.

1934 Lagonda M45 Le Mans Style Tourer, mechanics restored to the highest order, Le Mans style body recreated utilising aircraft aluminium. **Est. £32,000–36,000** *COYS*

> Miller's is a price
> GUIDE not a price LIST

l. **1934 Lagonda 16/80 Special 6-S Type Four Seater Sports Tourer,** good general condition throughout. **£21,000–23,000** *BKS*

LAGONDA Model	ENGINE cc/cyl	DATES	CONDITION		
			1	2	3
12/24	1421/4	1923-26	£14,000	£10,000	£8,000
2 litre	1954/4	1928-32	£28,000	£25,000	£19,000
3 litre	2931/6	1928-34	£35,000	£30,000	£22,000
Rapier	1104/4	1934-35	£13,000	£6,500	£5,000
M45	4429/6	1934-36	£35,000	£26,000	£18,000
LG45	4429/6	1936-37	£40,000	£30,000	£20,000
LG6	4453/6	1937-39	£40,000	£28,000	£20,000
V12	4480/V12	1937-39	£75,000	£50,000	£40,000

Prices are very dependent upon body type, originality and competition history.

1934 Lagonda M45 T7 Tourer, coachwork by Lagonda, excellent restored condition. Est. £55,000–65,000 *COYS*

1934 Lagonda M45 T9 Rapide Tourer, substantially restored throughout, excellent overall condition. Est. £43,000–50,000 *COYS*

1934 Lagonda M45 'Silent Travel' Saloon, 6 cylinder, 4453cc engine, requires restoration but complete and correct in every detail. £15,000–16,000 *COYS*

1936 Lagonda LG45 Rapide Style Sports Tourer, meticulous restoration to Rapide specifications including coachwork, instrumentation and engine, excellent condition. £56,000–59,000 *COYS*

LAGONDA Model	ENGINE cc/cyl	DATES	CONDITION		
			1	2	3
3 litre	2922/6	1953-58	£10,500	£7,000	£4,500
3 litre DHC	2922/6	1953-56	£14,000	£10,000	£8,500
Rapide	3995/6	1961-64	£11,000	£7,000	£4,500

1936 Lagonda LG45 French Grand Prix Team Car, a famous motor car with superb racing provenance, excellent condition, although requiring some small recommissioning. £170,000+ *BKS*

1936 Lagonda LG45 Drophead Coupé, 6 cylinder, 4453cc engine, excellent condition. £42,000–45,000 *COYS*

l. **1937 Lagonda LG45 Drophead Coupé,** 6 cylinder, 4467cc engine, good original condition. £27,000–29,000 *COYS*

Launched in 1935, the LG45 was available as a saloon, tourer or drophead coupé.

1937 Lagonda LG45 Pillarless 4 Door Saloon, 4 litre engine, bodywork is scruffy but sound, chassis good.
Est. £12,000–15,000 *BKS*

1955 Lagonda 3 Litre Drophead Coupé, coachwork by Tickford, appears basically sound and complete, requires total restoration.
£1,000–1,250 *BKS*

1938 Lagonda LG6 29.13hp 4½ Litre Drophead Coupé, non-runner, basically sound, complete and eminently restorable, twin side-mounted spare wheels, exposed twin horns, straightforward restoration.
£33,000–35,000 *BKS*

1950 Lagonda 2½ Litre Drophead Coupé, 6 cylinders, twin overhead camshaft, 2580cc, 105bhp at 5000rpm, 4 speed manual gearbox, hydraulically operated drums, rear brakes mounted inboard, independent front and rear suspension, right-hand drive, last run about 5 years ago, chromework requires attention, 2 owners from new, sympathetic restoration required.
£18,000–19,000 *C*

LAMBORGHINI

The famous charging bull insignia that adorns Lamborghini is a representation of the founder Ferrucio Lamborghini's zodiac sign Taurus – the Bull. It is no surprise that the most famous Lamborghini, the Miura, took its name from a Spanish fighting bull.

1968 Lamborghini Miura, Berlinetta coachwork by Bertone, 12 cylinders, 3929cc, excellent restored condition.
Est. £50,000–65,000 *COYS*

l. **1965 Lamborghini 350GT Coupé,** coachwork by Carrozzeria Touring, excellent condition throughout.
£50,000–55,000 *BKS*
120 examples of the 350GT were built.

r. **1971 Lamborghini Miura SV,** Berlinetta coachwork by Bertone, good example, ready for use.
£78,000–82,000 *COYS*

This car is one of just 7 right-hand drive Miura SVs made.

Lamborghini Miura

- Introduced in 1966, the Miura took the world by storm.
- Mid-engined 3929cc, V12 could produce 340bhp.
- Design team headed by Gianpaolo Dallara and bodywork by Bertone.
- Production ceased in 1972 after it is believed only 763 cars were built.

1973 Lamborghini Espada Series II, 12 cylinder, 3929cc engine, good condition throughout. **£10,000–11,000** *ADT*

l. **1973 Lamborghini 4 Litre Espada Series III,** V12 twin overhead camshaft, 3929cc, 365bhp at 7500rpm, 5 speed manual gearbox, front and rear disc brakes, front and rear unequal-length A-arm suspension, coil springs and anti-roll bar, right-hand drive, recorded mileage 33,000, sound and original example, service would be beneficial. **£9,000–10,000** *C*

LAMBORGHINI Model	ENGINE cc/cyl	DATES	CONDITION		
			1	2	3
350 GT fhc	3500/12	1964-67	£80,000	£50,000	£30,000
400 GT	4000/12	1966-68	£60,000	£50,000	£30,000
Miura LP400	4000/12	1966-69	£60,000	£50,000	£30,000
Miura S	4000/12	1969-71	£80,000	£60,000	£40,000
Espada	4000/12	1969-78	£18,000	£14,000	£10,000
Jarama	4000/12	1970-78	£22,000	£15,000	£13,000
Urraco	2500/8	1972-76	£18,000	£11,000	£8,000
Countach	4000/12	1974-82	£60,000	£40,000	£30,000

Countach limited editions are sought after.

LANCHESTER

1925 Lanchester Forty 40hp Limousine, coachwork by Windovers, 6 cylinder, single overhead camshaft, 6178cc engine, in unit with its 3 speed epicyclic gearbox, last on road c1958. **£8,000–9,000** *BKS*

Cross Reference
Restoration Projects

1930 Lanchester STR8 Replica Gunboat Tourer, 4¼ litre engine. **£20,000–22,500** *FHF*

1953 Lanchester LJ200 14hp Saloon, 4 cylinder in line engine, overhead valve, 1968cc, 60bhp at 4200rpm, 4 speed pre-selector manual gearbox, Girling hydromechanical front and rear brakes, independent torsion bar front, rigid axle with semi-elliptic leaf springs rear suspension, right-hand drive, 3 owners from new, replacement engine fitted, extremely original running condition. **£700–800** *C*

1934 Lanchester LA10 Drophead Coupé, unusual, probably unique body fitted prior to registration in 1934, good condition. **£6,200–6,600** *H&H*

This car is very rare.

LANCHESTER Model	ENGINE cc/cyl	DATES	CONDITION		
			1	2	3
LD10	1287/4	1946-49	£2,500	£1,500	£750
LD10 (Barker bodies)	1287/4	1950-51	£2,800	£1,500	£700

LANCIA

Founded in 1906 by Vincenzo Lancia, a well-respected racing driver, the factory was located in Turin. Lancia produced many famous models, the Alfa, Beta, Dialfa, Gamma and so on, using names derived from the Greek alphabet – the Lambda probably surpassing them all. The Eta, in 1913, was the first European car with electric lighting, although only offered as an extra.

The Lancia Stratos, a limited sports production model, launched in 1973, powered by the Fiat/Ferrari 246 Dino engine, had tremendous success on the international rally scene. It is highly sought by collectors and enthusiasts today.

1934 Lancia Augusta 12hp, 4 cylinder narrow V4 engine, unrestored sound example.
£3,750–4,250 *DB*

1928 Lancia Lambda 8th Series 4 Door Weymann Fabric Saloon, coachwork by Albany Carriage Company, aircraft style wicker front seats incorporating leather map wallets on their backs, original condition.
£22,000–24,000 *BKS*

c1936 Lancia Augusta Saloon, very good overall condition.
£5,750–6,500 *BKS*

1939 Lancia Aprilia 4 Door Pillarless Sports Saloon, 1486cc engine, right-hand drive, original interior trim in need of restoration, dry stored for many years, sound and very original example.
£3,600–4,000 *BKS*

1938 Lancia Astura 6th Series Lungo Mussolini/Hitler 'Pact of Steel', state parade cabriolet coachwork by Farina, 8 cylinder, 2972cc engine, fully restored, superlative condition.
£250,000+ *COYS*

Never offered before for public sale, this is a car which has a place in 20thC history.

1959 Lancia Flaminia GT Sports Coupé, coachwork by Touring of Milan, left-hand drive, thought to be complete apart from broken windscreen, unrestored.
Est. £3,500–5,500 *C*

1962 Lancia Flaminia GT 2.5 3C, coachwork by Touring of Milan, V6, 2458cc engine, converted to right-hand drive, very good overall condition.
£7,000–7,500 *COYS*

Lancia Flaminia

- Launched in 1957 as a replacement model for the Aurelia with pressed steel bodywork by Pininfarina.
- Featured the V6 2458cc engine which in standard form produced 102bhp at 4800 rpm.
- In 1959 Touring of Milan designed a GT Sports Coupé which had a top speed of 112mph.
- By 1960 the Flaminia 3C appeared with triple Weber carburettors producing 140bhp at 5400rpm, which could accelerate to 60mph in 12.7 seconds.

LANCIA Model	ENGINE cc/cyl	DATES	CONDITION 1	2	3
Theta	4940/4	1913-19	£24,000	£16,500	£8,000
Kappa	4940/4	1919-22	£24,000	£16,000	£8,000
Dikappa	4940/4	1921-22	£24,000	£16,000	£8,000
Trikappa	4590/4	1922-26	£25,000	£18,000	£10,000
Lambda	2120/4	1923-28	£35,000	£20,000	£10,000
Dilambda	3960/8	1928-32	£24,000	£16,000	£8,000
Astura	2604/8	1931-39	£25,000	£18,000	£9,000
Artena	1925/4	1931-36	£9,000	£5,000	£2,000
Augusta	1196/4	1933-36	£9,000	£4,000	£2,000
Aprilia 238	1352/4	1937-39	£10,000	£5,000	£3,000

1962 Lancia Flaminia Berlina, coachwork by Carrozzeria Pininfarina, good original condition and excellent provenance.
£8,400–8,800 *BKS*

1962 Lancia Flaminia Coupé 2.5, coachwork by Pininfarina, all alloy, overhead valve, V6 engine, 2458cc, 128bhp at 5100rpm, 4 speed manual transaxle gearbox, wishbones suspension, coil springs and anti-roll at front, de Dion axle, semi-elliptic leaf springs rear suspension, all-round disc brakes, left-hand drive.
£26,750–28,250 *C*

l. **1964 Lancia Flaminia Super Sport 2.8 3C,** coachwork by Zagato, 6 cylinder, 2775cc engine, maintained to a high standard, in very good condition.
Est. £18,000–25,000 *COYS*

1968 Lancia Flavia Convertible, coachwork by Vignale, recently retrimmed, in sound order, would probably benefit from an overhaul.
£3,000–3,400 *BKS*

Based on the Flavia Coupé 815 introduced in 1962, the convertible version was developed by Vignale on behalf of Lancia producing an attractive four seater sports car.

1968 Lancia Flavia Convertible, coachwork by Vignale, generally good, sound and serviceable order throughout.
£5,400–5,800 *BKS*

1976 Lancia Beta Coupé, 4 cylinder, 1592cc engine, 23,500 miles from new, excellent condition.
£3,400–3,800 *ADT*

1972 Lancia Fulvia Sport Coupé, coachwork by Zagato, 4 cylinders, 1300cc, rare right-hand drive, virtually unused since restoration.
£5,000–5,400 *COYS*

1976 Lancia Beta Spyder, 4 cylinder, 1995cc engine, very good all-round condition.
Est. £2,750–3,500 *ADT*

1978 Lancia Gamma 2500 Coupé, 5 speed manual gearbox, good condition.
Est. £1,800–2,000 *S*

1982 Lancia Monte Carlo 2 Door Coupé, coachwork by Pininfarina, very good condition throughout.
£3,300–3,800 *BKS*

1984 Lancia Gamma 2 Door Coupé, coachwork by Pininfarina, very good condition generally.
£2,000–2,400 *BKS*

LANCIA Model	ENGINE cc/cyl	DATES	CONDITION 1	2	3
Aprilia 438	1486/4	1939-50	£11,000	£6,000	£3,000
Ardea	903/4	1939-53	£10,000	£5,000	£3,000
Aurelia B10	1754/6	1950-53	£7,000	£5,000	£2,000
Aurelia B15-20-22	1991/6	1951-53	£10,000	£5,000	£2,500
Aurelia B24-B24S	2451/6	1955-58	£30,000	£15,000	£10,000
Aurelia GT	2451/6	1953-59	£15,000	£10,000	£7,000
Appia C10-C105	1090/4	1953-62	£6,000	£3,000	£2,000
Aurelia Ser II	2266/6	1954-59	£10,000	£5,000	£3,000
Flaminia Zagato	2458/6	1957-63	£18,000	£10,000	£7,000
Flaminia Ser	2458/6	1957-63	£12,000	£7,000	£5,000
Flavia 1500	1500/4	1960-75	£6,000	£4,000	£2,000
Fulvia	1091/4	1963-70	£3,000	£2,000	£1,000
Fulvia S	1216/4	1964-70	£3,500	£2,500	£1,500
Fulvia 1.3	1298/4	1967-75	£3,000	£2,000	£1,000
Stratos	2418/6	1969-71	£35,000	£18,000	£10,000
Flavia 2000	1991/4	1969-75	£3,000	£1,500	£500
Fulvia HF/1.6	1584/4	1969-75	£5,000	£2,000	£1,000
Beta HPE	1585/4	1976-82	£3,000	£1,500	£500
Beta Spyder	1995/4	1977-82	£4,000	£1,500	£800
Monte Carlo	1995/4	1976-81	£6,000	£3,000	£1,000
Gamma Coupé	2484/4	1977-84	£2,500	£1,500	£500
Gamma Berlina	2484/4	1977-84	£1,500	£800	£300

Competition history could cause prices to vary.

LAND ROVER

1948 Pre-Production Land Rover, requires sympathetic restoration, complete and original condition, non-factory doors.
£12,500–13,500 *S*

This Land Rover is one of the first 25 pre-production models.

1954 Land Rover Series 1, 86in Wheelbase, good overall condition for the year.
£2,200–2,400 *BKS*

This vehicle was once the property of Donald Campbell.

LAND ROVER Model	ENGINE cc/cyl	DATES	CONDITION 1	2	3
Ser 1	1595/4	1948-51	£5,000	£2,000	£1,000
Ser 1	1995/4	1951-53	£4,000	£2,000	£800
Ser 1	1995/4	1953-58	£4,000	£2,000	£500
Ser 1	1995/4	1953-58	£3,000	£1,800	£800
Ser 2	1995/4	1958-59	£2,000	£950	£500
Ser 2	1995/4	1958-59	£2,800	£1,200	£500
Ser 2	2286/4	1959-71	£2,000	£950	£500
Ser 2	2286/4	1959-71	£2,500	£1,200	£500
Range Rover	3528/V8	1970-	£5,000	£1,200	£600

Series 1 Land Rovers are now very sought after.

LA SALLE

La Salle was created by General Motors as a lower priced marque to be marketed in conjunction with Cadillac, using many Cadillac components.

La Salle, masterminded by Harley Earl in 1927, was by the late 1930s using body parts from Buick and other GM products. By 1940 the name had been dropped completely.

1929 La Salle Cabriolet, flat head V8 engine, downdraught carburation, excellent overall condition.
£40,000–42,500 *GAR*

Don't Forget!
If in doubt please refer to the 'How to Use' section at the beginning of this book.

r. **1931 La Salle Roadster,** coachwork by Fleetwood, V8, 353cu in engine, 95bhp at 3000rpm, 3 speed manual gearbox, drum brakes all-round, semi-elliptic leaf spring suspension front and rear, left-hand drive, excellent restored condition.
£57,000–60,000 *CNY*

This car is a National First Prize winner in both the Antique Automobile and Classic Car Clubs of America.

LEA-FRANCIS

R. H. Lea and G. J. Francis originally produced bicycles and the first motor car appeared from their Coventry factory in 1904. Full production of motor cars did not really start until 1920, and they were not a great success. An amalgamation with the Vulcan company in 1920 enabled Lea-Francis to use Meadows engines which led to a series of popular models. Lea-Francis survived after WWII but, crippled by the new purchase tax regulations amongst other reasons, the company ceased production in 1953.

1930 Lea-Francis Hyper Sports, Weyman body.
£8,000–12,500 *FHF*

l. **1950 Lea-Francis 2½ Litre Sports,** 4 cylinders, 2496cc, 110bhp at 5200rpm, 4 speed manual gearbox, drum brakes, independent front suspension, semi-elliptic leaf springs rear, right-hand drive, very good condition throughout.
£16,000–18,000 *C*

LEA-FRANCIS Model	ENGINE cc/cyl	DATES	CONDITION 1	2	3
12HP	1944/4	1923-24	£10,000	£5,000	£3,000
14HP	2297/4	1923-24	£10,000	£5,000	£3,000
9HP	1074/4	1923-24	£7,000	£4,000	£2,000
10HP	1247/4	1947-54	£10,000	£5,500	£3,000
12HP	1496/4	1926-34	£11,000	£6,000	£4,000
Various 6 cylinder models	1696/6	1927-29	£13,500	£9,500	£5,000
Various 6 cylinder models	1991/6	1928-36	£10,500	£8,750	£5,000
14HP	1767/4	1946-54	£6,000	£4,000	£2,000
1.5 litre	1499/4	1949-51	£10,000	£5,000	£2,500
2.5 litre	2496/4	1950-52	£12,000	£8,000	£4,000

LINCOLN

Founded in 1920, Henry Leland named his Lincoln Motor Company of Detroit after Abraham Lincoln. Due to financial problems, the company was soon sold to Henry Ford, shortly after which Leland resigned and the company was run by Henry Ford's son, Edsel. Elegant styling and first-rate engineering soon gained the company presidential patronage which started in 1924 and is still enjoyed today.

1929 Lincoln 'L' Sport Phæton, V8 side valve engine, 384cu in, 3 speed manual gearbox with overdrive, 4 wheel mechanical brakes, semi-elliptic leaf suspension front and rear, left-hand drive, excellent overall condition.
£35,000–37,000 *CNY*

1931 Lincoln Model K Dual Cowl Phæton,
V8 side valve 384cu in, engine, 120bhp at 2900rpm, 3 speed manual gearbox with free-wheeling device, semi-elliptic leaf spring suspension, left-hand drive, beautifully restored, optional side-mounted spare wheel covers, twin trip lights, single Pilot Ray.
£74,000–76,000 *CNY*

1931 Lincoln Model K Convertible Coupé,
V8 4 cylinder side valve engine, 6294cc, 120bhp at 2900rpm, 3 speed manual gearbox, drum brakes, semi-elliptic leaf spring suspension, left-hand drive, fully restored in USA to an exceptional standard.
£50,000–52,000 *C*

1939 Lincoln Zephyr V12 Fixed Head Coupé, completely overhauled 2 years ago, original 6 volt electrical system replaced by a 12 volt, resprayed, good condition throughout.
£16,000–17,000 *S*

1946 Lincoln Continental 4.7 Litre 2 Door Coupé, 3 speed manual transmission, electric windows, engine rebuilt, no known modifications from original specification, excellent condition throughout.
£13,500–14,500 *BKS*

This is one of only 265 of the 66H type with body style 57 made in 1946.

Lincoln Continental MkII

- Intended to be the ultimate luxury car to compete with Rolls-Royce and Bentley, each car was individually tested.
- Launched in 1955 it was powered by a 285bhp Lincoln V8 engine.
- The chrome plating was 3 times thicker than on other Ford cars, they were individually painted and the leather was bought from Scotland.
- Selling for $10,000 which was $2,000 more than Henry Ford had dictated, each car lost the company $1,000.
- Only about 3,000 MkIIs were built in a three-year production run.

1956 Lincoln Continental MkII, V8 engine, 368cu in, 285hp, 3 speed automatic gearbox, 4 wheel drum brakes, independent front suspension, live axle rear, left-hand drive, older restoration, good overall condition.
£15,000–17,000 *CNY*

1963 Lincoln 7 Litre Continental 4 Door Sedan, original paintwork in excellent condition, air conditioning, electric ally operated windows, quarter lights, door locks and seats.
£8,000–8,500 *BKS*

This car was first owned by Peter Sellers.

Cross Reference
American Feature Pages 65–68

1967 Lincoln Short Wheelbase Executive Limousine, coachwork by Lehmann Peterson, V8 engine, 462ci, 340bhp at 4600rpm, 3 speed automatic gearbox, 4 wheel hydraulic disc/drum brakes, independent front suspension, semi-elliptic leaf springs rear, left-hand drive, excellent original condition throughout.
£10,000–12,000 *CNY*

1967 Lincoln Continental Convertible, good general condition, some minor attention required.
£5,500–6,000 *BKS*

1980 Lincoln 7 Litre Stretched Limousine, 3 rows of seats, fitted cocktail cabinet, good condition throughout.
Est. £5,000–8,000 *BKS*

LINCOLN Model	ENGINE cu in/cyl	DATES	CONDITION 1	2	3
Première Coupé	368/8	1956-57	£6,000	£4,000	£2,000
Première Convertible	368/8	1956-57	£14,000	£8,000	£5,000
Continental Mk II	368/8	1956-57	£10,000	£6,000	£4,000
Continental 2 door	430/8	1958-60	£6,000	£4,000	£2,000
Continental Convertible	430/8	1958-60	£18,000	£10,000	£7,000

LOTUS

1959 Lotus Elite, 4 cylinders, 1216cc, good condition throughout.
Est. £16,000–18,000 *ADT*

Lotus Elite

- The Elite was the first Lotus coupé.
- Bodywork in glass fibre, it was the first monocoque glass fibre car generally available.
- Designed by Peter Kinwan-Taylor, it was a highly successful competition car.
- Less than 1,000 Coventry Climax engined Elites were built before production ceased in 1962.

1962 Lotus Elite Super 95, ZF gearbox, leather interior, superbly restored.
£28,500–29,500 *KSC*

1966 Lotus Elan S3 Fixed Head Coupé, mechanically in excellent condition, just over 26,000 miles from new.
£9,000–9,500 *BKS*

1963 Lotus Elan S1, excellent condition.
£18,000–20,000 *KSC*

1967 Lotus Elan S3 Fixed Head Coupé, little used for past few years, some recommissioning required.
£5,000–5,500 *BKS*

1970 Lotus Elan S4 SE Coupé, 4 cylinder twin cam engine, 1558cc, 115bhp at 5600rpm, 4 speed manual gearbox, 4 wheel disc brakes, independent double wishbone front suspension with combined shock absorbers and coil springs, independent rear suspension with Chapman strut, coil springs and trailing arm, right-hand drive, original black seats, dry storage for past 15 years.
£6,200–6,800 *C*

r. **1969 Lotus Elan S4 Fixed Head Coupé,** galvanised replacement chassis just fitted, excellent example.
£11,500–12,500 *KSC*

Lotus Elan Sprint

- The Elan Sprint was the final derivative of the Elan series.
- The Elan was launched in 1962, the S2 introduced in 1964, the fixed head coupé, S3 in 1965, and the more powerful S4 in 1969.
- The Sprint was introduced in 1970, the 1558cc, 4 cylinder engine produced 126bhp at 6500rpm, could accelerate to 60mph in 6.7 seconds and reach a top speed of 121mph.

1971 Lotus Elan Sprint, 4 cylinders, 1558cc, thoroughly restored over 8 years, very good example. **Est. £9,000–12,000** *COYS*

1972 Lotus Europa Twin Camshaft, good overall condition, ideal for road or race. **£7,000–7,400** *CGOC*

1972 Lotus Europa Twin Camshaft Special, 5 speed gearbox, totally rebuilt on new chassis, resprayed, original interior. **£12,500–13,500** *KSC*

1972 Lotus Europa Twin Camshaft Special, 4 speed gearbox, 21,000 miles from new, original paintwork, superb interior, totally original. **£11,500–12,500** *KSC*

1973 Lotus Europa Twin Camshaft, 4 cylinders, 1558cc engine, magnesium alloy wheels not original, good condition. **Est. £7,500–8,500** *ADT*

1979 Lotus Eclat 521,
5 speed gearbox, 60,000 miles
recorded, full history,
excellent original condition.
£4,250–4,750 *Bro*

1973 Lotus Europa Twin Camshaft Special,
5 speed gearbox, 150mph top speed from 186bhp.
£11,500–12,500 *KSC*

*This is a rare example of a Europa Special that
was modified for racing in about 1980.*

Cross Reference
Racing Cars

**1989 Lotus Esprit
Turbo,** with SE rear
spoiler, walnut
dashboard, Sony CD,
12,000 miles from new,
No. 24 of limited
edition of 40.
£15,500–16,500 *KSC*

1989 Lotus Esprit Turbo, with SE rear spoiler,
one of limited edition of 40.
£14,500–15,500 *KSC*

1990 Lotus Esprit Turbo SE, air conditioning, glass
sunroof, 27,000 miles, full history.
£20,500–21,500 *KSC*

A rebuilt car is not necessarily more valuable than a car in good original condition, even if the restoration has been costly.

l. **1992 Lotus Esprit Turbo 'Hi-Wing',**
leather interior, air conditioning, glass
sunroof, excellent example.
£23,500–24,500 *KSC*

1964 Lotus Cortina, 4 cylinders, 1588cc, standard specification, rear leaf springs from new, good unrestored condition.
£6,000–6,500   *COYS*

1990 Lotus Excel SE, leather interior, air conditioning, 23,000 miles from new.
£11,500–12,500   *KSC*

Cross Reference
Ford

*r .***1969 Lotus Cortina MkII,** good overall condition.
£2,400–2,800   *H&H*

LOTUS Model	ENGINE cc/cyl	DATES	CONDITION		
			1	2	3
Six		1953-56	£13,000	£7,000	£5,000
Seven S1 Sports	1172/4	1957-64	£12,000	£9,000	£4,500
Seven S2 Sports	1498/4	1961-66	£9,000	£7,000	£4,000
Seven S3 Sports	1558/4	1961-66	£9,000	£7,000	£4,000
Seven S4	1598/4	1969-72	£6,000	£4,500	£2,500
Elan S1 Convertible	1558/4	1962-64	£10,000+	£8,000	£4,500
Elan S2 Convertible	1558/4	1964-66	£9,000+	£6,500	£4,000
Elan S3 Convertible	1558/4	1966-69	£11,000+	£7,250	£5,000
Elan S3 FHC	1558/4	1966-69	£11,000	£6,000	£4,000
Elan S4 Convertible	1558/4	1968-71	£11,000+	£8,000	£5,000
Elan S4 FHC	1558/4	1968-71	£9,000	£6,250	£4,150
Elan Sprint Convertible	1558/4	1971-73	£10,000+	£7,500	£5,000
Elan Sprint FHC	1558/4	1971-73	£9,000	£6,250	£4,500
Europa S1 FHC	1470/4	1966-69	£4,000	£2,500	£1,500
Europa S2 FHC	1470/4	1969-71	£5,500	£3,000	£2,000
Europa Twin Cam	1558/4	1971-75	£8,000	£6,000	£4,000
Elan +2S 130	1558/4	1971-74	£8,000	£5,000	£4,000
Elite S1 FHC	1261/4	1974-80	£3,000	£2,500	£1,500
Eclat S1	1973/4	1975-82	£3,500	£3,000	£1,500
Esprit 1	1973/4	1977-81	£6,500	£5,000	£3,000
Esprit 2	1973/4	1976-81	£7,000	£4,000	£2,500
Esprit S2.2	2174/4	1980-81	£7,000	£5,500	£3,000
Esprit Turbo	2174/4	1980-90	£10,000	£6,500	£3,500
Excel	2174/4	1983-85	£5,000	£2,500	£1,800

Prices vary with some limited edition Lotus models.

MALDEN

r. **1898 Malden Runabout Steam Car,** 2 cylinder vertical engine, full elliptic leaf spring transversely mounted front suspension, full elliptic leaf spring rear, centre tiller drive, excellent condition.
Est. £16,500–23,500   *CNY*

The Malden Automobile Company built its first steam car in 1898, although it was not available for sale until the turn of the century.

This car is eligible for the famous London to Brighton run, it would also be ideal for one of the many events currently being organised for Victorian cars.

MARCOS

1970 Marcos Mantis 2+2 Sports Coupé,
chassis replaced, leather trim reconditioned,
very good restored condition.
Est. £10,000–14,000 *BKS*

1995 Mini Marcos, 4 cylinders, 1300cc, 670 miles,
'as new' example, excellent condition throughout.
Est. £3,900–4,500 *ADT*

MARCOS Model	ENGINE cc/cyl	DATES	CONDITION		
			1	2	3
1500/1600/1800	1500/1600/1800/4	1964-69	£8,000	£5,000	£2,500
Mini-Marcos	848/4	1965-74	£3,500	£2,500	£1,500
Marcos 2.5/3 litre	2500/3000/6	1969-71	£9,000	£5,000	£4,000
Mantis	2498	1970/71	£5,000	£3,000	£1,500

MARMON

Although a long-established engineering
company, Nordyke and Marmon did not
produce its first motor car until 1902.
Designed by Howard C. Marmon, production
models were offered for sale in 1905.
Successful in competitions, a Marmon Wasp
won the first Indianapolis 500 race in 1911,
and they enjoyed a good reputation for big,
well-built and comfortable motor cars. Car
production had ceased by the mid-1930s but
the Marmon name still survives today on
commercial vehicles.

**1933 Marmon V16 Type 143 Five
Passenger Victoria Coupé,** V16, 515cu in
engine, 250bhp at 3400rpm, 3 speed manual
gearbox, 4 wheel mechanical brakes, semi-
elliptic leaf springs suspension front and
rear, left-hand drive, complete restoration to
concours winning standard.
£65,000–68,000 *CNY*

l. **1923 Marmon Model 34 Speedster,** wire wheels, twin
rear mounted spares, optional front wheel brakes added,
rear-wing compartments, scuttle-mounted spotlights,
totally restored.
£29,000–31,000 *S*

MASERATI

The Maserati racing legend, Grand Prix
winners and sports cars, driven by some of
the all-time great drivers, ended in the late
1950s when Maserati withdrew from
competition, although some of their sports
cars continued for a few seasons, and in
the 1960s in private hands. The company
concentrated on the production of luxury
Grand Touring and sports cars, based around
the twin overhead camshaft, 6 cylinder,
3485cc engine. Famous models, the 5000GT
and the Quattroporte, were replaced in the
1960s by the Mistral and Sebring.
  Citroën acquired Maserati shortly after the
Ghibli was launched and a Citroën Maserati
SM was introduced in 1969. The company,
despite producing such super-cars as the
Bora and the Khamsin, was about to go out of
business when it was rescued and acquired
by Alejandro De Tomaso in 1975.

> *A rebuilt car is not necessarily more
> valuable than a car in good original
> condition, even if the restoration has
> been costly.*

1958 Maserati 3500 GT Coupé, bodywork
derusted and resprayed, engine reconditioned
and overhauled, left-hand drive, requires
finishing and recommissioning.
£8,000–8,500 *BKS*

l. **1959 Maserati Tipo 61 'Birdcage' 2.9 Litre Sports-Racing 2 Seater,** full FIA acceptance paperwork, in excellent all-round condition.
£250,000+ *BKS*

> **Cross Reference**
> Racing Cars

r. **1960 Maserati 3500GT 3.5 Litre 2 Door Coupé,** coachwork by Carrozzeria Touring of Milan, triple Weber carburettors, servo-assisted 4 wheel disc brakes, semi-elliptic rear suspension, extensively restored, good to very good condition generally.
Est. £20,000–25,000 *BKS*

One of only 28 right-hand drive versions built.

MASERATI Model	ENGINE cc/cyl	DATES	CONDITION 1	2	3
AG-1500	1488/6	1946-50	£30,000	£20,000	£10,000
A6G	1954/6	1951-53	£50,000	£35,000	£22,000
A6G-2000	1985/6	1954-57	£45,000	£35,000	£20,000
3500GT	3485/6	1957-64	£25,000	£15,000	£9,000
5000GT	4935/8	1960-65	£40,000	£20,000	£10,000
Sebring	3694/6	1962-66	£25,000	£18,000	£10,000
Quattroporte	4136/8	1963-74	£14,000	£10,000	£7,000
Mistral	4014/6	1964-70	£15,000	£10,000	£7,500
Mexico	4719/8	1965-68	£15,000	£12,000	£8,000
Ghibli	4719/8	1967-73	£20,000	£15,000	£12,000
Ghibli-spyder	4136/8	1969-74	£50,000	£40,000	£25,000
Indy	4136/8	1969-74	£15,000	£13,000	£9,000
Bora	4719/8	1971-80	£25,000	£18,000	£11,000
Merak	2965/6	1972-81	£16,000	£14,000	£9,000
Khamsin	4930/8	1974-81	£14,000	£10,000	£8,000

l. **1963 Maserati 3500GTi Spyder,** coachwork by Vignale, all-round disc brakes, 5 speed gearbox, Borrani wire wheels, very good condition throughout.
£46,000–48,000 *COYS*

One of only 250 Spyders designed by Vignale and built on a shorter wheelbase chassis.

r. **1964 Maserati 3500GTi ST Sports Coupé,** coachwork by Carrozzeria Touring, 5 speed manual gearbox, left-hand drive, good condition throughout.
£14,000–16,000 *BKS*

The 3.5 litre, 6 cylinder, twin overhead camshaft engine could produce 230bhp at 5500rpm and a top speed of 130mph.

1965 Maserati Quattroporte, right-hand drive, good overall condition.
£7,250–7,750 *Bro*

1965 Maserati Mistral, Spyder coachwork by Frua, 6 cylinders, 3692cc, twin cam engine, 5 speed ZF gearbox, 4 wheel disc brakes, low mileage, extremely original condition.
Est. £35,000–45,000 *COYS*

1966 Maserati 3700GTi Sebring Series II Coupé, coachwork by Vignale, 6 cylinders, 3692cc, much renovation work undertaken, repainted, interior retrimmed, good overall condition.
£17,000–18,000 *COYS*

Make the most of Miller's

Condition is absolutely vital when assessing the value of a vehicle. Top class vehicles on the whole appreciate much more than less perfect examples. Rare, desirable cars may command higher prices even when in need of restoration.

1968 Maserati Mexico Series I Sports Saloon, very sound, good working order, right-hand drive.
Est. £6,000–9,000 *BKS*

1968 Maserati Mistral Coupé, coachwork by Frua, straight 6, double overhead camshaft, 4014cc engine, Borg Warner 3 speed automatic gearbox, air conditioning, left-hand drive, good condition.
£11,400–12,000 *C*

1967 Maserati Mistral Fixed Head Coupé, coachwork by Frua, left-hand drive, good overall condition.
£21,000–23,000 *BKS*

1968 Maserati Mexico Series I 4.7 Litre Sports Saloon, very good working order, right-hand drive.
Est. £11,000–12,000 *BKS*

r. **1968 Maserati Mistral 4 Litre GT Coupé,** 5 speed ZF manual gearbox, Borrani wire wheels, bodily and mechanically excellent.
£20,000–22,000 *BKS*

l. **1970 Maserati Tipo 115 Ghibli 2 Door Berlinetta,** coachwork by Ghia, 4719cc, V8 engine and bodywork in excellent condition.
£20,000–22,000 *BKS*

r. **1970 Maserati Mistral Spyder,** coachwork by Frua, excellent overall condition.
£42,000–48,000 *C*

The Mistral Spyder was announced at the Geneva show in 1964, mechanically identical to the coupé but with a conventional boot lid and a retractable fabric roof. A total of 120 were built.

Maserati Bora

- The Bora, introduced in 1971, was Maserati's first mid-engined road going car.
- Powered by a 4719cc V8 engine with 4 camshafts producing 310bhp, it could accelerate to 60mph in 6.9 seconds.
- With a top speed of 165mph and a stylish body designed by Giorgetto Giugiaro, the Bora was phased out in 1980.

1971 Maserati Indy 4.7, right-hand drive, very good condition.
£15,000–16,000 *H&H*

l. **1972 Maserati Indy Coupé,** coachwork by Vignale, right-hand drive, good condition overall, would benefit from some cosmetic attention.
£7,000–7,500 *COYS*

MASERATI Model	ENGINE cc/cyl	DATES	CONDITION 1	2	3
AG-1500	1488/6	1946-50	£30,000	£20,000	£10,000
A6G	1954/6	1951-53	£50,000	£35,000	£22,000
A6G-2000	1985/6	1954-57	£45,000	£35,000	£20,000
3500GT	3485/6	1957-64	£25,000	£15,000	£9,000
5000GT	4935/8	1960-65	£40,000	£20,000	£10,000
Sebring	3694/6	1962-66	£25,000	£18,000	£10,000
Quattroporte	4136/8	1963-74	£14,000	£10,000	£7,000
Mistral	4014/6	1964-70	£15,000	£10,000	£7,500
Mexico	4719/8	1965-68	£15,000	£12,000	£8,000
Ghibli	4719/8	1967-73	£20,000	£15,000	£12,000
Ghibli-spyder	4136/8	1969-74	£50,000	£40,000	£25,000
Indy	4136/8	1969-74	£15,000	£13,000	£9,000
Bora	4719/8	1971-80	£25,000	£18,000	£11,000
Merak	2965/6	1972-81	£16,000	£14,000	£9,000
Khamsin	4930/8	1974-81	£14,000	£10,000	£8,000

1972 Maserati Indy 4.7, original right-hand drive, 5 speed gearbox, power-assisted steering, very good restored condition.
£15,000–16,000 *H&H*

1979 Maserati Kyalami, V8 twin overhead camshaft engine, 4200cc, 5 speed manual transmission, requires some body restoration.
£3,750–4,250 *DB*

1976 Maserati Merak SS, Berlinetta coachwork by Ital Design, ground up restoration, good condition.
£13,000–14,000 *COYS*

1980 Maserati Kyalami Sports Coupé, coachwork by Frua, right-hand drive, very good original condition.
£6,000–6,500 *BKS*

The Kyalami was created as a rescue measure for Maserati after the company's relationship with Citroën ended.

1980 Maserati Quattroporte III, V8 engine, 4930cc, 3 speed automatic gearbox, 4 wheel disc brakes, independent coil springs and telescopic shock absorbers all-round, left-hand drive, good condition.
£8,000–8,500 *C*

1987 Maserati 2500 Biturbo Spyder 2+2 Convertible Sports, coachwork by Zagato, servo-assisted disc braking all-round, central locking, electric windows, light alloy wheels, excellent low mileage condition.
£12,000–13,000 *S*

MATHIS

Make the Most of Miller's

Veteran Cars are those manufactured up to 31 December 1918. Only vehicles built before 31 December 1904 are eligible for the London/Brighton Commemorative Run. Vintage Cars are vehicles that were manufactured between 1 January 1919 and 31 December 1930.

Cross Reference
Restoration Projects

l. **c1932 Mathis TY 4 Door Saloon,** 4 cylinder side valve engine, 904cc, dry stored in a French barn for a number of years, requires total restoration.
£250–300 *S*

MATRA

1977 Matra Bagheera, 4 cylinders, 1442cc, imported into UK in 1984, 4 speed manual gearbox, very fair condition.
Est. £2,500–3,000 *ADT*

1965 Matra-Bonnet Djet V 2 Seater Sports, Gardini tuned 1108cc Renault engine, disc brakes, fibreglass bodywork, very good condition.
Est. £8,250–10,250 *BKS*

MAXWELL

The Maxwell Motor Company was one of the better known American manufacturers in the earlier days of motoring. They produced a large range of motor cars up until 1925.

MAYBACH

1938 Maybach SW38 Glaser Cabriolet, fully restored, excellent condition.
£235,000+ *BLK*

This car was once owned by German diplomat, Joachim von Ribbentrop.

l. **1911 Maxwell Model I 25hp 5 Seater Tourer,** 4 cylinders, 3248cc, good condition.
£15,000–17,000 *ADT*

MERCEDES-BENZ

One of the most desirable symbols in the motoring world is the famous three-pointed star of Mercedes-Benz. The sons of Gottlieb Daimler, Paul and Adolf, proposed the star as the emblem, as their father had once remarked that 'from here a star will rise (he was working at a picture of the factory) and my hope is that my family will benefit from it.'

When Daimler and Benz merged in 1926, the star became surrounded by the laurel wreath that featured on the Benz trademark. This new emblem has featured on all Mercedes-Benz passenger cars since.

1952 Mercedes-Benz 220S 2 Seater Drophead Coupé, good condition throughout.
£23,000–24,000 *S*

c1937 Mercedes-Benz 170V 4 Door Saloon, left-hand drive, condition generally sound, but some work required.
Est. £4,500–5,500 *BKS*

1958 Mercedes-Benz 219, right-hand drive, good condition.
£5,000–5,500 *COYS*

1958 Mercedes-Benz 220S Drophead Coupé, good general condition, recommissioning before use is recommended.
£17,000–18,000 *S*

Mercedes-Benz 220 Series

- Introduced in 1951, the 200 Series featured a 6 cylinder engine with valves set across the cylinder head, not in line.
- The 2195cc engine, with a single Solex carburettor, produced 80bhp at 4500rpm.
- The 220A of 1955 developed 96bhp from the same power unit.
- Initially the 220 was available only as a 4 door saloon, but 2 door coupé and cabriolet models were launched in 1956.
- The final derivative, the 220S, produced 120bhp and boasted a top speed of 100mph.

1955 Mercedes-Benz 300SL Gullwing Coupé, excellent original condition throughout.
£125,000+ *COYS*

1958 Mercedes-Benz 300SL, left-hand drive, good condition, engine rebuilt, some attention required.
Est. £80,000–85,000 *C*

r. **1962 Mercedes-Benz 190SL Roadster,** left-hand drive, factory hard top, fully restored.
£46,000–50,000 *BKS*

1960 Mercedes-Benz 300SL, very good condition throughout.
£80,000–85,000 *COYS*

MERCEDES-BENZ Model	ENGINE cc/cyl	DATES	1	2	3
300AD	2996/6	1951-62	£12,000	£10,000	£8,000
220A/S/SE Ponton	2195/6	1952-60	£10,000	£5,000	£2,000
220S/SEB Coupé	2915/6	1956-59	£9,000	£5,000	£3,500
220S/SEB Cabriolet	2195/6	1958-59	£22,000	£18,000	£7,000
190SL	1897/4	1955-63	£17,000	£13,000	£10,000
300SL 'Gullwing'	2996/6	1954-57	£120,000	£100,000	£70,000
300SL Roadster	2996/6	1957-63	£110,000	£90,000	£70,000
230/250SL	2306/ 2496/6	1963-68	£13,000	£9,000	£7,000
280SL	2778/6	1961-71	£14,000	£10,000	£8,000
220/250SE	2195/ 2496/6	1960-68	£8,000	£6,000	£3,000
300SE	2996/6	1961-65	£10,000	£8,000	£5,000
280SE Convertible	2778/6	1965-69	£20,000	£16,000	£12,000
280SE V8 Convertible	3499/8	1969-71	£25,000	£18,000	£15,000
280SE Coupé	2496/6	1965-72	£10,000	£5,000	£3,000
300SEL 6.3	6330/8	1968-72	£12,000	£7,000	£3,500
600 & 600 Pullman	6332/8	1964-81	£40,000+	£15,000	£8,000

1963 Mercedes-Benz 190SL, restored to the highest standard, excellent overall condition.
£28,000–30,000 *COYS*

1961 Mercedes-Benz 220SE, good condition.
£1,500–2,000 *H&H*

1960 Mercedes-Benz 190SL Roadster, with hard top, only one owner.
£20,000–25,000 *FHF*

1962 Mercedes-Benz 220SEB Convertible, 6 cylinder in line overhead camshaft engine, 2195cc, 130bhp at 5000rpm, disc brakes, 4 speed manual gearbox, upper/lower A-arms with coil springs front suspension, swing axles with coil springs rear, right-hand drive, good example with excellent provenance.
£13,250–13,750 *C*

l. **1965 Mercedes-Benz 220SEB Saloon,** good condition throughout.
£3,600–3,800 *BKS*

1968 Mercedes-Benz 300SEL, perfect working order, generally good condition.
Est. £4,750–5,500 *ADT*

1966 Mercedes-Benz 250SE, good overall condition.
£7,000–7,500 *HOLL*

l. **1968 Mercedes-Benz 600 Pullman 6 Door Limousine,** overall excellent condition.
£48,000–50,000 *S*

This car was formerly the property of Beatles member, Ringo Starr.

**1968 Mercedes-Benz 600 Four Door Pullman
Limousine,** left-hand drive, automatic gearbox,
restored condition.
£48,000–52,000 *BKS*

1969 Mercedes-Benz 280SEC 2 Door Coupé,
restored to very good overall condition.
Est. £11,500–12,500 *BKS*

1972 Mercedes-Benz 250CE, 6 cylinder,
2496cc engine, floorpan requires attention,
good condition.
£3,000–3,400 *ADT*

1970 Mercedes-Benz 280SE, 3.5 litre, 8 cylinders,
3499cc, good original condition.
£8,000–9,000 *COYS*

1972 Mercedes-Benz 280SE, one owner,
full service history.
£4,000–5,000 *VIC*

1972 Mercedes-Benz 280S, 6 cylinder,
2800cc engine, very good condition.
£1,900–2,200 *ADT*

1960 Mercedes-Benz 300D 'Adenauer' Saloon,
restored to very good condition.
£30,000–35,000 *BKS*

*Only 3,077 examples of the 300D were built in a
production span from 1957–62.*

> **Don't Forget!**
> *If in doubt please refer
> to the 'How to Use'
> section at the beginning
> of this book.*

l. **1968 Mercedes-Benz 280SE
Cabriolet,** 6 cylinders, 2800cc,
very good condition.
£16,500–17,000 *COYS*

1924 Rolls-Royce 3.2 Litre 20hp 5 Seater Open Tourer, overhauled, engine complete and original.
£19,000–20,000 *BKS*

1926 Rolls-Royce 20hp, three-quarter cabriolet de ville coachwork by Barker, pushrod 6 cylinder, 3127cc engine, excellent condition throughout.
Est. £28,000–32,000 *BKS*

1924 Rolls-Royce Silver Ghost.
£50,000–52,000 *BLE*

Ex-Maharaja's car.

1927 Rolls-Royce 20hp 4 Light Sports Saloon, 6 cylinder, 3127cc in line monobloc engine, pushrod operated overhead valves, good condition.
£14,500–15,500 *S*

1928 Rolls-Royce Phantom I Tourer, coachwork by Wilkinson of Derby, only 300 miles recorded since restoration, excellent condition.
£41,000–43,000 *BKS*

1928 Rolls-Royce Springfield Phantom I 40/50hp Ascot Dual Cowl Phæton, coachwork by Brewster, US specification, original and excellent example.
Est. £110,000–120,000 *BKS*

1928 Rolls-Royce 20 Four Seater Tourer, good general condition throughout.
£17,000–18,000 *BKS*

1929 Rolls-Royce Phantom I Convertible Sedan, coachwork by Hibbard & Darrin, 6 cylinder in line, 7668cc overhead valve engine, superb fully restored condition.
£112,000–120,000 *CNY*

1930 Rolls-Royce 20/25 3.7 Litre Continental Sports Saloon, coachwork by Barker, 6 cylinder, 3699cc overhead valve engine, superb condition with an interesting history.
£25,000–27,000 *BKS*

1931 Rolls-Royce 20/25 Maythorn Limousine, original D-back 6 light limousine, in storage for some time, sound structural condition, twin side-mounted spare wheels.
£17,000–18,500 *RCC*

1931 Rolls-Royce Phantom II Continental Sedanca Drophead Coupé, in the style of Gurney Nutting, superb useable condition.
Est. £65,000–80,000 *BKS*
Only 281 Phantom II Continental chassis were produced.

1931 Rolls-Royce 40/50hp Phantom II Croydon Convertible Coupé, coachwork by Brewster, excellent condition throughout.
£110,000+ *BKS*
Formerly owned by Charlie Chaplin.

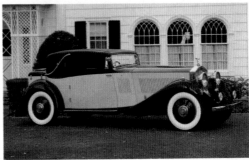

1933 Rolls-Royce Phantom II Fixed Head Coupé, coachwork by Gurney Nutting, 6 cylinder, 7668cc engine, 4 speed manual gearbox, drum brakes, excellent condition throughout.
£140,000+ *CNY*

1933 Rolls-Royce Phantom II Continental Close-Coupled Sports Saloon, coachwork by James Young, excellent condition throughout.
Est. £100,000–120,000 *S*

1932 Rolls-Royce 20/25 Limousine, coachwork by Thrupp & Maberly, 6 cylinder, 3164cc engine, 7 passenger limousine body, restored, excellent condition.
Est. £19,000–23,000 *ADT*

1933 Rolls-Royce Series Y 20/25 Foursome 2 Door Fixed Head Coupé, coachwork by Park Ward, long wheelbase chassis, good condition.
£24,000–26,000 *BKS*

1933 Rolls-Royce Phantom II Continental Sedanca de Ville, coachwork by Park Ward, winner of numerous awards, well patinated older restoration.
Est. £70,000–80,000 *S*

1933 Rolls-Royce Phantom II Continental Touring Saloon, coachwork by Barker & Co, sympathetic restoration, all original fittings.
£44,000–46,000 *S*

1934 Rolls-Royce Phantom II, coachwork by Barker & Co, very good restored condition.
£30,000–33,000 *S*

1934 Rolls-Royce 20/25 Sports Saloon, coachwork by Thrupp & Maberly, 6 cylinder overhead valve engine, 3699cc, very good condition, some attention required.
£15,000–16,000 *BKS*

1934 Rolls-Royce 20/25 Sports Saloon, coachwork by Hooper, excellent condition.
£24,000–26,000 *S*

1933 Rolls-Royce Phantom II Continental Faux Cabriolet, coachwork by Gurney Nutting, 6 cylinders, 7668cc, 4 speed manual gearbox, 4 wheel drum brakes, solid axle, semi-elliptic leaf springs suspension, right-hand drive.
£148,000–150,000 *CNY*

1932 Rolls-Royce 20/25 All Weather Tourer, coachwork by Barker & Co, 3.7 litres, 6 cylinders, 3699cc, collapsible Auster screen.
Est. £30,000–40,000 *COYS*

1935 Rolls-Royce 20/25 Two Door Fixed Head Coupé, coachwork by Henri Chapron, 3.7 litres, excellent condition throughout.
Est. £27,000–32,000 *BKS*

1935 Rolls-Royce Phantom II 40/50 Series T2 Sports Limousine, coachwork by Arthur Mulliner of Northampton, engine recently rebuilt.
£27,000–29,000 *BKS*

l. **1935 Rolls-Royce Phantom II 40/50 Sedanca de Ville,** coachwork by H. J. Mulliner & Co Ltd, general presentation to a high standard.
£37,000–39,000 *BKS*

1935 Rolls-Royce 20/25 Landaulette, coachwork by Thrupp & Maberly, 6 cylinders, 3699cc, 4 speed manual gearbox, very good condition.
£33,000–35,000 *BKS*

1939 Rolls-Royce Wraith Limousine, independent front suspension, very good restored condition.
£18,000–20,000 *S*

1958 Rolls-Royce Silver Cloud I Saloon,
6 cylinders, overhead inlet valve, side exhaust, 4887cc, 175bhp at 4500rpm, 4 speed automatic gearbox, 4 wheel drum brakes, left-hand drive, low mileage, mechanically restored, superb example.
£22,000–24,000 *CNY*

1954 Rolls-Royce Silver Dawn 4 Door Saloon, automatic transmission, good condition throughout.
£34,000–36,000 *BKS*

1937 Rolls-Royce 25/30 Sedanca de Ville, very good condition.
£24,000–25,000 *BLE*

1956 Rolls-Royce Silver Cloud I Drophead Coupé, coachwork by H. J. Mulliner, power steering, automatic transmission, electrically operated windows, altimeter, P-100 headlights mounted on front bumper, Everflex top, burr walnut picnic tables, left-hand drive, excellent condition throughout.
£340,000+ *S*

1962 Rolls-Royce Phantom V Two Door Coupé, coachwork by James Young, electrically operated windows, air conditioning, 45,000 miles, left-hand drive, excellent condition throughout.
£235,000+ *BLK*

*r.***1960 Rolls-Royce Silver Cloud II Drophead Coupé,** coachwork by H. J. Mulliner, luggage set, factory installed air conditioning, very good condition throughout.
£150,000+ *BLK*

1965 Rolls-Royce Silver Cloud III Drophead Coupé, restored, very good condition. **Est. £48,000–55,000** *S*

1965 Rolls-Royce Phantom V Seven Passenger Touring Limousine, very good condition throughout. **£55,000–57,000** *S*

1966 Rolls-Royce Silver Cloud III Continental Drophead Coupé, coachwork by Mulliner Park Ward, left-hand drive, cosmetic restoration, very good condition. **£110,000+** *BLK*

1968 Rolls-Royce Phantom VI Seven Seater Limousine, coachwork by Mulliner Park Ward, original air conditioning, 4 speed automatic gearbox, major mechanical service. **£52,000–55,000** *BKS*

1965 Rolls-Royce Silver Cloud III Four Door Cabriolet, long wheelbase, left-hand drive, superb condition. **£222,000+** *S*

1982 Rolls-Royce Silver Spirit, 56,000 miles, full service history. **£14,000–18,000** *VIC*

1974 Rolls-Royce Silver Shadow, 8 cylinders, 6750cc, good overall condition. **£6,400–6,800** *ADT*

1966 Rolls-Royce Phantom V Seven Passenger Limousine, coachwork by Mulliner Park Ward, left-hand drive, 31,000 miles, excellent condition. **£46,000–48,000** *S*

1966 Rolls-Royce Phantom V State Landaulette, coachwork by Mulliner Park Ward, part-glazed roof, power-operated top, burr walnut trim, cocktail cabinet with Waterford crystal set, excellent condition. **£200,000+** *S*

1985 Rolls-Royce Camargue, 8 cylinders, 6750cc, very well maintained, full service history, 21,000 miles, excellent condition. **£50,000–55,000** *ADT*

1947 Rover 12hp Open 4 Seater Tourer,
4 cylinder in line engine, overhead valves, 1496cc,
4 speed synchromesh gearbox, semi-elliptic spring
suspension front and rear, excellent condition.
£8,000–8,400 *C*

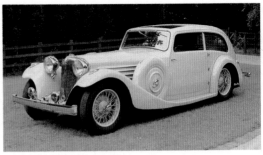

1934 SS1 Four Seater Airline Coupé, 6 cylinders,
1608cc, synchromesh gearbox, restored, maintained
to the highest standards.
£28,000–32,000 *COYS*

**1938 SS100 Jaguar 'Grey Lady' Fixed Head
Coupé,** restored to original specification, excellent
condition, good provenance.
Est. £140,000–160,000 *BKS*

1939 SS Jaguar 100 2½ Litre Sports Roadster,
6 cylinder engine with side valves and pushrods,
restored to excellent condition.
Est. £65,000–75,000 *BKS*

1948 Triumph 2000 Roadster, 4 cylinders, 2088cc,
3 speed gearbox, low mileage, original and unspoilt
example, excellent condition.
£11,000–12,000 *COYS*

1938 Talbot T150C 'Lago Special' Cabriolet,
4 litre engine, 4 speed Wilson preselector gearbox,
sprung steering wheel, superb overall condition.
Est. £115,000–130,000 *BKS*

1958 Triumph TR3A, 4 cylinders, 1991cc,
mechanically overhauled, interior retrimmed and
replaced, very good condition throughout.
Est. £10,500–12,000 *ADT*

1930 Sunbeam 18.2hp Sportsman Coupé,
6 cylinders, 2194cc, mechanically and bodily
restored, one of only 50 built, excellent condition.
Est. £16,000–20,000 *COYS*

1960 Triumph TR3A Open Sports,
4 cylinders, 1991cc, excellent condition,
undergone a complete body-off restoration.
£12,750–13,500 *COYS*

1971 Triumph Herald 13/60 Convertible,
4 cylinder, overhead valve engine, 1296cc,
4 speed manual gearbox, front disc brakes, rear
drum, independent coil spring front suspension,
transverse leaf spring rear.
£3,000–3,500 *C*

1974 Triumph Stag, 8 cylinders, 2997cc,
automatic gearbox, engine overhauled,
good useable condition.
£3,300–3,600 *ADT*

1974 Triumph TR6, 6 cylinders, 2498cc, 4 speed
manual gearbox, engine, paintwork and interior
in good condition, full service history.
Est. £7,500–9,500 *ADT*

The TR6 was in production for more than 7 years.

1925 Vauxhall 30/98 Special Two Seater,
counterbalanced crank engine, well-known
example in excellent condition throughout.
£80,000–85,000 *BKS*

**1976 Triumph Stag Sports Convertible with
Hard Top,** 90° V8 single overhead camshaft,
2997cc, 145bhp at 5500rpm, automatic gearbox,
front disc brakes, rear drum, independent front
and rear suspension, excellent condition.
£7,500–8,000 *C*

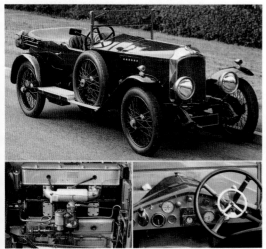

1923 Vauxhall 30/98 Velox Fast Tourer,
110bhp, engine overhauled, completely
restored, in excellent condition.
£120,000+ *BKS*

**1977 VW Beetle Cabriolet 1303S Four Seater
Cabriolet,** coachwork by Karmann, 1584cc,
60bhp, only 18,000 miles, excellent condition.
£9,000–10,000 *COYS*

1925 Morris Cowley Bullnose Van, with
3 alternative bodies, excellent restored condition.
£14,750–15,250 *Mot*

The tourer body version of the **1925 Morris
Cowley Bullnose,** *featured above.*

**1973 Range Rover
'Camper' by Carmichael,**
V8 overhead valve, 3528cc,
engine, 178bhp at 4750rpm,
automatic gearbox, disc
brakes, radius arms front
suspension, Panhard rod
and coil springs rear, very
low mileage, excellent
all-round condition.
£15,000–16,000 *C*

1936 Austin 7 Pick-Up, converted from
a saloon car, good condition.
£2,000–3,000 *SW*

1922 Ford Model T Motor Bus, 4 cylinders
2890cc, 20hp, 2 speeds, recently re-commissioned.
£14,500–15,500 *C*

1927 Albion EB24 Shooting Brake, coachwork by
J. W. Fleet, 4 cylinders, 4 speed gearbox, ready for use.
£30,000–32,000 *BKS*

1938 Austin 7 5cwt Delivery Van,
fully restored, engine rebuilt,
5000 miles, very good condition.
£4,800–5,200 *MAW*

1912 Autocar Type XXI Passenger Bus,
2 cylinders, 2639cc, magneto ignition, 3 speed
gearbox, seats for 14 passengers, very good condition.
£13,500–14,000 *S*

1931 Caravan Car Cruiser, excellent
restored condition.
£3,000–4,000 *SW*

c1980 ERA Replica Child's Racing Car, 5hp Briggs & Stratton petrol engine, metal bodied.
£2,250–2,650 *S*

A Tri-ang Veteran Style Pedal Car, restored.
£330–360 *HOLL*

1989 Aston Martin Junior Volante, Honda 320cc 8hp Type GXV 160 engine.
£5,200–6,200 *BKS*

1949 Austin Pathfinder, superb condition throughout, restored to full working order.
£2,600–2,900 *ADT*

1967 Jomoro Child's Single Seater Racing Car, Briggs & Stratton 1.5hp engine.
£1,400–1,600 *BKS*

c1945 Austin J40 Child's Pedal Car, resprayed in blue livery.
£575–425 *AAV*

1968 Lotus Formula One Child's Racing Car, petrol engine, excellently restored, very rare.
£8,500–9,500 *CNY*

An Alfa Romeo P3 Child's Racing Car, modelled on the 'Monoposto' Grand Prix racer.
£1,800–2,000 *BKS*

1966 Chaparral 2F Child's Racing Car, petrol engine, gullwing doors, excellently restored.
Est. £8,000–12,000 *CNY*

1995 Ferrari F40 Child's Electric 2 Seater, 12volts, plastic body, fittings on tubular steel chassis.
£450–500 *CARS*
The full-sized Ferrari Mondial is used for comparison.

c1970 BRM Child's Pedal Car, styled on the Marlboro sponsored GP machines, glass reinforced plastic body, 45in (114cm) long.
£190–210 *BKS*

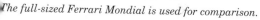

1968 Abarth 850 TC Corsa Saloon, 4 cylinders, 982cc, single Weber 36 DCD7 carburettor, 90bhp, 5 speed gearbox, Girling front disc brakes and Bilsten gas-filled dampers, foam-filled fuel tank, five-point safety harness, racing seat, steel roll cage with door bars, Campagnolo alloy wheels, fire extinguisher, excellent condition. Est. £18,000–24,000 *COYS*

1964–65 AC Cobra 5 Litre Competition Roadster. £175,000+ *BKS*

1924–80 Alfa Romeo RL with RLTF Targa Florio Modifications, excellent condition. Est. £56,000–60,000 *BKS*

1974 Renault Alpine A110 1600 SI Two Seater Sports Coupé, Koni dampers, very good condition. Est. £12,000–18,000 *BKS*

1937 Alvis 4.3 Litre Sports Racing 2 Seater, shortened chassis, very good overall condition. £44,000–45,000 *BKS*

Built as a special by Harold Barr in the late 1950s.

1981 Audi Quattro 2.2 Litre Turbo Charged 4 Wheel Drive Long Wheelbase International Rally Car, 5 cylinders, very good condition. Est. £11,000–13,000 *BKS*

r. **1957 AC Ace Bristol Open Sports,** 6 cylinders, 1998cc, 125bhp, completely restored, steel crankshaft, Cosworth pistons, excellent condition throughout. Est. £45,000–55,000 *COYS*

A highly competitive car with 48 race results in recent years, including class wins. With FIA papers.

1985 Audi Quattro Sport Group B Works Rally Car, full factory rally specification with new 400/450bhp works engine, 5 speed gearbox with bullet clutch, original Kevlar Carbon body with chrome moly roll cage.
Est. £40,000–45,000 *BKS*

1964 Austin Healey 3000 MkIII 3 Litre Sports 2+2, 2912cc, built to works rally specification, aluminium body, side exit exhaust, front wing vents, good condition.
Est. £30,000–35,000 *BKS*

l. **1964 Ex-Works Austin Healey 3000 MkIII Two Seater Competition Sports,** 6 cylinders, 2912cc, 3 double choke Weber carburettors, 4 wheel disc brakes, superb condition.
Est. £60,000–80,000 *COYS*

1959 Austin Healey 3000 Mark I Competition Roadster with hard top, 6 cylinders, 2994cc.
Est. £15,000–20,000 *COYS*

1965 Brabham BT14 Formula Libra, Lotus twin cam engine, restored to as new condition.
£28,000–30,000 *Car*
One of only 10 made with chassis No. FL-2-65.

1922 Bentley 3 Litre TT Car, 4 cylinders, 2996cc, 4 speed and reverse gearbox, excellent condition.
£69,000–72,000 *C*

1972 Brabham-Ford BT38 1.6 Litre Formula 2 Hillclimb Single Seater, very good condition.
Est. £12,000–15,000 *BKS*

1967 Brabham BT21B, 4 cylinders, 1038cc, excellent condition.
£16,500–17,500 *COYS*

1972 Brabham BT38 Formula 2 Single Seater Rolling Chassis and Gearbox.
Est. £9,500–12,500 *BKS*

1964 BRM P261 Formula One/Tasman Single Seater Racing, excellent condition throughout.
£220,000+ *BKS*

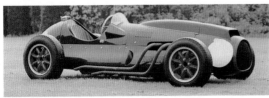

1953 Cooper-Bristol Formula 2 Single Seater,
6 cylinders, 1971cc, immaculate, ready to race condition.
£48,000–50,000 *COYS*

1957 Cooper-Climax T43 Formula 2 Single Seater, 1.5 litres, very good overall condition.
£26,000–28,000 *BKS*

1969 Crosslé 16F Formula Ford, 1600cc engine, restored in 1993, condition as new.
£12,500–14,500 *Car*

1959 Elva Formula Junior, BMC A engine,
4 cylinders, 994cc, excellent all-round condition.
£29,000–34,500 *C*

1970 Chevron-BMW B8 Racing Coupé,
new BMW racing engine, rebuilt chassis,
very good condition.
Est. £35,000–40,000 *BKS*

1968 Chevron B8 BMW GT Racing Car, 2 litre race engine, needs attention.
£30,000–35,000 *Car*

1965 Ford Mustang Fastback Racing Saloon,
V8 engine, 400bhp, entirely stripped and rebuilt.
£15,000–16,000 *BKS*

1975-76 Ferrari 312T Formula One GP Single Seater, one of only 5 built.
£210,000+ *BKS*

r. **1964 Ferrari 250 Le Mans,** Berlinetta coachwork by Pininfarina, excellent provenance, superb condition throughout, original Scuderia Filipinetti livery, ready to be driven, excellent restored condition throughout.
£400,000+ *COYS*

l. **1966/84 Ford GT40 MkIIA Sports-Racing Coupé,** 8 cylinders, 6998cc, finished to definitive 1966 Mark IIA configuration, complete with all authentic parts. **£84,000–88,000** *COYS*

1993-95 Jaguar XJ220C 3.5 Litre Turbocharged 2 Door Competition Coupé, engine rebuilt by TWR, completely restored to running condition. **Est. £60,000–90,000** *BKS*

1921 Ford Model T Racer, 4 cylinder in line engine, 3 speed manual gearbox, 4 wheel drum brakes. **£6,750–7,500** *C*

1963 Lightning Formula Junior, 1100cc Ford MAE engine, good condition. **£14,000–16,000** *Car*

1959 Kieft-Climax Sports-Racing, 4 cylinders, 1098cc, fair to good condition, last sports-racer built by the company. **£10,000–12,000** *COYS*

1959 Lister-Chevrolet Costin-Bodied 5.7 Litre Sports-Racing 2 Seater, rebuilt engine, good provenance, ready to race. **£120,000+** *BKS*

1969 Lola-Chevrolet T70 GT MkIIIB 5.7 Litre Group 6 Competition Coupé, V8 Chevrolet engine, 500bhp, Hewland LG600 gearbox, 4 Weber 461DA down draught carburettors, renovated, well known provenance, excellent condition. **Est. £70,000–90,000** *BKS*

1987 Lola T87-30, rebuilt carbon fibre body, good overall condition. **Est. £20,000–22,000** *S*
This car was designed and built for the French team, Larrousse, for their debut in Formula I in 1987.

1956 Lotus 11 Sports, 4 cylinder, 1098cc Coventry Climax FWA engine, Austin A35 gearbox, drum brakes fitted to front, ready to race condition, full documentation including FIA papers.
£21,000–23,000 *COYS*

c1960 Lotus-Coventry Climax FPF Type 18 Formula One Grand Prix Single Seater.
£32,000–34,000 *BKS*

1968 Lotus 51C Ex-Works Formula Ford, 1600cc engine, restored, as new condition.
£13,500–15,000 *Car*

1962 Lotus 23 Uprated to B Specification, 4 cylinders, double overhead camshaft, 1594cc, 180bhp, 5 speed manual gearbox, 4 wheel disc brakes.
Est. £32,000–38,000 *C*

1965 Lotus Cortina MkI Ex-Works, 4 cylinders, 1588cc, original in every respect.
£36,000–38,000 *COYS*

1938 Maserati 6cm 1.5 Litre Racing Vetturetta, part dismantled, highly original, restored, in running order, ready for race preparation.
£140,000+ *BKS*

1987 March Leyton House Formula One, V8 Ford Cosworth, DFV 3000cc engine, Hewland 5 speed gearbox.
£45,000–47,000 *C*

1954 Maserati 250F 2½ Litre Formula One Grand Prix Single Seater, a well-known car with good provenance, excellent condition.
£600,000+ *BKS*

c1960 Maserati Tipo 61 'Birdcage' 2 Seater Sports-Racing Spyder, 2 litre engine, very good condition.
£450,000+ *BKS*

l. **1955 Maserati 300S Open Sports-Racing,** coachwork by Fantuzzi, 6 cylinders, 2993cc, coil spring wishbone front suspension, de Dion axle leaf spring, rear, excellent competition record, superb condition.
£400,000+ *COYS*

1986 Maserati 450S Replica Sports-Racing 2 Seater, by Wymondham Engineering, for the Cannonball Run in the US, mechanically excellent. **£40,000–42,000** *BKS*

1956 Moretti Tipo 1500 E GT Golden Arrow Based Mille Miglia Barchetta, excellent overall condition. **Est. £30,000–40,000** *BKS*

1959 Osca Formula Junior, 4 cylinder Fiat engine, 1089cc, 88bhp at 7500rpm, excellent condition. **Est. £35,000–40,000** *C*

1973 Porsche 911 Carrera RS Lightweight Coupé, club competition specification, well-known car. **Est. £22,000`–28,000** *BKS*

500 Carrera RS were introduced in 1973 and proved so popular that it enabled them to race in Group 3.

1932 Riley Special Single Seater Racing Car, 4 cylinders, 1496cc, VSCC car, excellent condition. **£16,000–18,000** *C*

1987 Ralt TR31 Single Seater, 4 cylinders, 2000cc, refitted with Volkswagen engine, very good condition. **£8,000–9,000** *COYS*

This car was supplied new for 1987 season and raced.

r. **1935 Riley TT Sprite Open Sports-Racing,** 6 cylinders, 1808cc, 75bhp, well known racing car, excellent condition throughout. **£28,000–30,000** *COYS*

1946 Strang Formula 3-500, 499cc engine. **£7,250–7,750** *DB*

The first 500cc car to be completed in 1946 for a new formula.

1971 Surtees-Chevrolet TS8 Formula 5000 Single Seater, 5 litre V8 engine, well presented, potentially competitive. **Est. £20,000–30,000** *BKS*

1980 Formula Monza Single Seater, 499cc, modified Fiat 500F engine believed to produce around 50bhp, 4 speed gearbox, good condition. **£600–800** *COYS*

1960 Lotus Team Elite Replica 2 Seater Sports, 1216cc Coventry Climax Series II FWE engine, rebuilt as an ultra-lightweight racer. **Est. £18,000–24,000** *BKS*

1995 Jaguar C-Type Replica, by Heritage, 4.2 litre, 6 cylinder engine, triple 45DCOE Weber carburettors, 185bhp, Jaguar suspension. **Est. £29,500–32,500** *ADT*

1979/92 Daytona Spyder 2 Seater Sports Roadster, Jaguar 5.3 litre V12 fuel injected engine, Getrag gearbox, 40,000 miles, excellent condition. **£9,500–10,000** *BKS*

1990 GTD 40 Two Seater Sports Coupé, replica of the Ford GT40, Ford 90° V8 small block engine, 4950cc, 250bhp at 6000rpm, air conditioning, right-hand drive, professionally built. **Est. 18,000–22,000** *C*

1956-57 Talbot-Maserati Dubonnet Barquette de Course, 6 cylinder twin camshaft 2.5 litre engine, 230bhp, very good condition with excellent provenance. **Est. £250,000–300,000** *BKS*

1970/1980s L & R Roadsters D-Type Sports Racing 2 Seater, 3.4 Litre XK engine with triple Weber carburettors, fibreglass coachwork, concours standards. **Est. £18,000–22,000** *BKS*

1966 Austin Healey 3000 MkIII Works Replica, 3 litre 6 cylinder engine, triple twin-choke Weber carburettors, 200bhp, overdrive on 3rd and 4th gears body-off restoration, converted to right-hand drive. **£22,000–24,000** *BKS*

c1982 Ford GT40 Replica, by KVA, 6 cylinders, 3100cc, 220bhp, new exhaust system very good condition throughout. **£9,250–9,750** *COYS*

1964 Mercedes-Benz SL Pagoda Hard Top,
occasional rear seat, rare white steering wheel,
restored, history.
£16,000–17,000 *UMC*

1965 Mercedes-Benz 230SL, left-hand drive,
very good restored condition.
£13,000–13,500 *CFI*

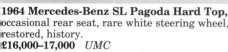

1965 Mercedes-Benz 230SL, 6 cylinder, 2281cc
engine, very good condition mechanically, repainted.
Est. £13,750–15,500 *ADT*

1966 Mercedes-Benz 230SL Roadster,
6 cylinder, 2300cc engine, 150bhp at 5500rpm,
4 speed manual gearbox, front disc brakes, rear
drum brakes, independent front suspension,
single joint swing axle rear, coil springs, left-
hand drive, low mileage, excellent virtually
unused condition.
£42,000–45,000 *CNY*

1968 Mercedes-Benz 280SL Convertible,
right-hand drive, no known modifications to
original specification, good condition throughout.
£11,000–12,000 *BKS*

1969 Mercedes-Benz 280SL, 6 cylinder,
2778cc engine, well maintained, good
condition throughout.
£18,000–19,000 *ADT*

l. **1970 Mercedes-Benz 280SL,**
6 cylinder, 2778cc engine,
very good overall condition.
£11,000–12,000 *ADT*

Don't Forget!
*If in doubt please refer
to the 'How to Use'
section at the beginning
of this book.*

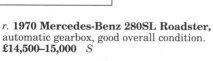

r. **1970 Mercedes-Benz 280SL Roadster,**
automatic gearbox, good overall condition.
£14,500–15,000 *S*

1970 Mercedes-Benz 280SL, 6 cylinder, 2778cc engine, excellent condition.
£16,000–17,000 *COYS*

1974 Mercedes-Benz 450SEL, fully restored condition.
Est. £5,500–6,500 *ADT*

1976 Mercedes-Benz 280CE Coupé, right-hand drive, automatic gearbox, original example requiring some restoration.
£1,400–1,800 *C*

1977 Mercedes-Benz 450SEL Saloon, 6.9 litre engine, good overall condition, some restoration required.
£2,800–3,200 *S*

1977 Mercedes-Benz 450SLC, high mileage, major body restoration, history.
£6,000–8,000 *UMC*

1978 Mercedes-Benz 450SEL, 6.9 litre engine, right-hand drive, good condition throughout.
£3,300–3,800 *COYS*

1978 Mercedes-Benz 450SEL, 8 cylinder, 6834cc engine, right-hand drive, very good condition throughout.
£5,000–5,500 *COYS*

1978 Mercedes-Benz 450SEL, 6.9 litre engine, excellent condition throughout.
Est. £6,250–7,500 *ADT*

Mercedes-Benz 450SEL 6.9 Litre

- The 6.9 litre 450SEL was launched in 1975 using the long wheelbase 450 body shell.
- The 6834cc, V8 engine produced 286bhp using Bosch fuel injection.
- It could accelerate to 60mph in 7.4 seconds with a top speed of around 140mph.
- The 450SEL 6.9 litre cost almost twice as much as the ordinary 450SEL.
- Production ceased in 1979.

1979 Mercedes-Benz 450SEL Saloon, 6.9 litre engine, excellent condition throughout
£5,500–5,900 *BKS*

1979 Mercedes-Benz 450SEL, 6.9 litre, 8 cylinder, 6834cc engine, electric sunroof, air conditioning with climate control, electric windows, rear head rests, front arm rests and cruise control, very good condition with some restoration.
£10,300–10,800 *ADT*

1981 Mercedes-Benz 450SEL, 6.9 litre engine, paintwork stripped down and resprayed, good overall condition.
Est. £7,000–10,000 *S*

1972 Mercedes-Benz 350SL, alloy wheels, full history, optional rear seat.
£10,000–12,000 *VIC*

1974 Mercedes-Benz 350SL, left-hand drive, manual gearbox, good original condition.
£10,750–11,250 *Bro*

r. **1972 Mercedes-Benz 350SL,** 8 cylinder, 3499cc engine, full service history, good condition throughout, hard top requires some minor work.
£7,400–7,800 *ADT*

1979 Mercedes-Benz 230, 4 cylinder, 2307cc engine, very good condition.
£1,900–2,300 *ADT*

1972 Mercedes-Benz 350SC, good condition throughout.
£6,000–7,000 *H&H*

1972 Mercedes-Benz 350SL 2 Door Convertible, rust-free bodywork would benefit from cosmetic attention, no modifications from original specification.
Est. £8,000–9,000 *BKS*

Miller's is a price GUIDE not a price LIST

1973 Mercedes-Benz 350SL 2 Seater Sports, good original condition throughout.
£5,500–6,000 *BKS*

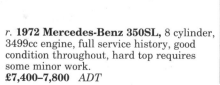

1975 Mercedes-Benz 350SL, 8 cylinder, 3500cc engine, recent total respray, good condition throughout.
Est. £6,750–7,500 *ADT*

1979 Mercedes-Benz 350SL Sports Coupé
3.5 litre, V8 engine, hard top, good condition, some small areas of corrosion.
Est. £7,000–9,000 *BKS*

1980 Mercedes-Benz 450SLC, 8 cylinder, 4520cc engine, some restoration, good condition.
£5,250–5,600 *ADT*

1984 Mercedes-Benz 380SL, automatic gearbox, air conditioning, high mileage, good overall condition.
£8,500–9,500 *CFI*

1979 Mercedes-Benz 450SL, 4.5 litre, V8 engine, automatic gearbox, later alloy wheels, good restored condition.
£10,250–10,750 *Mot*

1981 Mercedes-Benz 500SLC Special Edition Coupé, 4973cc, overhead camshaft, V8 engine, very good condition throughout.
£21,000–22,000 *BKS*

1980 Mercedes-Benz 450SL, hard top, alloy wheels, full service history, excellent condition.
£12,500–13,500 *SJR*

1984 Mercedes-Benz 500 SEC Coupé, leather trim, air conditioning, cruise control, ABS, alloy wheels, electric seats and sunroof, good condition.
£8,750–9,250 *Mot*

1990 Mercedes-Benz 190 Evolution II, 16,000 recorded miles, excellent condition.
£31,000–33,000 *BKS*

l. **1984 Mercedes-Benz 500 SEC,** good overall condition.
£6,000–6,500 *H&H*

MERCURY

1966 Mercury Monterey Convertible, V8 cast iron block, 390cu in engine, automatic gearbox, power steering, good original condition.
£5,000–5,400 *ADT*

MESSERSCHMITT

Designed by Fritz Fend, the Messerschmitt Kabinenroller was produced at the Messerschmitt aeroplane factory at Regensburg, Germany. Introduced in 1953, it was not available in the UK until 1955.

Powered by a Fichtel & Sachs 174cc engine which produced 9bhp, the KR175 was superseded in 1955 by the 191cc engined KR200. The KR175 could achieve 60mph from the single cylinder engine. Today the Messerschmitt is highly sought-after by collectors despite handlebar steering and cable-operated brakes.

l. **1959 Messerschmitt KR200 Cabin Scooter,** good original condition, requires recommissioning.
Est. £4,500–5,500 *BKS*

> **Cross Reference**
> Microcars

> **Make the most of Miller's**
>
> *Condition is absolutely vital when assessing the value of a vehicle. Top class vehicles on the whole appreciate much more than less perfect examples. Rare, desirable cars may command higher prices even when in need of restoration.*

l. **1959 Messerschmitt KR200 Kabinenroller,** museum stored, very good condition.
£4,000–4,400 *COYS*

METZ

1912 Metz 22 3 Litre Runabout, left-hand drive, original boa horn, excellent restored condition.
Est. £12,000–13,000 *H&H*

1914 Metz Two Seater, 4 cylinder engine, variable speed transmission, unrestored condition.
£3,000–4,000 *DB*

MG

The MGB was launched in September 1962 to supersede the MGA which by then had sold 100,000 units. Mechanically it was similar to the MGA but now featured the BMC B Series 4 cylinder, 1798cc engine which, with 95bhp, gave the MGB a top speed of about 105mph. It could accelerate to 60mph in 12.2 seconds and cost £950 when new.

It was a very popular car and in 1965 the MGB GT was introduced which was equally successful both at home and in the USA. The MGC was offered between 1967 and 1969 powered by the 2912cc, 6 cylinder engine from the Austin 3 litre.

Despite the introduction of the MGB GT V8 in the early 1970s, the increasingly tight controls governing the importation of cars to America led to changes including the infamous big black rubber bumpers which finally ended the MGB's 18 year production run in 1980. The final 1,000 cars, sold in 1981, were designated LE, limited editions, the roadsters were finished in bronze with gold stripes and the GTs in pewter with silver stripes; 420 and 580 respectively were built.

Probably the archetypal classic car, the MGB is as popular now as it ever was.

1934 MG N-Type Magnette, 6 cylinders, 1409cc, fully rebuilt, Godfrey K150 supercharger, VSCC blue form and FIA papers, distinguished history.
£28,000–30,000 *COYS*

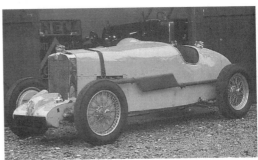

1934 MG Q-Type, 4 cylinder, 746cc supercharged engine, pre-selector 4 speed gearbox with overload clutch, 4 wheel 12in cable-operated drum brakes, semi-elliptic leaf spring suspension with sliding trunnions, right-hand drive, well maintained over past 30 years since restoration, good running order throughout, original example with fine provenance.
£60,000–65,000 *C*

1935 MG PA/PB Racing Special 'Bonagazoo', 4 cylinder, 939cc supercharged engine, 4 speed manual gearbox, 4 wheel drum brakes, semi-elliptic leaf spring suspension all round, right-hand drive, aluminium 2 seater body, shortened and lightened PA chassis, PB engine and gearbox fitted with Marshall supercharger.
Est. £18,000–22,000 *C*

This car is a well-known racing MG.

1939 MG TA Tickford Drophead Coupé, fully restored, excellent restored condition, taken many awards.
£32,000–35,000 *OCC*

The TA Tickford was produced for 1938 and replaced in 1939 by the TB. War stopped production after a total of over 400 examples had been produced by Salmons & Sons of Newport Pagnell.

1937 MG TA 2 Seater Sports Tourer, extensively restored, full engine and ancillary rebuild, reupholstered, twin trumpet horns, twin aero screens.
Est. £10,000–12,000 *BKS*

MG SA

- The MG SA Saloon was introduced in 1936.
- The 6 cylinder overhead valve engine produced 75bhp. The 2288cc engine was later increased to 2322cc.
- Available with saloon, open tourer or drophead coupé bodywork.
- Production ceased at the outbreak of WWII after a total of 2738 vehicles had been built.

1938 MG SA Saloon, rare 'barn discovery', straightforward restoration project.
£12,000–12,500 *BKS*

1948 MG TC, excellent condition throughout.
£20,000–22,000 *CFI*

1950 MG TD, excellent overall condition.
£10,750–11,250 *BLE*

This car was once the property of film star Rock Hudson.

1951 MG TD 2 Seater Sports, left-hand drive, paintwork faded, straightforward restoration required.
£7,200–7,800 *BKS*

The successor to the MG TC was the TD model with improved box section chassis, rack-and-pinion steering, independent front suspension with disc wheels and a synchronised gearbox.

1950 MG TD MkI, original right-hand drive, rebuilt from existing parts in 1990, with new parts fitted as required, original tonneau hood and side screens in good condition, mechanics very sound, very good condition.
£13,000–14,000 *SJR*

Cross Reference
Restoration Projects

1952 MG TD MkII, restored to high standard, good condition.
£9,250–9,750 *CGOC*

1953 MG TF, 4 cylinders, 1247cc, extensively restored, engine completely rebuilt.
£14,250–15,000 *COYS*

1954 MG TF 1250, original right-hand drive, well restored to original specifications with new frame, history.
£14,250–14,750 *Mot*

1954 MG TF 1500, original right-hand drive, good overall condition.
£13,500–14,000 *H&H*

1954 MG TF 1250, leather interior, totally rebuilt to show condition.
£13,750–14,250 *Mot*

1955/1993 MGA Le Mans Copy, built to highest possible standard.
£13,750–14,500 *H&H*

Produced in aluminium, this MGA has taken over 2,000 hours to rebuild making it almost totally a 'manufactured' car. The engine has been modified considerably, lightened and balanced, with the main modifications in the head gasket to the block. It is also fitted with a Le Mans oil cooler, steel wheels, and a 20 gallon fuel tank.

1956 MGA Roadster 1500, left-hand drive, fully restored to excellent condition in 1987, engine rebuilt.
£8,250–8,750 *Mot*

1956 MGA 1500 Roadster, 1492cc, totally restored, stainless steel exhaust system, engine and transmission rebuilt excellent condition.
£9,500–10,500 *H&H*

1958 MGA, 1500cc, solid wood floors, good mechanics, painted wire wheels, chrome boot rack, excellent condition.
£12,750–13,250 *SJR*

MGA

- Launched in 1955, the MGA replaced the traditionally styled T series sports cars.
- Powered by the new BMC 4 cylinder engine of 1489cc, it produced initially 68bhp at 5500rpm.
- The power rating was increased to 72bhp which could propel the MGA to 60mph in 15 seconds with a top speed of 97mph.
- Superseded by the MGA 1600 in 1969, the car was available as both a roadster and a fixed head coupé with a slightly better performing 1588cc engine.

1960 MGA Fixed Head Coupé,
very good condition.
Est. £5,000–6,000 *HOLL*

1960 MGA 1600, 4 cylinders, 1588cc,
chassis-up rebuild to original specification.
£12,500–13,250 *ADT*

1960 MGA Roadster MkI, 1600cc,
good paintwork, chrome wire
wheels, chrome 'knock-on spinners',
engine in good condition.
£13,500–14,000 *SJR*

1960 MGA MkI Fixed Head Coupé,
excellent mechanics, original right-hand
drive, chrome wire wheels, good condition.
£10,250–10,750 *SJR*

1968 MG 1300, 4 cylinders, 1275cc, standard
example, superb original order, under 20,000
recorded miles.
£3,200–3,600 *ADT*

1962 MGB 2 Seater Roadster, not used since
major restoration, original factory specification,
requires running in following engine rebuild.
Est. £7,000–8,500 *BKS*

1964 MGB Roadster, 4 cylinders, 1798cc,
mostly original, full respray, mechanically
without fault, retrimmed, only 43,000 miles.
£4,200–4,600 *ADT*

1967 MGB MkI, chrome wire wheels and
bumpers, original right-hand drive, new front
wings and rear wing sections, some restoration,
excellent condition.
£8,750–9,250 *SJR*

1968 MGC GT, 6 cylinders, 2912cc, Minilite style alloy wheels, fully restored, very good condition.
£4,000–5,000 *ADT*

1968 MGC Roadster, 3000cc, excellent restored condition.
£9,000–10,000 *SW*

1968 MGC GT, very good condition.
£4,250–5,000 *H & H*

1969 MGB 2 Seater Sports Roadster, fully rebuilt, excellent condition throughout.
£8,200–8,600 *BKS*

Since its rebuild, this car has been on display in the Haynes Motor Museum at Sparkford, Somerset.

l. **1969 MGB GT,** 1797cc, 4 cylinders, very good condition.
£4,250–5,000 *H & H*

MG Model	ENGINE cc/cyl	DATES	CONDITION 1	2	3
TC	1250/4	1946-49	£13,000	£11,000	£7,000
TD	1250/4	1950-52	£13,000	£9,000	£5,000
TF	1250/4	1953-55	£15,000	£13,000	£8,000
TF 1500	1466/4	1954-55	£16,000	£14,000	£9,000
YA/YB	1250/4	1947-53	£5,500	£2,750	£1,500
Magnette ZA/ZB	1489/4	1953-58	£3,000	£2,000	£500
Magnette Mk III/IV	1489/4	1958-68	£2,500	£850	£350
MGA 1500 Roadster	1489/4	1955-59	£9,000	£6,500	£3,500
MGA 1500 FHC	1489/4	1956-59	£7,000	£5,000	£3,000
MGA 1600 Roadster	1588/4	1959-61	£11,000	£9,000	£4,500
MGA 1600 FHC	1588/4	1959-61	£7,000	£5,000	£3,000
MGA Twin Cam Roadster	1588/4	1958-60	£17,000	£12,000	£9,000
MGA Twin Cam FHC	1588/4	1958-60	£14,000	£9,000	£7,000
MGA 1600 Mk II Roadster	1622/4	1961-62	£12,000	£10,000	£4,000
MGA 1600 Mk II FHC	1622/4	1961-62	£9,000	£7,000	£3,000
MGB Mk I	1798/4	1962-67	£7,000	£4,000	£1,200
MGB GT Mk I	1798/4	1965-67	£5,000	£3,500	£1,000
MGB Mk II	1798/4	1967-69	£7,500	£4,000	£1,500
MGB GT Mk II	1798/4	1969	£4,500	£2,500	£850
MGB Mk III	1798/4	1969-74	£6,500	£4,000	£1,100
MGB GT Mk III	1798/4	1969-74	£4,500	£2,500	£1,000
MGB Roadster (rubber bumper)	1798/4	1975-80	£6,000	£4,500	£1,200
MGB GT	1798/4	1975-80	£4,000	£3,000	£1,000
MGB Jubilee	1798/4	1975	£5,000	£3,000	£1,200
MGB LE	1798/4	1980	£8,500	£4,750	£2,250
MGB GT LE	1798/4	1980	£6,000	£3,750	£2,000
MGC	2912/6	1967-69	£8,000	£6,500	£4,000
MGC GT	2912/6	1967-69	£6,000	£4,500	£2,000
MGB GT V8	3528/8	1973-76	£9,000	£6,000	£3,000
Midget Mk I	948/4	1961-62	£4,000	£2,000	£850
Midget Mk II	1098/4	1962-66	£3,000	£2,000	£850
Midget Mk III	1275/4	1966-74	£3,200	£2,000	£850
Midget 1500	1491/4	1975-79	£3,000	£2,000	£850

All prices are for British right hand drive cars. Deduct 10-15% for left hand drive varieties, even if converted to right hand drive.

1971 MGB Roadster, very good restored condition.
£5,800–6,200 *ADT*

1973 MGB GT, very good overall condition.
£3,800–4,200 *ADT*

1975 MGB Roadster, good sound condition.
£4,400–4,800 *ADT*

1977 MGB V8 Roadster, 8 cylinders, 3528cc,
totally original and in excellent condition.
Est. £9,000–10,000 *ADT*

1981 MGB GT 2+2 LE Coupé, meticulously
maintained, unrestored as new condition.
£8,400–8,800 *S*

1979 MGB Roadster, genuine and original
one-owner car, with service history.
£3,800–4,200 *HOLL*

1979 MGB Roadster, cosmetic
restoration, 47,000 miles.
£4,400–4,800 *ADT*

1980 MGB GT, very good condition throughout.
£3,800–4,200 *ADT*

MINI

Launched in 1959, the Austin Seven, or Mini as it was soon to be known, was a revolution designed by Alec Issigonis. It used the BMC 4 Series engine of 848cc and took 24 seconds to reach 60mph.

John Cooper the racing car manufacturer developed the Mini, available in 997cc, 1071cc and ultimately with a 1275cc engine, and the Mini Cooper S was to claim many competition prizes including the Monte Carlo Rally in 1964. The Cooper S engine produced about 75bhp and could easily reach 100mph. The main difference between the Morris and the Austin Mini Coopers was the front grille, the slats being narrower on the Austin.

Mini Coopers are still available new today, and John Cooper's Garage in Sussex will still convert one to 'S' configuration.

1959 Austin Seven Mini, 4 cylinder, 848cc engine, restored to as new condition, believed to be earliest and most original survivor.
£12,000–12,500 *COYS*

Chassis 103 was the third Mini to be produced at Longbridge on 4th May, 1959.

1966 Austin Mini Cooper S MkI, undergone a complete restoration, carefully stored.
£4,400–4,800 *COYS*

1963 Austin Mini Super De Luxe, recorded mileage of 34,000, one family owned from new, good throughout and mostly original.
£1,800–2,200 *ADT*

1968 Austin Mini Cooper MkII, 998cc engine, excellent example of original mini.
£2,750–3,250 *H&H*

1969 Austin Mini Cooper S, 4 cylinder, 1275cc engine, restored to good original condition.
£3,750–4,250 *ADT*

l. **1979 Austin Mini Van,** recorded mileage 58,000, excellent condition.
£1,800–2,000 *CC*

MINI Model	ENGINE cc/cyl	DATES	CONDITION 1	2	3
Mini	848/4	1959-67	£2,000	£900	-
Mini Countryman	848/4	1961-67	£1,800	£900	-
Cooper Mk I	997/4	1961-67	£6,000	£3,000	£1,500
Cooper Mk II	998/4	1967-69	£4,000	£3,000	£1,500
Cooper S Mk I	var/4	1963-67	£6,500	£4,000	£2,000
Cooper S Mk II	1275/4	1967-71	£5,500	£4,000	£2,000
Innocenti Mini Cooper	998/4	1966-75	£4,500	£2,000	£1,000

1973 Austin Morris Pick-up, very rare example, in good condition.
£1,800–2,200 *KSC*

1987 Austin Mini City E, 998cc engine, 4 speed manual gearbox, right-hand drive, registration No. H15.
1962 Austin Mini 850, registration No. HER5.
£15,000–15,800 each *C*

1967 Mini Moke,
good overall condition.
£2,000–2,300 *H&H*

1971 Austin Mini Bug MkII Special, by Stimpson, 1098cc engine with full road-going equipment, rare specially constructed open 2 seater.
Est. £800–900 *HOLL*

MONTEVERDI

Monteverdi of Binningen near Basel was a distributor of Ferrari and Lancia cars. Peter Monteverdi, son of the founder of the company, began to design and manufacture racing cars from 1959, and built Switzerland's first Formula 1 car in 1961. Sports and GT cars were also built. In 1967 a new luxury model, the 375L, was launched, designed to compete with the Ferrari and Maserati.

These were high performance luxury cars possessing various body styles and luxuriously appointed. Production probably never exceeded 80 cars a year.

MOON

Joseph Moon, born in Scotland, had a manufacturing plant at St Louis in the USA. The first production car appeared in 1905. Good reliable cars were produced, most with attractive streamlined bodies, but the business was acquired by New Era Motors in 1929. Moon disappeared in 1931 following the collapse of the new parent company.

1970 Monteverdi 375L Sports Coupé, 7 litre overhauled engine, subject of extensive recent restoration, right-hand drive.
£9,500–10,000 *BKS*

1930 Moon, coachwork by Brainsby of Peterborough, 4½ litre, 8 cylinder, 92cc engine, straight 8 manual gearbox, unrestored condition.
£5,000–5,500 *DB*
Thought to be a unique 2 seater.

MORGAN

Founded by H. F. S. Morgan in 1910, the
Morgan reputation was won on the race
tracks with a series of three-wheeled motor
cars. Powered by V-twin motorcycle engines
mounted externally between the two front
wheels, the Morgans soon established their
reputation for both speed and reliability.

The Grand Prix, Aero and Super Sports,
powered mainly by JAP, Blackburne, Anzani
or Matchless engines, continued in production
until the four-wheeled Morgans appeared.

Three-wheel Morgans still compete (and
win) today and are highly sought after by
collectors and enthusiasts alike.

1922 Morgan Aero, 8hp Anzani engine,
Binks 2 jet carburettor engine.
£14,000–15,000 *FHD*

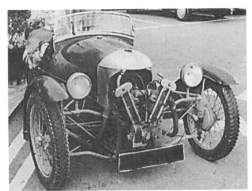

1930 Morgan 2 Seater Super Sports, 'barn-
stored' for many years, recently unearthed in
most original and sound but unrestored condition.
£14,500–15,000 *BKS*

**1929 Morgan Three-Wheeler Aero Style
Sports 2 Seater,** water-cooled V-twin JAP,
c1000cc, 2 speed chain drive gearbox, 3 wheel
drum brakes, independent sliding pillar front
suspension, quarter elliptic rear, right-hand
drive, not in running condition, displayed in
motor museum for many years.
£5,000–5,500 *C*

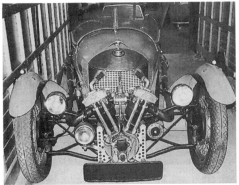

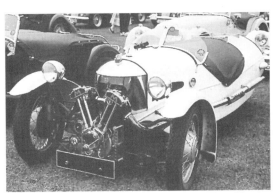

1933 Morgan MX2 Super Sports, Matchless V-twin,
990cc, overhead valve engine.
£15,000–16,000 *FHD*

1934 Morgan 3 Wheeler MX4 Super Sports,
water-cooled V-twin Matchless, 990cc, overhead
valve engine, compression ration 6.1, 3 speed chain
drive gearbox, 3 wheel drum brakes, independent
sliding pillar front suspension, quarter-elliptic
springs rear, right-hand drive, very well presented,
excellent restored condition throughout.
£19,000–20,000 *C*

r. **1933 Morgan Super Sports,** JAP engine.
£18,000–20,000 *FHD*
This car lapped Brooklands at over 100mph.

MORGAN Model	ENGINE cc/cyl	DATES	CONDITION 1	2	3
4/4 Series I	1098/4	1936-50	£10,000	£7,000	£6,000
Plus 4	2088/4	1950-53	£13,000	£9,000	£7,000
Plus 4	1991/4	1954-68	£12,000	£10,000	£7,000
4/4 Series II/III/IV	997/4	1954-68	£9,000+	£6,000	£4,000
4/4 1600	1599/4	1960 on	£14,000	£9,000	£6,000
Plus 8	3528/8	1969 on	£17,000	£13,500	£10,000

1938 Morgan 4/4 Series I, Climax engine, Meadows gearbox.
£9,000–13,000 *FHD*

1939 Morgan 4/4 Drophead Coupé, 4 cylinders, 1122cc, 35bhp at 4500rpm, 4 speed manual gearbox, 4 wheel drum brakes, independent coil front suspension, semi-elliptic rear, right-hand drive, undergone extensive restoration including the bodywork, paintwork and upholstery.
£13,500–14,250 *C*

c1952 Morgan +4 Flat Rad 2 Seater, Vanguard engine, Moss gearbox.
£15,000–19,000 *FHD*

1953 Morgan Flat Rad Drophead Coupé, Vanguard engine, Moss gearbox.
£15,000–19,000 *FHD*

117 Flat Rad drophead coupés were built until 1954.

1953 Morgan +4 Four Seater, 1990cc Triumph engine, unused for 20 years.
£9,750–10,250 *DB*

c1962 Morgan 4/4 Series IV, Ford 109E, 1340cc engine.
£8,000–12,000 *FHD*

206 were built between 1961–63.

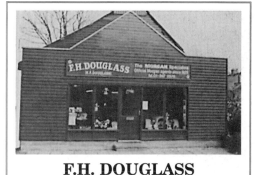

1964 Morgan +4+ Hard Top.
£22,000–28,000 *FHD*

*Twenty-six hard top Morgans were
made, and only a few survive.*

1968 Morgan 4/4, Ford 1600GT Cortina engine,
4 speed gearbox.
£8,000–12,000 *FHD*

r. **1973 Morgan 4/4 Two Seater,**
4 cylinder, 1600cc engine, good
unrestored condition.
£10,500–11,500 *DB*

1978 Morgan 4/4, Ford 1600 GT engine,
4 speed gearbox.
£7,000–12,000 *FHD*

**1967 Morgan 4/4 Two Seater 1.5 Litre
Sports,** engine reconditioned, chrome wire
wheels, chassis up restoration, chassis
replaced with new factory unit, all panels
and ash frame were renewed as needed.
£11,000–12,000 *BKS*

> **Miller's is a price
> GUIDE not a price LIST**

l. **1987 Morgan 4/4,** Ford CVH 1600 engine,
5 speed gearbox.
£13,000–17,000 *FHD*

1976 Morgan +8 Lightweight, 3.5cc Rover
V8 engine, Rover 4 speed gearbox, alloy panels.
£19,000–23,000 *FHD*

This is one of only 19 ever made.

c1990 Morgan +8, 3.9 litre engine,
pre-catalytic converter.
£22,500–26,000 *FHD*

MORRIS

William Morris, later Lord Nuffield, built
his success upon emulating American
mass-production techniques, including
sourcing the components from outside
manufacturers, and turning his factory
into an assembly plant. Morris also
adopted the Ford theory of aggressive price
cutting during the depression period which
enabled the Morris Cowley to become one
of the best selling cars of 1920s.

The Bullnose Morris was nicknamed
from the sound styling of the radiator
between 1913 and 1926. By 1927 a flat
squared-off radiator was adopted but not
before Morris had easily outsold other
British makers, most importantly their
arch rival Austin.

1924 Morris Cowley 11.9hp 2 Seater with Dickey,
correct rear wheel braking only, suction wipers, bulb
horn, runs well.
£8,250–8,750 *BKS*

1925 Morris Cowley 4 Seater Tourer,
full set of side screens, luggage rack with
basket, excellent example.
£11,000–11,500 *BKS*

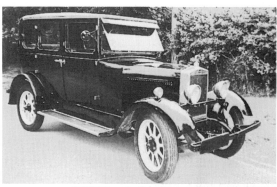

1928 Morris Cowley, very good condition.
£7,500–8,000 *CC*

**1923 Morris Cowley 11.9hp Bullnose 2 Seater
and Dickey,** fully restored, in good running order
with no major known modifications.
Est. £8,750–9,250 *S*

1929 Morris Cowley 4 Seater Tourer,
excellent condition.
£11,500–12,000 *CC*

1931 Morris Minor Tourer, coachwork by Burlington
Carriage Co Ltd, 4 cylinder, side valve engine, 847cc,
8hp, 3 speed manual gearbox, 4 wheel drum brakes,
semi-elliptic suspension, small rear bench seat, right-
hand drive, in running condition.
£2,400–2,600 *C*

1932 Morris Minor Special Coupé, totally
rebuilt, sound and sympathetically restored.
£5,200–5,600 *ADT*

*Costing £170 when new, as opposed to the £110
charged for the standard 2 seater, this special
coupé is a rare 'top-of-the-range' model.*

1932 Morris Minor 2 Seater Tourer.
£4,500–5,000   *CC*

1935 Morris 8 Pre-Series 4 Seater Tourer.
£5,750–6,250   *CC*

Morris 8

- The Morris 8 was introduced in 1934 to compete with the Austin Seven.
- 918cc four cylinder engine could just top 60mph.
- Available in 2 and 4 door saloon versions and 2 or 4 seater open tourers.
- 164,000 Series I models were sold between 1934 and 1937 and a further 54,000 MkIIs were produced.
- Morris 8 was superseded by the Series E in 1938.

1934 Morris 8 Four Door Saloon, outstanding condition, recently undergone major refurbishment including new carpets, headlining and sunroof.
£3,300–3,800   *H&H*

1935 Morris 8 Four Seater Tourer, 4 cylinder, side valve engine, 918cc, 8hp, 3 speed manual gearbox, 4 wheel hydraulic drum brakes, semi-elliptic suspension, right-hand drive, complete with tool roll, jack, starting handle, radiator blind, spare wheel and cover mounted on the rear, very sound.
£5,600–6,200   *C*

1935 Morris 8 Saloon, 4 cylinder, 918cc engine, bodywork in excellent order, minor refurbishment required.
£2,200–2,600   *ADT*

MORRIS Model	ENGINE cc/cyl	DATES	CONDITION		
			1	2	3
Prices given are for saloons					
Cowley (Bullnose)	1550/4	1913-26	£12,000	£8,000	£6,000
Cowley	1550/4	1927-39	£8,000	£6,000	£4,000
Oxford (Bullnose)	1803/4	1924-27	£14,000	£10,000	£6,000
Oxford	1803/4	1927-33	£10,000	£8,000	£6,000
16/40	2513/4	1928-33	£8,000	£7,000	£6,000
18	2468/6	1928-35	£9,000	£7,000	£5,000
8 Minor	847/4	1929-34	£5,500	£4,000	£2,000
10/4	1292/4	1933-35	£5,000	£3,000	£1,500
25	3485/6	1933-39	£10,000	£8,000	£5,000
Eight	918/4	1935-39	£4,000	£3,000	£1,500
10HP	1140/4	1939-47	£4,500	£3,000	£1,500
16HP	2062/6	1936-38	£5,000	£3,500	£2,000
18HP	2288/6	1935-37	£5,000	£3,500	£2,500
21HP	2916/6	1935-36	£6,000	£4,000	£2,500

A touring version of the above is worth approximately 30% more and value is very dependent on body type and has an increased value if coachbuilt.

1935 Morris 8 Two Door 2 Seater Tourer, unused for approximately 10 years, some attention required.
£3,400–3,700 *HOLL*

1935 Morris 12 Saloon, museum stored for 10 years, runs very well.
£3,300–3,600 *H&H*

1937 Morris 8 Series I, all-steel panels, luggage rack at the rear, new wood roof, largely original, very sound condition.
£2,400–2,600 *H&H*

1937 Morris 10/4, 4 cylinder, overhead valve engine, good useable original condition.
£3,400–3,600 *DB*

1938 Morris 8 Series II Tourer, good overall condition, replacement soft hood and side screens are required.
£3,750–4,250 *S*

1947 Morris 8 Series E Saloon, 4 cylinder, 918cc engine, bodily and structurally good, solid and largely original, all mechanicals refurbished.
£2,400–2,800 *ADT*

1953 Morris Oxford Saloon, very good original condition.
£1,300–1,600 *S*

1970 Morris Oxford, excellent overall condition.
£2,000–2,500 *SW*

Morris Minor

The Morris Minor Series MM was first introduced in 1948 with a 918cc, 4 cylinder, side valve engine which was evolved from the Morris 8. Designed by Alec Issigonis it was one of the first cars to employ a monocoque construction and do away with a separate chassis.

In 1951 Morris Motors merged with the Austin Motor Company to form the British Motor Corporation, or BMC. This resulted in the Morris Minor Series II being given an A Series, ohv, 803cc engine as used in the Austin A30. The Series II began production in 1952, although not all Morris Minors were fitted with the new engine until it was standardised in 1953. In October 1953 the Traveller was introduced joining the Saloon and Tourer models already in production.

The Morris Minor 1000 was introduced in 1956, powered by an 948cc, ohv engine producing 37bhp at 4750rpm. It had a much improved 4 speed gearbox and did away with the old-fashioned type split windscreen. By late 1960, 100,000 Minors had been produced, and no significant further changes were made to the model until 1963 when the larger 1098cc engine was introduced, giving the Minor a top speed of 73mph.

Sales fell during the late sixties and production finally ceased in 1971.

1950 Morris Minor 1000 Convertible, very good overall condition.
£6,250–6,750   *CCon*

1949 Morris Minor Series MM, needing light restoration, very correct and in good running order.
£1,000–1,200   *ADT*

1954 Morris Minor Series II, original order and will require some attention.
£600–700   *ADT*

1954 Morris Minor 2 Door Convertible, paintwork with minor blemishes, new carpets, original and in good condition.
£4,000–4,400 *BKS*

1954 Morris Minor GPO Telephone Engineers Van, 1 litre, 1000cc engine in place of 803cc original, fully equipped, traditional moulded rubber wings, totally rebuilt.
Est. £3,000–4,000 *BKS*

Cross Reference
Commercial Vehicles

l. **1955 Morris Minor Series II,** 803cc engine, fair condition.
£1,200–1,500 *MOR*

> *A rebuilt car is not necessarily more valuable than a car in good original condition, even if the restoration has been costly.*

1955 Morris Minor Series II Convertible De Luxe, well presented original car.
£4,600–4,800 *BKS*

1956 Morris Minor Series II, 4 cylinders, 803cc, good condition throughout.
Est. £1,250–1,750 *ADT*

1956 Morris Minor 1000 Convertible, very good condition throughout.
£4,250–4,750 *CCon*

1957 Morris Minor 1000 Four Door Saloon, one owner from new, original condition.
£1,200–1,600 *HOLL*

1958 Morris 1000, restored, retrimmed interior, new convertible roof and hood.
£4,500–4,800 *Bro*

1958 Morris 1000 Saloon, 948cc, 38,000 miles recorded, very good condition throughout.
£2,200–2,500 *H&H*

1957 Morris Minor 1000 Saloon,
good original condition.
£2,500–2,700 *H&H*

1957 Morris Minor 1000 Traveller, 1098cc
engine in place of the original 948cc unit, all
woodwork repaired or replaced, retrimmed,
overhauled gearbox.
£3,800–4,000 *BKS*

1959 Morris Minor 4 Door Saloon, needs some
cosmetic attention, generally good.
£3,200–3,400 *BKS*

1959 Morris Minor 1000 Convertible,
excellent overall condition.
£4,250–4,750 *CCon*

1966 Morris Minor 1000 Convertible,
total restoration, engine rebuilt,
good condition throughout.
£3,500–4,000 *H & H*

1965 Morris Minor Van, restored.
£1,500–2,000 *ESM*

1961 Morris Minor 1000 Convertible, 1098cc engine, fully restored.
£7,000–7,500 *CCon*

l. 1966 Morris Minor
1000 Convertible,
excellent overall condition.
£4,250–4,750 *CCon*

Don't Forget!
*If in doubt please
refer to the 'How
to Use' section at
the beginning of
this book.*

1967 Morris 1000 Four Door Saloon,
only 12,850 miles, excellent condition.
£3,500–4,000 *H&H*

1967 Morris Minor 1000 Convertible,
very good overall condition.
£3,250–3,750 *CCon*

1967 Morris Minor Traveller Estate,
excellent restored condition.
£4,250–4,750 *CCon*

1968 Morris Minor 2 Door Saloon,
1098cc engine, good condition.
£2,200–2,450 *ESM*

1969 Morris Minor 1000 Convertible, very good condition throughout.
£4,500–5,000 *CCon*

1969 Morris Minor 1000 Convertible, 1100cc engine, fully restored.
£6,000–6,500 *MOR*

1969 Morris Minor 1000 Convertible, very good overall condition.
£3,250–3,750 *CCon*

1968 Morris Minor 1000 Four Door Saloon, 47,000 recorded miles, very smart condition.
£2,800–3,000 *Bro*

1969 Morris 1000 Traveller, very good original condition.
£2,000–2,500 *H&H*

1969 Morris 1000 Two Door Saloon, fully restored to very high standard.
£2,200–2,500 *H&H*

1969 Morris Minor Convertible, 4 cylinders, 1098cc, good running order.
£2,400–2,800 *ADT*

MORRIS Model	ENGINE cc/cyl	DATES	CONDITION 1	2	3
Minor Series MM	918/4	1948-52	£2,000	£1,200	£500
Minor Series MM Conv	918/4	1948-52	£4,000	£1,800	£800
Minor Series II	803/4	1953-56	£2,000	£1,000	£500
Minor Series II Conv	803/4	1953-56	£4,000	£2,500	£1,000
Minor Series II Est	803/4	1953-56	£3,000	£1,250	£800
Minor 1000	948/4	1956-63	£1,750	£925	£250
Minor 1000 Conv	948/4	1956-63	£3,000	£2,000	£750
Minor 1000 Est	948/4	1956-63	£2,000	£1,200	£350
Minor 1000	1098/4	1963-71	£2,000	£950	£250
Minor 1000 Conv	1098/4	1963-71	£3,500	£2,250	£750
Minor 1000 Est	1098/4	1963-71	£3,000	£1,200	£400
Cowley 1200	1200/4	1954-56	£1,675	£1,000	£300
Cowley 1500	1489/4	1956-59	£1,750	£950	£350
Oxford MO	1476/4	1948-54	£2,000	£850	£250
Oxford MO Est	1476/4	1952-54	£3,000	£1,500	£350
Series II/III	1489/4	1954-59	£2,000	£1,200	£300
Series II/III/IV Est	1489/4	1954-60	£2,250	£1,350	£250
Oxford Series V Farina	1489/4	1959-61	£1,800	£800	£250
Oxford Series VI Farina	1622/4	1961-71	£1,750	£750	£200
Six Series MS	2215/6	1948-54	£2,500	£1,500	£500
Isis Series I/II	2639/6	1955-58	£2,500	£1,300	£450
Isis Series I/II Est	2639/6	1956-57	£2,600	£1,350	£500

l. **1970 Morris Minor 4 Door Saloon.** £450–500 *HOLL*

1969 Morris Minor 1000 Convertible, 1098cc engine, rebuilt, original excellent condition. £5,500–6,500 *MOR*

Cross Reference Commercial Vehicles

1970 Morris Minor 4 Door Saloon, good condition. £2,200–2,400 *ESM*

1971 Morris Minor 1000 Convertible, engine fully restored. £4,500–5,000 *MOR*

1971 Morris Minor Van, 27,000 recorded miles, very good original condition. £2,500–2,750 *ADT*

NAPIER

Throughout the 19th century Napier manufactured precision engineering products including printing presses. Initially based in Lambeth, Montague Napier worked on designing and producing their first motor car at the turn of the century.

Napier cars enjoyed much success including a 24-hour Brooklands record which stood for nearly 18 years. Napier made Aero engines during WWI but despite the manufacture of high quality vehicles the company ceased production in 1924.

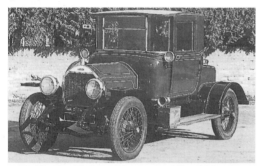

1912 Napier T46 2.7 Litre 15hp Fixed Head Coupé, Napier petrol and oil pressure gauges, Stewart speedometer, replica fixed head body, Willocq-Bottin headlamps, Rudge-Whitworth wire wheels, only 200 miles since its rebuild, recommissioning recommended before road use.
£11,000–13,000 *BKS*

1909 Napier 30hp 3 Position Cabriolet, coachwork by May & Jacobs of Guildford, 6 cylinder engine, excellent condition.
£55,000–57,000 *BKS*

NASH

1950 Nash Rambler Convertible, 6 cylinder, 184cu in engine, 85bhp at 3800rpm, 3 speed manual gearbox, 4 wheel hydraulic drum brakes, semi-elliptic leaf spring suspension front and rear, left-hand drive, only 28,000 miles from new, excellent restored condition.
£6,000–7,000 *CNY*

NSU

NSU first built cars in 1905, continuing at Neckarsulm and Heilbronn until 1931. The Heilbronn factory was sold to Fiat, and the firm concentrated on production of motorcycles. In 1958 they recommenced building cars, their first being the Prinz, a small rear-engined car with vertical twin cylinder air-cooled overhead camshaft engine of 598cc.

1965 NSU Sport Prinz 2 Seater Coupé, styling by Bertone for Drauz Karosseriewerke, right-hand drive, manual 4 speed and reverse gearbox, bodywork fully restored to original specification, interior original.
£3,300–3,600 *BKS*

OLDSMOBILE

Founded by Ransom Eli Olds at Lansing, Michigan, around 1896. Despite a fire at their factory in 1901 Oldsmobiles were the first truly mass-produced motor cars.

The Curved Dash model with a single cylinder, 1564cc, 5bhp engine and 2 speed epicyclic transmission was a great success selling over 5,000 units in 1904 alone. More models appeared but R. E. Olds left the company in the same year to form REO. Oldsmobile is now part of the General Motors Empire.

c1968 Oldsmobile Toronado 10 Seater Limousine, good restored condition.
£3,000–3,300 *S*

This vehicle is one of only 2 limousines of its type believed to have been converted from standard Toronado estate cars. It is said to seat 10 persons.

OLDSMOBILE Model	ENGINE cc/cyl	DATES	CONDITION		
			1	2	3
Curved Dash	1600/1	1901-04	£14,000	£13,000	£11,000
30	2771/6	1925-26	£9,000	£7,000	£4,000
Straight Eight	4213/8	1937-38	£12,000	£8,000	£5,000

PACKARD

Founded by James Ward Packard in Warren, Ohio, Packard was producing cars by the turn of the century. Always built to the highest standards, Packard, Peerless and Pierce-Arrow were considered to be on a par with Rolls-Royce.

The factory moved to Detroit in 1903 following a takeover by Henry Joy. Packard produced some excellent motor cars during the 1920s and '30s and by the 1950s had bought the ailing Studebaker company. This led to the demise of Packard in 1958.

1928 Packard Model 526 5th Series Two Seater Roadster with Dickey Seat, good condition throughout.
Est. £27,000–30,000 *BKS*

The replica period roadster body with dickey seat, by Long of Kinver, was constructed to replace the original saloon.

1930 Packard Type 840 De Luxe Coupé, immaculate condition throughout.
£24,000–26,000 *S*

1931 Packard Model 840 Dual Cowl Phæton, straight 8384.8cu in engine, 120bhp at 3200rpm, 4 speed manual gearbox, 4 wheel drum brakes, semi-elliptic leaf springs suspension front and rear, left-hand drive, restored.
£90,000–95,000 *CNY*

This car is a genuine Dual Cowl Phæton.

1937 Packard 120 Four Door Sedan, right-hand drive, chassis and mechanics good, needs restoring, rewiring and cosmetic attention.
£2,500–3,500 *CGB*

Don't Forget!

If in doubt please refer to the 'How to Use' section at the beginning of this book.

1936 Packard Fifteenth Series 6 Two Seater Drophead with Dickey Seat, in need of restoration, in running order but mechanical recommissioning recommended.
Est. £4,000–7,000 *S*

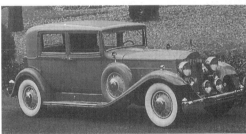

1932 Packard Model 905 Club Sedan Twin Six, V12, 445ci engine, 160bhp at 3200rpm, 3 speed manual gearbox, drum brakes, semi-elliptic leaf spring suspension front and rear, left-hand drive, excellent condition.
£49,500–52,000 *CNY*

This Packard is fitted with rare Club Sedan coachwork.

PACKARD Model	ENGINE cc/cyl	DATES	CONDITION		
			1	2	3
Twin Six	6946/12	1916-23	£25,000	£20,000	£13,000
6	3973/6	1921-24	£20,000	£15,000	£12,000
6, 7, 8 Series	5231/8	1929-39	£35,000	£25,000	£14,000
12	7300/12	1936-39	£40,000	£30,000	£18,000

PANTHER

Founded in 1972 at Weybridge in Surrey by Bob Jankel, the first car produced, the J72, was powered by a Jaguar engine and looked very much like the pre-war SS100 sports car.

Despite the introduction of other models; including the Lima, the company ran into financial trouble and was taken over by a Korean company in 1981. The Lima was relaunched as the Kallista and sold well, mainly because it was several thousand pounds cheaper than when it was originally introduced.

1987 Panther Kallista, V6 Ford Engine, alloy body, leather interior, only 6,000 miles recorded, excellent condition.
£7,000–9,000   *VIC*

l. **1990 Panther Solo 2 Litre 2+2 Coupé,** air conditioning, as new condition, from a famous collection.
Est. £19,000–21,000   *BKS*

One of 12 UK specification Panther Solos delivered before this supercar project was halted in October 1990.

PIERCE-ARROW

r. **1914 Pierce-Arrow 48B 2 Seater Gentleman's Roadster,** 6 cylinder, 8600cc engine, totally restored in America, mint condition throughout.
£64,000–68,000   *COYS*

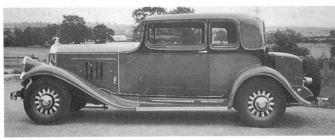

l. **1932 Pierce-Arrow Model 54 Club Brougham,** 6 litre, straight 8 engine, good condition throughout, no modifications from maker's specification.
£15,500–16,500   *BKS*

PEUGEOT

Armand Peugeot, in association with Léon Serpollet, produced a steam car as early as 1889. The first petrol-driven Peugeots were powered by Panhard-built Daimler engines and success followed. A factory was built at Audincourt and by the turn of the century Peugeot were manufacturing their own engines.

The Bugatti-designed Peugeot Bébé, launched in 1913, was a milestone in French motoring history, as was the Austin Seven in the UK.

1899 Peugeot 4 Seater Phæton, twin horizontal cylinder, 8hp engine, 3 speed and reverse chain drive gearbox, drum and transmission brakes, semi-elliptic suspension front and rear, tiller steering, found in totally original and unrestored condition, completely stripped to a bare chassis and restored, rebuilt transmission and engine, requires some recommissioning before use.
£32,000–34,000   *C*

PEUGEOT Model	ENGINE cc/cyl	DATES	CONDITION 1	2	3
153	2951/4	1913-26	£5,000	£4,000	£2,000
163	1490/4	1920-24	£5,000	£4,000	£2,000
Bebe	676/4	1920-25	£7,000	£6,000	£3,000
156	5700/6	1922-24	£7,000	£5,000	£3,000
174	3828/4	1922-28	£7,500	£5,000	£2,000
172	714/4	1926-28	£4,000	£3,000	£1,500
183	1990/6	1929-30	£4,000	£3,000	£1,500
201	996/4	1930-36	£4,000	£3,000	£1,500
402	2140/4	1938-40	£4,000	£3,000	£1,000

Right hand drive cars will always achieve more interest than left hand drive. Good solid cars.

1905 Peugeot Rear Entrance Tonneau, single cylinder, 7/8hp engine, 3 speed manual gearbox, rear wheel drum brakes, semi-elliptic suspension, right-hand drive, replica coachwork, wooden spoked wheels, wooden mudguards, fully rebuilt.
£9,500–10,000 *C*

1914 Peugeot 'Bebe' 856cc Open 2 Seater, replica coachwork in the style of Henri Gauthier, 4 cylinders, very good original condition.
£20,000–21,000 *BKS*

1921 Peugeot Type 161 Quadrillette Tandem Two Seater, excellent condition throughout.
£19,000–20,000 *S*

1924 Peugeot 190S Tourer, 4 cylinder side valve engine, an unrestored 'discovery'.
£2,500–2,750 *DB*

Cross Reference
Restoration Projects

1973 Peugeot 504 GL Cabriolet, 4 cylinder, 1971cc engine, good overall condition, no known modifications from the original factory specification.
Est. £3,500–4,500 *S*

1972 Peugeot 304 Convertible,
4 cylinders, 1288cc, sound condition,
but requires further restoration.
£500–550 *ADT*

1923–29 Peugeot 'The Lockhart Special', well
known VSCC competition car, not in running order
but with set of spare parts.
Est. £4,500–5,500 *S*

PHOENIX

The Phoenix company was originally
based in Caledonian Road, Kings Cross
before moving to Letchworth in 1911.
They made their first light car as early
as 1904.

1907 Phoenix 8hp Skiff Sports 2 Seater.
£6,000–7,000 *BKS*

PONTIAC

Although an early motor manufacturer,
Pontiac products were sold as Oaklands by
founder Edward Murphy. Pontiac-badged
cars, sold under the slogan 'Chief of the
Sixes', were not launched until 1926. They
were extremely successful and the Oakland
name was soon dropped.

Now part of General Motors, it is
interesting to note that Pontiac is one of the
few marques to have been 'created' rather
than bought as a company.

PLYMOUTH

1965 Plymouth Sport Fury 2 Door Coupé,
2 owners from new, engine and brake rebuild,
original and unmarked interior, rust free.
£3,900–4,400 *BKS*

1926 Pontiac Type 6-27 Landaulette Sedan,
6 cylinder, 3050cc engine, hickory spoked wheels,
restored, landaulette-style roof added.
Est. £12,000–13,500 *ADT*

**1974 Pontiac Firebird Trans Am SD 455
Coupé,** coachwork by Fisher Body Corporation,
very good condition throughout.
£3,800–4,200 *BKS*

1954 Pontiac Star Chief Convertible, left-hand
drive, hardly used since full body-off restoration.
£15,000–20,000 *CGB*

PONTIAC Model	ENGINE cc/cyl	DATES	CONDITION		
			1	2	3
Six-27	3048/6	1926-29	£9,000	£7,000	£4,000
Silver Streak	3654/8	1935-37	£12,000	£9,000	£5,500
6	3638/6	1937-49	£7,000	£4,000	£3,500
8	4078/8	1937-49	£7,000	£4,000	£3,500

PORSCHE

Porsche, surprisingly, was not founded as a company until 1948. Ferdinand Porsche, one of the most famous names in German motoring history, had worked for, designed or inspired most German manufacturers at some time. This work included the pre-WWII 16 cylinder Auto Union Grand Prix cars, the Tiger Tank and the Volkswagen Beetle.

The first Porsche sports cars, created by his son Ferry, were effectively highly-tuned Volkswagens. Success followed the introduction of the 356, the 911 followed and the rest is history.

> ## Porsche 356
> - 356 designation meant that it was the 356th project worked on.
> - Launched in 1949 it originally featured the 1086cc Volkswagen engine.
> - By 1955 in its final form the engine was 1582cc, flat 4 cylinder, producing 74bhp and a top speed of 109mph.
> - The 356A of 1955 was, at that time, the fastest German production car.

1963 Porsche 356B Carrera 2 Coupé, 4 cylinder, 1966cc engine, engine rebuilt, excellent original condition.
Est. £28,000–35,000 *COYS*

1955 Porsche 356A 2 Door Coupé, some attention to the floorpan needed, generally good condition.
£8,800–9,400 *BKS*

1959 Porsche 356A Cabriolet, 4 cylinder, 1600cc engine, manual gearbox, good condition throughout.
£15,500–16,500 *BKS*

1960 Porsche 356B Cabriolet, coachwork by Reutter, 4 cylinder, 1582cc engine, concours winning condition throughout.
£37,000–39,000 *COYS*

1961 Porsche 356B Super 90 Roadster, coachwork by d'Ieteren Frères, left-hand drive, never restored but preserved in excellent condition.
£24,000–26,000 *COYS*

1961 Porsche 356B Super 90 Roadster, 4 cylinder, 1600cc engine, very good order both bodily and mechanically, re-upholstered interior.
£17,000–18,000 *ADT*

r. **1973 Porsche 911 Carrera RS Touring Sports Coupé,** left-hand drive, manual gearbox, fully restored, good condition throughout.
Est. £18,000–20,000 *BKS*

1969 Porsche 911E 2 Door Sports Coupé, the body, chassis and transmission in perfect condition, 5-spoke Fuchs alloy wheels.
Est. £8,500–12,000 *BKS*

1974 Porsche 911S Targa, rust free, rebuilt engine.
£5,000–6,000 *CFI*

1973 Porsche Carrera RS 2.7 Litre Coupé, 6 cylinder, 2687cc engine, good, unrestored example, excellent condition for its age.
£28,000–30,000 *COYS*

Porsche 911 RS

- Designed as a sports car that can be driven to the track, raced, and driven home.
- RS (Rennsport) was a 911S derivative but with lightened bodywork.
- 2.7 litre, flat 6 cylinder, fuel injected engine produced about 210bhp.
- It could accelerate to 60mph in just over 5 seconds with a top speed of nearly 160mph.

1974 Porsche 911 Targa, 4 cylinder, 2700cc engine, very good condition throughout.
Est. £7,750–9,000 *ADT*

1974 Porsche 911 Carrera.
£10,000–15,000 *FHF*

PORSCHE Model	ENGINE cc/cyl	DATES	CONDITION 1	2	3
356	var/4	1949-53	£15,000	£8,000	£5,000
356 Cabriolet	var/4	1951-53	£20,000	£14,000	£10,000
356A	1582/4	1955-59	£11,500	£7,000	£3,000
356A Cabriolet	1582/4	1956-59	£15,000	£9,000	£7,000
356A Speedster	1582/4	1955-58	£25,000	£19,000	£14,000
356 Carrera	1582/ 1966/4	1960-65	£28,000	£20,000	£15,000
356C	1582/4	1963-65	£13,000	£9,000	£5,000
356C Cabriolet	1582/4	1963-64	£17,000	£12,000	£7,000
911/911L/T/E	1991/6	1964-68	£9,000	£6,000	£4,000
912	1582/4	1965-68	£6,500	£5,000	£2,000
911S	1991/6	1966-69	£12,000	£8,000	£5,500
911S	2195/6	1969-71	£12,000	£9,000	£6,000
911T	2341/6	1971-73	£10,000	£7,000	£5,000
911E	2341/6	1971-73	£10,000	£7,000	£5,000
914/4	1679/4	1969-75	£4,000	£3,000	£1,000
914/6	1991/6	1969-71	£6,000	£3,500	£1,500
911S	2341/6	1971-73	£15,000	£9,000	£7,500
Carrera RS lightweight	2687/6	1973	£32,000	£28,000	£16,000
Carrera RS Touring	2687/6	1973	£30,000	£26,000	£17,000
Carrera 3	2994/6	1976-77	£14,000	£9,000	£7,000
924 Turbo	1984/4	1978-83	£4,500	£3,000	£1,500
928/928S	4474/4664/V8	1977-86	£9,000	£6,000	£3,500
911SC	2993/6	1977-83	£10,000	£7,000	£5,000

Sportomatic cars are less desirable.

c1988 Porsche 959 2.85 Litre Twin-Turbocharged 4 Wheel Drive Sports Coupé, good condition throughout. Est. £150,000–190,000 *BKS*

RAILTON

1934 Railton Terraplane Saloon, a rare and early example, fair condition, requires some restoration. £4,000–4,400 *S*

RELIANT

Probably best known as the manufacturer of three-wheeler cars, both saloon and commercial vehicles, the first four-wheel product was the Sabre in 1961. An export/manufacturing deal was made with the Israelis where the car was designated Sabra. The Sabra was not a great success, unlike the Scimitar launched in 1964.

In 1968 the Ogle-designed GTE hatchback was introduced with a fibreglass body, like all Reliants, but featuring the Ford V6, 2994cc engine, producing 135bhp.

The Reliant GTE, almost a sports estate car, was probably best known when HRH Princess Anne bought one. About 16,000 Scimitars were built in the seventeen-year production period.

1960 Reliant Sabra Sports Prototype, 4 cylinder, 1700cc engine, rebuilt using genuine parts, 3 speed column change gearbox. £3,800–4,200 *ADT*

1988 Porsche 959, flat 6 cylinders, double overhead camshaft, 4 valves per cylinder, twin KKK turbo chargers, 2849cc, 450bhp at 6500rpm, 6 speed manual gearbox, with permanent four-wheel drive, power-assisted self-ventilated disc brakes with ABS, suspension with unequal length upper and lower A-arms, coil springs, anti-roll bar with electronically controlled height adjustment, left-hand drive, hydraulically boosted rack-and-pinion steering, special safety tyres, top speed of around 190mph, excellent condition. £190,000+ *C*

1937 Railton Cobham Sports Saloon, 8 cylinder, 4168cc engine, very good overall condition. Est. £8,500–10,000 *ADT*

1976 Reliant Scimitar GTE, automatic, replacement reconditioned engine, vinyl upholstery.
Est. £2,500–3,500 *ADT*

1975 Reliant Scimitar GTE 3 Litre, V6 Ford engine and gearbox, average condition.
£900–1,000 *DB*

> **Miller's is a price GUIDE not a price LIST**

1978 Reliant Scimitar GTE SE6, manual gearbox, maintained to a high standard.
£1,600–1,800 *H&H*

1985 Reliant Scimitar SS1, CVH 1600cc Escort engine, 35,000 miles recorded, good condition.
Est. £2,500–3,500 *ADT*

RELIANT Model	ENGINE cc/cyl	DATES	CONDITION 1	2	3
Sabre 4 Coupé & Drophead	1703/4	1961-63	£4,500	£2,750	£1,000
Sabre 6 " "	2553/6	1962-64	£5,000	£3,250	£1,000
Scimitar GT Coupé SE4	2553/6, 2994 V6	1964-70	£4,500	£2,500	£1,000
Scimitar GTE Sports Estate SE5/5A	2994/V6	1968-75	£4,500	£2,000	£750
Scimitar GTE Sports Estate SE6/6A	2994/V6	1976-80	£6,000	£3,500	£1,250
Scimitar GTE Sports Estate SE6B	2792/V6	1980-86	£8,000	£5,000	£2,000
Scimitar GTC Convertible SE8B	2792/V6	1980-86	£9,000	£8,000	£5,500

RENAULT

1906 Renault 20/30hp Limousine, 4 cylinder, side valve, 4398cc engine, 4 speed gearbox, rear wheel brakes, leaf springs suspension front and rear, right-hand drive, engine rebuilt, perfect running order.
£55,000–58,000 *C*

r. **1904 Renault 14/20hp Roi De Belges 5 Person Tourer,** restored to usuable condition.
Est. £50,000–70,000 *S*

RENAULT Model	ENGINE cc/cyl	DATES	CONDITION 1	2	3
40hp	7540/6	1919-21	£30,000	£20,000	£10,000
SR	4537/4	1919-22	£10,000	£7,000	£5,000
EU-15.8HP	2815/4	1919-23	£5,000	£3,000	£2,000
GS-IG	2121/4	1920-23	£5,000	£3,000	£2,000
JP	9123/6	1922-29	£25,000	£20,000	£15,000
KJ	951/4	1923-29	£6,000	£4,000	£2,000
Mona Six	1474/6	1928-31	£7,000	£5,000	£3,000
Reinastella	7128/8	1929-32	£25,000	£20,000	£15,000
Viva Six	3181/6	1929-34	£10,000	£7,000	£3,000
14/45	2120/4	1929-35	£7,000	£5,000	£2,000
Nervahuit	4240/8	1931	£12,000	£10,000	£7,000
UY	1300/4	1932-34	£7,000	£5,000	£2,000
ZC/ZD2	4825/8	1934-35	£12,000	£10,000	£7,000
YN2	1463/4	1934-39	£7,000	£5,000	£2,000
Airline Super and Big 6	3620/6	1935	£10,000	£8,000	£5,000
18	2383/4	1936-39	£9,000	£5,000	£3,000
26	4085/6	1936-39	£12,000	£8,000	£5,000

Veteran pre-war models like the 2 cylinder AX, AG and BB are very popular, with values ranging between £6,000 and £15,000. The larger 4 cylinder cars like the AM, AZ, XB and VB are very reliable and coachbuilt examples command £25,000+.

1910 Renault 8hp AX 2 Seater, twin cylinder water-cooled engine, restored, good overall condition.
Est. £12,000–13,000 *BKS*

1912 Renault CE 20/30 Tourer, coachwork by The Regent Carriage Co, 4 cylinders, side valve engine cast in 2 blocks of twin cylinders, 5026cc, 24.8hp, 4 speed gearbox with reverse, rear wheel drum brakes, semi-elliptic leaf springs suspension front and rear, right-hand drive, full set of brass lamps, hand horn, twin spare tyres and a Shell petrol can, fully restored, excellent condition.
£40,000–43,000 *C*

1960 Renault Dauphine, 4CV, 1090cc engine, 3 speed gearbox, left-hand drive, has been dry-stored, in running order.
£1,000–1,100 *ADT*

r. **1931 Renault Model KZ6 13.9hp Saloon,** 4 cylinder, side valve, 2120cc engine, 3 speed gearbox, to right-hand drive specification, original in all major respects.
Est. £4,000–5,000 *BKS*

RENAULT Model	ENGINE cc/cyl	DATES	CONDITION 1	2	3
4CV	747/ 760/4	1947-61	£3,500	£2,000	£850
Fregate	1997/4	1952-60	£3,000	£2,000	£1,000
Dauphine	845/4	1956-66	£1,500	£1,000	£350
Dauphine Gordini	845/4	1961-66	£2,000	£1,000	£450
Floride	845/4	1959-62	£3,000	£2,000	£600
Caravelle	956/ 1108/4	1962-68	£4,500	£2,800	£750
R4	747/ 845/4	1961-86	£2,000	£1,500	£350
R8/R10	1108/4	1962-71	£1,800	£750	£200
R8 Gordini	1108/4	1965-66	£8,000	£5,000	£2,000
R8 Gordini	1255/4	1966-70	£8,000	£5,500	£2,500
R8S	1108/4	1968-71	£2,000	£1,200	£400

1962 Renault Caravelle Cabriolet, 4 cylinder, 956cc engine, rare model, full body and engine restoration, excellent condition.
£2,200–2,600 *COYS*

1978 Renault-Alpine 2.7 Litre Model A 310 Two Door Coupé, excellent condition throughout, GRP bodywork.
Est. £7,000–8,000 *BKS*

1988 Renault-Alpine A110, 1600cc, good restoration with history.
£16,250–16,750 *CGOC*

| Cross Reference |
| Racing Cars |

1983 Renault-Alpine A310 2+2 Sports Coupé, outstanding condition throughout.
Est. £10,000–12,000 *BKS*

REO

Oldsmobile, makers of one of the most successful early mass-produced motor cars, the Curved Dash Oldsmobile, had been founded by R. E. Olds. He left the company in 1904 when he was forty due to a disagreement with the board of directors. He was persuaded to abandon his plans for retirement and instead founded the REO company.

Ransom Eli Olds produced many famous cars and commercial vehicles, although motor car production ceased in 1936. He died in 1950 aged 86.

1925 REO T6 Roadster with Rumble Seat, 6 cylinders, 3926cc, good condition throughout.
Est. £10,500–12,500 *ADT*

RILEY

The first Riley was initially hand-built by Percy Riley in 1898. One of four Riley sons, Percy, was responsible for the design and building of the first Riley engines as well. The first four-wheeled automobile was sold in 1905 and, despite a confusing and complex range of models, Riley Motor Manufacturing Company survived.

By the 1930s Riley were making arguably some of the best-looking and performing sports cars of the era, enjoying much competition success. Acquired by Lord Nuffield in 1938 Riley soon became a badge engineering excercise and had disappeared by the 1960s.

1931 Riley Monaco Plus Ultra 9hp Saloon, engine and transmission believed to have been rebuilt, bodywork and interior will require restoration.
Est. £3,500–4,500 *BKS*

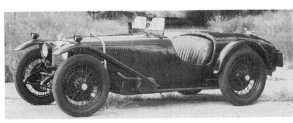

l. **1929 Ex-Works Riley 9 Brooklands Open Sports,** 4 cylinder, 1087cc engine, distinguished competition history, in excellent condition.
£30,000–32,000 *COYS*

RILEY Model	ENGINE cc/cyl	DATES	CONDITION		
			1	2	3
9hp	1034/2	1906-07	£9,000	£6,000	£3,000
Speed 10	1390/2	1909-10	£10,000	£6,000	£3,000
11	1498/4	1922-27	£7,000	£4,000	£2,000
9	1075/4	1927-32	£10,000	£7,000	£4,000
9 Gamecock	1098/4	1932-33	£14,000	£10,000	£6,000
Lincock 12hp	1458/6	1933-36	£9,000	£7,000	£5,000
Imp 9hp	1089/4	1934-35	£35,000	£28,000	£20,000
Kestrel 12hp	1496/4	1936-38	£8,000	£5,000	£2,000
Sprite 12hp	1496/4	1936-38	£40,000	£35,000	£20,000

Many Riley 9hp 'Specials' available ideal for VSCC and club events.

1934 Riley Kestrel 9hp Sports Saloon, bodily and mechanically well restored. **£10,000–11,000** *S*

1934 Riley 9 Special, 4 cylinder, 1087cc engine, rebuilt to a very good standard, VSCC blue form. Est. **£9,250–10,500** *ADT*

1933 Riley Earl of March Special Roadster. **£20,000–25,000** *FHF*

1936 Riley Sprite 1½ Litre 2 Seater Sports, engine and transmission rebuilt, bodywork generally presentable, matching engine and chassis numbers. Est. **£38,000–40,000** *BKS*

1937 Riley Lynx Sprite, 4 cylinder, 1496cc engine, completely restored, including chromework, excellent condition. **£20,000–22,000** *COYS*

r. **1947 Riley RMA Convertible,** very good overall condition. **£9,750–10,250** *Bro*
This car is one of only 8 built by AMC.

RILEY Model	ENGINE cc/cyl	DATES	CONDITION		
			1	2	3
1½ litre RMA	1496/4	1945-52	£5,000	£3,500	£1,500
1½ litre RME	1496/4	1952-55	£5,000	£3,500	£1,500
2½ litre RMB/F	2443/4	1946-53	£9,000	£7,000	£3,000
2½ litre Roadster	2443/4	1948-50	£13,000	£11,000	£9,000
2½ litre Drophead	2443/4	1948-51	£20,000	£18,000	£10,000
Pathfinder	2443/4	1953-57	£3,500	£2,000	£750
2.6	2639/6	1957-59	£3,000	£1,800	£750
1.5	1489/4	1957-65	£3,000	£2,000	£850
4/68	1489/4	1959-61	£1,500	£700	£300
4/72	1622/4	1961-69	£1,600	£800	£300
Elf I/II/III	848/4	1961-66	£1,500	£850	£400
Kestrel I/II	1098/4	1965-67	£1,500	£850	£400

1952 Riley 1.5 Litre, largely original car but 4 cylinder, 1496cc engine rebuilt, requires some attention.
£3,400–3,600 *ADT*

1954 Riley 2½ Litre RMA, good overall condition.
£2,000–3,000 *H&H*

1949 Riley 2½ Litre RM Roadster, to original specification in all major respects, good overall condition.
Est. £9,000–11,000 *BKS*

1965 Riley Elf 2 Door Saloon, mechanically excellent, bodywork and interior good, non-original carpets.
£1,700–1,900 *BKS*

The Mini was made not only in Austin and Morris form but also appeared as the Wolseley Hornet in 1962, and with built-out boot and traditional Riley radiator as the Riley Elf.

ROCHDALE

c1960 Rochdale 2 Door GT Coupé, good partly restored condition.
£800–900 *BKS*

ROCHET-SCHNEIDER

r. **1914 Rochet-Schneider,** very good condition.
£26,000–28,000 *GAR*

ROLLS-ROYCE

The first cars built by Henry Royce were made as early as 1904. In 1906, the Hon Charles Rolls agreed to market all of Royce's vehicles and Rolls-Royce was formed. A new site was bought at Derby and a factory built with a public flotation raising the capital required. The first car, the 40/50, was soon developed into the Silver Ghost and, built to the highest standards then, is still sought-after by collectors today.

Rolls-Royce owners are well served today by the owners' club, and, although expensive, spare parts are relatively easy to obtain. Coachbuilt bodies are the most desirable. Some reproduction bodies exist and history and provenance can easily be confirmed with careful research.

Post-war Rolls-Royces are extremely good value for money and, although not very economical, they will provide luxury, prestigious travel for the cost of a modern hatchback.

1923 Rolls-Royce 20hp Barker Open Tourer, repainted, all numbers match, turned aluminium dashboard, excellent condition.
£36,000–37,000 *H&H*

This car was supplied new to the Nawab of Bahawalpur.

1925 Rolls-Royce Silver Ghost Landaulette,
coachwork by Hooper, original condition, would
benefit from sympathetic restoration retaining
as much originality as possible.
£45,000–48,000 *BKS*

1928 Rolls-Royce Phantom I Playboy.
£65,000–70,000 *BLE*

1926 Rolls-Royce Phantom I, 6 cylinder
engine in 2 blocks of 3, overhead valves, 7668cc,
4 speed manual gearbox, 4 wheel drum servo-
assisted brakes, right-hand drive.
£16,500–17,000 *C*

1927 Rolls-Royce 20hp Barker Style Tourer,
6 cylinders, 3127cc, fully restored to high standard,
very good condition throughout.
Est. £23,000–28,000 *COYS*

1928 Rolls-Royce Phantom I Sedanca de Ville,
coachwork by Broughton.
£59,000–61,000 *BLE*

Rolls-Royce Phantom I

- Introduced in 1926 to replace the Silver Ghost.
- 7668cc, 6 cylinder engine with overhead valves
  produced 100bhp.
- Pressed steel chassis with coachwork to order,
  the Phantom I could achieve 75mph.
- Over 2,000 were built at Derby and about
  1,200 in America at the Springfield works.

**1926 Rolls-Royce Phantom I Seven Seater
Tourer,** coachwork by Joseph Cockshoot of
Manchester, very good overall condition.
Est. £50,000–55,000 *BKS*

1926 Rolls-Royce Barker 20hp Tourer.
£35,000–45,000 *FHF*

1927 Rolls-Royce Phantom I 40/50 Tourer, coachwork by Labourdette, running and driving well, requires cosmetic restoration.
£55,000–58,000 *S*

Make the Most of Miller's
Veteran Cars are those manufactured up to 31 December 1918. Only vehicles built before 31 December 1904 are eligible for the London/Brighton Commemorative Run. Vintage Cars are vehicles that were manufactured between 1 January 1919 and 31 December 1930.

1928 Rolls-Royce Phantom I 'Newmarket' Open 4 Seater Tourer, coachwork by Brewster, 6 cylinder engine in 2 blocks of 3, overhead valves, 7668cc, 4 speed manual gearbox, 4 wheel drum servo-assisted brakes, semi-elliptic leaf springs front suspension, cantilever leaf springs rear, left-hand drive, very good overall condition.
Est. £65,000–75,000 *C*

1928 Rolls-Royce Phantom I.
£64,000–66,000 *BLE*

1929 Rolls-Royce 20hp Limousine, coachwork by Park Ward, remarkably original condition, period interior fittings.
Est. £16,000–20,000 *BKS*

1928 Rolls-Royce 20hp Doctor's Coupé, coachwork by Windovers, originally with a Weymann 4 door saloon body, good condition, would benefit from cosmetic attention.
Est. £28,000–30,000 *S*

Confirmation has been obtained that the change in coachwork occurred before the war.

1930 Rolls-Royce 20/25 Sedanca De Ville, coachwork by Thrupp & Maberly, 3.7 Litre engine, engine rebuilt.
£22,500–23,500 *ADT*

c1928 Rolls-Royce Phantom I Dual Cowl Open Tourer, rear Auster screen, little known history, good general condition.
£33,000–35,000 *COYS*

1929 Rolls-Royce Phantom I 40/50 Limousine, coachwork by Windovers, restored to original specification, polished aluminium wheel discs all-round.
£42,000–44,000 *S*

1932 Rolls-Royce Phantom II Continental 4 Door Saloon, coachwork by Thrupp & Maberly, good condition throughout.
£48,000–50,000 *S*

1930 Rolls-Royce 20/25 Landaulette, coachwork by H. J. Mulliner of Chiswick, engine replaced, good general condition.
Est. £25,000–30,000 *BKS*

1930 Rolls-Royce Phantom II Sedanca de Ville, coachwork by Windovers, good overall condition.
Est. £60,000–70,000 *S*

1930 Rolls-Royce 20/25 Saloon, coachwork by William Arnold, 6 cylinders, 3669cc, refurbished, resprayed, interior woodwork polished, head lining replacement.
£19,000–22,000 *ADT*

William Arnold were prominent coachbuilders from 1910 to 1948. Some 50–60 bodies were built by them for Rolls-Royce between 1919 and 1936.

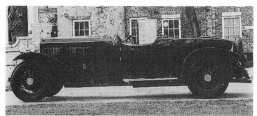

1932 Rolls-Royce Phantom II Continental Boat-Tail Tourer, coachwork by James Pearce, body built in 1970, requires some remedial work.
£32,000–35,000 *BKS*

1932 Rolls-Royce 20/25 Sports Saloon, coachwork by Freestone & Webb, 4 doors, 4 lights, twin side-mounted spare wheels, Lucas P80 headlamps, twin electric trumpet horns.
Est. £18,000–22,000 *BKS*

l. **1933 Rolls-Royce 20/25 Sports Saloon,** coachwork by Thrupp & Maberly, requires cosmetic attention.
£15,000–16,000 *RCC*

ROLLS-ROYCE Model	ENGINE cc/cyl	DATES	CONDITION 1	2	3
Silver Ghost 40/50	7035/6	pre-WWI	£350,000	£120,000	£50,000
Silver Ghost 40/50	7428/6	post-WWI	£110,000	£70,000	£35,000
20hp (3 speed)	3127/6	1922-25	£29,000	£23,000	£15,000
20hp	3127/6	1925-29	£30,000	£24,000	£15,000
Phantom I	7668/6	1925-29	£50,000	£28,000	£22,000
20/25	3669/6	1925-26	£30,000	£18,000	£13,000
Phantom II	7668/6	1929-35	£40,000	£30,000	£20,000
Phantom II Continental	7668/6	1930-35	£60,000	£40,000	£28,000
25/30	4257/6	1936-38	£24,000	£18,000	£12,000
Phantom III	7340/12	1936-39	£38,000	£28,000	£14,000
Wraith	4257/6	1938-39	£38,000	£32,000	£25,000

Prices will vary considerably depending on heritage, originality, coachbuilder, completeness and body style. A poor reproduction body can often mean the value is dependent only upon a rolling chassis and engine.

1935 Rolls-Royce 20/25 Saloon with Division,
coachwork by H. J. Mulliner of Chiswick,
very good condition throughout.
Est. £18,000–22,000 *BKS*

1934 Rolls-Royce 20/25 6 Light Saloon,
coachwork by Thrupp & Maberly, sound
condition, original upholstery.
£18,000–19,000 *RCC*

1935 Rolls-Royce 20/25 Saloon,
coachwork by Mulliner.
£19,000–20,000 *DB*

1935 Rolls-Royce 20/25 Sports Saloon,
coachwork by Thrupp & Maberly, unused for some
time, requires attention, complete, running and
driving, cylinder head requires attention.
£11,000–12,000 *RCC*

1936 Rolls-Royce 25/30 Seven Seater Limousine,
coachwork by Hooper, with sliding division,
stainless steel exhaust, extensively overhauled.
£20,000–25,000 *VIC*

**1937 Rolls-Royce Phantom III Touring
Limousine,** restored to highest standards.
£30,000–34,000 *S*

1937 Rolls-Royce Phantom III Limousine,
coachwork by Park Ward, exceptionally original
car, original Philco radio, good overall condition.
£22,000–23,000 *RCC*

1937 Rolls-Royce 25/30 Tourer, 6 cylinders,
4257cc, overhead valve, non-original body,
new leather trim, rebuilt engine.
£11,500–12,500 *Mot*

1937 Rolls-Royce 25/30 Limousine, coachwork
by Barker, all aluminium body, sunroof, occasional
seats, new leather interior, carpets, head lining
and chrome, very good restored condition.
£16,500–17,500 *Mot*

r. **1947 Rolls-Royce Silver Wraith Hooper
Touring Limousine,** razor-edge 'Teviot' styling,
correct P100 headlamps, centre spot, sound condition,
runs well, complete and correct, requires attention.
£9,500–10,500 *RCC*

1953 Rolls-Royce Silver Wraith Drophead Coupé, coachwork by Park Ward, paintwork in good condition, hood and upholstery renewed, excellent condition.
Est. £45,000–55,000 *C*

1952 Rolls-Royce Phantom IV Sedanca de Ville, coachwork by Hooper, glass division, telephone, picnic tables, cocktail bar, good mechanical condition.
£168,000–172,000 *C*

1952 Rolls-Royce Silver Wraith Sedanca de Ville, coachwork by H. J. Mulliner, completely restored to original specification, superb example, excellent condition.
£27,000–30,000 *COYS*

1954 Rolls-Royce Silver Dawn Saloon, no known modifications from factory specifications, very good overall condition.
£17,000–18,000 *S*

l. **1953 Rolls-Royce Silver Wraith 7 Seater Limousine,** coachwork by Hooper, brakes overhauled, fair condition overall.
Est. £12,500–13,500 *S*

ROLLS-ROYCE Model	ENGINE cc/cyl	DATES	CONDITION		
			1	2	3
Silver Wraith LWB	4566/				
	4887/6	1951-59	£22,000	£15,000	£9,000
Silver Wraith SWB	4257/				
	4566/6	1947-59	£18,000	£12,000	£9,000
Silver Wraith Drophead	4257/				
	4566/6	1947-59	£50,000	£35,000	£25,000
Silver Dawn St'd Steel	4257/				
	4566/6	1949-52	£25,000	£15,000	£10,000
Silver Dawn St'd Steel	4257/				
	4566/6	1952-55	£30,000	£20,000	£15,000
Silver Dawn Coachbuilt	4257/				
	4566/6	1949-55	£35,000	£25,000	£18,000
Silver Dawn Drophead	4257/				
	4566/6	1949-55	£60,000	£50,000	£30,000
Silver Cloud I	4887/6	1955-59	£18,000	£10,000	£8,000
SCI Coupé Coachbuilt	4887/6	1955-59	£30,000	£20,000	£15,000
SCI Conv (HJM)	4887/6	1955-59	£80,000	£60,000	£40,000
Silver Cloud II	6230/8	1959-62	£19,000	£10,000	£8,000
SCII Conv (HJM)	6230/8	1959-62	£80,000	£75,000	£40,000
SCII Conv (MPW)	6230/8	1959-62	£60,000	£40,000	£32,000
Silver Cloud III	6230/8	1962-65	£25,000	£12,000	£10,000
SCIII Conv (MPW)	6230/8	1962-65	£70,000	£45,000	£35,000
Silver Shadow	6230/				
	6750/8	1965-76	£14,000	£8,000	£6,000
S Shadow I Coupé (MPW)	6230/				
	6750/8	1965-70	£15,000	£10,000	£8,000
SSI Drophead (MPW)	6230/				
	6750/8	1965-70	£33,000	£25,000	£18,000
Corniche fhc	6750/8	1971-77	£15,000	£11,000	£8,000
Corniche Convertible	6750/8	1971-77	£28,000	£22,000	£18,000
Camargue	6750/8	1975-85	£35,000	£25,000	£18,000

1955 Rolls-Royce Silver Dawn Saloon, 6 cylinders, 4566cc, overhead inlet valves, 145bhp at 4000rpm, 4 speed automatic gearbox, 4 wheel drum brakes, independent coil front suspension, semi-elliptic leaf springs rear, left-hand drive, comprehensive cosmetic restoration, repainted, new leather upholstery, restored interior woodwork and chrome. **£25,000–27,000** *CNY*

Rolls-Royce Silver Dawn

- The Silver Dawn was introduced in 1949.
- It was the first Rolls-Royce to be offered with a factory fitted steel body.
- The 4257cc in line 6 cylinder engine produced 135bhp, later increased to 4566cc.
- Based on the MkVI Bentley, it was the first Rolls-Royce designed for the owner-driver.

1954 Rolls-Royce Silver Dawn Standard Steel Saloon. **£35,000–40,000** *PJF*

1956 Rolls-Royce Silver Cloud Hearse, bodywork requires attention. **£7,000–8,000** *S*

1957 Rolls-Royce Silver Cloud I Standard Steel Saloon, 4887cc, good original condition. **£8,500–9,500** *HCC*

1958 Rolls-Royce Silver Cloud I Convertible, adapted by H. J. Mulliner. **£100,000–120,000** *PJF*

1957 Rolls-Royce Silver Cloud I Standard Steel Saloon, right-hand drive, good condition throughout. **£15,000–17,000** *BKS*

1962 Rolls-Royce Silver Cloud II Long Wheelbase with Division, excellent condition. **Est. £26,000–29,000** *C*

1962 Rolls-Royce Silver Cloud III, 8 cylinders, 6230cc, good original condition, some cosmetic attention required. **Est. £14,000–16,000** *ADT*

r. **1963 Rolls-Royce Silver Cloud III Standard Steel Saloon,** good condition throughout. **£18,000–20,000** *S*

1964 Rolls-Royce Silver Cloud III Standard Steel Saloon, excellent condition.
£35,000–45,000 *PJF*

1964 Rolls-Royce Silver Cloud III Convertible, professional conversion to the 'Mulliner adaptation' design, very high standard.
£32,000–35,000 *COYS*

1962 Rolls-Royce Silver Cloud II, restored, excellent condition.
£21,000–23,000 *C*

1964 Rolls-Royce Silver Cloud III Long Wheelbase with Division, coachwork by Park Ward, fully restored to as close as new as possible.
£35,000–38,000 *COYS*

Rolls-Royce Silver Cloud III

- The MkIII was the last of the Silver Cloud series.
- The 6230cc, V8 engine could accelerate to 60mph in just over 10 seconds.
- Over 2,000 were made with factory pressed steel bodies and about 250 had a long wheelbase chassis.
- Only a few had customer coachbuilt bodies including the Mulliner Park Ward 'Chinese Eye' 4 headlamp version.

1964 Rolls-Royce Silver Cloud III, 8 cylinders, 6230cc, excellent all-round condition.
£16,000–18,000 *ADT*

1965 Rolls-Royce Silver Cloud III Drophead Coupé, coachwork by Mulliner Park Ward, totally rebuilt, excellent condition.
£56,000–58,000 *S*

1967 Rolls-Royce Phantom V Limousine, coachwork by Mulliner Park Ward, V8 engine, 6230cc, 200bhp at 4000rpm, 4 speed automatic gearbox, drum brakes, independent coil springs and wishbones front suspension, live rear axle, semi-elliptic leaf springs rear, lever arm hydraulic dampers, left-hand drive, very good overall condition.
£40,000–42,000 *CNY*

1966 Rolls-Royce Silver Shadow 2 Door Fixed Head Coupé, 6750cc engine, fair condition.
£7,500–8,000 *S*

1969 Rolls-Royce Silver Shadow 2 Door,
coachwork by Mulliner Park Ward, V8 engine,
6250cc, automatic gearbox, unrestored condition.
£8,250–8,750 *DB*

1970 Rolls-Royce Silver Shadow, 8 cylinders,
6230cc, very good condition.
£5,500–6,000 *ADT*

**1969 Rolls-Royce Phantom VI Seven Seater
Limousine,** coachwork by Hooper, very good
condition throughout.
£52,000–56,000 *S*

1972 Rolls-Royce Silver Shadow,
8 cylinders, 6750cc, carefully maintained,
good condition throughout.
Est. £11,500–12,500 *ADT*

1978 Rolls-Royce Silver Shadow II, 8 cylinders,
6750cc, very good condition throughout.
£8,500–9,000 *ADT*

1973 Rolls-Royce Corniche Convertible,
good overall condition.
£20,000–22,000 *H&H*

1974 Rolls-Royce Silver Shadow, 8 cylinders,
6750cc, very good original condition.
£6,400–6,800 *ADT*

1974 Rolls-Royce Corniche Drophead Coupé,
less than 14,000 miles from new, good original
condition throughout.
£27,000–30,000 *COYS*

1978 Rolls-Royce Silver Shadow II, well
maintained, good condition throughout.
£14,500–16,000 *S*

l. **1975 Rolls-Royce Silver Shadow,** V8 engine,
6750cc, automatic gearbox, good condition.
£7,250–7,750 *DB*

1981 Rolls-Royce Camargue 2 Door Saloon,
coachwork by Mulliner Park Ward, engine replaced
by a reconditioned unit, bodywork good.
Est. £22,000–24,000 *BKS*

1989 Rolls-Royce Silver Spur Turbo,
V8 engine, 6750cc, 3 speed automatic
gearbox, a factory built 'one-off'.
Est. £40,000–46,000 *C*

1981 Rolls-Royce Corniche Convertible,
one owner, full history.
£36,000–37,000 *BLE*

ROSENGART

1934 Rosengart Type LR4, 750cc, Austin 7
derivative built in France, running, requires
restoration.
£1,000-1,500 *DB*

ROVER

John Stanley manufactured bicycles under
the Rover name and in 1888 produced an
electric tricycle which was, arguably, the
first motor vehicle built at Coventry.

When Owen Clegg joined the company
in 1910 production methods were
revolutionised. The company went from
strength to strength producing solid reliable
vehicles for middle England. The merger
with Leyland in 1966 enabled Rover to
continue the production of luxury cars.

1929 Rover 10/25hp Weymann Cabriolet,
folding roof, dummy hood irons, bodywork
restored, interior original.
Est. £4,500–4,800 *BKS*

1931 Rover 10/25 Weymann 4 Door Saloon,
restored some years ago,
very good condition throughout.
£5,000–5,500 *H&H*

1932 Rover 10 Special 4 Door Saloon,
original upholstery, running well, bodywork
in good condition.
£5,250–5,750 *S*

l. **1936 Rover 14hp 4 Door Saloon,**
some recommissioning undertaken,
still requires some attention.
£3,800–4,400 *S*

ROVER Model	ENGINE cc/cyl	DATES	CONDITION 1	2	3
10hp	998/2	1920-25	£5,000	£3,000	£1,500
9/20	1074/4	1925-27	£6,000	£4,000	£2,000
10/25	1185/4	1928-33	£6,000	£4,000	£2,500
14hp	1577/6	1933-39	£6,000	£4,250	£2,000
12	1496/4	1934-37	£7,000	£4,000	£1,500
20 Sports	2512/6	1937-39	£6,000	£4,000	£2,500

1938 Rover Sports Saloon, very good overall condition.
£6,000–7,000 *H&H*

1948 Rover P3 Sports Saloon, very good original condition.
£8,750–9,250 *Bro*

1948 Rover P2-10, 4 cyclinders, 1389cc, good original car.
£2,000–2,500 *ADT*

1951 Rover Cyclops, good original condition.
£5,000–6,000 *SW*

This car is known as 'Cyclops' because of the single front-mounted spotlight on the grille.

1960 Rover 100 Four Door Saloon, solid body, worn leather interior, good overall condition.
£1,250–1,500 *BKS*

1961 Rover 100, good condition, reconditioned engine, with history.
£2,800–3,200 *Mot*

1967 Rover P5B, 8 cylinders, 3531cc, reconditioned automatic gearbox.
£4,600–4,900 *ADT*

1970 Rover P5B 3.5 Litre Saloon, original factory specification, good condition throughout, extremely original car.
Est. £3,000–4,000 *S*

1973 Rover P5B 3.5 Litre Saloon, V8 engine, automatic gearbox, very good condition throughout, good history, winner of 'Best of Show' in 1995.
£3,750–4,250 *Mot*

1972 Rover P5B 3.5, full history available, restored.
£5,200–5,400 *S*

This car won first prize at the P5 Club in 1988 and 1989.

1971 Rover 3500 P6, very good original condition throughout.
£2,000–2,300 *ADT*

1972 Rover 3500 V8, only 15,000 miles from new, outstanding condition.
£3,900–4,400 *ADT*

l. **1973 Rover P5B Saloon,** rebuilt engine, reconditioned automatic gearbox, good overall condition, some minor attention required.
£2,800–3,200 *ADT*

ROVER Model	ENGINE cc/cyl	DATES	CONDITION 1	2	3
P2 10	1389/4	1946-47	£2,900	£2,000	£500
P2 12	1496/4	1946-47	£3,200	£2,300	£600
P2 12 Tour	1496/4	1947	£6,500	£3,000	£1,000
P2 14/16	1901/6	1946-47	£4,000	£2,800	£700
P2 14/16 Sal	1901/6	1946-47	£3,700	£2,500	£700
P3 60	1595/4	1948-49	£3,000	£2,000	£800
P3 75	2103/6	1948-49	£4,000	£3,000	£800
P4 75	2103/6	1950-51	£2,800	£1,000	£800
P4 75	2103/6	1952-64	£2,500	£900	£800
P4 60	1997/4	1954-59	£2,300	£750	£800
P4 90	2638/6	1954-59	£2,900	£1,100	£500
P4 75	2230/6	1955-59	£2,500	£900	£400
P4 105R	2638/6	1957-58	£3,000	£1,600	£500
P4 105S	2638/6	1957-59	£3,000	£1,600	£250
P4 80	2286/4	1960-62	£2,500	£900	£500
P4 95	2625/6	1963-64	£3,000	£1,600	£500
P4 100	2625/6	1960-62	£3,200	£1,500	£500
P4 110	2625/6	1963-64	£3,250	£1,600	£500
P5 3 litre	2995/6	1959-67	£3,500	£2,000	£550
P5 3 litre Coupé	2995/6	1959-67	£5,000	£3,500	£750
P5B (V8)	3528/8	1967-74	£6,000	£4,000	£900
P5B (V8) Coupé	3528/8	1967-73	£6,000	£4,250	£1,250
P6 2000 SC Series 1	1980/4	1963-65	£2,200	£800	-
P6 2000 SC Series 1	1980/4	1966-70	£2,000	£800	-
P6 2000 SC Auto Series 1	1980/4	1966-70	£1,500	£600	-
P6 2000 TC Series 1	1980/4	1966-70	£2,000	£900	-
P6 2000 SC Series 2	1980/4	1970-73	£2,000	£900	-
P6 2000 SC Auto Series 2	1980/4	1970-73	£1,500	£800	-
P6 2000 TC Series 2	1980/4	1970-73	£2,000	£900	-
P6 3500 Series 1	3500/8	1968-70	£2,500	£1,400	-
P6 2200 SC	2200/4	1974-77	£1,750	£850	-
P6 2200 SC Auto	2200/4	1974-77	£2,500	£1,000	-
P6 2200 TC	2200/4	1974-77	£2,000	£1,000	-
P6 3500 Series 2	3500/8	1971-77	£3,000	£1,700	-
P6 3500 S Series 2	3500/8	1971-77	£2,000	£1,500	-

SAAB

1980 Saab 99 Turbo, very good condition.
£3,000–3,300 *H&H*
This is one of the later 145bhp models, and is believed to be one of the 500 homologation specials built by the factory.

1967 Saab Sonnett II V4 Sports Coupé, 1815cc, Sport and Rally modifications, with FIA and RAC papers, close ratio gearbox, limited slip differential, roll cage, fire extinguishers and cut-out switch.
Est. £7,000–8,000 *BKS*

Cross Reference
Racing Cars

SAAB Model	ENGINE cc/cyl	DATES	CONDITION 1	2	3
92	764/2	1950-53	£2,000	£1,000	£500
92B	764/2	1953-55	£2,000	£1,000	£500
93-93B	748/3	1956-60	£2,000	£1,000	£500
95	841/3	1960-68	£2,000	£1,000	£500
96	841/3	1960-68	£2,000	£500	-
96 Sport	841/3	1962-66	£2,000	£500	-
Sonnett II	1698/4	1967-74	£2,000	£800	-
95/96	1498/4	1966-80	£1,500	£500	-
99	1709/4	1968-71	£1,500	£1,000	-
99	1854/4	1970-74	£1,500	£1,000	-
99	1985/4	1972-83	£3,000	£1,000	£500
99 Turbo	1985/4	1978-83	£3,000	£1,000	£500

SECQUEVILLE-HOYAU

The Secqueville-Hoyau car company was established in 1919 in Gennevilliers, Seine, and manufactured luxury small cars which were built to exacting standards with very good quality workmanship.

r. **1922 Secqueville-Hoyau Sports 2 Seater with Dickey,** 4 cylinder, 1250cc engine, rated at 10hp, 4 speed manual gearbox, rear wheel drum brakes, semi-elliptic leaf springs suspension, right-hand drive, sporting body with V-screen and weather equipment for front passengers, some restoration, Marchal headlamps.
£11,000–12,000 *C*

Prior to car production, the company made aircraft components and during WWI they built Bugatti aero engines under licence which has led to speculation that their own car was designed by Bugatti himself.

SINGER

Although George Singer, of sewing machine fame, originally produced bicycles in Coventry, he built his first true motor car in 1905. These vehicles were basically Lea-Francis products built under licence with White & Poppe engines.

The first Singer-engined model, the 10hp, was introduced in 1912. Success continued after WWI, with the Singer Nine gaining a creditable record at the Le Mans 24-hour race.

In 1956 the Singer company was acquired by the Rootes Group, and badge-engineered products followed until 1970 when the marque was finally phased out.

1934 Singer Le Mans 9hp 2 Seater Sports, original specification, original fitted radiator stone guard, folding windscreen with 2 cowl scuttle, sprung steering wheel, cut-away doors, large slab petrol tank with twin side stone guard, twin rear-mounted spare wheels, extensive body-off restoration.
£10,000–11,000 *S*

SINGER Model	ENGINE cc/cyl	DATES	CONDITION 1	2	3
10	1097/4	1918-24	£5,000	£2,000	£1,000
15	1991/6	1922-25	£6,000	£3,000	£1,500
14/34	1776/6	1926-27	£7,000	£4,000	£2,000
Junior	848/4	1927-32	£6,000	£3,000	£1,500
Senior	1571/4	1928-29	£7,000	£4,000	£2,000
Super 6	1776/6	1928-31	£7,000	£4,000	£2,000
9 Le Mans	972/4	1932-37	£12,000	£8,000	£5,000
Twelve	1476/6	1932-34	£10,000	£7,000	£6,000
1.5 litre	1493/6	1934-36	£3,000	£2,000	£1,000
2 litre	1991/6	1934-37	£4,000	£2,750	£1,000
11	1459/4	1935-36	£3,000	£2,000	£1,000
12	1525/4	1937-39	£3,000	£2,000	£1,000

1934 Singer Le Mans 1 Litre Sports 2 Seater Speed Model, fully restored to high standard, excellent condition throughout.
£11,000–11,500 *BKS*

1947 Singer 9 Two Door 4 Seater Roadster, 4 cylinders, 1074cc, single overhead camshaft engine, good condition.
Est. £4,500–5,500 *ADT*

SIZAIRE-BERWICK

1914 Sizaire-Berwick 20hp Malvern Torpedo Tourer, 4 cylinder, in line, side valve monobloc engine, 4060cc, 4 speed gearbox with reverse, right-hand change, internal footbrake expanding on rear wheels, internal handbrake expanding on transmission, front and rear semi-elliptic suspension, Sizaire-Berwick patent worm and roller, excellent condition, some minor attention required.
£38,000–40,000 *C*

The photograph shows the late actor, Jack Warner, at the wheel, Mr Warner having been a test driver for Sizaire-Berwick in 1913.

1951 Singer 4 Seater Tourer, superb condition.
£8,000–8,500 *H&H*

This car was completely rebuilt regardless of cost, and was given the award for the best roadster at the Singer Owners' Club National Rally.

SS

1934 SSI Four Seater Tourer, very good condition throughout, maintained to highest standards.
£24,000–26,000 *COYS*

1934 SSI, 6 cylinders, non-original 16hp engine, excellent overall condition.
£27,000–28,000 *S*

1936 SSII Four Seater Coupé, 4 cylinders, 1608cc, maintained to highest standards, outstanding condition.
Est. £20,000–24,000 *COYS*

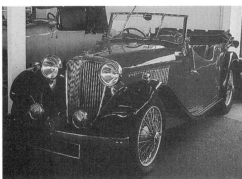

1934 SSII Four Seater Tourer, 4 cylinder, side valve engine, 1608cc, 38bhp at 4000rpm, 4 speed manual gearbox, 4 wheel drum brakes, semi-elliptic suspension, right-hand drive, in running condition though not used on the road for past few years, sound example, requires some cosmetic renovation.
£12,500–14,000 *C*

1938 SS Jaguar 100 Roadster, 6 cylinders, 2664cc, resprayed, retrimmed, superb condition. **Est. £70,000–80,000** *COYS*

AUSTIN SWALLOW

1932 Austin 7 Swallow Saloon, very good condition, many original features.
£10,000–11,000 *ASR*

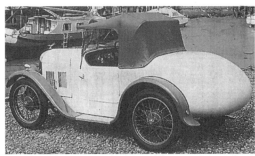

1929 Austin 7 Swallow Sports, very original, sympathetically restored.
£10,500–11,500 *ASR*

Cross Reference
Austin
Jaguar
Standard

Austin Swallow

- The Austin Swallow was the first car produced by the Swallow Sidecar and Coachbuilding Co, who became SS cars, SS Jaguar and the Jaguar Car Co.
- Priced about 70% higher than the standard Austin, the Swallow was aimed at the top end of the small car market and had many luxury features.
- The 2 seater sports version was produced between 1927 and 1932, and the 4 seater saloon between 1929 and 1932.
- Swallow also built luxury bodies for Standard 9, Wolseley Hornet, Swift and Fiat 9hp chassis.

AUSTIN Model	ENGINE cc/cyl	DATES	CONDITION		
			1	2	3
7 Swallow 2 Seater Sports	747/4	1927-32	£11,000	£8,500	£7,000
7 Swallow 4 Seater Saloon	747/7	1929-32	£10,000	£7,500	£6,000

STANDARD

The Standard Company was barely sixty years old when it was closed by British Leyland in 1963.

Founded by R. W. Maudslay in Coventry, Standard began modestly, and by the end of the Great War were producing very good and popular motor cars. They were joined by Captain John Black in the late 1920s who reorganised and transformed the company. The 'Flying' series are collected today by enthusiasts and they have a very active club.

1930 Standard Swallow 4 Seater Saloon, very well finished, restored to concours standard.
£14,500–15,500 *S*

STANDARD Model	ENGINE cc/cyl	DATES	CONDITION 1	2	3
SLS	1328/4	1919-20	£5,000	£4,000	£1,000
VI	1307/4	1922	£5,000	£4,000	£1,000
SLO/V4	1944/4	1922-28	£5,000	£4,000	£1,000
6V	2230/6	1928	£10,000	£8,000	£5,000
V3	1307/4	1923-26	£4,000	£3,000	£1,000
Little 9	1006/4	1932-33	£4,000	£2,000	£1,000
9	1155/4	1928-29	£5,500	£3,000	£1,000
Big 9	1287/4	1932-33	£4,500	£3,250	£2,000
15	1930/6	1929-30	£6,000	£4,000	£2,000
12	1337/6	1933-34	£4,000	£3,000	£1,500
10hp	1343/4	1933-37	£4,000	£2,500	£1,000
9	1052/4	1934-36	£4,000	£2,500	£1,000
Flying 9	1131/4	1937-39	£3,000	£1,800	£750
Flying 10	1267/4	1937-39	£3,250	£2,000	£750
Flying 14	1176/4	1937-48	£4,000	£2,000	£1,000
Flying 8	1021/4	1939-48	£4,000	£1,800	£750

1924 Standard Coleshill 2 Seater Tourer, good running order.
Est. £6,000–6,500 *S*

1931 Standard-Avon Coupé, 4 cylinders, 1005cc, good unspoilt condition, good running order.
£4,500–5,000 *ADT*

Based on the Standard Little 9 chassis with sporting coachwork of high quality manufacture.

1933 Standard Little 9, 4 cylinders, 1052cc, good general condition.
£3,400–3,800 *ADT*

1934 Standard 9, good condition.
£2,750–3,250 *CC*

l. **1935 Standard 12hp De Luxe,** 4 cylinder, side valve 1479cc engine, good original condition.
£1,800–1,900 *DB*

STANDARD Model	ENGINE cc/cyl	DATES	CONDITION 1	2	3
12	1609/4	1945-48	£2,000	£950	£250
12 DHC	1509/4	1945-48	£3,200	£2,000	£500
14	1776/4	1945-48	£3,000	£950	£250
Vanguard I/II	2088/4	1948-55	£1,800	£750	£150
Vanguard III	2088/4	1955-61	£1,500	£750	£150
Vanguard III Est	2088/4	1955-61	£2,000	£800	£150
Vanguard III Sportsman	2088/4	1955-58	£2,000	£800	£200
Vanguard Six	1998/6	1961-63	£1,500	£700	-
Eight	803/4	1952-59	£1,250	£500	-
Ten	948/4	1955-59	£1,400	£800	-
Ensign I/II	1670/4	1957-63	£1,000	£800	-
Ensign I/II Est	1670/4	1962-63	£1,000	£850	-
Pennant Companion	948/4	1955-61	£1,800	£850	£300
Pennant	948/4	1955-59	£1,650	£825	£250

1936 Standard Light 12, good general condition.
£2,000–2,500 *H&H*

1937 Standard Flying 12, 4 cylinders, 1608cc,
long storage, requires recommissioning.
£4,000–4,400 *ADT*

1954 Standard 10, 4 cylinders, 948cc, original car,
low mileage, good example.
Est. £500–650 *ADT*

1952 Standard Vanguard 1A, very good condition.
£2,200–2,600 *H&H*

1958 Standard Pennant, 4 cylinders,
948cc, recorded mileage of 19,000,
very good original condition.
£2,000–2,300 *ADT*

STANLEY

**1904 Stanley 8hp Model CX Steam
Runabout,** polished wooden wheels, separate
pilot fuel feed system, solid steel drum boiler,
good running order.
£12,500–13,500 *BKS*

STUDEBAKER

**1931 Studebaker President Model 81 Four
Seasons Roadster,** straight 8 engine, 337cu in,
122bhp at 3200rpm, 3 speed gearbox, 4 wheel
drum brakes, semi-elliptic leaf springs
suspension, left-hand drive, total nut and bolt
restoration, dual trip lights, single Pilot Ray,
stone guard, trunk, auxiliary tail lamp, Kelsey
Hayes stainless steel wire spoked wheels,
Lalique mascot.
£57,000–60,000 *CNY*
National Prize Winner in USA.

**1932 Studebaker President Four Seasons
Roadster,** straight 8 engine, 337cu in, 122bhp at
3200rpm, 3 speed gearbox, 4 wheel drum brakes,
semi-elliptic leaf springs front and rear, left-hand
drive, 29,000 miles from new, very original
overall condition.
£54,000–58,000 *CNY*

SUNBEAM

By the turn of the century the Sunbeam Bicycle Company had produced its first motor car, with a single cylinder 4 horsepower engine. A twin cylinder motor followed in 1901, and the Wolverhampton based company was on its way to producing not only good, high quality road cars, but also sensational racing cars. The famous designer, Louis Coatalen, built the cars raced by, amongst others, Sir Henry Segrave, and a Sunbeam was the first British motor car to win a Grand Prix – France in 1923.

The Company was acquired by the Rootes Group before WWII, and the name survived until 1982.

1913 Sunbeam 12/16hp 4 Seater Tourer, comprehensive mechanical restoration, good condition. **£30,000–32,000** *BKS*

1921 Sunbeam 24hp Standard Tourer, coachwork by factory, excellent condition throughout. **Est. £38,000–50,000** *COYS*

1926 Sunbeam 14/40 Folding Head Coupé with Dickey Seat, coachwork by Martin Walter of Folkstone, good overall condition, requires some attention. **£10,500–11,500** *BKS*

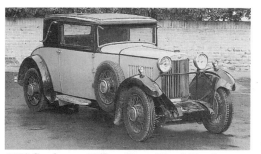

1930 Sunbeam 16 Two Door Fixed Head Coupé with Sunshine Roof, good unrestored condition. **£8,750–9,500** *BKS*

1933 Sunbeam 20hp Sportsman's Saloon, 6 cylinders, 2526cc, excellent condition throughout. **£6,400–6,800** *ADT*

> **Make the Most of Miller's**
> *Veteran Cars are those manufactured up to 31 December 1918. Only vehicles built before 31 December 1904 are eligible for the London/Brighton Commemorative Run. Vintage Cars are vehicles that were manufactured between 1 January 1919 and 31 December 1930.*

l. **1950 Sunbeam-Talbot 80 1.2 Litre 4 Door Saloon,** 1185cc Hillman Minx engine, with overhead valves, right-hand drive, one previous owner, excellent condition throughout. **£4,000–4,400** *BKS*

SUNBEAM Model	ENGINE cc/cyl	DATES	CONDITION 1	2	3
12/16	2412/4	1909-11	£20,000	£14,000	£10,000
16/20	4070/4	1912-15	£32,000	£22,000	£15,000
24	4524/6	1919-22	£28,000	£18,000	£10,000
3 litre	2916/6	1925-30	£48,000	£30,000	£20,000
16	2040/6	1927-30	£16,000	£12,500	£10,000
20	2916/6	1927-30	£22,000	£15,000	£10,500
Speed 20	2916/6	1932-35	£15,000	£10,000	£8,000
Dawn	1627/4	1934-35	£8,000	£5,000	£3,500
25	3317/6	1934	£10,000	£8,000	£4,000

Prices can vary depending on replica bodies, provenance, coachbuilder, drophead, etc.

1954 Sunbeam-Talbot 90 Drophead Coupé, 4 cylinders, 2267cc, repainted, good mechanical condition.
Est. £6,000–7,000 *ADT*

1955 Sunbeam-Talbot 90 MkIII A, dry stored since 1981, surprisingly good condition.
£2,750–3,000 *H&H*

l. **1954 Sunbeam Alpine MkI Roadster,** replacement 4 cylinder engine, 2267cc, overhead valve, gearbox converted to floor change, good condition.
Est. £8,500–9,500 *BKS*

1955 Sunbeam Alpine MkIII Sports Roadster, excellent restored condition.
£12,000–13,000 *BKS*

1969 Sunbeam Venezia, coachwork by Touring, totally original excellent condition.
Est. £9,000–10,000 *ADT*

SUNBEAM Model	ENGINE cc/cyl	DATES	CONDITION 1	2	3
Talbot 80	1185/4	1948-50	£3,500	£2,250	£1,000
Talbot 80 DHC	1185/4	1948-50	£6,000	£4,500	£2,000
Talbot 90 Mk I	1944/4	1949-50	£4,000	£2,100	£750
Talbot 90 Mk I DHC	1944/4	1949-50	£7,000	£4,750	£2,000
Talbot 90 II/IIa/III	2267/4	1950-56	£5,000	£3,000	£1,500
Talbot 90 II/IIa/III DHC	2267/4	1950-56	£6,000	£4,500	£2,250
Talbot Alpine I/III	2267/4	1953-55	£9,000	£7,500	£3,750
Talbot Ten	1197/4	1946-48	£3,500	£2,000	£750
Talbot Ten Tourer	1197/4	1946-48	£7,000	£4,000	£2,000
Talbot Ten DHC	1197/4	1946-48	£6,500	£4,000	£2,000
Talbot 2 litre	1997/4	1946-48	£4,000	£2,500	£1,000
Talbot 2 litre Tourer	1997/4	1946-48	£7,500	£4,000	£2,250
Rapier I	1392/4	1955-57	£1,200	£700	£300
Rapier II	1494/4	1957-59	£1,800	£900	£300
Rapier II Conv	1494/4	1957-59	£3,000	£1,500	£450
Rapier III	1494/4	1959-61	£2,000	£1,200	£400
Rapier III Conv	1494/4	1959-61	£3,500	£1,600	£600
Rapier IIIA	1592/4	1961-63	£2,000	£1,200	£400
Rapier IIIA Conv	1592/4	1961-63	£3,600	£1,700	£650
Rapier IV/V	1592/ 1725/4	1963-67	£2,000	£700	£250
Alpine I-II	1494/4	1959-62	£6,000	£3,500	£1,800
Alpine III	1592/4	1963	£6,500	£4,000	£1,250
Alpine IV	1592/4	1964	£6,500	£4,000	£1,250
Alpine V	1725/4	1965-68	£7,000	£4,000	£1,250
Harrington Alpine	1592/4	1961	£8,000	£4,750	£1,250
Harrington Le Mans	1592/4	1962-63	£10,000	£6,500	£3,000
Tiger Mk I	4261/8	1964-67	£12,000	£9,000	£5,000
Tiger Mk II	4700/8	1967	£10,000	£7,500	£5,000
Rapier Fastback	1725/4	1967-76	£1,100	£700	£250
Rapier H120	1725/4	1968-76	£1,500	£800	£300

l. **1965 Sunbeam Tiger Harrington Sports Coupé,** Webasto sunroof, rebuilt, excellent overall condition.
Est. £18,000–19,000 *BKS*

> *A rebuilt car is not necessarily more valuable than a car in good original condition, even if the restoration has been costly.*

1966 Sunbeam Tiger MkI 260, 8 cylinders, 4200cc, excellent mechanical condition, converted to right-hand drive when imported to UK in 1980s.
Est. £8,000–11,000 *COYS*

1967 Sunbeam Alpine 1725cc GT Sports 2 Seater, less than 30,000 miles recorded, garaged and unused since 1983, very good all-round condition.
£5,750–6,250 *BKS*

TALBOT

The talbot company was incorporated in 1902 to build French Clement vehicles in England. The first all-British Talbot appeared in 1906.

George Roesch, a well-known Swiss engineer, joined the company in 1916, and went on to design some first class motor cars. At this time Clement-Talbot was acquired by Darracq, and a takeover of Sunbeam soon followed forming the STD (Sunbeam-Talbot-Darracq) organisation.

1937 Talbot BD 105 Four Seater Open Tourer, replica coachwork in the style of Vanden Plas c1986, excellent condition throughout.
Est. 30,000–40,000 *BKS*

Launched in 1931, the Talbot 105 was fitted with a 6 cylinder engine of 2960cc, which developed 105bhp at 4500rpm with a compression ratio of 6.6:1 in touring form. For racing, however, the compression ratio was increased to 10.2:1 and output increased to 140bhp.

1935 Talbot T120 Two Door Cabriolet, very good condition.
Est. £41,000–55,000 *BKS*

This car is a fine example of one of the great French sporting marques.

1925 Talbot 10/23 Two Seater with Dickey, original condition, requires some restoration.
£4,000–4,400 *S*

TALBOT Model	ENGINE cc/cyl	DATES	CONDITION		
			1	2	3
25hp and 25/50	4155/4	1907-16	£35,000	£25,000	£15,000
12hp	2409/4	1909-15	£22,000	£15,000	£9,000
8/18	960/4	1922-25	£8,000	£5,000	£2,000
14/45	1666/6	1926-35	£16,000	£10,000	£5,000
75	2276/6	1930-37	£22,000	£12,000	£7,000
105	2969/6	1935-37	£28,000	£20,000	£15,000

Higher value for tourers and coachbuilt cars.

TOLEDO

1901 Toledo Runabout 6½hp Model B Steam Car, restored to highest standards.
£24,000–26,000 *BKS*

TOYOTA

The Toyota 2000GT was a true sporting GT car built for Toyota by Yamaha and only 337 were produced. They were only marketed in Japan and the USA, but were raced in the US with some success, and are highly sought-after by the Japanese and Americans. There are only two of these cars in this country, but one or two do come up for auction in the USA each year.

Toyotas from the 1970s are still relatively cheap to buy and maintain and most spares are still available from Toyota GB. They are mechanically robust, but the bodywork usually suffered badly from rust in the English climate. Interest in early Toyotas has grown steadily during the past two or three years, and Celicas and Crowns have been shown at many Classic Car Shows.

Peter D. Hunter

1972 Toyota Crown Coupé, excellent condition.
£1,400–1,600 *TEC*

1972 Toyota Crown Super, very good condition.
£1,000–1,200 *TEC*

1977 Toyota Celica 1600GT, very good condition.
£1,600–1,900 *TEC*

1974 Toyota Crown Coupé, excellent condition.
£1,400–1,600 *TEC*

1974 Toyota Celica 1600ST, excellent condition.
£1,200–1,400 *TEC*

l. **1977 Toyota Celica 2000GT Liftback,** superb condition.
£1,600–1,900 *TEC*

TOYOTA Model	ENGINE cc/cyl	DATES	CONDITION		
			1	2	3
Celica TA22 & TA23 Coupé	1588/4	1971-78	£1,400	£600	£350
RA28 Liftback	1968/4	1971-78	£1,400	£600	£350
Plus a premium of £200–500 for a Twin-Cam GT.					

1972 Toyota Crown Coupé, excellent condition.
£1,400–1,600 *TEC*

1967 Toyota Corona 1.5 Litre 1500 Four Door Saloon, manual transmission, only 42,400 miles, condition throughout commensurate with mileage, excellent condition.
£2,500–2,800 *BKS*

1966 Toyota 2000GT Coupé, an early example, very good overall condition.
£38,000–40,000 *BKS*

TOYOTA Model	ENGINE cc/cyl	DATES	CONDITION		
			1	2	3
Crown MS65, MS63, MS75, Saloon, Estate, Coupé	2563/6	1972-75	£1,200	£500	£300
Plus a premium of £200–400 for the Coupé.					

TRABANT

Introduced in 1959 by VEB Sachsenring Automobilwerk of Zwickau in East Germany (the German Democratic Republic), the first Trabant model – the Model 50 – replaced the Zwickau P70. Initially the 500cc, twin cylinder, 2 stroke engine was based on the P70 engine, but in 1962 the capacity was increased to 594cc. Like the P70, the Trabant featured a glass fibre body and front wheel drive.

1986 Trabant P601 Two Door Saloon, left-hand drive, good condition.
£1,400–1,600 *BKS*

TRIUMPH

1947 Triumph Renown, 4 cylinders, 1776cc, fair to good overall condition.
Est. £1,000–1,500 *ADT*

1934 Triumph Southern Cross Roadster, excellent overall condition.
£10,000–12,500 *FHF*

1946 Triumph 1800 Roadster, 4 cylinders, 1776cc, extensive restoration, excellent condition throughout.
£12,000–13,000 *ADT*

1948 Triumph Roadster, 2000cc engine, fully restored throughout.
£13,500–14,750 *WEC*

1948 Triumph Roadster, 2000cc, fully restored throughout.
£13,500–14,750 *WEC*

1949 Triumph Roadster, 2000cc, USA import, right-hand drive, requires restoration.
£6,000–7,000 *WEC*

Triumph Roadster

- The Roadster appeared in 1946 and was the first vehicle to be produced after Triumph had been acquired by Standard.
- Powered by a 4 cylinder overhead valve engine of 1776cc producing 65bhp.
- The Roadster was the last production car to feature a dickey seat.

TRIUMPH Model	ENGINE cc/cyl	DATES	CONDITION 1	2	3
Super 7 & 8 Saloon	747/4 & 832/4	1927-34	£5,000	£3,000	£1,000
Super 7 & 8 Tourer	747/4 & 832/4	1927-34	£6,000	£4,000	£1,400
Super 9 Saloon	1018/4	1932-33	£6,000	£3,000	£1,000
Super 9 Tourer	1018/4	1932-33	£7,000	£5,000	£1,500
Southern Cross	1018/4	1932-34	£7,000	£5,000	£1,500
Gloria Saloon 9.5 &10.8hp	1087 & 1232/4	1934-37	£9,000	£5,000	£2,000
Gloria Tourer 9.5 & 10.8hp *	1232/4 & 1991/6	1934-37	£15,000	£10,000	£3,000
Gloria Southern Cross 10.8hp	1232/4 & 1991/6	1935-36	£17,000	£11,000	£3,500
Gloria Saloon 2L	1991/6	1935-36	£15,000	£8,000	£4,000
Vitesse Saloon	1767/4	1937-38	£9,000	£5,000	£2,000
Vitesse Saloon	1991//6	1937-38	£14,000	£7,000	£3,500
Dolomite Saloon	1767/4	1937-39	£9,000	£5,000	£2,000
Dolomite Saloon	1991/6	1937-39	£14,000	£7,000	£3,500
Dolomite Roadster	1767/4	1938-39	£17,000	£11,000	£5,000

* Including Monte Carlo

1949 Triumph Roadster, 2000cc engine, excellent original example.
£10,000–12,000 *WEC*

1975 Triumph 2000 Saloon MkII, some light restoration, excellent condition bodily and mechanically.
£2,400–2,800 *H&H*

1954 Triumph TR2, 4 cylinders, 1911cc, professionally restored, superb condition.
£10,000–11,000 *ADT*

1955 Triumph TR2, excellent condition throughout.
£10,000–10,500 *H&H*

1964 Triumph 2000 Saloon Automatic, 12,200 miles from new, very good original condition.
£3,800–4,200 *H&H*

1977 Triumph 2500 TC, 6 cylinders, 2498cc, very sound and original.
Est. £700–1,200 *ADT*

l. **1977 Triumph 2500S Estate,** excellent overall condition.
£3,500–4,500 *SW*

1977 Triumph Dolomite, 30,000 miles from new, full service history, very good original condition. £1,400–1,600 *Bro*

1960 Triumph TR3A, Californian, twin Weber carburettors, rust free. £4,600–5,000 *CFI*

TRIUMPH Model	ENGINE cc/cyl	DATES	CONDITION 1	2	3
1800/2000 Roadster	1776/ 2088/4	1946-49	£12,000	£7,500	£3,500
1800	1776/4	1946-49	£5,000	£2,000	£1,000
2000 Renown	2088/4	1949-54	£5,000	£2,000	£1,000
Mayflower	1247/4	1949-53	£2,000	£1,000	£500
TR2 long door	1247/4	1953	£10,000	£8,000	£5,000
TR2	1247/4	1953-55	£9,000	£6,000	£5,000
TR3	1991/4	1955-57	£9,000	£8,500	£3,500
TR3A	1991/4	1958-62	£9,500	£8,500	£3,500
TR4	2138/4	1961-65	£9,000	£6,000	£3,000
TR4A	2138/4	1965-67	£9,000	£6,500	£3,000
TR5	2498/6	1967-68	£10,000	£8,500	£4,000
TR6 (PI)	2498/6	1969-74	£9,000	£7,500	£3,500
Herald	948/4	1959-61	£1,000	£400	£150
Herald FHC	948/4	1959-61	£1,500	£550	£300
Herald DHC	948/4	1960-61	£2,000	£800	£350
Herald 'S'	948/4	1961-64	£800	£400	£150
Herald 1200	1147/4	1961-70	£1,100	£500	£200
Herald 1200 FHC	1147/4	1961-64	£1,400	£800	£300
Herald 1200 DHC	1147/4	1961-67	£2,000	£900	£350
Herald 1200 Est	1147/4	1961-67	£1,300	£700	£300
Herald 12/50	1147/4	1963-67	£1,200	£600	£250
Herald 13/60	1296/4	1967-71	£1,300	£600	£200
Herald 13/60 DHC	1296/4	1967-71	£2,000	£1,200	£400
Herald 13/60 Est	1296/4	1967-71	£1,500	£650	£300
Vitesse 1600	1596/6	1962-66	£2,000	£1,250	£550
Vitesse 1600 Conv	1596/6	1962-66	£2,800	£1,350	£600
Vitesse 2 litre Mk I	1998/6	1966-68	£1,800	£800	£300
Vitesse 2 litre Mk I Conv	1998/6	1966-68	£3,000	£1,500	£650
Vitesse 2 litre Mk II	1998/6	1968-71	£2,000	£1,500	£300
Vitesse 2 litre Mk II Conv	1998/6	1968-71	£4,000	£1,750	£650
Spitfire Mk I	1147/4	1962-64	£2,000	£1,750	£300
Spitfire Mk II	1147/4	1965-67	£2,500	£2,000	£350
Spitfire Mk III	1296/4	1967-70	£3,500	£2,500	£450
Spitfire Mk IV	1296/4	1970-74	£2,500	£2,000	£350
Spitfire 1500	1493/4	1975-78	£3,500	£2,500	£750
Spitfire 1500	1493/4	1979-81	£4,500	£3,000	£1,200
GT6 Mk I	1998/6	1966-68	£5,000	£4,000	£1,200
GT6 Mk II	1998/6	1968-70	£6,000	£4,500	£1,400
GT6 Mk III	1998/6	1970-73	£7,000	£5,000	£1,500
2000 Mk I	1998/6	1963-69	£2,000	£1,200	£400
2000 Mk III	1998/6	1969-77	£2,000	£1,200	£500
2.5 PI	2498/6	1968-75	£2,000	£1,500	£900
2500 TC/S	2498/6	1974-77	£1,750	£700	£150
2500S	2498/6	1975-77	£2,500	£1,000	£150
1300 (FWD)	1296/4	1965-70	£800	£400	£150
1300TC (FWD)	1296/4	1967-70	£900	£450	£150
1500 (FWD)	1493/4	1970-73	£700	£450	£125
1500TC (RWD)	1296/4	1973-76	£850	£500	£100
Toledo	1296/4	1970-76	£850	£450	£100
Dolomite 1500	1493/4	1976-80	£1,350	£750	£125
Dolomite 1850	1854/4	1972-80	£1,450	£850	£150
Dolomite Sprint	1998/4	1976-81	£5,000	£4,000	£1,000
Stag	2997/8	1970-77	£9,000	£4,250	£2,000
TR7	1998/4	1975-82	£4,000	£1,200	£500
TR7 DHC	1998/4	1980-82	£5,000	£3,500	£1,500

1960 TR3A, good, well maintained, original car.
£8,250–8,750 *CGOC*

1962 Triumph Spitfire, 4 cylinders, 1147cc,
restored to very good condition.
Est. £3,750–4,500 *ADT*

1966 Triumph TR4A, 4 cylinders, 2138cc,
excellent condition throughout.
£8,250–8,750 *ADT*

1966 Triumph Spitfire MkII, 4 cylinders, 1147cc,
good overall condition.
Est. £1,750–2,250 *ADT*

1966 Triumph TR4A Sports, 2138cc, overdrive
gearbox, wire wheels, restored to very good condition.
£5,200–5,800 *H&H*

1966 Triumph TR4A, independent rear
suspension, well restored to original condition.
£9,000–9,250 *KSC*

1971 Triumph GT6,
good overall condition.
£2,000–2,500 *H&H*

r. **1973 Triumph Spitfire,** body off rebuild,
new hood and tonneau, concours condition.
£5,000–5,300 *SJR*

1980 Triumph 1500 Spitfire, carefully
maintained, good running order throughout.
£1,750–1,900   *H&H*

1979 Triumph Spitfire 1500, overdrive hard top,
soft top and tonneau cover, 15,500 miles recorded,
very good original condition.
£5,400–5,800   *ADT*

1971 Triumph Stag, early example,
repainted some years ago, will require
some recommissioning.
£3,200–3,500   *C*

1973 Triumph Stag, 8 cylinders, 2997cc, properly
maintained in original order, a good example.
Est. £5,500–6,500   *ADT*

Triumph Stag

- Introduced in 1970, the Stag was a
  luxury high performance sports car.
- Based on the Triumph 2000
  saloon car, it was styled by
  Giovanni Michelloti.
- Featuring a 3 litre, V8, overhead
  camshaft engine producing 145bhp.
- Although it suffered from a
  reputation for unreliability, the
  Stag had a top speed of 120mph.
- Production ceased in 1977.

1972 Triumph Stag,
good original condition.
£5,000–6,000   *VIC*

l. **1973 Triumph Stag MkII
2 Door Convertible,** 27,000 miles
since new short engine was fitted,
good condition throughtout.
£3,800–4,200   *ADT*

Don't Forget!
*If in doubt please refer to the
'How to Use' section at the
beginning of this book.*

r. **1975 Triumph Stag MkII 2 Door
Sports Convertible,** 2997cc, V8 engine,
automatic gearbox, power-assisted
steering, alloy wheels, factory hard top,
good condition throughout.
£3,700–4,100   *ADT*

Dexter Brown, 'Tour de France 1956', Stirling Moss in action, acrylic on canvas, mounted, framed and glazed, 36 x 48in (91 x 120cm).
Est. £3,500–4,000 *BKS*

Le Mans 1927, 'Accident à la Maison Blanché', watercolour and gouache, signed, dated and captioned by the artist, mounted, framed and glazed, 21 x 26in (53 x 66cm).
£7,500–8,000 *BKS*

F. Gordon Crosby, French Grand Prix 1921, Jimmy Murphy Duesenberg, watercolour, signed, 1928, 17 x 27in (43 x 69cm), mounted & framed.
£10,000–12,000 *BKS*

A coachbuilt Phaeton-style Hispano-Suiza tourer at speed on a country road, watercolour, pencil and gouache, c1932, 23 x 28in (60 x 71cm).
£4,200–5,200 *BKS*

F. Gordon Crosby, 'Grand Prix de l'ACF 1923', depicting Segrave in the 2 litre Sunbeam, watercolour, signed and dated 1929, 28 x 38in (71 x 96cm), mounted and framed.
£11,000–12,000 *BKS*

F. Gordon Crosby, 'Brookland's Picnic', pre-WWI setting, charcoal, watercolour and gouache, unsigned, mounted, framed and glazed, 26 x 33in (66 x 59cm).
£19,000–20,000 *BKS*

Bryan de Grineau, RAC Tourist Trophy 1933, watercolour and gouache heightened in white, signed and dated, 16½ x12in (42 x 30.5cm).
£6,000–6,500 *C*

Frederick Gordon Crosby, 'Brooklands – Flying Finish', watercolour and gouache, signed, 1914, 12½ x 21¼in (31.5 x 54cm).
£10,000–12,000 *C*

Michael Wright, Monaco Grand Prix 1936 – Alfa Romeo, watercolour and gouache, signed and inscribed, 22 x 16in (56 x 40cm).
£1,000–1,100 *BKS*

Nicholas Watts, Victory for Porsche – Le Mans 1970, print, one of an edition of 850, signed by Richard Attwood, Hans Hermann and the artist, 25 x 33in (63 x 84cm).
£90–100 *MPG*

Gavin Macleod, 'Moody Blue', Damon Hill in the 1995 Williams, print, 19½ x 27in (49.5 x 68.5cm).
£40–50 *MPG*

Francesco Scianna, a study of the Lancia Aurelia at speed, gouache, ink and pastel, signed, mounted, framed and glazed, 19 x 25in (48 x 63.5cm).
Est. £180–250 *BKS*

Michael Turner, Graham Hill in the high-wing Gold Leaf Lotus at the 1968 Mexican Grand Prix, watercolour and gouache, signed, 18 x 24in (46 x 61cm).
£4,000–4,500 *BKS*

Gavin Macleod, 'Italian Farewell', depicting Villeneuve's last race, print, one of an edition of 600, 22 x 33in (56 x 84cm).
£55–65 *MPG*

Nicholas Watts, 'Monaco Maestro', print, one of an edition of 850, 25 x 33in (63 x 84cm).
£70–80 *MPG*

Guy Lipscombe, a print depicting an early Mercer racing car at speed, inscribed and dated '1912' on reverse, 12½in (32cm) square.
£250–275 *BKS*

A Dunlop advertising display, lithographic cut-out mounted on plywood, c1930.
£450–550 *BKS*

A British Automobile Racing Club full member's badge, chrome plated and enamelled, stamped Membership No. '1053', c1950.
£75–95 *CARS*

A collection of Morgan coasters, c1990, 5in (12.5cm) wide.
50p–£1 each *FAL*

An Order of the Road chrome plated and enamelled member's badge.
£20–25 *CARS*

A British Racing Drivers' Club full member's badge, chrome plated and enamelled, c1930.
£350–400 *CARS*

Two showroom signs:
l. Riley, c1950. **£150–200**
r. MG, c1950. **£175–225** *MSMP*

A Brooklands Junior Club badge, chrome plated and enamelled, c1930.
£200–250 *CARS*

A Brooklands member's brass badge, c1990.
£50–75 *CARS*

A British Automobile Racing Club full member's badge, chrome plated and enamelled, stamped on reverse, c1925.
£450–500 *CARS*

A Bentley Drivers' Club chrome plated brass badge, in the form of a wheel spinner, c1960.
£25–35 *CARS*

An Order of the Road chrome plated and enamelled badge, c1950.
£125–150 *CARS*

An Alfa Romeo double-sided banner, post-WWII.
£400–440 *BKS*

A Brighton & Hove Motor Club chrome badge, c1930.
£250–300 *CARS*

British Motor Racing Marshals' Club chrome plated brass badge, enamelled, 1950s.
£100–150 *CARS*

A National Motorists' Association chrome plated and enamelled car badge, with motto on base plate 'Omnium Saluti', late 1930s.
£200–250 *CARS*

A Brighton & Hove Motor Club member's chrome and enamel, badge, c1950.
£40–50 *CARS*

An RAC associate member's enamelled, badge, c1930.
£45–55 *CARS*

An RAC associate member's badge, with enamelled central boss, early 1930s.
£80–100 *CARS*

An RAC full member's badge, pierced chromed brass on blue steel backing plate, c1950.
£30–40 *CARS*

An RAC associate member's nickel plated brass badge, early 1920s.
£125–150 *CARS*

An RAC associate member's badge, silver-dipped chromed brass with glass enamelled Union flag central boss, base stamped with membership number, late 1920s.
£80–100 *CARS*

An RAC full member's chromed brass badge, showing King Edward VII, and the Queen's crown, c1965.
£50–65 *CARS*

A pair of AA light car or motorcycle badges, WWI, 4⅛in high.
£280–300 *MSMP*

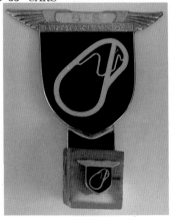

An RAC full member's nickel plated brass badge, with King Edward VII, and the King's crown, 1912–20.
£150–200 *CARS*

A Brooklands Society member's chrome and enamelled badge, and a lapel pin version, 1990s.
Badge **£20–25**
Pin **£8–10** *CARS*

An RAC full member's chrome plated brass with glass enamel badge, c1960.
£50–65 *CARS*

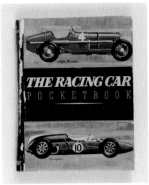

Motor Racing Facts, 1970.
£10–12 *GPCC*

The Encyclopedia of Motor Sport, by E. N. Georgano, 1971.
£90–120 *GPCC*

The Racing Car Pocket Book, by Denis Jenkinson, 1962.
£8–12 *GPCC*

Jack Brabham's Motor Racing Book, 1960, signed.
£30–45 *GPCC*

Jim Clark, Portrait of a Great Driver, by Graham Gauld, 1968.
£20–25
Jim Clark – The Legend Lives, signed.
£75–100 *GPCC*

The Modern Boys Book of Racing Cars, and *The Modern World Book of Motors*.
£150–160 *BKS*

James Hunt Against All Odds, by James Hunt and Eoin Young, 1977, signed.
£40–50 *GPCC*

Theme Lotus, 1956–1986, From Chapman to Ducarouge, by Doug Nye, signed by Innes Ireland, Mario Andretti, Peter Gethin, Peter Collins, and 10 others associated with Team Lotus.
£100–150 *GPCC*

World Championship, and *Champion Year*, 1959.
£18–25 each *GPCC*

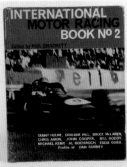

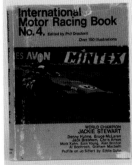

Motor Racing and Motor Rally Directory, 1957, 2nd edition.
£15–20 *GPCC*

International Motor Racing Book No. 2, 1968.
£10–15 *GPCC*

International Motor Racing Book, No. 4, 1970.
£10–15 *GPCC*

The Raleigh 7-17 Sports Tourer
brochure, 1934, 8½ x 9in
(21.5 x 23cm).
£25–30 *DM*

The Gordon Three Wheeler brochure,
1956, 8½ x 5½in (21.5 x 14cm).
£25–30 *DM*

The BSA Three Wheeler brochure,
1935, 9 x 8in (23 x 20.5cm).
£30–40 *DM*

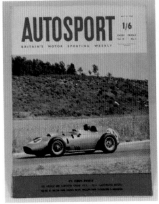

Autosport magazine, 1959.
£50–65 for full year *GPCC*

The Scootacar brochure, 1958,
8 x 5in (20.5 x 12.5cm).
£10–15 *DM*

Heinkel de Luxe Cruiser brochure, 1959,
6 x 8in (15 x 20.5cm).
£10–15 *DM*

Autosport magazine, 1963.
£45–50 for full year *GPCC*

The Morgan brochure, 1934,
5½ x 8½in (14 x 21.5cm).
£50–55 *DM*

Autosport magazine, 1984.
£35–40 for full year *GPCC*

Autosport magazine, 1955.
£65–80 for full year *GPCC*

Autosport magazine, 1977.
£45–50 for full year *GPCC*

Autosport magazine, 1993.
£35–40 for full year *GPCC*

A Goodyear double-sided wall mounted enamel sign, c1930.
£300–350 *MSMP*

Note the different tread pattern on reverse.

A Bosch spark plug enamel sign, excellent condition, c1950, 18 x 12in (45.5 x 30.5cm).
£90–100 *BCA*

A Carless Petrol enamel sign, c1920, 18 x 22in (45.5 x 56cm).
£100–120 *BCA*

A National Batteries enamel sign, inscribed 'For Price Power Performance', c1940.
£40–60 *BCA*

A KLG Sparking Plugs enamel sign, c1920, 18 x 12in (45.5 x 30.5cm).
£35–45 *BCA*

An Aeroshell Lubricating Oil double-sided hanging enamel sign, c1920.
£290–320 *MSMP*

A John Bull Tyres enamel sign, c1930, 18 x 22in (45.5 x 56cm).
£75–85 *BCA*

A Cleveland Petrols enamel sign, c1930, 20in (51cm) square.
£85–95 *BCA*

An enamel sign, inscribed Pratts 'On top in all Road Tests', c1930.
£30–50 *BCA*

An AA Garage shield-shaped enamel sign.
£110–120 *MR*

A Mobiloil "A" can-shaped enamel sign, c1930.
£240–280 *MSMP*

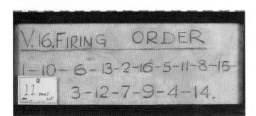

A section of asbestos wall taken from the BRM office at Bourne, with V16 firing order, framed and glazed.
Est. £1,200–1,500 *BKS*

A refrigerator, covered in Formula One logos etc, 66in (167.5cm) high.
£90–100 *BKS*

A set of Sparco racing overalls issued to Michael Schumacher, 1994 season.
£4,500–5,000 *BKS*

A pair of Ayrton Senna's 1989 racing overalls, Nomex, by Stand 21, France.
£14,000–15,000 *C*

A pair of Alain Prost's 1985 racing overalls, Nomex, by Stand 21, France.
Est. £3,000–5,000 *C*

r. A victory champagne bottle, signed by Ayrton Senna and Alain Prost, 1989.
£4,000–4,500 *BKS*

The original steering wheel from the Marlboro McLaren Honda driven to victory by Ayrton Senna in the San Marino Grand Prix, Imola, 1988, together with full-authentication certificate.
Est. £7,500–9,500 *BKS*

One of the helmets worn by Ayrton Senna in 1986, last worn by him when qualifying for the Australian Grand Prix in that year.
£43,500–45,000 *C*

There is a mark from the impact of a large stone above the visor.

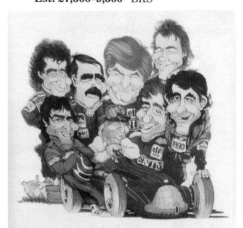

'The Magnificent Seven & The Master', pencil and watercolour depicting 7 world champions and Juan Fangio, signed by all drivers, published by the Adelaide News, framed and glazed.
Est. £5,500–7,000 *BKS*

A motor racing helmet, by Geno of Paris, worn by Duncan Hamilton, red painted aluminium shell, 1950s.
Est. £280–350 *BKS*

A Ferrari helmet, by Arai, worn by Nigel Mansell, Nos. SA009/86.99, dated '02/89', 1989.
£4,800–5,200 *BKS*
Worn by Nigel Mansell during the 1989 season and when he won the Brazilian Grand Prix.

A helmet, by Arai, worn by Nigel Mansell, signed, finished in sponsors' colours, 1992.
£6,000–7,000 *C*
Worn at the German Grand Prix and at Spa in 1992.

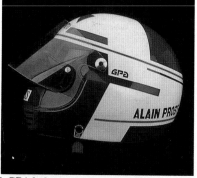

A GPA helmet, worn by Alain Prost, finished in blue and white with sponsors decals.
Est. £5,000–8,000 *C*

A Bieffe-Marlboro helmet, worn by Gerhard Berger in the Hungarian Grand Prix, signed 'Berger 94'.
£2,400–3,600 *BKS*

A Team-Lotus helmet, worn by Ayrton Senna when making a commercial, 1985.
£3,800–4,400 *BKS*

An original nose-cone section body panel, from Michael Schumacher's Championship car, Nos. 194/05/040:4 No. 03, 1994.
Est. £2,400–3,400 *BKS*

A Williams FW07 cockpit cover, from Alan Jones' World Championship winning car, good condition, 1980.
£1,600–2,200 *BKS*

An original nose section from the Hill-Shadow DN1A, No. '12', driven at the Monaco Grand Prix, 1973.
£250–300 *BKS*

A Saudia Williams original engine cover panel, from Keke Rosberg's Championship car, 1982.
£420–500 *BKS*

C. Vieweg, World Champions of Formula 1 – Phil Hill to Alan Jones, 2 original watercolours on fine art paper, mounted, framed and glazed, largest 21 x 36in (53 x 91cm).
£1,400–1,800 *BKS*

An Oldfield Dependence
oil combination tail and
number plate lamp,
c1908, 7in (18cm) high.
£35–40 *FAL*

A Lucas King of the
Road oil combination
rear and number
plate lamp, c1920,
9in (23cm) high.
£45–50 *FAL*

A Lucas King of the
Road car lamp, c1980,
12in (30.5cm) high.
£90–110 *FAL*

A Lalique dragonfly glass mascot, signatures
to base and tail, together with original Breves
Galleries invoice, dated 'November 4th 1937'.
£1,800–2,000 *BKS*

A Lalique comet clear glass mascot,
No. 1123, etched 'R. Lalique France'
to end of tail, 1925.
£15,000–16,000 *FFA*

A French mermaid glass
mascot, mounted an
illuminated base, marked
'Lumière et Cie', c1920,
6in (15cm) high.
£300–350 *S*

A Lalique Hirondelle swallow
clear and frosted glass mascot,
No. 1143, moulded signature
'R. Lalique' to base, 1928.
£2,500–3,500 *FFA*

A Lalique owl clear and frosted glass
mascot, No. 1181, etched signature
'R. Lalique' to base.
£45,000–50,000 *FFA*

A Lalique Tête d'Aigle clear
and frosted glass mascot,
moulded signature, 1928.
£2,000–3,000 *FFA*

A Lalique Tête de Coq clear
and frosted glass mascot, No.
1137, impressed 'Lalique', 1928.
£1,000–1,500 *FFA*

A Lalique Epsom horse's head mascot in clear and frosted glass, moulded signature.
£15,000–20,000 *FFA*

Introduced 5 June 1929 for Epsom.

A Lalique peacock's head mascot in clear and frosted glass, introduced 3 February 1928.
£5,500–6,000 *FFA*

A Lalique ram's head mascot in clear and frosted glass, impressed signature, introduced 3 February 1928.
£5,500–6,000 *FFA*

A Lalique dragonfly mascot in clear and frosted glass, moulded signature, introduced 12 April 1928.
£3,500–4,000 *FFA*

A solid nickel Spirit of Ecstasy mascot, signed 'Charles Sykes', for a Rolls-Royce Silver Ghost, c1923, 5½in (14cm) high.
£625–675 *S*

A Lalique Longchamps horse's head mascot in clear and frosted glass, moulded signature, introduced 12 June 1929.
£4,500–5,000 *FFA*

An Egyptian Ailee nickelled bronze, by H. Bonnot, 1920s, 7in (18cm) high.
Est. £800–1,000 *S*

A Scooter Girl chromed bronze mascot by A. Renevey, c1930, 5in (13cm) high.
Est. £400–480 *S*

A Rolls-Royce solid cast bronze chromium plated Spirit of Ecstasy mascot, c1938.
£250–300 *CARS*

A Le Genie nickel plated bronze mascot by M. Virot, designed 1921, 6¼in (16cm) high.
Est. £1,400–1,600 *S*

l. A Riley Ski Lady mascot, 1930–37, 5in (13cm) high, on a marble base.
£750–850
c. A Farman Icarus mascot, by Colin George, with foundry stamp, 1922–30, wingspan 7in (18cm), on a marble base.
£900–950
r. A nickel plated skier mascot, 1928–29, 5¾in (14.5cm) high.
£700–750 *S*

An elephant radiator bronze mascot, c1910, 6in (15cm) high.
£600–650 *BCA*

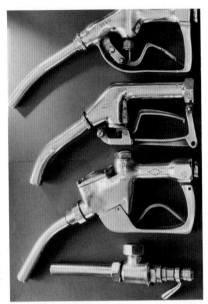

An Avery Hardoll petrol pump, restored, c1960.
Repro Globe £80–85
Pump £300–325 *MSMP*

A Gilbert & Barker roadside petrol pump, reproduction Shell pump globe, c1920.
£1,000–1,200 *BKS*

A Gilbert & Barker pump, restored, c1925.
£580–640 *MSMP*

A collection of petrol pump guns, 1920–50.
£15–25 each *MSMP*

Three petrol pump glass globes:
l. Shell Economy. **£150–170**
c. Shell Economy. **£160–180**
r. Super Shell. **£175–200** *BKS*

A Shell Derv globe, c1969.
£280–320 *MSMP*

A Kent pump globe, c1965, 17in (43cm) wide.
£140–160 *MSMP*

Three petrol pump glass globes:
l. Super Shell. **£220–240**
c. Shell Economy. **£180–200**
r. Shell. **£180–200** *BKS*

A Major Supreme petrol pump globe, c1970.
£180–220 *MSMP*

A Fina Diesel pump globe, c1970.
£180–220 *MSMP*

A Cleveland 50/50 Mixture globe, c1960.
£280–320 *MSMP*

An Essolene petrol pump globe, c1935.
£280–320 *MSMP*

A Tractor Vapourising Oil Shell-Mex BP Ltd glass pump globe, c1929, 17in (43cm) high.
£180–220 *MSMP*

A Cleveland Motor Diesel pump glass globe, c1970, 16½in (42cm) high.
£280–320 *MSMP*

A six-person picnic set, by
J. C. Vickery, suitable for a pre-
war Rolls-Royce Silver Ghost,
patented 1909, 25in (63cm) wide.
£2,500–3,000 *S*

A two-person tea basket, by
B. Altman, New York, with
fitments including kettle and
burner, c1920, 15½in (39cm) wide.
£1,300–1,400 *S*

An 'en route' drinks and picnic
set, c1910, 20½in (52cm) wide.
£1,800–2,000 *S*

A four-person picnic set,
with kettle and burner,
sandwich box in ceramic
and metal, cutlery in lid,
by Asprey, c1920.
£1,200–1,500 *BKS*

An overnight vanity case, by Mappin
& Webb, with 6 silver-topped bottles
and 2 silver back brushes, vesta case,
ink bottle, writing case, valuables box,
shoehorn, 1913, 16in (40.5cm) wide.
£1,000–1,100 *S*

A Coracle four-person picnic set,
with kettle and burner, glasses,
1910–14, 22in (56cm) wide.
£4,200–4,600 *S*

A two-person Rexine covered
picnic set, by Mappin & Webb,
c1908, 18in (46cm) wide.
£3,000–3,500 *S*

A two-person picnic set,
by J. C. Vickery, in a
sloped case, c1900–09.
£2,000–2,500 *BKS*
*The sloped lid doubled as
a foot-rest.*

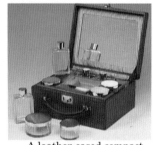

A leather-cased compact
vanity case, by Finnigans,
with silver-topped bottles.
£500–600 *BKS*

A Coracle four-person picnic
set, with 2 Thermos flasks,
wicker drinks bottles, cups
and saucers, glasses, the
cutlery housed in the lid.
£1,000–1,500 *BKS*

A six-person wicker picnic
set, with drinks bottles,
glasses, kettle and burner,
the cutlery housed in the lid.
£1,800–2,000 *BKS*

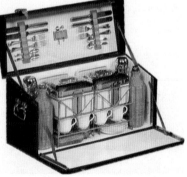

A four-person Rexine picnic case, with
3 wicker covered bottles, glasses,
ceramic butter jar, cups and saucers,
enamel plates, 2 flasks and 3 food
boxes, the cutlery housed in the lid,
1920s, 22½in (57cm) wide.
£2,000–2,500 *S*

A six-person black leather picnic set, with kettle and spirit stove.
£1,500–1,600 *BKS*

A Louis Vuitton lady's vanity and overnight case, 1920s, 19½in (49.5cm) wide.
£1,200–1,500 *S*

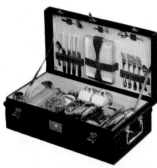

A Coracle four-person picnic set, 1920s, 23½in (60cm) wide.
£1,400–1,500 *S*

A six-person wicker picnic set, by Drew & Sons, with kettle and spirit burner, c1908–14.
£7,500–8,000 *FFA*

A two-person picnic set, by Drew & Sons, with step-board case, c1910, 14½in (37cm) wide.
£2,000–2,500 *S*

A two-person picnic set, by J. C. Vickery, c1905–09.
£1,200–1,600 *FFA*

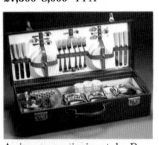

A six-person picnic set, by Drew & Son, with fitted interior, c1910, 30⅝in (78cm) wide.
£5,000–5,500 *S*

A Coracle four-person picnic set, with copper kettle, c1909–14.
£2,800–3,500 *FFA*

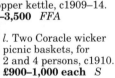

l. Two Coracle wicker picnic baskets, for 2 and 4 persons, c1910.
£900–1,000 each *S*

A six-person picnic set, by Drew & Sons, with table linen, c1905–09.
£8,500–9,000 *FFA*

A Coracle four-person running-board picnic set, in a wooden case, c1907–10.
£3,000–3,500 *FFA*

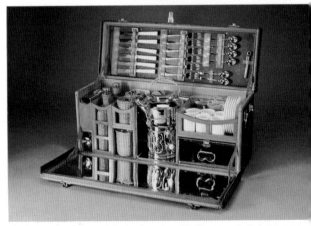

A six-person 'en route' picnic set, with honey oak lined interior, decorated kettle and burner, saucepan, glasses, bottles, condiments jars, 1908–10, 27in (69cm) wide.
£16,000–17,000 *S*

An original poster for the Monaco Grand Prix 1935, after Geo Ham, depicting a Mercedes W25 style racing car, linen-backed, 40 x 30in (101.5 x 76cm).
£3,100–3,400 *BKS*

An original poster for the British Grand Prix 1954 at Silverstone, full colour and photographic design, 30 x 20in (76 x 51cm).
£240–280 *BKS*

An original poster advertising the Grand Prix d'Europe, Reims, 1951, artwork by Marcel Gaglio, 32 x 24in (81.5 x 61cm).
Est. £500–800 *C*

An original poster for the British Empire Trophy Race excellent condition, 1935, 30 x 20in (76 x 51cm), unframed.
£390–420 *BKS*

An original poster for the British Grand Prix, Aintree, 1955, after Roy Nockolds, 30 x 20in (76 x 51cm).
Est. £280–350 *BKS*

An original poster for the BARC Goodwood Whitsun Trophy, with the Maserati 250F and BRM, c1955, 30 x 20in (76 x 51cm).
£280–300 *BKS*

An original poster for the British Grand Prix at Silverstone, 1951, after Royman Brown, depicting the BRM V16, Ferrari 4.5 and Alfa 159, 30 x 20in (76 x 51cm).
£500–540 *BKS*

An original poster for the British Empire Trophy Race, Brooklands, excellent condition, unframed, 30 x 20in (76 x 51cm).
£260–290 *BKS*

An original poster for the BRDC 500 Mile Race, Brooklands, 1932, excellent condition, 30 x 20in (76 x 51cm).
£380–420 *BKS*

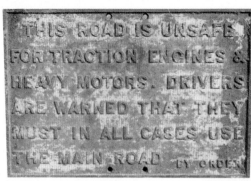

A cast iron road sign, c1900,
20 x 31in (51 x 79cm).
£80–90 *MSMP*

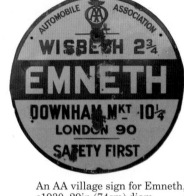

A Trial's Championship bronze trophy,
by Frederick Gordon Crosby, mounted
on a marble plinth, signed, 1930.
Est. £12,000–14,000 *BKS*

A motor car glass and silver-plated
cruet set, c1910, 4¾in (12cm) long.
£240–260 *BCA*

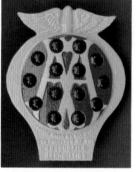

An AA offside reflector,
c1920, 9in (23cm) high.
£45–55 *MSMP*

An AA village sign for Emneth,
c1930, 29in (74cm) diam.
£75–85 *MSMP*

An Edwardian racing car
deskpiece, silver-plated, inkwell
missing, signed 'W. Furick'.
£1,500–1,600 *CSK*

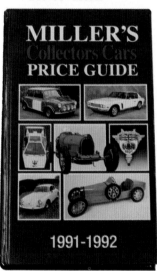

Miller's Collectors Cars Price Guide,
signed by racing drivers including
Ayrton Senna and Nigel Mansell, 1991.
£750–850 *LJ*

An AA village sign for Puckeridge
c1915, 34in (86.5cm) high.
£225–275 *MSMP*

A dashboard aneroid
barometer, early 1930s.
£270–300 *BCA*

Two clockwork toy models of Sunbeam
'Silver Bullet', and Napier 'Bluebird', by
Gunthermann, c1931, 18in (40cm) long.
Est. £180–220 each *C*

A St. Christopher dashboard silver
and green enamel mascot, c1950,
2in (5cm) diam.
£130–150 *BCA*

A Schweiz Veteranen-
Rallye Grand Prix
pewter trophy, 1959,
5¼in (13.5cm) high.
£25–30 *COB*

1971 Triumph TR6, 6 cylinders, 2498cc, restored throughtout, replacement engine.
£8,600–9,200 *ADT*

Triumph TR6

- Introduced as the best in the TR Series in 1969, the TR6 remained in production until 1976.
- Featuring a straight six cylinder, 2.5 litre engine, the early models produced 150bhp.
- Later models were detuned and, although retaining the fuel injection system, they produced 124bhp.
- American export models had twin Solex carburettors.
- Often considered the last of the true traditional British sports cars.

1981 Triumph TR8 Convertible, good condition.
Est. £5,000–7,000 *BKS*

1980 Triumph TR7 Two Seater Sports Convertible, good condition, overall high standard.
£3,800–4,200 *S*

TVR

l. **1992 TVR Chimaera,** 8 cylinders, 3952cc, 17,000 miles recorded, full history.
£24,000–25,000 *ADT*

TVR developed many models, popular variants being the 2500, the Vixen, and the Griffith. In 1992 the Chimaera 2 seater open sports car was produced, developed from the later series Griffith.

TVR Model	ENGINE cc/cyl	DATES	CONDITION 1	2	3
Grantura I	1172/4	1957-62	£4,000	£3,000	£2,000
Grantura II	1558/4	1957-62	£4,500	£3,000	£2,000
Grantura III/1800S	1798/4	1963-67	£5,000	£3,000	£2,200
Tuscan V8	4727/8	1967-70	£12,000	£7,000	£6,000
Vixen S2/3	1599/4	1968-72	£5,000	£3,000	£1,500
3000M	2994/6	1972-79	£7,000	£4,000	£3,000
Taimar	2994/6	1977-79	£7,500	£5,000	£3,500

VANDEN PLAS

Make the most of Miller's

Condition is absolutely vital when assessing the value of a vehicle. Top class vehicles on the whole appreciate much more than less perfect examples. Rare, desirable cars may command higher prices even when in need of restoration.

l. **1978 Vanden Plas Allegro 1500,** 67,000 miles recorded, excellent condition throughout.
£900–1,000 *Mot*

VANDEN PLAS Model	ENGINE cc/cyl	DATES	CONDITION 1	2	3
3 litre I/II	2912/6	1959-64	£4,000	£2,000	£700
4 litre R	3909/6	1964-67	£4,000	£2,500	£700
1100 Princess	1098/4	1964-67	£2,000	£1,000	£250
1300 Princess	1275/4	1967-74	£2,200	£1,500	£500

Don't Throw Away A Fortune!
Invest In
Miller's Price Guides

Please send me the following editions

❑ **Miller's Collectables Price Guide 1996/1997** -- £16.99

❑ **Miller's Antiques Price Guide 1997** – £21.99

❑ **Miller's Classic Motorcycles Price Guide 1997/1998** – £12.99

❑ **Miller's Pine & Country Furniture Buyer's Guide** – £17.99

❑ **Miller's Art Nouveau & Art Deco Buyer's Guide** – £17.99

If you do not wish your name to be used by Miller's or other carefully selected organisations for promotional purposes, please tick this box ❑

I enclose my cheque/postal order for £.................post free (UK only)
Please make cheques payable to *'Reed Book Services Ltd.'*
or please debit my Access/Visa/Amex/Diners Club account number

Expiry Date............/............

NAME *Title   Initial   Surname*

ADDRESS

Postcode

SIGNATURE

Photocopy this page or write the above details on a separate sheet and send it to Miller's Direct, 43 Stapleton Road, Orton Southgate, Peterborough, PE2 6TD or telephone the Credit Card Hotline 01733 371999. Lines open from 9:00 to 5:00. Registered office: Michelin House, 81 Fulham Road, London SW3 6RB. Registered in England number 1974080

CODE: W104

VAUXHALL

In 1903 the Vauxhall Iron Works Company Ltd produced its first vehicle, a 5hp standard light car. They moved their car production to Luton in 1905 and have been there ever since. Superb motor cars, engineered by Laurence Pomeroy, were built and the company was acquired by General Motors in 1925.

The mainstay of Vauxhall production, the light six, was replaced by a more modern looking series in 1935. Vauxhalls of the 1950s showed some very stylish saloons, heavily influenced by transatlantic tastes, notably the Velox and Wyvern ranges.

Vauxhall, with Opel, are one of the largest manufacturers in Europe today.

1903 Vauxhall Voiturette, single horizontal cylinder, 970cc, water-cooled, 5hp engine, 2 speed epicyclic gearbox, single chain drive, external contracting rear brakes, coil spring suspension front and rear, side tiller steering, good running order, regularly used, very good all-round condition.
£30,000–32,000 *C*

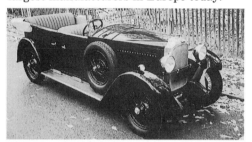

1929 Vauxhall 20/60 Princeton 4 Seater Tourer, new paint and upholstery, sound overall condition, extremely presentable.
Est. £18,000–20,000 *BKS*

1931 Vauxhall 14hp Saloon, fully restored condition.
£8,000–8,400 *CC*

l. **1932 Vauxhall Cadet 26hp,** full professional body-off restoration, good condition in all respects.
£6,000–6,500 *ADT*

1939 Vauxhall 14hp Type 5.
£2,500–3,000 *DB*

VAUXHALL Model	ENGINE cc/cyl	DATES	CONDITION 1	2	3
D/OD	3969/4	1914-26	£32,000	£24,000	£18,000
E/OE	4224/4	1919-28	£100,000	£60,000	£25,000
Eighty	3317/6	1931-33	£10,000	£8,000	£5,000
Cadet	2048/6	1931-33	£7,000	£5,000	£3,000
Lt Six	1531/6	1934-38	£5,000	£4,000	£1,500
14	1781/6	1934-39	£4,000	£3,000	£1,500
25	3215/6	1937-39	£5,000	£4,000	£1,500
10	1203/4	1938-39	£4,000	£3,000	£1,500

l. **1975 Vauxhall Victor 2.3S,** manual gearbox, good condition.
£700–750 *H&H*

> *A rebuilt car is not necessarily more valuable than a car in good original condition, even if the restoration has been costly.*

r. **1957 Vauxhall Velox,** recently restored to very high standard.
£2,500–3,000 *C*

1965 Vauxhall Viva, 4 cylinders, 1057cc, low mileage, unrestored.
£450–500 *DB*

1977 Vauxhall Magnum Saloon 1800, 67,000 miles, with history, very good original condition.
£600–650 *Mot*

VAUXHALL Model	ENGINE cc/cyl	DATES	CONDITION 1	2	3
Wyvern LIX	1500/4	1948-51	£2,000	£1,000	£500
Velox LIP	2200/6	1948-51	£2,000	£1,000	£500
Wyvern EIX	1500/4	1951-57	£2,000	£1,320	£400
Velox EIPV	2200/6	1951-57	£3,000	£1,650	£400
Cresta EIPC	2200/6	1954-57	£3,000	£1,650	£400
Velox/Cresta PAS/PAD	2262/6	1957-59	£2,850	£1,300	£300
Velox/Cresta PASY/PADY	2262/6	1959-60	£2,700	£1,500	£300
Velox/Cresta PASX/PADX	2651/6	1960-62	£2,700	£1,300	£300
Velox/Cresta PASX/PADX Est	2651/6	1960-62	£2,700	£1,300	£300
Velox/Cresta PB	2651/6	1962-65	£1,600	£800	£100
Velox/Cresta PB Est	2651/6	1962-65	£1,600	£800	£100
Cresta/Deluxe PC	3294/6	1964-72	£1,500	£800	£100
Cresta PC Est	3294/6	1964-72	£1,500	£800	£100
Viscount	3294/6	1964-72	£1,700	£900	£100
Victor I/II	1507/4	1957-61	£2,000	£1,000	£250
Victor I/II Est	1507/4	1957-61	£2,100	£1,100	£300
Victor FB	1507/4	1961-64	£1,500	£900	£200
Victor FB Est	1507/4	1961-64	£1,600	£1,000	£300
VX4/90	1507/4	1961-64	£2,000	£900	£150
Victor FC101	1594/4	1964-67	£1,600	£900	£150
Victor FC101 Est	1594/4	1964-67	£1,800	£1,000	£200
101 VX4/90	1594/4	1964-67	£2,000	£1,500	£250
VX4/90	1975/4	1969-71	£1,000	£600	£100
Ventora I/II	3294/6	1968-71	£1,000	£375	£100
Viva HA	1057/4	1963-66	£1,000	£350	£100
Viva SL90	1159/4	1966-70	£1,000	£350	£100
Viva Brabham	1159/4	1967-70	£1,200	£500	£100
Viva	1600/4	1968-70	£500	£350	£100
Viva Est	1159/4	1967-70	£500	£400	£100

VOLKSWAGEN

Developed by Ferdinand Porsche and incorporating designs from TATRA, the first air-cooled, 984cc engined Volkswagen was introduced to Adolf Hitler's Nazi Party in 1938. Originally only developed as a prototype vehicle it was turned into a production model in the mid-1940s and eventually exported in 1947, when it became known as the Volkswagen Beetle, the 'people's car'.

In 1949, a VW Beetle was given to the Karmann design house and after a few alterations the Karmann Cabriolet was launched and has since become a much sought-after classic.

In 1954, the Beetle engine was uprated to 1192cc and 3 years later the design received its first major facelift with the split rear window being replaced by a small oval one. The flat windscreen was withdrawn in 1976 in favour of the curved design which had been used in certain models for a number of years. By 1979 production of the Beetle ended in Germany after nearly twelve million Beetles had been built. Although production of the Beetle has never stopped entirely, it is now made in Mexico under the name Fusca.

The Beetle, or Bug as it is affectionately known, can truly be heralded as one of the most popular cars ever produced.

R. P. Saxton

1955 Volkswagen Beetle, 4 cylinders, 1200cc, oval rear window, Alpine White paintwork, semaphore indicators, blade bumpers, lowered suspension, period roof-rack, left-hand drive, very good condition.
£3,200–3,400 *PC*

1964 Volkswagen Beetle, 4 cylinders, 1192cc, very good partly restored condition.
£3,000–3,500 *ADT*

1973 Volkswagen Beetle, 4 cylinders, 1300cc, 30hp, original Texas Yellow paintwork, Empi 8-spoke alloy wheels, very good condition.
£1,400–1,600 *PC*

1965 Volkswagen 21 Window Samba Split Screen Camper, 1500cc, US specification front bumper, lowered suspension, full length ragtop sunroof, fridge and cooker, very good condition.
£4,200–4,400 *PC*

A rebuilt car is not necessarily more valuable than a car in good original condition, even if the restoration has been costly.

l. **1971 Volkswagen Beetle 1300 Saloon**, 1284cc, 23,000 miles recorded, good original condition throughout.
£3,500–4,000 *H&H*

VOLKSWAGEN Model	ENGINE cc/cyl	DATES	CONDITION 1	2	3
Beetle (split rear screen)	1131/4	1945-53	£5,000	£3,500	£2,000
Beetle (oval rear screen)	1192/4	1953-57	£4,000	£2,000	£1,000
Beetle (slope headlamps)	1192/4	1957-68	£2,500	£1,000	£600
Beetle DHC	1192/4	1954-60	£6,000	£4,500	£2,000
Beetle 1500	1493/4	1966-70	£3,000	£2,000	£1,000
Beetle 1302 LS	1600/4	1970-72	£2,500	£1,850	£850
Beetle 1303 S	1600/4	1972-79	£3,000	£2,000	£1,500
1500 Variant/1600	1493/ 1584/4	1961-73	£2,000	£1,500	£650
1500/1600	1493/ 1584/4	1961-73	£3,000	£2,000	£800
Karmann Ghia/I	1192/4	1955-59	£5,000	£3,000	£1,000
Karmann Ghia/I DHC	1192/4	1957-59	£8,000	£5,000	£2,500
Karmann Ghia/I	1192/4	1960-74	£5,500	£3,000	£1,800
Karmann Ghia/I DHC	1192/4	1960-74	£7,000	£4,500	£2,000
Karmann Ghia/3	1493/4	1962-69	£4,000	£2,500	£1,250

1977 Volkswagen Cabriolet, 4 cylinders, 1584cc, good condition throughout.
£4,400–4,800 *ADT*

1966 Volkswagen Karmann Ghia 1600 Coupé, excellent overall condition.
£5,750–6,250 *Bro*

1972 Volkswagen Karmann Ghia Coupé, maintained to a very high standard, subject of a major refurbishment.
Est. £4,000–4,500 *S*

r. **1973 Volkswagen Karmann Ghia Coupé,** left-hand drive, restored but with original engine, good overall condition.
£2,300–2,600 *H&H*

VOLVO

Latin for 'I go', the first Volvo was produced in 1927. Designed by Helmer Masolle and engineered by Gustav Larson and Assar Gabrielsson the Volvo was built in Göteborg, Sweden, aimed solely at the Swedish market.

Post-war rally success made Volvo a byword for fast reliable machines with excellent road holding. Popular classic Volvos include the Amazon and the PV444, of which over 196,000 were built during a fourteen-year production run.

The P1800 Ghia-styled sports coupé immortalised by Simon Templar, 'The Saint', is one of the most desirable and sought-after Volvos today.

1960 Volvo P544 Two Door Sports Saloon, very good condition throughout.
£4,800–5,200 *BKS*

1961 Volvo 122S Amazon, good original condition.
£1,500–2,000 *H&H*

1962 Volvo 122S, 4 cylinders, 1780cc, interior and paintwork in good condition.
Est. £2,800–3,200 *ADT*

1966 Volvo 122S, 4 cylinders, 1800cc, original body in excellent condition.
£2,600–2,900 *ADT*

1967 Volvo 131 Two Door, very good condition throughout.
£3,000–4,000 *H&H*

VOLVO Model	ENGINE cc/cyl	DATES	CONDITION		
			1	2	3
PV444	1800/4	1958-67	£4,000	£1,750	£800
PV544	1800/4	1962-64	£4,000	£1,750	£800
120 (B16)	1583/4	1956-59	£3,000	£1,000	£300
121	1708/4	1960-67	£3,500	£1,500	£350
122S	1780/4	1960-67	£4,500	£1,500	£250
131	1780/4	1962-69	£4,000	£1,500	£350
221/222	1780/4	1962-69	£2,500	£1,500	£300
123Gt	1986/4	1967-69	£3,000	£2,500	£750
P1800	1986/4	1960-70	£3,500	£2,000	£1,000
P1800E	1986/4	1970-71	£4,000	£2,500	£1,000
P1800ES	1986/4	1971-73	£5,000	£3,000	£1,000

l. **1967 Volvo P1800S Sports Coupé,** fully restored.
Est. £2,800–3,500 *BKS*

> **Don't Forget!**
> *If in doubt please refer to the 'How to Use' section at the beginning of this book.*

1969 Volvo 121, 4 cylinders, 1986cc, good running order throughout.
£1,800–2,200 *ADT*

1967 Volvo 1800S, 4 cylinders, 1778cc, very good sound condition.
£1,750–2,000 *ADT*

1968 Volvo 1800S, fully restored condition.
Est. £3,500–4,500 *ADT*

1969 Volvo P1800S 2 Litre 2 Seater Coupé, highly original, low mileage example.
£3,300–3,700 *C*

> **Make the Most of Miller's**
> *Veteran Cars are those manufactured up to 31 December 1918. Only vehicles built before 31 December 1904 are eligible for the London/Brighton Commemorative Run. Vintage Cars are vehicles that were manufactured between 1 January 1919 and 31 December 1930.*

1971 Volvo P1800E, manual gearbox with overdrive, very good overall condition.
£4,750–5,250 *Bro*

1973 Volvo 1800ES, 4 cylinders, 1986cc, good general condition.
£2,400–2,800 *ADT*

1977 Volvo 244 Automatic, fair to good overall condition.
£1,300–1,500 *H&H*

WANDERER

1938 Wanderer W25K Roadster, 6 cylinders, 1949cc supercharged, thoroughly restored with great attention to historical detail, maintained to a high standard.
£80,000–85,000 *COYS*

This car was designed by Ferdinand Porsche.

WILLYS-KNIGHT

c1928 Willys-Knight 4 Door Open Tourer, complete in all major respects, fair condition, engine seized, restoration project.
£3,400–3,800 *S*

This car is one of about 7 survivors in the UK. It bears a 'Heaton Chapel, Manchester' plaque, indicating its UK manufacture.

1926 Willys Whippet Tourer, good overall condition.
£5,800–6,200 *H&H*

c1928 Willys-Knight, received considerable attention in recent years, good general condition.
£7,400–7,800 *COYS*

1930 Willys-Knight Great Six Model 66B 'Plaid Side' Roadster, 6 cylinder in line engine, Knight sleeve valve, 255cu in, 82bhp at 3200rpm, 3 speed manual gearbox, 4 wheel mechanical brakes, semi-elliptic leaf spring suspension, left-hand drive, immaculately restored example, covered only 9 miles since restoration.
£54,000–56,000 *CNY*

WINTON

The Winton Motor Carriage Company was founded by a Scotsman, Alexander Winton, in 1896. In their first year of production, 1898, 25 cars were built. The factory was at Cleveland, Ohio, and Winton enjoyed much competition, both on the track and in endurance, with much success.

Despite this, Winton cars ceased production in 1925. They continued to make marine diesel engines and became part of General Motors.

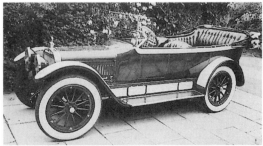

1916 Winton Six Model 22A 7 Passenger Touring, original and excellent condition.
£22,000–24,000 *BKS*

WOLSELEY

1912 Wolseley 12/16hp Tourer, good running order prior to recent fire damage, original specification.
£6,500–6,900 *BKS*

1909 Wolseley-Siddeley 14hp Tourer, pair-cast cylinders, 4 cylinders, 3 speed manual transmission, shaft final drive, full 4/5 seater tourer body with Auster screen for rear seat passengers, electric lighting, bodywork said to be original to the car, right-hand drive.
Est. £21,000–23,000 *BKS*

> **Cross Reference**
> Restoration Projects

1902 Wolseley 10hp, rear entrance, excellent condition.
£40,000–44,000 *WOL*

WOLSELEY (Veteran & Vintage) Model	ENGINE cc/cyl	DATES	CONDITION		
			1	2	3
10	987/2	1909-16	£16,000	£12,500	£9,000
CZ (30hp)	2887/4	1909	£18,000	£13,000	£9,000
15hp and A9	2614/4	1920-27	£12,000	£10,000	£8,000
20 and C8	3921/ 3862/6	1920-27	£11,000	£8,000	£6,000
E4 (10.5hp)	1267/ 1542/4	1925-30	£6,000	£4,000	£3,000
E6 and Viper and 16hp	2025/6	1927-34	£15,000	£12,000	£8,000
E8M	2700/8	1928-31	£18,000	£15,000	£12,000
Hornet	1271/4	1931-35	£10,000	£8,000	£4,500
Hornet Special	1271/ 1604/6	1933-36	£12,000	£8,000	£5,000
Wasp	1069/4	1936	£7,000	£5,000	£3,500
Hornet	1378/6	1936	£8,000	£6,000	£4,000
21/60 and 21hp	2677/ 2916/6	1932-39	£11,000	£6,000	£4,000
25	3485/6	1936-39	£8,500	£5,500	£4,000
12/48	1547/4	1937-39	£5,000	£3,000	£2,000
14/56	1818/6	1937-39	£6,000	£4,000	£2,000
18/80	2322/6	1938-39	£7,500	£5,500	£4,000

Early Wolseley cars are well made and very British and those with coachbuilt bodies command a premium of at least +25%.

1922 Wolseley H7 Model, 7hp, well restored.
£10,000–12,000 *WOL*

1919 Wolseley Stellite 9hp, completely restored to current superb condition.
£20,000–22,000 *WOL*

1925 Wolseley 11/22 Two Seater with Dickey, original equipment, excellent condition.
£11,000–13,000 *WOL*

1923 Wolseley 15/40 Landaulette,
4 cylinders, 2614cc, considerably restored, very good overall condition.
Est. £18,000–20,000 *ADT*

r. **1928 Wolseley 16/45hp 2 Seater with Dickey Convertible,** chassis in good condition, 2056cc engine in running order, electrical equipment requires attention, restoration project.
£7,400–7,800 *S*

1930 Wolseley 21hp Messenger, fully restored, excellent condition.
£14,000–15,000 *WOL*

1936 Wolseley 12 Sports Saloon, ex-police car,
good overall condition.
£7,500–8,500 *FHF*

1948 Wolseley 8hp, good condition throughout.
£2,500–3,500 *WOL*

1937 Wolseley 18/80, left-hand drive, good condition.
£5,000–6,000 *WOL*

WOLSELEY Model	ENGINE cc/cyl	DATES	CONDITION 1	2	3
8	918/4	1939-48	£3,000	£2,000	£1,000
10	1140/4	1939-48	£3,500	£2,000	£1,000
12/48	1548/4	1939-48	£4,000	£2,000	£1,250
14/60	1818/4	1946-48	£4,500	£2,500	£1,500
18/85	2321/6	1946-48	£6,000	£3,000	£2,000
25	3485/6	1946-48	£7,000	£4,000	£2,500
4/50	1476/4	1948-53	£2,500	£1,000	£450
6/80	2215/6	1948-54	£3,000	£1,500	£750
4/44	1250/4	1952-56	£2,500	£1,250	£750
15/50	1489/4	1956-58	£1,850	£850	£500
1500	1489/4	1958-65	£2,500	£1,000	£500
15/60	1489/4	1958-61	£2,000	£700	£400
16/60	1622/4	1961-71	£1,800	£800	£400
6/90	2639/6	1954-57	£2,500	£1,000	£500
6/99	2912/6	1959-61	£3,000	£1,500	£750
6/110 MK I/II	2912/6	1961-68	£2,000	£1,000	£500
Hornet (Mini)	848/4	1961-70	£1,500	£750	£400
1300	1275/4	1967-74	£1,250	£750	£400
18/85	1798/4	1967-72	£950	£500	£250

1954 Wolseley 4/44, well restored condition.
£2,500–3,000 *WOL*

1956 Wolseley 15/50, 39,000 miles, full history.
£2,900–3,100 *CC*

1957 Wolseley 15/50 1.5 Litre Saloon, only 29,000 miles recorded, very good original condition.
£2,200–2,400 *BKS*

Wolseley (Post-War)

After WWII Wolseley cars were badge-engineered Morris vehicles. For example, the Wolseley 8 was basically the Morris 8 and the Wolseley 4/50 and 6/80 were Morris Oxfords.

The 4/44 featured the MG TD engine detuned to produce 46bhp, and were quite well-known as police cars. Wolseley, with their more upmarket image, even produced their own version of the Mini, the Hornet. The badge-engineering continued until 1975, when the Wolseley name finally and sadly disappeared.

1965 Wolseley 1100 Saloon, 17,000 miles, original and concours condition throughout.
£4,000–4,400 *S*

1959 Wolseley 15/60 Saloon, 4 cylinders, 1489cc, good condition throughout, original in many respects.
£1,500–1,800 *ADT*

1968 Wolseley Hornet MkIII, good overall condition.
£900–1,000 *H&H*

1971 Wolseley 16/60 Saloon, excellent condition throughout.
£1,600–1,800 *H&H*

COMMERCIAL VEHICLES

1924 Morris Commercial Light Tonner Van,
4 cylinder, 1802cc, 13.9hp engine, very good
overall condition.
£8,800–9,600 *ADT*

1926 Austin 12/4 Pick-Up Truck,
in good overall condition.
£9,000–10,000 *FHF*

l. **1926 Rolls-Royce 20hp Delivery Van,**
full body restoration.
£19,750–20,250 *Bro*

1930 Morris Cowley Light Van,
in good order throughout.
£4,200–4,600 *H&H*

c1932 Citroën C4 Light Commercial Truck,
very good condition throughout, fully restored.
£5,000–5,500 *C*

1937 Bedford WLG Flat Bed Truck, very good
condition all-round, cosmetic attention received.
£7,000–7,400 *S*

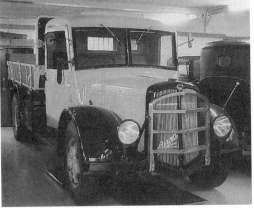

1946 Berna 3½ Ton Three-Way Tipper, direct
injection 4 cylinder diesel, 5.3 litre, 65bhp,
5 speed with synchromesh on top 2 gears,
pneumatic drum brakes, semi-elliptic all-round
suspension, left-hand drive, overhauled,
mechanically in excellent condition.
£3,600–4,200 *C*

1948 Jowett Bradford Pick-Up,
fair to good condition.
£1,000–1,500 *HOLL*

1953 Austin A40 Devon Pick-Up,
very well restored.
£4,750–5,250 *Bro*

1959 Austin A35 Van, stored for the majority of its
life in less than ideal conditions, body needs tidying.
£425–450 *ADT*

1960 Saurer Alpenwagen IIIA, coachwork by
Ramseier & Jenzer, in line 6 cylinder diesel,
8720cc engine, 135bhp, 8 gear pneumatic,
preselector gearbox, live axle front and rear
suspension, 4 wheel drum brakes, left-hand drive,
overhauled, mechanically in excellent condition.
£13,200–14,600 *C*

1968 Austin A35 Van, in good overall condition.
Est. £1,000–1,500 *LF*

1959 Ford 100E Van, very good
restored condition.
£1,200–1,500 *HOLL*

1981 Reliant Mighty Ant TW9 Tipper Truck,
very good condition.
£3,250–3,500 *S*

CYCLE CARS

1901 Royal Enfield Quadricycle, De-Dion
Bouton single vertical cylinder, 2¾hp engine,
largely original condition.
£8,000–8,500 *C*

*This car is eligible for the RAC London to Brighton
Veteran Car Run.*

1903 Quadrant 3hp Three-Wheeled Forecar,
3hp, single cylinder engine, surface carburettor,
atmospheric inlet valves, ignition by coil and
battery, single speed belt drives to rear wheel,
fitted with clutch, subject of careful restoration
some 30 years ago.
£12,000–12,500 *BKS*

FIRE APPLIANCES

1896 Shand Mason Steam Fire Engine, overall appearance indicating careful storage and very little use.
£12,500–13,000 *BKS*

1942 Leyland Merryweather Fire Engine, 4 cylinders, 33.3hp, overall chassis is sound, turntable operated ladders, condition is generally good.
£2,500–3,000 *ADT*

MICROCARS

1966 Trojan 200cc Bubble Car, 16,000 miles recorded, one previous owner, excellent restored condition.
Est. £4,000–5,000 *BKS*

1963 Scootacar MkI, Villiers 197cc, 2 stroke engine.
£1,500–2,000 each *ScR*

About 750 Scootacars of this model were produced. There was also a MkII and MkIII version with a different body shape, making the total production of Scootacars in the region of 950. They were manufactured at the Hunslet Locomotive works in Leeds during the late 1950s.

MILITARY VEHICLES

1959 Willys Jeep General Purpose 0.25 Ton 4x4, completely original and good throughout.
Est. £4,000–5,000 *BKS*

1951 Dodge M37 4x4 Truck, fair to good overall condition.
£1,800–2,100 *DB*

1956 Volvo TP21 Military 4x4 Radio/Command Car, 3.6 litre engine, very good all-round condition.
£4,400–4,800 *BKS*

1942 Daimler Scout Car Dingo MkII, 6 cylinder DB18 engine, rebuilt, full restoration from chassis up.
£4,400–4,800 *S*

REPLICA VEHICLES

1972 Replica Alfa Romeo Giulia 2000 GTAM,
4 cylinders, 1962cc, 180bhp, twin Weber 45 DCOE
carburettors, thorough restoration including
modifying body to GTAM specification.
Est. £5,800–7,000 *ADT*

1990 Replica Bugatti, 4 cylinders, 1600cc, based
on Volkswagen Beetle running gear and engine,
good overall condition.
£2,400–2,600 *ADT*

1973 Replica Ferrari Daytona Spyder,
coachwork by Autokraft Restorations, 5 speed
gearbox, right-hand drive, running gear based
on Daimler Double 6, good overall condition.
Est. £15,000–17,000 *ADT*

1978 Daytona Spyder Replica, by Robin Hood.
£11,750–12,250 *BLE*

1989 Proteus C-Type, superb fibreglass body,
excellent condition in every respect.
£11,000–12,000 *COYS*

**1966 Jaguar D-Type 'Short Nose' Competition
(Remanufactured),** all aluminium, constructed
from an original Jaguar.
£63,000–68,000 *BLK*

1967/89 Jaguar D-Type Replica, 3.8 litre,
6 cylinders, 3781cc, triple SU carburettors, 4 speed
manual gearbox, aluminium tub, GRP long nose,
finned rear, wrap-around windscreen.
Est. £10,000–12,000 *ADT*

Based on Jaguar running gear.

**1963/88 Wingfield 3.8 Litre D-Type Sports
2 Seater,** engine converted to dummy dry-
sump appearance, excellent overall condition.
£33,000–34,000 *BKS*

Based on a 1963 production Jaguar E-Type.

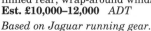

r. **1990 Jaguar D-Type Replica,**
6 cylinder, 3781cc engine, hard
pressed to distinguish from
an original.
Est. £58,000–65,000 *COYS*

1987 Jaguar D-Type 'Short Nose' Replica,
6 cylinder, 3797cc engine, restored, in very fine
order throughout.
Est. £16,500–18,500 *ADT*

1989 Riley MPH Replica, complete history with
warranted 5,500 mileage, outstanding condition.
£7,500–8,000 *S*

1953 Wolseley Replica Police Car,
as new condition.
£5,000–6,000 *SW*

RESTORATION PROJECTS

1948 AC 2 Litre Saloon, for restoration.
Est. £1,800–2,000 *HOLL*

**1935 Alvis Speed 20SC 3 Position Drophead
Coupé,** as found, poor mechanical order, with
engine and brakes seized, largely complete,
ready for restoration.
£13,300–13,600 *S*

1936 Bentley 4¼ Litre Pillarless Saloon,
coachwork by Van Vooren, splendid 'barn find'
Derby Bentley.
£8,800–9,400 *BKS*

c1935 BMW 319 2 Seater Sports Cabriolet,
6 cylinders, overhead valve, 1911cc, 4 speed
manual gearbox, 4 wheel drum brakes, single
transverse leaf spring front suspension, semi-
elliptic rear, right-hand drive.
£3,500–3,900 *C*

*Substantial work and money have already been
spent to date including; body-off check of the
chassis, rebuilding axles, hubs, brakes, springs
and shock absorbers, the engine rebuilt, rebored,
new pistons, crankshaft, main bearings and big
ends refurbished.*

> **Don't Forget!**
> *If in doubt please refer to the
> 'How to Use' section at the
> beginning of this book.*

1935/49 BMW Open Sports, 6 cylinder, 1971cc
engine, with nearly all the major components.
£7,600–8,200 *COYS*

1937 Daimler Straight 8 Limousine, coachwork by H. J. Mulliner, good original condition.
£5,600–6,000 *S*

1930 Dennis G7 Fire Engine Converted to Mobile Crane, for restoration.
£1,100–1,300 *DB*

1970 Jaguar E-Type Series II 2+2 Fixed Head Coupé, will require minor recommissioning all round.
£6,800–7,200 *S*

1931 Rolls-Royce Phantom II Rolling Chassis, 6 cylinders, overhead valve, 7668cc, 120bhp at 2750rpm, 4 speed manual gearbox, 4 wheel drum brakes, semi-elliptic leaf spring suspension, left-hand drive.
£19,000–20,000 *C*

This left-hand drive AJS chassis with original engine has been run since its total rebuild.

1920 Rochet-Schneider Truck, 4 cylinder, side valve, 3500cc engine, unrestored.
£4,800–5,200 *DB*

This vehicle was formerly a coal truck.

1921 Rover 8 Two Seater, engine dismantled, unearthed after 35 years storage.
£2,250–2,500 *DB*

1931 Star 18.50 Comet Coachbuilt Coupé,
engine requires attention, original and sound
condition, straightforward restoration.
Est. £800–1,200 *S*

1951 Singer Nine Roadster, 4 cylinder
engine with overhead chain driven camshaft,
needs total restoration.
Est. £800–1,000 *BKS*

TRACTORS

1954 David Brown 25D, fitted with hydraulic
lift, PTO pulley and full lighting set.
£850–875 *HSS*

1942 Case Model D, 4 cylinder, overhead
valve petrol/TVO engine, American Bosch
magneto and rear PTO.
£2,000–2,200 *HSS*

1946/47 Series 1 Mk 2 Field-Marshall, contractors
model, full lighting set, H. D. Marshall winch, high
top gear and differential lock.
£5,000–5,400 *HSS*

1964 McCormick International B614,
diesel fitted with hydraulics, PTO,
tipping pipe and full lighting set.
£1,200–1,300 *HSS*

**1946 McCormick International W9
Standard,** with pulley, rear PTO, and fitted
International magneto.
£3,800–4,200 *HSS*

ROAD ROLLERS

Marshall Sons & Co Ltd Diesel Roadroller,
Perkins P4 diesel and scarifier.
£3,200–3,600 *HSS*

RACING & RALLY CARS

Historic racing started in the mid-1960s. It grew from the desire of a few enthusiasts to race older cars in a somewhat more relaxed and less frenetic atmosphere than modern contemporary racing. It also helped that these older cars were cheaper to buy, since they were now uncompetitive in current events. Of course, once historic racing became established the prices of the cars escalated, but it was still possible to buy and race an historic car on a limited budget.

When the classic car boom of the late 1980s arrived, in came the entrepreneurs and investors, and the prices went through the roof. This had the effect of removing some of the cars from the race track and into hermetically sealed warehouses. A few people made a great deal of money, and some cars changed hands for four or five times their true worth. It couldn't last, and it didn't.

With the recession the market went into free-fall, but now prices seem to have stablised at around their mid-1980s level. There has also been a subtle change in the market. In the past the buyers came from three distinct groups; the investors, the collectors and the racers. Now the investors and collectors seem to have disappeared, leaving just the racers. However, the problem with the racers is that they only buy cars in the autumn and winter – they are racing in the summer and also they never have any money – they spent it all going racing. This has the effect of keeping prices both seasonal and reasonable. There is a great deal of fun to be had with an old racing car, get out there and enjoy.

Chris Alford

1937-39 Alta 1.4 Litre Supercharged I.S. Voiturette Racing Single Seater, 4 cylinders, 1500cc engine, 180bhp, all-independently suspended twin-tube chassis, Lancia-like system with coil springs on vertical pillars.
Est. £60,000–80,000 *BKS*

1961 Ausper Mk 3 Formula Junior, 1100cc Ford MAE engine, restored, very good condition.
£19,000–21,000 *Car*

1983 BMW 3.5 Litre 635 CSi Coupé Group A Competition Touring Car, nominally 330bhp version of the Munich 3.5 litre, 6 cylinder, twin overhead camshaft, fuel-injected power unit, engine rebuilt, bodywork very good, to original race specification.
Est. £12,000–14,000 *BKS*

1957 Cooper T43 Ex-Jack Brabham, 1.5 litre FPF engine No. 1001, chassis No. FII–3–57, restored in 1993 by Neil Twyman, FIA papers, 'as new' condition.
£54,000–57,000 *Car*

This car has been raced by Roy Salvadori, Sir Jack Brabham and Bruce McLaren.

1964 DRW Mark 5 Sports-Racing Spyder, 1 litre engine, widely used in recent seasons in Hill-Climb and Sprint Championships.
Est. £15,000–20,000 *BKS*

1974 Dastle Mk 16 Formula 4, 1600cc, Ford CVH engine, rebuilt from a pre-1974 Formula Ford to 750MC Formula Four specification.
£4,500–5,000 *Car*

1971 Elden Mk 8 Formula Ford Chassis No. 1, ex-works car driven by Tony Brise, 23 wins in 1971, restored by Elden, ready to race.
£15,000–18,000 *Car*

1961 Elfin Formula Junior, Ford Cosworth MAE 1100cc engine, front wheel drive, VW gearbox turned through 180°, 6 drum brakes, 4 on the front, restored by Rod Tolhurst to 'as new' condition.
£20,000–24,000 *Car*

1964 Ford Anglia 105E Rally and Saloon Racecar, 1496cc Asper Cortina engine bored to 1560cc and balanced, 135bhp, extensive race history.
Est. £6,500–7,500 *S*

1973 Dastle Mk 10 Formula 3, Lotus twin cam engine, restored by Geoff Rumble, ready to race.
£12,000–14,000 *Car*

1935 ERA R4A 2 Litre Single Seater Racing Voiturette, a well-known car with excellent provenance and in good overall condition.
Est. £240,000–260,000 *BKS*

1963 Ford Anglia Rally Car 1200cc, full rally specification, completed 2 Monte Carlo Retro events.
£5,500–6,000 *Car*

1970 Gropa GP6, 1800cc Cosworth FVC engine, Hewland FT 200 gearbox, restored by Malcolm Ricketts in 1989, excellent condition.
£37,000–40,000 *Car*

1974 GRD 74B Formula Atlantic,
Ford BDA engine, very good condition,
ready to race.
£19,000–22,000 *Car*

c1986 Jaguar Lynx D-Type Short Nose,
finished in British Racing green, with green
leather interior.
£45,000–55,000 *VIC*

r. **1969 Lenham P70 GT,** very good condition.
£33,000–35,000 *Car*
*This rare gullwing coupé racing car could be
converted into an excellent road car.*

1928–34 LA VSCC Special, 750cc supercharged
MG/Austin 7 engine, very good condition.
£25,000–30,000 *Car*
This car won the Spiro Trophy in 1994

**1955–56 Ex-Joaquin Palacios/Rodolfo Bay
3.8 Litre Jaguar D-Type Sports Racing
Two Seater.
Est. £500,000+** *BKS*

*This well prepared D-Type Jaguar has been rebuilt
specifically for Historic sports car racing by Le
Mans-winning specialist Paul Lanzante.*

1983–84 3 Litre Turbo-Charged Lancia-Ferrari LC2 Group C Corsa Competition Coupé, designed by Ing. GianPaolo Dallara, Abarth-built turbo-charged Ferrari 268C/308C V8 engine, carbon/Kevlar composite bodywork.
Est. £120,000–180,000 *BKS*

It is claimed the body weighs a mere 810kg.

1956 Lotus 11, 4 cylinder, 1098cc engine, in ready to race condition, full documentation including FIA papers.
£22,000–24,000 *COYS*

1958–59 3.8 Litre Lister-Jaguar Appendix J Sports-Racing Two Seater, rebuilt in the early 1990s by specialist John Pearson.
Est. £130,000–160,000 *BKS*

1960 Lotus 7 Series One, BMC engine, restored by Neil Twyman in 1993 and raced by him in HSCC events, 'as new' condition.
£14,000–16,000 *Car*

1960 Lotus Elite, 4 cylinder, 1216cc engine, Weber carburettors, external oil cooler, 4 speed close ratio ZF gearbox, lowered suspension, competition springs, fibreglass bucket seat, roll cage, lightweight fuel tank, Perspex side and rear screens, 13in (33cm) wheels, well presented car.
£19,000–20,000 *COYS*

l. **1960 Ex-Sir Gawaine Baillie/Michael Parkes Le Mans 1.3 Litre Lotus Elite 2 Door Competition Coupé,** restored, mechanical work carried out by Doug Lawson.
£30,000–35,000 *BKS*

1963 Lotus 23B, 4 cylinder, 1594cc engine, fully restored with documentary evidence, fine example. **£36,000–38,000** *COYS*

1965 Lotus Elan S2 GTS, twin cam 175bhp engine, very good condition, ready to race, prepared with the help of Tony Thompson. **£22,000–25,000** *Car*

1969 Lotus 61 Formula Ford, restored by Peter Van Vervalien, good condition. **£14,000–16,000** *Car*

This car was raced by Jackie Stewart and Jocken Rindt in 1969 and in 1994 by Peter Van Vervalien.

1955–61 Maserati Tipo V12 Engined 3 Litre 150S/63 Sports-Racing 2 Seater, excellent provenance, a classic 'barn find' for restoration. **Est. £92,000–98,000** *BKS*

c1971 McLaren-Chevrolet M18 5 Litre, Formula 5000 Single Seater, completely rebuilt and restored, new moulded glass fibre nose body section. **Est. £25,000–30,000** *BKS*

1969 Merlyn Mk 14 Formula Atlantic, Ford/Lotus twin cam engine, restored, ready to race. **£17,000–20,000** *Car*

1948 MG TC T-Type Racer, 1250cc full Brown & Gammonds race specification engine, restored to 'as new' condition. **£15,000–18,000** *Car*

r. 1971 Royale-Ford RPII Formula 3 Single Seater, 1.6 litre engine, completely restored. **Est. £8,000–10,000** *BKS*

1975 Royale RP 21, 1600cc Formula
Ford engine, good condition.
£4,000–6,000 *Car*

**c1929 'The Stinson Special' Single Seater
Sprint Car,** one of the few original American
sprint cars in the UK, discovered unrestored,
bodywork unpainted.
Est. £8,000–9,000 *BKS*

**1932 Vernon-Crossley 1100cc Sports
Racing Car,** rebuilt engine requires
running-in, rewired, bodywork and
transmission good, VSCC Blue Form.
Est. £11,000–11,500 *BKS*

1982 Van Dieman RF 82 Formula Ford,
original, useable condition.
£2,000–3,500 *Car*

1989 Westfield Lotus 7 Early Series,
Panasports fuel cell, excellent condition.
£9,000–10,500 *CFI*

**1959 Volpini Formula
Junior,** 1100cc Fiat engine,
very good condition.
£19,000–21,000 *Car*

l. **1988 Westfield 11
Lotus 11 Replica,**
very good example.
£6,500–7,000 *Car*

AUTOMOBILE ART

Donington, 1935, acrylic on board with framed edging, back-drop style, 48 x 96in (122 x 244cm).
£480–520 *BKS*

Steven Massey, The Rolls-Royce is Silent, pen and ink with watercolour, after a 1908 design by G. Studdy, with facsimile signature, 11 x 14in (28 x 36cm), mounted, framed and glazed.
£270–290 *S*

Roy Nockolds, Alpine Rally, 1952, hand-colourist's proof, 37 x 27in (94 x 69cm).
£740–780 *S*

Frederick Gordon Crosby, XI Grand Prix de l'ACF, Dieppe, 1908, signed, watercolour and charcoal heightened with white, 28 x 17½in (71 x 44cm), mounted, framed and glazed.
£24,000–26,000 *S*

Bob Murray, Sir Henry Birkin, watercolour study, 24in (61cm) square, mounted, framed and glazed.
£490–510 *BKS*

Don't Forget!
If in doubt please refer to the 'How to Use' section at the beginning of this book.

Frederick Gordon Crosby, Rallye des Alpes, signed, pencil and charcoal, highlighted with white, 24 x 30in (61 x 76cm), mounted, framed and glazed.
Est. £3,000–4,000 *BKS*

Phil May, British Empire Trophy Race, 1937, watercolour and charcoal highlighted with white, signed and captioned by the artist, mounted, framed and glazed, 15 x 19in (38 x 48.5cm).
£80–90 *BKS*

Phil May, Targa Florio, 1929, watercolour and gouache, signed, 9 x 12in (23 x 30.5cm).
Est. £150–200 *CSK*

l. Julian Webster, James Hunt – Marlboro McLaren, full-colour pastel drawing, signed, unframed, 15 x 22in (38 x 56cm).
£160–180 *BKS*

Roy Nockolds, Monte Carlo Rally 1955, hand-colourist's proof, (89 x 66cm), unframed.
£300–325 *S*

Nick Watts, Porsche 908, oil on canvas, mounted, framed and glazed, 20 x 29in (52 x 74cm).
£1,600–1,700 *BKS*

Dion Pears, Brabham Repco, oil on board, signed, mounted, framed and glazed, 28 x 38in (50 x 66cm).
Est. £520–620 *BKS*

Roy Nockolds, Winning Jaguar
XKC At Le Mans 1951, limited
edition No. 1/50, 19¾ x 29½in
(50 x 75cm), framed and
glazed, together with limited
edition certificate.
Est. £150–200 *S*

Michael Wright, Grand Prix de
l'ACF – 1906, Sziz's Renault,
pencil and watercolour, signed,
17 x 25in (43 x 61cm).
£720–740 *C*

Russell Brockbank, ERA,
monotone watercolour and gouache
highlighted with white, signed,
mounted, framed and glazed,
original artwork illustration
published in *Speed,* c1936.
£450–480 *BKS*

Delahaye 135, Le Mans setting,
original sketch, pencil and blue
crayon on drafting paper,
facsmile signature stamp,
mounted, framed and glazed,
14 x 20in (35.5 x 51cm).
£380–420 *BKS*

F. Munger, Sunbeam 1924,
depicting Campbell driving
car No. 12, original study,
watercolour, signed, mounted,
framed and glazed, 12 x 9in
(30.5 x 23cm).
Est. £350–400 *BKS*

Bob Murray, Airborne Salute,
Spitfire Mark Vb flying over
Aston Martin DB4 GT Zagato,
original watercolour and
gouache, mounted, framed and
glazed, 24 x 20in (61 x 51cm).
£850–875 *BKS*

Peugeot Grand Prix 1913, a
pencil and blue crayon sketch
on drafting paper, 14 x 20in
(35.5 x 51cm), mounted,
framed and glazed.
£570–650 *BKS*

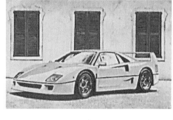

l. Ferrari F40, original acrylic on
board of the car against Italian
Villa setting, 47¼ x 76¾in
(120 x 195cm).
£280–300 *BKS*

Louis Berger, La Ballet Russe,
depicting arrival at the theatre,
original painting, watercolour
and Indian ink, signed, mounted,
framed and glazed, c1920,
23 x 18in (59 x 46cm).
Est. £2,500–2,800 *BKS*

Dion Pears, Alan Jones driving
Williams-Saudia in wet weather
conditions, signed, oil on canvas,
28 x 38in (71 x 96.5cm), framed.
Est. £600–750 *BKS*

Dion Pears, BRDC 500 mile
race, Brooklands 1929, depicting
No. 31, the 4½ litre Bentley of
Barclay & Clement and No. 32,
the supercharged 4½ litre
Bentley driven by Birkin,
watercolour, signed, 21 x 31in
(53 x 78cm) framed and glazed.
£340–360 *S*

Geo Ham, Berlinette Bleue,
signed, watercolour and gouache
highlighted with white,
12 x 15in (30.5 x 38cm),
mounted, framed and glazed.
£450–480 *BKS*

Jaguar D-Type, acrylic on board,
backdrop style painting, 47 x 77in
(120 x 195cm), with framed edging.
£650–675 *BKS*

AUTOMOBILIA

A Gladiator radiator, Type 3, No. 109, with filler cap and manufacturer's plaque, finished in black, 19½in (49.5cm) wide.
Est. £200–300 *C*

l. A Gabriel copper and brass exhaust whistle, with manufacturer's trade label 'Gabriel Horn MFG. Co Cleveland, patd. Oct. 24. 1905', 34in (86.5cm) long.
£180–200 *C*

A marble bust, entitled 'The Racing Driver', by Pineschi, base repaired, c1927, 12in (30.5cm) high, on a marble base.
£1,800–2,000 *S*

A Jaguar 2.4 litre 6 cylinder Motor Show display engine, sectioned and mounted on a stand together with standard gearbox in unit, non-overdrive with bell housing, cast 29 November, 1955.
£1,250–1,500 *BKS*

This is one of the very first 2.4 litre XK series saloon car engines.

An original steering wheel from Ayrton Senna's Marlboro McLaren Honda MP4/4, driven to victory in the San Marino Grand Prix, Imola, 1988, with full authentication certificate from McLaren International, with signatures including Ron Dennis, Gordon Murray and co-director, mounted on framed display board.
£9,250–9,500 *BKS*

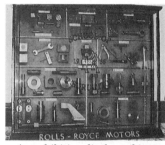

An exhibition display cabinet, inscribed 'Rolls-Royce School of Instruction 1935', containing engineering apprentice pieces from all stages of training.
£1,800–1,900 *BKS*

An Oldfield Dependence brass mirror, with adjustable brass swivel bracket, suitable for Rolls-Royce or similar, c1905.
£220–260 *BKS*

Badges

A BARC Brooklands member's badge, un-numbered, enamelled in colours.
£380–400 *C*

> **Miller's is a price GUIDE not a price LIST**

A Jaguar Drivers' Club chromed brass membership badge, in the form of a steering wheel with a lion's head boss and red enamelled legend to base riband, c1960.
£25–35 *CARS*

A British Monte Carlo Rally Drivers' Association chrome badge, manufacturer's stamp 'Spencer, London', 4in (10cm) high.
£150–160 *CSK*

l. A BARC Brooklands 120mph member's car badge, by Spencer of London, No. 888, awarded to A. W. von der Becke, dated 19.9.1936, filed to base mounting, inscribed to reverse, scratched and defaced.
£1,800–1,900 *BKS*

A British Racing Drivers' Club enamel badge, by Marples & Beasley, inscribed 'Silverstone Club', Birmingham, No. 856, 5½in (14cm) high.
£320–340 *S*

An early Rolls-Royce Enthusiasts' Club member's badge, by Darby's, Birmingham, cleaned and rechromed, 5in (12.5cm) high.
£160–180 *S*

An American Rolls-Royce Owners' Club member's enamel badge, slight chip to enamel, 3¾in (9.5cm) diam.
£160–180 *S*

An Automobile Club Ardennais bronze member's badge, c1918, 5¾in (14.5cm) high, on a turned wooden base.
£330–350 *S*

Brochures

An Automobile Club of Palestine chromium-plated badge, depicting a camel set within a steering wheel, 4¾in (12cm) high.
£550–575 *CSK*

A Motor Union member's brass badge, No. 205, with stepped flange mount stamped with maker's details, c1909, 7in (18cm) high.
£510–530 *S*

An Austin Healey 100S four page green sales brochure, c1950.
£100–150 *PMB*

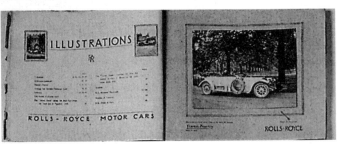

A Rolls-Royce 40/50 Silver Ghost sales catalogue, 1912–13, embossed card covers cord bound, with 6 colour and 10 sepia tipped-in plates, 88pp, with prices, 4to.
£600–625 *S*

l. A *Motor* magazine, early 1930s.
£8–10 *PMB*

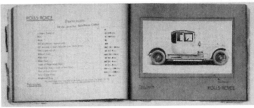

A Ford Galaxie multi-page sales catalogue, c1960.
£12–15 *PMB*

A Rolls-Royce 40/50 Silver Ghost sales catalogue, January 1914, embossed card covers cord bound, with 6 colour and 8 sepia tipped-in plates, 94pp, 4to, some wear and tears to covers.
£480–500 *S*

Bronzes

A bronze sculpture, by Frank Biele, depicting Lautenschlager's Mercedes which won the French Grand Prix in 1914, stamped and inscribed to base, mounted on green polished marble plinth, with Perspex glazed cover, 22in (56cm) wide.
£1,500–2,000 *BKS*

Clothing

A pair of Mirovich Lumina goggles, for cyclists and automobilists, excellent condition, boxed, with 2 spare lenses.
£270–290 *BKS*

r. An oakleaf leather motoring coat, double-breasted and blanket-lined, with detachable woollen lining, complete with zip-up map pocket and belt, c1915.
£250–275 *S*

Garage Equipment

An Alfred Diggle Reliance battery charging plant, 1920s.
£200–220 *BKS*

An Aeroshell double-sided sign, finished in red, yellow, blue and white, with decorative scrollwork mounting bracket, and a Shell Aviation Spirit lubricant can.
£640–660 *C*

Miller's is a price GUIDE not a price LIST

A collection of Morris, Ford and Wolseley oil cans, 1930s.
£65–£75 *GAZ*

An original Michelin tyre compressor, complete with M. Bibendum and gauge, 1920s.
£520–550 *HOLL*

A Wilmot-Breedon calorimeter, 1930s.
£20–30 *GAZ*

Horns

A coiled brass bulb horn, with flared trumpet, plaited wire hose and rubber bulb, 56in (142cm) long.
£290–310 *S*

A Heaths In-Lux-Way coiled bulb horn, nickel-plated with fly-mesh, mounting bracket and size 14 rubber bulb, 19¾in (50cm) long.
£310–330 *S*

A French Le Testophone 4 trumpet horn, in working order, with block mounting bracket, polished brass fitted to a hose with leather and brass bellows, by Guillaume, Paris.
£2,200–2,400 *S*

A boa constrictor snake's head horn, with original glass eyes, tongue and paint, with rubber bulb, mounted on a wooden display base, patented 1907, 78in (198cm) long.
£1,400–1,500 *S*

Instruments

Two dashboard instruments, a speedometer with milometer, with Rolls-Royce logo blacked out, and a rev counter, by A. T. Speedometer Co Ltd, West Kensington, W14, each with numerals on a black background, bevelled glass and brass case.
£1,400–1,500 *C*

A lever 17-jewelled motorist's pocket watch, by S Smith & Son, with white enamel dial, Roman numerals and blued steel hands, c1920, bezel 2⅜in (6cm) diam, with velvet lined dashboard mounting case.
£140–150 *S*

An 8-day car clock, by Jaeger for Delage, Swiss made, the nickel plated face with Roman numerals, blued steel hands, bezel 3¼in (8cm) diam, with mounting bracket.
£110–125 *S*

r. An SS speedometer, by S. Smith & Sons, silvered dial with 5–100mph scale, 1930s, bezel 4½in (11.5cm) diam.
£260–280 *S*

A silver keyless lever chronograph watch, by Stauffer Son & Co, Chaux de Fonds, the matt gilded movement with mechanism visible on the backplate, white enamel dial with Roman numerals, subsidiary dials for seconds and minutes, small red mark at 8 on minutes, plain case, the back engraved 'Automobile Club Gordon-Bennett Cup Race Ireland 1903', c1905.
£1,400–1,500 *S*

Lighting

A pair of Lucas QK596 (SS100) headlands, fully restored, c1938.
£2,000–2,500 *FFA*

A pair of Scintilla triple lens rear lamps, c1930.
£1,500–2,000
A pair of Scintilla double lens rear lamps.
£800–1,200 *FFA*

A pair of Lucas R100 electric headlamps, each chromed pillar mounted case with ribbed reflector, Rolls-Royce centre badge, clear glass lens 10⅞in (27.5cm) diam.
£850–880 *S*

A pair of Bleriot acetylene headlamps, each polished brass fork mounted case, marked and signed 'Bleriot', slight damage, 1904, bevelled lens 10in (25.5cm) diam.
£1,100–1,250 *S*

A pair of Bleriot copper and brass projectors, with bevelled glass lenses, rear mounting brackets, labelled 'patent 21572 1896 and patent 7L3 1900, L. Bleriot Brevette Déposé, France', c1905, 13in (33cm) high.
£1,100–1,200 *C*

Louis Bleriot manufactured oval style projectors until c1908, but reminded patrons of his pioneering design work by quoting earlier patent numbers.

A pair of Edwardian square-sided lamps, electrically illuminated, each brass body with flange mount, 2 square lenses with ruby door lenses, damaged, c1905.
Est. £300–400 *S*

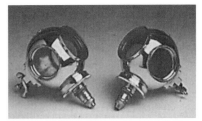

A pair of nickel 'diver's helmet' rear lamps, restored.
£330–350 *BKS*

A Scintilla triple rear lamp, type SPR1, the chromed case with 3 original lenses mounted on a Bakelite backplate, c1930.
£610–660 *S*

A pair of acetylene brass Lucas King of the Road headlamps, self-generating.
Est. £700–750 *BKS*

An acetylene motorcycle headlamp, generator, rubber hose and mount, by Powell and Hanmer.
£200–220 *BKS*

A pair of Meteor anti-dazzle driving lights, by James Neale & Sons, restored.
Est. £300–350 *BKS*

A J. & R. Oldfield Dependence brass rear lamp, with circular bevelled edge red lens, clear rectangular side markers, c1910.
£160–180 *BKS*

This style of lamp was not only manufactured in various series but was offered in either steel or brass construction. Good brass examples, therefore, command higher prices.

A pair of Marchal fluted bull's-eye headlamps, fully restored, c1930.
£1,500–2,000 *FFA*

A pair of brass acetylene headlamps, fully restored, c1909.
£2,500–3,500 *FFA*

Lighting

Early lighting was candle powered and rather ineffective. Although oil lamps were also used, Lucas developed the principle of adding water to calcium carbide, thus producing acetylene gas which, when lit, burns very brightly.
Lucas lamps are very collectable, as are P&H, (Powell & Hanmer). Lucas bought out P&H in 1929.
Other quality lamp manufacturers that today command high prices include Bleriot, Grebel, Zeiss and Marchal. By the outbreak of WWI electric lighting had been developed, and was becoming the favoured means of illumination.

A self-generating acetylene headlamp, by J. Rothschild & Fils, brass body with fork mounts, c1900, lens 8¾in (22cm) diam.
Est. £500–600 *S*

A pair of ornate self-generating acetylene lamps, each nickel plated brass case with three-tiered chimney, faceted 'port & starboard' side lenses, heavy mounting bracket, c1903, bevelled lens 3¾in (9.5cm) diam.
Est. £500–600 *S*

A pair of American Rushmore sidelamps, each drum-shaped brass body with side flange mount, mirrored reflector and simple flat chimney, one reflector missing, lenses replaced, one cracked, each strip lens 4in (10cm) diam.
Est. £280–340 *S*

A pair of Rotax sidelamps, No. 1176, converted to electricity, c1907.
Est. £350–420 *S*

A pair of Carl Zeiss chromium plated headlamps, with mounting bracket and screw, reeded lenses, slight damage, 12in (30.5cm) high.
£720–760 *C*

Luggage & Picnic Sets

A Coracle four-person picnic set, the black leather cloth covered case with brass handles, with accessories, c1920, 24¾in (63cm) wide.
Est. £2,900–3,400 *S*

A Coracle four-person running board type picnic set, the black leather cloth covered wooden case with brass handles, catches and lock, the lid fitted with rubber step board material with brass edging, wicker partitioned interior with accessories, c1908, 32¼in (82cm) wide.
Est. £3,500–4,200 *S*

Mascots

A blue leather vanity/overnight case, by Mappin & Webb, the vanity unit lined with silk, velvet-lined jewellery compartment and tin box, c1930, 12½in (32cm) wide, with foul weather cover.
Est. £1,000–1,500 *S*

A two-person wicker picnic basket, by Barrett & Sons, some fitments replaced, c1910, 15¼in (39cm) wide, with leather carrying harness.
Est. 1,200–1,400 *S*

A silver plated Alsation's head mascot, engraved 'Asprey, London', c1920, 4¾in (12cm) high, on a turned wooden base.
£200–250 *S*

A nickel plated brass Amilcar Pegasus mascot, stamped 'Darel', c1926, 6in (15cm) long, mounted on a radiator cap.
Est. £350–450 *S*

A Lalique 'Sanglier' mascot, fumée glass, etched on base damaged, 1930s, 3½in (9cm) long.
Est. £900–1,000 *S*

A bronze car mascot, depicting a figure with seven-league boots fitted with spurs, repaired, c1920, 6¼in (16cm) high, on a shaped marble base.
Est. £1,200–1,400 *S*

A chrome plated diving frog car mascot, by A Renevy, c1930, 6¾in (17cm) long, on a radiator cap.
£780–820 *S*

A gilt bronze car mascot, by Bione, depicting Pierrot sitting on the moon, c1910.
Est. £550–600 *BKS*

A French bronze Tête de Chien Policier mascot, by E. Bregeon, signed, c1925, 4¼in (11cm) high, mounted on a wooden base.
£230–280 *S*

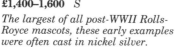

A Rolls-Royce Silver Ghost Spirit of Ecstasy solid-nickel mascot, signed, marked 'Rolls-Royce Ltd. Feb 6, 1911', 5½in (14cm), mounted on a radiator cap above a wooden base.
£1,400–1,600 *S*

The largest of all post-WWII Rolls-Royce mascots, these early examples were often cast in nickel silver.

A silvered-bronze Pegasus mascot, by Gaston Broquet, signed, No. 413, with 'Elie Victor Buchet' monogram to the front, c1920, 4½in (11.5cm) high, on a display base.
Est. £1,500–1,700 *S*

A French nickel-plated squirrel mascot, by Max le Verrier, c1920, 5in (12.5cm) high, mounted on a radiator cap.
Est. £360–420 *S*

A nickel-plated hornet mascot, stamped 'Asprey London', c1920, mounted on a radiator cap.
£540–580 *BKS*

A French nickel-plated bronze elephant in the egg mascot, early 1920s, 3¾in (9.5cm) high, mounted on a radiator cap.
Est. £1,200–1,400 *S*

A Rolls-Royce Spirit of Ecstasy kneeling mascot, 3⅓in (9cm) high.
£400–425 *S*

Earlier examples could be fitted to a Rolls-Royce 25/30 and Phantom III.

An Indian head mascot, with opaque composition face and chromed surround, stamped 'Blackstone MFG Co Inc Copyright 1950'.
£125–150 *BKS*

Designed for illumination and extremely rare.

A lilac tinted glass frog mascot, by René Lalique, on Brèves Galleries metal mounting surmounting an oak plinth, moulded mark 'Lalique'.
£2,000–3,000 *BKS*

A chrome-plated diving girl car mascot, 1920–38, 6¾in (17cm) high, mounted on a radiator cap.
£250–280 *BKS*

A frosted-glass mascot, by Red Ashay, depicting lovers embracing, nickel radiator mount, on a pre-WWII radiator cap, excellent condition and good patination.
£800–900 *BKS*

A brass monkey in a circle mascot, by M. Abit, stamped, c1920, 4¼in (11cm) high, on a wooden base.
£320–350 *S*

A French lilac tinted glass St Christophe mascot, by René Lalique, on a chrome-plated illuminating base, complete with electrical fittings, damaged, stamped 'Brèves Galleries Knightsbridge', mounted on a ceramic base, c1930.
£450–500 *BKS*

An Art Deco Lalique Archer intaglio mascot, some damage, 4¾in (12cm) high.
£500–540 *HAM*

A French satin glass Vitesse mascot, by René Lalique, embossed 'R. Lalique', c1925, 7¼in (18.5cm) high.
£6,000–6,500 *S*

Pedal Cars

A Morgan 4/4 pedal car, steel chassis and two-tone fibreglass body, folding windscreen, working lights and horn, c1993, 49in (124.5cm) long.
£700–800 *MM*

A Morgan 4/4 one third scale pedal car, with steel chassis and fibreglass body, opening bonnet, c1994, 49in (124.5cm) long.
£500–600 *MM*

A Maserati 250F child's electric car, aluminium bodywork on tubular steel frame, drum brakes, coil sprung front suspension, opening bonnet, wood-rim racing style wheel, forward and reverse gears, 66in (167.5cm) long.
£6,500–6,800 *BKS*

This scale replica was one of two believed to have been built for the Orsi family.

A Bugatti T52 child's electric car, cast-alloy spoked wheels, pneumatic tyres, polished front axle, fully detailed working brakes, opening louvred bonnet, outside handbrake and spare wheel, excellent unused condition, 66in (167.5cm) long.
£3,300–3,600 *BKS*

Photographs

A black and white photograph of Bluebird, signed 'Malcolm Campbell', 1935, 7½ x 9½in (19 x 24cm).
Est. £200–250 *CSK*

An autographed photograph of Jim Clark, in a Lotus at Silverstone, 14 x 19½in (35.5 x 49.5cm), mounted on board.
£700–750 *CSK*

An autographed black and white photograph of Jackie Stewart and Graham Hill, c1965, 6½ x 8½in (16.5 x 21.5cm).
£675–825 *CSK*

An autographed black and white photograph of Colin Chapman and Jim Clark within a victory wreath, 6½ x 8½in (16.5 x 21.5cm).
£725–775 *CSK*

Posters

A study of Jackie Stewart in the BRM at the German Grand Prix at Nürburgring, 1966, by Michael Cooper, signed to mount, framed and glazed, 16 x 20in (40.5 x 51cm).
£200–250 *BKS*

A view of the start at Le Mans from the pits balcony, on the stroke of 4pm, c1956, mounted, framed and glazed.
£80–120 *BKS*

An Englebert Ambassador advertising poster, depicting a V-12 9.4 litre Hispano-Suiza at a polo match, rubber stamped with '22 Mars 1935', 27½ x 19¾in (70 x 50cm), framed and glazed with Perspex.
£700–730 *S*

After Michael Turner, Sebring – April 1st, 1967, original poster for the event, full colour depicting racing scene, 20 x 24in (51 x 61cm).
£350–400 *BKS*

After Roy Nockolds, an original colour lithograph poster for the Brooklands 500 Mile Race 1935, 30 x 20in (76 x 51cm).
£420–460 *BKS*

r. Geo Ham, Grand Prix de Pau 1957, an original colour lithograph poster, 22 x 16in (56 x 40.5cm).
£220–260 *BKS*

After Geo Ham, Monaco Grand Prix 1933, a full colour lithograph poster depicting a Bugatti at the tunnel exit, 40 x 28in (101.5 x 71cm), framed and glazed.
Est. £3,000–3,500 *BKS*

An ADAC – Eifel – Rennen poster, 1956, by Van Husen, 33 x 23½in (84 x 60cm).
Est. £225–300 *S*

A Pneu Vélo Michelin colour lithograph poster, mounted on cloth, pre-1907, 10¼ x 15in (26 x 38cm).
£480–500 *BKS*

A Grand Prix de Nimes 1947, full-colour lithograph poster, mounted on display-board backing, some fading and wear, 40 x 30in (101.5 x 76cm).
£840–880 *BKS*

Prints

Whilst motor racing paintings command high prices at auction, prints can be obtained at a fraction of the price of an original artwork. Artists' proofs, limited editions and prints signed by the artist, the drivers featured, or other appropriate contemporary personalities, are highly prized and whilst not inexpensive are proving to be a good investment.

Monte Carlo Rally, original post-war print depicting Renault Gordini on the event, c1954, with 2 other prints.
£140–160 *BKS*

After Gamy, Renault 1911, a hand coloured lithograph depicting a rendezvous in the Bois de Boulogne, mounted.
Est. £350–380 *BKS*

After Walter Thor, Vive le Sport!, a full colour lithograph, c1906, 26 x 32in (66 x 81.5cm), mounted, framed and glazed.
£120–150 *BKS*

After Geo Ham, Rallye Monte Carlo 1932, an original full colour lithographed print depicting the winning Hotchkiss, with sketch illustrations to the border, 25 x 32in (63.5 x 81.5cm), mounted, framed and glazed.
£375–425 *BKS*
This was the year that Geo Ham was himself a competitor.

After Gamy, Grand Prix de l'Amerique Indianapolis 1913 – Goux le Gagnant sur Peugeot, a hand coloured lithograph, mounted, 19 x 38in (48.5 x 96.5cm).
Est. £600–650 *BKS*

Migalet, Two Thoroughbreds, signed and dated '86', limited edition print, 21 x 29in (55 x 75cm), framed and glazed.
Est. 150–200 *S*

Roy Nockolds, ERA R4D At Shelsley Walsh, 1947, limited edition, 20 x 29in (50 x 75cm), with limited edition certificate.
£150–200 *S*

After Albert Beerts, Les Desconfits, a print depicting a Renault style limousine passing a stranded horsedrawn carriage in a snow scene, mounted, c1912.
Est. £260–280 *BKS*

After Alan Stammers, J-M.
Fangio and Stirling Moss
Mercedes Benz 1955, a
limited edition monotone
print entitled 'The Train',
signed by both drivers.
Est. £800–900 *BKS*

After A Moynk, Proces-Verbal;
and Poursuite, printed by
Dietrich & Cie, Bruxelles,
a pair of lithographs in colours,
18½ x 36¼in (47 x 92cm).
Est. £450–650 *CSK*

After Baxon, Leon Thery's
Richard-Brassier, 1905 Coupe
Gordon Bennett, a monotone
lithograph, 20½ x 32½in
(52 x 82.5cm).
Est. £500–800 *CSK*

Petrol Pumps & Globes

r. A hand cranked Bowser
petrol pump, No. N35727,
finished in Shell livery
with a modern plain glass
globe, 16 gallon gauge,
replica price flag, hose
without nozzle, pump
80¾in (205cm) high.
Est. £500–600 *S*

l. A hand cranked petrol
pump, probably an Avery-
Hardol Model CH1, black
and yellow with polished
brass cylinder, with
National Benzole guarantee
replica flag, 82¾in (210cm)
high, with modern three-
sided National Benzole
glass globe.
Est. £400–500 *S*

A Super Premium glass petrol
pump globe, c1960, 14in
(35.5cm) high.
£240–260 *MSMP*

l. An Avery skeleton pump,
finished in Shell livery with
polished brass work, complete
with hose and nozzle.
Est. £350–420 *S*

> **Miller's is a price
> GUIDE not a price LIST**

Signs

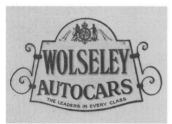

A Wolseley Autocars double-sided
sign, finished in white with green
text, 18 x 30in (45.5 x 76cm).
£490–510 *C*

An enamel advertising sign, for
Humber Motor Cycles, blue script
motif on white ground, chipped,
c1914, 20 x 40in (51 x 101.5cm).
£200–220 *BKS*

A Good Year double-sided
enamel sign, 1950s.
£50–60 *GAZ*

Trophies

r. A Victorian silver cup,
hallmarked 'London 1879',
reconstituted and represented
as the Assen Automuseum
Concours award trophy in
1984, on a turned wooden base,
14in (35.5cm) high.
Est. £600–800 *BKS*

l. A DAC trophy, the brass
globular bowl with a baluster
stem, foliate decorated base,
applied with enamel ADAC
badge and engraved, 1928,
10½in (26.5cm) high.
£220–250 *CSK*

A silver salver, with
piecrust rim and scrolled
feet, crest to centre,
inscribed with
signatures relating to
the motor industry and
'1896–1920', hallmarked
'Sheffield 1921', 14¼in
(36cm) diam.
£450–550 *BKS*

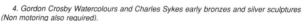

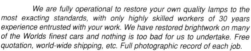

GLOSSARY

We have attempted to define some of the terms that you will come across in this book. If there are any terms or technicalities you would like explained or you feel should be included in future please let us know.

All-weather - A term used to describe a vehicle with a more sophisticated folding hood than the normal Cape hood fitted to a touring vehicle. The sides were fitted with metal frames and transparent material, in some cases glass.

Berline - See Sedanca de Ville.

Boost - The amount of pressure applied by a supercharger or turbocharger.

Brake Horsepower - Bhp - This is the horse power of the combustion engine measured at the engine flywheel (See Horsepower).

Brake - A term dating from the days of horse drawn vehicles. Originally the seating was fore and aft, with the passengers facing inwards.

Cabriolet - The term Cabriolet applies to a vehicle with a hood which can be closed, folded half way, or folded right back. The Cabriolet can be distinguished from the Landaulette as the front of the hood reaches the top of the windscreen whereas the Landaulette only covers the rear quarter of the car.

Chain drive - A transmission system in which the wheels are attached to a sprocket, driven by a chain from an engine powered sprocket usually on the output side of a gearbox.

Chassis - A framework to which the car body, engine, gearbox, and axles are attached.

Chummy - An open top 2 door body style usually with a single door, 2 seats in the front and one at the rear.

Cloverleaf - A 3 seater open body style usually with a single door, 2 seats in the front and one at the rear.

Concours - *Concours d'Elegance* is a competition to show cars in their perfect state. Concours has become a byword for a vehicle in excellent condition.

Cone Clutch - One in which both driving and driven faces form a cone.

Convertible - A general term (post-war) for any car with a soft top.

Continental - This is a car specifically designed for high speed touring, usually on the Continent. Rolls-Royce and Bentley almost exclusively used this term during the 1930s and post-WWII.

Coupé - In the early Vintage and Edwardian period, it was only applied to what is now termed a Half Limousine or Doctor's Coupé which was a 2 door, 2 seater. The term is now usually prefixed by Drophead or Fixed Head.

Cubic Capacity - The volume of an engine obtained by multiplying the bore and the stroke.

De Ville - Almost all early coachwork had an exposed area for the driver to be in direct control of his horses, and so the motor car chauffeur was believed to be able to control the vehicle more easily if he was open to the elements. As the term only refers to part of the style of the car, i.e. the front, it is invariably used in connection with the words Coupé and Sedanca.

Dickey Seat - A passenger seat, usually for 2 people contained in the boot of the car without a folding hood (the boot lid forms the backrest). Known in America as a rumble seat.

Doctor's Coupé - A fixed or folding head coupé without a dickey seat and the passenger seat slightly staggered back from the driver's to accommodate the famous black bag.

Dog Cart - A horsedrawn dog cart was originally used to transport beaters and their dogs to a shoot (the dogs were contained in louvred boxes under the seats, the louvres were kept for decoration long after the dogs had gone).

Dos-à-dos - Literally back-to-back, i.e. the passenger seating arrangement.

Drophead Coupé - Originally a 2 door 2 seater with a folding roof, see Roadster.

Dry Sump - A method of lubricating engines, usually with 2 oil pumps, one of which removes oil from the sump to a reservoir away from the engine block.

Engine - Engine sizes are given in cubic centimetres (cc) in Europe and cubic inches (cu in) in the USA. 1 cubic inch equals 16.38cc (1 litre = 61.02cu in).

Fixed Head Coupé - FHC, a coupé with a solid fixed roof.

Golfer's Coupé - Usually an open 2 seater with a square-doored locker behind the driver's seat to accommodate golf clubs.

Hansom - As with the famous horse drawn cab, an enclosed 2 seater with the driver out in the elements either behind or in front.

Horsepower - The unit of measurement of engine power. One horsepower represents the energy expended in raising 33,000lb by one foot in 60 seconds.

Landau - An open carriage with a folding hood at each end which would meet in the middle when erected.

Laudaulette - Also Landaulet, a horsedrawn Landaulette carried 2 people and was built much like a coupé. A Landau was a town carriage for 4 people. The full Landau was rarely built on a motor car chassis because the front folding hood took up so much room between the driver's seat and the rear compartment. The roof line of a Landaulette has always been angular, in contrast to the Cabriolet and the folding hood, and very often made of patent leather. A true Landaulette only opens over the rear compartment and not over the front seat at all.

Limousine - French in origin, always used to describe a closed car equipped with occasional seats and always having a division between the rear and driver's compartments. Suffixes and prefixes are often inappropriately used with the term Limousine and should be avoided.

Monobloc engine - An engine with all cylinders cast in a single block.

Monocoque - A type of construction of car bodies without a chassis as such, the strength being in the stressed panels. Most modern mass produced cars are built this way.

OHC - Overhead camshaft, either single (SOHC) or double (DOHC).

OHV - Overhead valve engine.

Phæton - A term dating back to the the days of horsedrawn vehicles for an open body, sometimes with a Dickey or Rumble Seat for the groom at the rear. It was an owner/driver carriage and designed to be pulled by 4 horses. A term often misused during the Veteran period but remains in common use, particularly in the United States.

Post Vintage Thoroughbred (PVT) - A British term drawn up by the Vintage Sports Car Club (VSCC) for selected models made in the vintage tradition between 1931 and 1942.

Roadster - An American term for a 2 seater sports car. The hood should be able to be removed totally rather than folded down as a drophead coupé.

Roi des Belges - A luxurious open touring car with elaborately contoured seat backs, named after King Leopold II of Belgium. The term is sometimes wrongly used for general touring cars.

Rotary engine - An engine in which the cylinder banks revolve around the crank, for example the Wankel engine with its rotating piston.

Rpm - Engine revolutions per minute.

Rumble Seat - A folding seat for 2 passengers, used to increase the carrying capacity of a standard 2 passenger car.

Runabout - A low powered light open 2 seater from the 1900s.

Saloon - A 2 or 4 door car with 4 or more seats and a fixed roof.

Sedan - See Saloon.

Sedanca de Ville - A limousine body with the driving compartment covered with a folding or sliding roof section, known in America as a Town Car.

Sociable - A cycle car term meaning that the passenger and driver sat side-by-side.

Spider/Spyder - An open 2-seater sports car, sometimes a 2+2 (2 small seats behind the 2 front seats).

Station Wagon - See Brake.

Supercharger - A device for forcing fuel/air into the cylinder for extra power.

Surrey - An early 20thC open 4 seater with a fringed canopy. A term from the days of horse drawn vehicles.

Stanhope - A term from the days of horsedrawn vehicles for a single seat 2 wheel carriage with a hood. Later, a 4 wheeled 2 seater, sometimes with an underfloor engine.

Stroke - The distance a piston moves up-and-down within the cylinder. This distance is always measured in millimetres.

Tandem - A cycle car term, the passengers sat in tandem, with the driver at the front or at the rear.

Targa - A coupé with a removable centre roof section.

Tonneau - A rear entrance tonneau is a 4 seater with access through a centrally placed door at the rear. A detachable tonneau meant that the rear seats could be removed to make a 2 seater. Tonneau nowadays usually means a waterproof cover over an open car used when the roof is detached.

Torpedo - An open tourer with an unbroken line from the bonnet to the rear of the body.

Tourer - An open 4 or 5 seater with 3 or 4 doors, folding hood, with or without sidescreens, generally replaced the term torpedo, with seats flush with the body sides. This body design began in about 1910, but by 1920 the word tourer was used instead - except in France, where 'torpédo' continued until the 1930s.

Veteran - All vehicles manufactured before 31st December 1918, only cars built before 31st March 1904 are eligible for the London to Brighton Commemorative Run.

Victoria - Generally an American term for a 2 or 4 seater with a very large folding hood. If a 4 seater, the hood would only cover the rear seats.

Vintage - Any vehicles manufactured between the end of the veteran period and 31st December 1930. See Post Vintage Thoroughbred.

Vis-à-Vis - Face-to-face, an open car where one or 2 passengers sit opposite each other.

Voiturette - A French term meaning a very light car, originally used by Léon Bollée.

Wagonette - A large car for 6 or more passengers, in which the rear seats faced each other. Entrance was at the rear, and the vehicles were usually open.

Weyman - A system of construction employing Rexine fabric panels over a Kapok filling to prevent noise and provide insulation.

Wheelbase - The distance between the centres of the front and rear wheels.

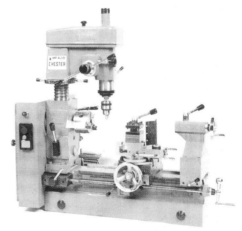

MOTOR BOOKS

Leading specialists in automotive books for enthusiasts throughout the world.
Many thousands of general, technical, tuning and rating books in our catalogue for £1.00

MOTOR BOOKS, 33 St Martin's Court, St Martin's Lane, London WC2N 4AL	Tel: 0171-836 5376/6728/3800	Fax: 0171-497 2539
MOTOR BOOKS, 8 The Roundway, Headington, Oxford OX3 8DH	Tel: (01865) 66215	Fax: (01865) 63555
MOTOR BOOKS, 241 Holdenhurst Road, Bournemouth BH8 8DA	Tel: (01202) 396469	Fax: (01202) 391572
MOTOR BOOKS, 10 Theatre Square, Swindon SN1 1QN	Tel: (01793) 523170	Fax: (01793) 432070

MAIL ORDER: *Inland:* add 10% of order value, minimum £1.50, maximum £3.00. Orders over £50.00 post free.

Overseas: add 15% of order value on orders up to £150.00, minimum £5.00. Add 10% of order value

on orders over £150.00. For large orders we prefer insured parcel post (usually by air) which we will quote for.

CREDIT CARDS: Visa, Access, Mastercard, Eurocard, Diners Club, TSB, AMEX Please quote full card number and expiry date.

Official technical books. These are all originals or unedited re-issues of official factory publications, including workshop manuals and parts catalogues. Far more detailed than the condensed literature widely available, they are essential possessions for owners and restorers and are highly recommended.

Audi Fox Official Service Manual: 1973–79. 562 pages, 1,020 illus/diagrams, 27 pages of electrical wiring diagrams. SB. (XO92) (ISBN 083760 0979) £24.95

Austin A40 Mks I & II Official Workshop Manual. Pub. 1968. Full procedures for all service and repair tasks. 280 pages, photos and drawings. HB. (AKD927H) (No ISBN) £19.95

Austin Healey 100/6 & 3000 Official Workshop Manual. Covers 100/6, 3000 Mks I & II. Plus Mk II and Mk III sports convertible (series BJ7 and BJ8). Detailed upkeep and repair, tools, general info. 400 pages, fully illustrated. SB. (AKD1179H) (ISBN 094820 7477) £21.95

Daimler 2.5 V-8 & 250 Saloon Official Service Manual. Detailed upkeep and repair, tools, general information. 548 pages, photos, drawings, SB. (E1002) (ISBN 185520 0082) £24.95

Daimler 2.5 V-8 & 250 Saloon Official Parts Catalogue. Fully illustrated and indexed guide to all parts. 328pp, drawings. SB. (D4) (ISBN 185520 0090) £24.95

Ford Capri Official Workshop Manual 1974 on. Covers: 1300cc, 1600cc, 2000cc, 2300cc, 3000cc. 600 pages. Well illus. SB. (ISBN 185520 2018) £29.95

Ford Capri 2.8 Injection Official Workshop Manual. Supplement to the above. 84 pages, illustrated. SB. (ISBN 185520 2026) £7.95

Jaguar XK120, XK140, XK150, XK150S & Mk VII, VIII & IX Official Service Manual. Massive publication compiled from 9 different previous official manuals. 784 pages, photos, drawings, wiring diagrams. SB. (ISBN 187064 2279) £46.95

Jaguar Mk 2 Official Service Manual. 4th edition covering all 2.4, 3.4, 3.8, 240 and 340 models. 545 pages, drawings. SB. (E121/7) (ISBN 187064 2953) £29.95

Jaguar E-Type V-12 Series 3 Official Service Manual. Well illustrated with drawings, charts and diagrams. Ringbinder (E165/3) (ISBN 185520 0015) £27.95

Jaguar S-Type Parts Catalogue. Covers 3.4 & 3.8 models. 248 pages, drawings, diagrams. SB. (J35) (ISBN 185520 1569) £24.95

Jaguar E-Type Series 1 4.2 litre Official Parts Catalogue. 308 pages, drawings, diagrams. SB. (J37) (ISBN 187064 2112) £35.95

Jaguar E-Type V-12 Series 3 Open 2 Seater Official Parts Catalogue. All parts illustrated and numbered. 240 pages, drawings. SB. (RTC9014) (ISBN 186982 6841). £15.95

Land Rover Series 1 Official Workshop Manual. Covers all petrol and diesel models up to 1958. 384 pages, drawings, charts. SB. (4291) (ISBN 090707 3980). £21.95

Land Rover Discovery Official Workshop Manual. A detailed guide to maintenance, etc. Covers petrol models V-8, 3.5 & 3.9 and diesel models Mpi and 200 Tdi. 844 pages. Over 1,000 illustrations. SB. (ISBN 185520 312X) £39.95

Land Rover Series 1 1948–53 Official Parts Catalogue. Section 1 – 1948–51 models, Section 2 – 1952–53 models, Section 3 – extra equipment. Covers home and export models: part numbers and illustrations. 446 pages (4051) SB. (ISBN 185520 1194). £19.95

Land Rover Series 1 1954–58 Official Parts Catalogue. 86, 88, 107 & 109 petrol and diesel models. Covers home and export. Contains part numbers and illustrations. 442 pages. (4107) SB. (ISBN 185520 1070). £19.95

High Performance Lotus Cortina Official Workshop Manual 1969. Information on all repair and adjustment procedures on the Mk 2. 316 pages, illustrated with photos and diagrams. SB. (ISBN 185520 1461). £27.95

MG Midget Series TD & TF Official Workshop Manual. Covers all components and tasks in great detail, for both minor and major repairs. 240 pages, photos, drawings, diagrams. SB. (AKD580A) (ISBN 185520 2115). . £17.95

MG Midget/Sprite 948cc, 1098cc, 1275cc Official Workshop Manual. Covers Sprite Mks II, III, IV; Midget Mks I, II, III up to and including car no. Gan 5-153920 (1974 models) 330 pages. Fully illustrated. SB. (AKD4021) (No ISBN) £18.95

MGB Official Workshop Manual. Maintenance, lubrication chart, general data, engine tuning, all components, service tools, plus emission control supplement. Pub. 76. 425 pages, diagrams. SB. (AKD3259) (ISBN 185520 1747). £21.95

MGC Workshop Manual. Covers the six-cylinder MGC 1967–69. Full maintenance, repair, troubleshooting, tune-up instructions. 336 pages, drawings. SB. (ISBN 185520 1852) £15.95

MGB Tourer, GT & V-8 Official Parts Catalogue, up to Sept 1976. All parts numbered, illustrated. 440 pages. SB. (AKM0039) (ISBN 094820 706X). . £21.95

Mini Official Workshop Manual (1959–76). 9th edition. The complete professional or amateur mechanic's guide to all repair and servicing procedures. Covers Saloon, Countryman, Traveller, Clubman, Estate, 1275GT, Van Pick-up, Moke, Cooper 'S'. 362 pages. SB. (AKD4935) (ISBN 185520 1488). £19.95

Morris Minor Series MM, Series II & 1000 Official Workshop Manual. Highly detailed maintenance and repair instructions for service supervisors, qualified & less experienced mechanics. Pub. 70. 440 pages, drawings. SB. (AKD530) (ISBN 185520 1577) . . . £16.95

Range Rover (Two Door) Official Repair Operation Manual. Covers years 1970–85. Detailed instructions for all components, also incorporating 5 speed and automatic gearbox supplement. 508 pages, drawings. SB. (AKM3630) (ISBN 185520 1224). £33.95

Triumph Dolomite Sprint Official Workshop Manual. Detailed repair, maintenance and servicing procedures for all components. 258 pages, drawings. SB. (AKM3629) Edn 2. (ISBN 185520 2824). £27.95

Triumph TR4 Official Workshop Manual (Incorporating supplement for TR4A). The complete professional or amateur mechanic's guide to all repair and servicing procedures. 360 pages, photos and drawings. SB. (510322) (ISBN 094820 7957). £23.95

Triumph Stag Official Repair Operation Manual. Complete guide to all components and their repair and upkeep. Pub. 1977. 640 pages, drawings. SB. (AKM3966) (ISBN 185520 0139). . £24.95

Triumph TR2 & TR3 Official Spare Parts Catalogue. All parts illustrated, identified and numbered. 4th edition. 369 pages, drawings. SB. (501653) (ISBN 090707 3999). £18.95

Volkswagen 1200 Official Workshop
Manual 1961–65. Covers types 11, 14 &
15 (Beetle, Beetle Convertible, Karmann
Ghia Coupé, Karmann Ghia Convertible).
1,364 pages, 2,622 illus/diagrams, 10
pages of electrical wiring diagrams. SB.
(V165) (ISBN 083760 3900) £64.95

Austin A40 Devon/Dorset WSM. . . . £17.95
Austin A40 Somerset WSM £24.95
Austin A55 MkII & A60/Oxford V & VI/
  Wolseley 15/60 & 16/60 WSM £32.95
AustinMorris & Vanden Plas etc.
  1100/1300 WSM £19.95
Austin Healey 100 BN1 & BN2 WSM . . . .
  . . . . £19.95
Austin Healey 100/4 Parts £28.95
Austin Healey 3000 MkII 61–67 Parts . . . .
  . . . . £28.95
Austin Healey 3000 MkII 62–68 Parts . . . .
  . . . . £33.95
Austin Healey 100/6 & 3000 WSM . £21.95
Austin Healey 100/6 Parts £28.95
Austin Healey Sprite MkI 'Frogeye' WSM .
  . . . . £17.95
Austin Healey Sprite I/II & Midget I
  Body Parts £15.95
Austin Healey Sprite I/II & Midget I
  Mechanical Parts £34.95
Austin Healey Sprite Mk 2, 3 & 4 &
  Midget WSM £18.95
Austin Healey Sprite Mk 3 & 4 Parts £18.95
Bentley Mk VI Parts £72.95
BMW 1502/2002 WSM £97.00
BMW 2500/3.3 Litre WSM £97.00
BMW 320/323i 6 cyl (2 vols) WSM . . £87.95
BMW 520 6 cylinder WSM £67.95
BMW 518-520 4 cylinder WSM £60.95
BMW 628/630/633Csi WSM £97.00
BMW 728/730/733i (2 vols) WSM . £109.95
Citroën 12 & 15 WSM £19.95
Citroën 2CV (2 vols) £49.90
Citroën 2CV Parts £31.00
Daimler 2.5L V8 & 250 Saloon WSM£29.95
Daimler 2.5L V8 & 250 Saloon Parts£24.95
Daimler Dart Parts £19.95
Datsun 280ZX (S130) £54.95
Fiat Uno All Models £68.95
Fiat X1/9 Technical Data WSM £26.95
Fiat 500 1957–72 WSM £31.95
Ford Anglia/Prefect/Popular 1939–59 £28.95
Ford Anglia 100E WSM £27.95
Ford Capri 1.3/1.6/2.0/2.3 & 3.0 from
  1974 WSM £29.95

Ford Capri 2.8i Supplement WSM . . £7.95
Jaguar 1.5, 2.5, 3.5 1946–48 WSM . £14.95
Jaguar Mk V Parts £33.00
Jaguar XK 120/140/150 & Mk 7/8/9 WSM .
  . . . . £46.95
Jaguar XK 120 Parts £38.95
Jaguar XK 140 Parts £36.95
Jaguar XK 150 Parts (2 vols) £73.95
Jaguar Mk 2/240/340 WSM £29.95
Jaguar Mk 2 3.4, 3.8, 340 Parts £33.95
Jaguar Mk 2 2.4 Parts £43.95
Jaguar Mk 10 & 420G WSM (HC) . . £31.95
Jaguar S-Type WSM £27.95
Jaguar E-Type 3.8/4.2 Ser. 1/2 WSM£35.95
Jaguar E-Type V12 Ser. 3 WSM . . . £25.95
Jaguar 420 WSM £27.95
Jaguar XJ6 Ser. 1 WSM £29.95
Jaguar XJ6 Ser. 2 WSM £29.95
Jaguar XJ12 Ser. 2 WSM £29.95
Jaguar XJ6 & XJ12 Ser. 3 WSM . . . £52.00
Jaguar XJS V12 (+HE Supp) WSM . £36.95
Jaguar Mk 2 3.4/3.8/340 Parts £33.95
Jaguar E-Type Ser. 1 Parts £19.95
Jaguar E-Type 4.2 Ser. 1 Parts £19.95
Jaguar E-Type Ser. 2 GT Parts £24.95
Jaguar XJ6 Ser. 1 Parts £16.95
Jaguar XJ6 Ser. 2 Parts £29.95
Jaguar XJ6 Ser. 3 Parts £29.95
Lamborghini Espada WSM £27.95
Lamborghini Diablo WSM £46.00
Lamborghini Countach 5000 WSM . £27.95
Lamborghini Countach 5000 Parts . £27.95
Lamborghini Countach 5000 4V Parts . . . .
  . . . . £27.95
Lamborghini Urraco 3 Litre WSM . . £27.95
Lamborghini Urraco P250 WSM . . . £29.95
Lamborghini Urraco P250 Parts . . . £27.95
Lancia Delta & HF WSM £49.00
Lancia Delta HF/Prisma/Integrale
  4WD WSM £91.95
Lancia Fulvia Ser. 1 WSM £52.80
Lancia Fulvia Ser. 2 Supplement WSM . . .
  . . . . £18.95
Lancia Beta WSM £33.00
Lancia Montecarlo WSM £35.95
Lancia Flaminia WSM £33.95
Lancia Flavia WSM £33.95
Lancia Stratos WSM £36.95
Lancia Stratos Parts £36.95
Lancia Thema WSM £64.95
Lancia Dedra WSM £69.00
Lancia Prisma WSM £64.95
Lotus Cortina Mk 2 WSM £27.95
Maserati Ghibli WSM £27.95

Maserati Bora WSM	£27.95
Maserati 3500GT WSM	£23.00
Maserati 3500GT Parts	£27.95
Maserati Biturbo WSM	£75.95
Mazda RX2 WSM	£22.95
Mazda RX3 WSM	£29.95
Mazda RX7 to 1985 WSM	£29.95
Mercedes Benz 170 (M136) 1950–53 WSM	£63.00
Mercedes Benz 190 1956–61 WSM	£42.00
Mercedes Benz 190SL Supplement WSM	£26.95
Mercedes Benz 180/220/220S Supplement to 190 WSM	£42.00
Mercedes Benz 300SL WSM	£63.00
Mercedes Benz 190C–300SEL from '59 WSM	£42.00
Mercedes Benz 108, 109, 111, 113 WSM	£42.00
MG Midget TD & TF WSM	£17.95
MG Midget Mk 1, 2 & 3 WSM	£17.95
MG Midget 1500 WSM	£17.95
MGA WSM	£18.95
MGA 1500 Parts	£18.95
MGA 1600 Parts	£20.95
MGB & GT to Sept '76 WSM	£21.95
MGB & GT 1978 on WSM	£16.95
MG Midget Mk 2 & 3 Parts	£17.95
MGB Tourer GT & V8 to Sept '76 Parts	£19.95
MGB Tourer & GT Sept '76 on Parts	£13.95
Mini 1959–76 WSM	£19.95
Morris Oxford Series 'MO' WSM	£24.95
Reliant Scimitar GTE SE5	£41.95
Reliant Scimitar GTE SE6	£41.95
Reliant SST & SS1 WSM	£33.95
Reliant SST & SS1 Parts	£29.00
Renault 8 WSM	£37.95
Renault Dauphine WSM	£35.00
Riley 1 1/2 – 2 1/2 WSM	£26.95
Riley 1 1/2 Parts	£32.95
Land Rover Series 1 WSM	£21.95
Land Rover Series 1 1948–53 Parts	£19.95
Land Rover Series 1 1954–58 Parts	£19.95
Land Rover Series 2 & 2A WSM	£46.90
Land Rover Series 3 WSM	£23.95
Land Rover Series 3 Parts	£12.95
Land Rover 90/110 Defender to 1993 WSM	£39.95
Range Rover 1970–85 WSM Parts	£24.95
Range Rover 1986–93 WSM	£49.95
Rover P4 WSM	£43.95
Rover 3 & 3.5L Saloon & Coupé WSM	£28.95

Rover 3 & 3.5L Saloon & Coupé Parts	£28.95
Rover 2000 & 2200 (P6) WSM	£25.95
Rover 2000 Series 2 Parts	£15.95
Rover 2200 Parts	£17.95
Rover 3500 & 3500S (P6) WSM	£26.95
Rover 3500 & 3500S (P6) Parts	£23.95
Standard Eight & Ten	£25.95
Sunbeam Alpine Series I to V WSM	£33.00
Sunbeam Alpine Series I to V Parts	£34.00
Triumph Dolomite Sprint WSM	£27.95
Triumph Dolomite Range from 1976 Parts	£29.95
Triumph TR2 & 3 WSM	£23.95
Triumph TR4 & TR4A WSM	£23.95
Triumph TR6 WSM	£24.95
Triumph Spitfire 1, 2, 3, Vitesse 6 & Herald WSM	£20.95
Triumph Spitfire Mks I & II Parts	£28.95
Triumph Spitfire 4 WSM	£17.95
Triumph Spitfire 1500 WSM	£17.95
Triumph Stag WSM	£24.95
Triumph TR2 & 3 Parts	£18.95
Triumph TR4 Parts	£18.95
Triumph TR6 Parts	£18.95
Triumph TR7 1975–78 Parts	£19.95
Triumph TR7 1979 on Parts	£19.95
Triumph Spitfire Mk 3 Parts	£15.95
Triumph Spitfire 1500 (75+) Parts	£15.95
Triumph Stag Parts	£22.95
Volvo P1800 WSM	£34.95
Volvo P1800ES WSM	£39.95
Volvo Amazon 120 WSM	£41.95
Volvo 121/122S WSM	£28.95
Volvo PV544 (P210) WSM	£40.95
Wolseley 1500 & Riley 1.5 WSM	£25.95

Postage on all manuals/parts inland . £5.00

We can also supply many handbook reprints for the above range of vehicles as well as the original factory manuals for many other vehicles old and new.

DIRECTORY OF CAR CLUBS

If you would like your Club to be included in next year's directory, or have a change of address or telephone number, please inform us by 30th June 1997. Entries will be repeated unless we are requested otherwise.

A C Owners Club, R A Morpeth, The Clovers, Mursley, Buckinghamshire MK17 0RT

A40 Farina Club, Membership Secretary, 2 Ivy Cottages, Fullers Vale, Headley Down, Bordon, Hampshire GU35 8NR

ABC Owners Club, D S Hales, The Hedgerows, Sutton St Nicholas, Hereford & Worcester HR1 3BU Tel: 01432 880726

Alexis Racing and Trials Car Register, Duncan Rabagliati, 4 Wool Road, Wimbledon, London SW20 0HW

Alfa Romeo 1900 Register, Peter Marshall, Mariners, Courtlands Avenue, Esher, Surrey KT10 9HZ

Alfa Romeo Owners Club, Michael Lindsay, 97 High Street, Linton, Cambridgeshire CB1 6JT

Alfa Romeo Section (VSCC Ltd), Allan & Angela Cherrett, Old Forge, Quarr, Nr Gillingham, Dorset SP8 5PA

Allard Owners Club, Miss P Hulse, 1 Dalmeny Avenue, Tufnell Park, London N7

Alvis Owners Club, 1 Forge Cottages, Bayham Road, Little Bayham, Lamberhurst, Kent TN3 8BB

Alvis Register, Mr J Willis, The Vinery Wanborough Manor, Nr Guildford, Surrey GU3 2JR Tel: 01483 810308

Amilcar Salmson Register, R A F King, Apple House, Wildmoor Lane, Sherfield on Lodden, Hampshire RG27 0HA

Armstrong Siddeley Owners Club Ltd, Peter Sheppard, 57 Berberry Close, Bourneville, Birmingham, West Midlands B30 1TB

Association of British Volkswagen Clubs, Dept PC, 66 Pinewood Green, Iver Heath, Buckinghamshire SL0 0QH

Association of Healey Owners, Don Griffiths, The White House, Hill Pound, Swanmore, Hampshire SO32 2PS Tel: 01489 895813

Association of Old Vehicle Clubs in Northern Ireland Ltd, Trevor Mitchell, Secretary, 38 Ballymaconnell Road, Bangor, Co Down, Northern Ireland BT20 5PS Tel: 01247 467886

Association of Singer Car Owners, Anne Page, 39 Oakfield, Rickmansworth, Hertfordshire WO3 2LR Tel: 01923 778575

Aston Martin Owners Club Ltd, Jim Whyman, AMOC Ltd, 1A High Street, Sutton, Nr Ely, Cambridgeshire CB6 2RB Tel: 01353 777353

Atlas Register, 38 Ridgeway, Southwell, Nottinghamshire NG25 0DJ

Austin A30-35 Owners Club, Andy Levis, 26 White Barn Lane, Dagenham, Essex RM10 9LH Tel: 0181 517 0198

Austin Atlantic Owners Club, 124 Holbrook Road, Stratford, London E15 3DZ Tel: 0181 534 2682 (home) 0171 833 7907 (work)

Austin Big 7 Register, R E Taylor, 101 Derby Road, Chellaston, Derbyshire DE73 1SB

1100 Club, Paul Vincent, 32 Medgbury Road, Swindon, Wiltshire SN1 2AS

Austin Cambridge/Westminster Car Club, Mr J Curtis, 4 Russell Close, East Budleigh, Budleigh Salterton, Devon EX9 7EH Tel: 01395 446210

Austin Eight Register, Ian Pinniger, 3 La Grange Martin, St Martin, Jersey, Channel Islands JE3 6JB

Austin Gipsy Register 1958–1968, Mike Gilbert, 24 Green Close, Rixon, Sturminster Newton, Dorset DT10 1BJ

Austin J40 Car Club, B G Swann, 19 Lavender Avenue, Coudon, Coventry CV6 1DA

Austin Maxi Club, Mrs C J Jackson, 27 Queen Street, Bardney, Lincolnshire LN3 5XF

Austin Seven Mulliner Register, Mike Tebbett, Little Wyche, Walwyn Road, Upper Colwall, Nr Malvern, Hereford & Worcester WR13 6PL

Austin Seven Owners Club (London), Mr and Mrs Simpkins, 5 Brook Cottages, Riding Lane, Hildenborough, Kent TN11 9QL

Austin Seven Sports Register, C J Taylor, 222 Prescot Road, Aughton, Ormskirk, Lancashire L39 5AQ

750 Motor Club Ltd, Courthouse, St Winifreds Road, Biggin Hill, Kent TN16 3H Tel: 01959 575812

Austin Seven Van Register 1923–29, N B Baldry, 32 Wentworth Crescent, Maidenhead, Berkshire SL6 4RW

Austin Sheerline & Princess Club, Ian Coombes, 44 Vermeer Crescent, Shoeburyness, Essex S53 9TJ

Austin Swallow Register, G L Walker, School House, Back Way, Great Haseley, Oxfordshire OX44 7JP

Austin Ten Drivers Club Ltd, Mrs Patricia East, Brambledene, 53 Oxted Green, Milford, Godalming, Surrey GU8 5DD

Austin Healey Club, Colleen Holmes, Dept CC, 4 Saxby Street, Leicester, Leicestershire LE2 0ND

Austin Healey Club, Mike Ward, Midland Centre, 9 Stag Walk, Sutton Coldfield, West Midlands B76 1JZ Tel: 0121 382 3223

Battery Vehicle Society, Keith Roberts, 29 Ambergate Drive, North Pentwyn, Cardiff, Wales CF2 7AX

Bean Car Club, G Harris, Villa Rosa, Templewood Lane, Farnham Common, Buckinghamshire SL2 3H

Bentley Drivers Club, 16 Chearsley Road, Long Crendon, Aylesbury, Buckinghamshire HP18 9AW

Berkeley Enthusiasts Club, Paul Fitness, 9 Hellards Road, Stevenage, Hertfordshire SG1 3PN Tel: 01438 724164

Biggin Hill Car Club, Peter Adams, Jasmine House, Jasmine Grove, Anerley, London SE20 Tel: 0181 778 3537

BMW Car Club, PO BOX 328, Andover, Hampshire SP10 1YN Tel & Fax: 01264 337883

BMW Drivers Club, Sue Hicks, Bavaria House, PO Box 8, Dereham, Norfolk NR19 1TF Tel: 01362 694459

Bond Owners Club, Stan Cornock, 42 Beaufort Avenue, Hodge Hill, Birmingham, West Midlands B34 6AE

Borgward Drivers Club, Ian Cave, Nateley House, Ridgway, Pyrford, Woking, Surrey GU22 8PW Tel: 01932 342341

Brabham Register, Ed Walker, The Old Bull, 5 Woodmancote, Dursley, Gloucestershire GL11 4AF Tel: 01453 543243

Bristol Austin Seven Club, 1 Silbury Hill Cottages, West Kennett, Marlborough, Wiltshire SN8 1QH

Bristol Microcar Club, 123 Queens Road, Bishopsworth, Bristol, Avon BS13 8QB. Tel: 0117 964 2901

Bristol Owners Club, John Emery, Uesutor, Marringdean Road, Billingshurst, Sussex RH14 9HD

British Ambulance Preservation Society, Roger Leonard, 21 Victoria Road, Horley, Surrey RH6 9BN

British Automobile Racing Club, Thruxton Circuit, Andover, Hampshire SP11 8PN Tel: 01264 772607 & 772696/7

British Racing and Sports Car Club, Brands Hatch, Fawkham, Dartford, Kent DA3 8NG

British Saab Enthusiasts, Mr M Hodges, 75 Upper Road, Poole, Dorset BH12 3EN

British Salmson Owners Club, John Maddison, 86 Broadway North, Walsall, West Midlands WS1 2QF Tel: 01922 29677

Brooklands Society Ltd, Reigate Lodge, Chartway, Reigate, Surrey RG2 0NZ

Brough Superior Club, P Staughton, Secretary, 4 Summerfields, Northampton, Northamptonshire NN4 9YN

BSA Front Wheel Drive Club, Godfrey Slatter (Membership Secretary), 14 Calstone, Calne, Wiltshire SN11 8PZ Tel: 01249 822322

Buckler Car Register, Stan Hibberd, 52 Greenacres, Woolton Hill, Newbury, Berkshire RG15 9TA Tel: 01635 254162

Bugatti Owners Club Ltd, Sue Ward, Prescott Hill, Gotherington, Cheltenham, Gloucestershire GL52 4RD

Bullnose Morris Club, Richard Harris, P O Box 383, Hove, Sussex BN3 4FX

C A Bedford Owners Club, G W Seller,
7 Grasmere Road, Benfleet, Essex SS7 3HF
Cambridge-Oxford Owners Club, COOC Membership,
6 Hurst Road, Slough, Berkshire SL1 6ND
Capri Club International, Field House, Ipsley Church
Lane, Redditch, Hereford & Worcester B98 0AJ
Tel: 01527 502066
Capri Drivers Association, Mrs Moira Farrelly,
Secretary, 9 Lyndhurst Road, Coulsdon,
Surrey CR5 3HT
Chiltern Vehicle Preservation Group,
Chiltern House, Aylesbury, Buckinghamshire HP17 8BY
Tel: 01296 651283
Citroen Car Club, P O Box 348, Bromley, Kent BR2 2QT
2 CVGB Deux Chevaux Club of GB, PO Box 602, Crick,
Northampton, Northamptonshire NN6 7UW
Citroen Traction Owners Club, Steve Reed,
1 Terwick Cottage, Rogate, Nr Petersfield,
Hampshire GU31 5EG
Clan Owners Club, Chris Clay, 48 Valley Road,
Littleover, Derbyshire DE23 6HS
Tel: 01332 767410
Classic and Historic Motor Club Ltd, Tricia Burridge,
The Smithy, High Street, Ston Easton, Bath, Avon BA3 4DE
Classic Corvette Club (UK), Ashley Pickering,
The Gables, Christchurch Road, Tring,
Hertfordshire HP23 4EF
Classic Crossbred Club, Alan Easto, 7 Wills Hill,
Stanford Le Hope, Essex SS17 7AY
Tel: 01375 679943
Classic Saloon Car Club, 7 Dunstable Road, Luton,
Bedfordshire LU1 1BB
Tel: 01582 31642
Classic Z Register, Lynne Godber, Thistledown,
Old Stockbridge Road, Kentsboro, Wallop, Stockbridge,
Hampshire SO20 8LB
Tel: 01264 781979
Club Alfa Romeo 2600/2000 International, Roger
Monk, Knighton, Church Close, West Runton, Cromer,
Norfolk NR27 9QY
Club Lotus, Lotus Lodge, P O Box 8, Dereham,
Norfolk NR19 1TF Tel: 01362 694459
Club Marcos International, Mrs I Chivers, Membership
Secretary, 8 Ludmead Road, Corsham,
Wiltshire SN13 9AS Tel: 01249 713769
Club Peugeot UK, Club Regs 504 Cab/Coupe,
Beacon View, Forester Road, Soberton Heath,
Southampton, Hampshire SO32 3QG Tel: 01329 833029
Club Peugeot UK (General Secretary),
2 Sunnyside, Priors Hill, Tinsbury, Bath, Avon, BA3 1HE
Club Triumph, Derek Pollock, 86 Waggon Road, Hadley
Wood, Hertfordshire EN14 0PP Tel: 0181 440 9000
Club Triumph Eastern, Mr D A Davies,
72 Springwater Road, Eastwood, Leigh-on-Sea,
Essex SS9 5BJ
Clyno Register, J J Salt, New Farm, Startley,
Chippenham, Wiltshire SN15 Tel: 01249 720271
Commercial Vehicle and Road Transport Club,
Steven Wimbush, 8 Tachbrook Road, Uxbridge,
Middlesex UB8 2QS
Connaught Register, Duncan Rabagliati,
4 Wool Road, Wimbledon, London SW20 0HW
Cortina Mk II Register, Mark Blows, 78 Church
Avenue, Broomfield, Chelmsford, Essex CM1 7HA
Cougar Club of America, Barrie S Dixon,
11 Dean Close, Partington, Greater Manchester M31 4BQ
Crayford Convertible Car Club, Rory Cronin,
68 Manor Road, Worthing, Sussex BN11 4SL
Tel: 01903 212828
Crossley Climax Register, Mr G Harvey,
7 Meadow Road, Basingstoke, Hampshire RG21 3LL
Crossley Register, Malcolm Jenner, Willow Cottage,
Lexham Road, Great Dunham, Kings Lynn,
Norfolk PE32 2LS
DAF Owners Club, S K Bidwell (Club Secretary),
56 Ridgedale Road, Bolsover, Chesterfield,
Derbyshire S44 6TX
Daimler and Lanchester Owners Club,
John Ridley, Trewyn Manor, Pandy, Abergavenny, Gwent,
Wales NP7 7PG Tel: 01873 890737
De Tomaso Drivers Club, Chris Statham, 2–4 Bank Road,
Bredbury, Stockport, Cheshire SK6 1DR
Tel: 0161 430 5052
Delage Section VSCC Ltd, Peter Jacobs, 17 The Scop,
Almondsbury, Bristol, Avon BS12 4DU
Delahaye Club GB, A F Harrison, 34 Marine Parade,
Hythe, Kent CT21 6AN Tel: 01303 261016
Dellow Register, Douglas Temple Design Group,
4 Roumelia Lane, Bournemouth, Dorset BH5 1EU
Tel: 01202 304641

Diva Register, Steve Pethybridge, 8 Wait End Road,
Waterlooville, Hampshire PO7 7DD Tel: 01705 251485
DKW Owners Club, C P Nixon, Rose Cottage, Rodford,
Westerleigh, Bristol, Avon BS17
Droop Snoot Group, 41 Horsham Avenue
Finchley, London N12 9BG Tel: 0181 368 1884
Dunsfold Land Rover Trust, Dunsfold, Surrey GU8 4NP
Tel: 01483 200058
Dutton Owners Club, Rob Powell, 20 Burford Road,
Baswich, Stafford, Staffordshire ST17 0BT
Tel: 01785 56835
Elva Owners Club, R A Dunbar, Maple Tree Lodge,
The Hawthorns, Smock Alley, West Alley,
West Chiltington, Sussex RH20 2QX
ERA Club, Guy Spollon, Arden Grange,
Tanworth-in-Arden, Warwickshire B94 5AE
F and F B Victor Owners Club, Wayne Parkhouse,
5 Farnell Road, Staines, Middlesex TW18 4HT
F-Victor Owners Club, Alan Victor Pope,
34 Hawkesbury Drive, Mill Lane, Calcot,
Reading, Berkshire RG3 5ZR
Tel: 01635 43532
Facel Vega Owners Club, Roy Scandrett,
Windrush, 16 Paddock Gardens, East Grinstead,
Sussex RH19 4AE
Fairthorpe Sports Car Club, Tony Hill,
9 Lynhurst Crescent, Uxbridge, Middlesex UB10 9EF
Ferrari Club of GB, Betty Mathias, 7 Swan Close,
Blake Down, Kidderminster, Hereford & Worcester DY10 3JT
Tel: 01562 700009
Fiat 130 Owners Club, Michael Reid, 28 Warwick
Mansions, Cromwell Crescent, London SW5 9QR
Tel: 0171 373 9740
Fiat Dino Register, Mr Morris, 59 Sandown Park,
Tunbridge Wells, Kent TN2 4RT
Fiat Motor Club (GB), H A Collyer, Barnside, Chilkwell
Street, Glastonbury, Somerset BA6 8D Tel: 01458 31443
Fiat Osca Register, Mr M Elliott, 36 Maypole Drive,
Chigwell, Essex IG7 6DE Tel: 0181 500 7127
Fiat Twin-Cam Register, 3 Anderson Place, Bagshot,
Surrey GU19 5LX
Fire Service Preservation Group, Andrew Scott,
50 Old Slade Lane, Iver, Buckinghamshire SL0 9DR
Five Hundred Owners Club Association,
David Docherty, 'Oakley', 68 Upton Park, Chester,
Cheshire CH2 1DQ Tel: 01244 382789
Ford 105E Owners Club, Sally Harris, 30 Gower Road,
Sedgley, Dudley, West Midlands DY3 3PN
Tel: 01902 671071
Ford Avo Owners Club, D. Hensley, 11 Sycamore Drive,
Patchway, Bristol, Avon BS12 5DH
Ford Capri Enthusiasts Register, Liz Barnes,
46 Manningtree Road, South Ruislip, Middlesex HA4 7LB
Tel: 0181 842 0102
Ford Classic and Capri Owners Club, Roy Lawrence,
15 Tom Davies House, Coronation Avenue, Braintree,
Essex CM7 1EP Tel: 01376 43934
Ford Corsair Owners Club, Mrs E Checkley,
7 Barnfield, New Malden, Surrey KT3 5RH
Ford Cortina 1600E Enthusiasts Club, D Wright,
32 St Leonards Avenue, Hove, Sussex BN3 4QL
Ford Cortina 1600E Owners Club, Dave Marston,
23 Cumberland Road, Bilston, West Midlands WV14 6LT
Tel: 01902 405055
Ford Escort 1300E Owners Club, Robert Watt,
65 Lindley Road, Walton on Thames, Surrey KT12 3EZ
Ford Executive Owners Register, Jenny Whitehouse,
3 Shanklin Road, Stonehouse, Coventry,
Warwickshire CV3 4EE
Ford Granada Mk 1 Owners Club, Paul Bussey,
Bay Tree House, 15 Thornbera Road, Bishops Stortford,
Hertfordshire CM23 3NJ
Ford GT Owners, c/o Riverside School, Ferry Road,
Hullbridge, Hockley, Essex SS5 6ND
Ford Mk II Independent O/C, 173 Sparrow Farm Drive,
Feltham, Middlesex TW14 0DG Tel: 0181 384 3559
Ford Mk III Zephyr and Zodiac Owners Club,
John Wilding, 10 Waltondale, Telford, Shropshire TF7 5NQ
Tel: 01952 580746
Ford Model 'T' Ford Register of GB, Mrs Julia Armer,
3 Strong Close, Keighley, Yorkshire BD21 4JT
Tel: 01535 607978
Ford RS Owners Club, PO Box 135, Newport, Gwent,
Wales NP6 2YU Tel: 01633 412626
Ford Sidevalve Owners Club, Membership Secretary,
30 Earls Close, Bishopstoke, Eastleigh,
Hampshire SO50 8HY
Ford Y&C Model Register, Bob Wilkinson, Castle Farm,
Main Street, Pollington, Goole, Humberside DN14 0DJ
Tel: 01405 860836

Frazer-Nash Section of the VSCC, Mrs J Blake, Daisy Head Farm, South Street, Caulcott, Bicester, Oxfordshire OX6 3NE

Friends of The British Commercial Vehicle, c/o BCVM, King Street, Leyland, Preston, Lancashire PR5 1LE

Gentry Register, Frank Tuck, 1 Kinross Avenue, South Ascot, Berkshire SL5 9EP Tel: 01990 24637

Gilbern Owners Club, P C Fawkes, 24 Mayfield, Buckden, Huntingdon, Cambridgeshire PE18 9SZ Tel: 01480 812066

Ginetta Owners Club, Dave Baker, 24 Wallace Mill Gardens, Mid Calder, Livingstone, West Lothian, Scotland EH53 0BD Tel: 01506 8883129

Gordon Keeble Owners Club, Ann Knott, Westminster Road, Helmdon, Brackley, Northamptonshire NN13 5QB Tel: 01280 702311

Granada Mk II and Mk III Enthusiasts' Club, 10 Alder Grove, Halesowen, West Midlands B62 9TL Tel: 0121 426 2346 (Mobile 0860 423126)

Grand Prix Contact Club, David Hayhoe, 26 Broom Road, Shirley, Croydon, Surrey CR0 8NE Tel: 0181 777 4835

Gwynne Register, H K Good, 9 Lancaster Avenue, Hadley Wood, Barnet, Hertfordshire EN4 0EP

Heinkel Trojan Owners and Enthusiasts Club, Y Luty, Carisbrooke, Wood End Lane, Fillongley, Coventry, Warwickshire CV7 8DF

Hillman Commer Karrier Club, A Freakes, Kingfisher Court, Bridge Road, East Molesey, Surrey KT8 9HL Tel: 0181 941 0604

Historic Commercial Vehicle Society HCVS, Iden Grange, Cranbrook Road, Staplehurst, Kent TN12 0ET

Historic Lotus Register, Mike Marsden, Orchard House, Wotton Road, Rangeworthy, Bristol, Avon BS17 5NA

Historic Rally Car Register RAC, Martin Jubb 38 Longfield Road, Bristol, Avon BS7 9AG

Historic Sports Car Club, Cold Harbour, Kington Langley, Wiltshire SN15 5LY

Historic Volkswagen Club, 11a Thornbury Lane, Church Hill, Redditch, Hereford & Worcester B98 7RP Tel: 01527 591883

Holden UK Register, GRC Hardy, Clun Felin, Woll's Castle, Haverfordwest, Pembrokeshire, Dyfed, Wales SA62 5LR

Honda S800 Sports Car Club, Chris Wallwork, 23a High Street, Steeton, Yorkshire BD20 6NT Tel: 01535 53845

Hotchkiss Association GB, Michael Edwards, Wootton Tops, Sandy Lane, Boars Hill, Oxford, Oxfordshire OX1 5HN Tel: 01865 735180

HRG Association, I J Dussek, Little Allens, Allens Lane, Plaxtol, Sevenoaks, Kent TN15 0QZ

Humber Register, R N Arman, Northbrook Cottage, 175 York Road, Broadstone, Dorset BH18 8ES

Imp Club, Jackie Clark, Cossington Field Farm, Bell Lane, Boxley, Kent ME14 3EG Tel: 01634 201807

Isetta Owners Club, Alan Tozer, The Spinney, Fairmile, Henley-on-Thames, Oxfordshire RG9 6AE

Jaguar Car Club, R Pugh, 19 Eldorado Crescent, Cheltenham, Gloucestershire GL50 2PY

Jaguar Drivers Club, JDC Jaguar House, Stuart Street, Luton, Bedfordshire LU1 2SL Tel: 01582 419332

Jaguar Enthusiasts Club, G G Searle, Sherborne, Mead Road, Stoke Gifford, Bristol, Avon BS12 6PS Tel: 0117 969 8186

Jaguar/Daimler Owners Club, 130/132 Bordesley Green, Birmingham, West Midlands B9 4SU

Jensen Owners Club, Caroline Clarke, 45 Station Road, Stoke Mandeville, Buckinghamshire HP22 5UE Tel: 01296 614072

Jensen Owners Club, Brian Morrey, Selwood, Howley, Nr Chard, Somerset Tel: 01460 64165

Jowett Car Club, Ian Priestly, Membership Secretary, 626 Huddersfield Road, Wyke, Bradford, Yorkshire BD12 8JR

Junior Zagato Register, Kenfield Hall, Petham, Nr Canterbury, Kent CT4 5RN Tel: 01227 700555

Jupiter Owners Auto Club, Steve Keil, 16 Empress Avenue, Woodford Green, Essex IG8 9EA Tel: 0181 505 2215

Karmann Ghia Owners Club GB, Eliza Conway, 269 Woodborough Road, Nottingham, Nottinghamshire NG3 4JT

Kieft Racing and Sports Car Club, Duncan Rabagliati, 4 Wool Road, Wimbledon, London SW20 0HW

Lagonda Club, Colin Bugler (Hon Secretary), Wintney House, London Road, Hartley Wintney, Hampshire RG27 8RN Tel & Fax: 01252 845451

Lancia Motor Club, Dave Baker, (Membership Secretary), Mount Pleasant, Penrhos, Brymbo, Wrexham, Clwyd, Wales LL11 5LY

Land Rover Register (1947–1951), Membership Secretary, High House, Ladbrooke, Leamington Spa, Warwickshire CV33 0BT

Land Rover Series One Club, David Bowyer, East Foldhay, Zeal Monachorum, Crediton, Devon

Land Rover Series Two Club, P O Box 1609, Yatton, Bristol, Avon

Landcrab Owners Club International, Bill Frazer, PO Box 218, Cardiff, Wales

Lea Francis Owners Club, R Sawers, French's, High Street, Long Wittenham, Abingdon, Oxfordshire OX14 4QQ

Les Amis de Panhard et Levassor GB, Denise Polley, 11 Arterial Avenue, Rainham, Essex RM13 9PD

Lincoln-Zephyr Owners Club, Colin Spong, 22 New North Road, Hainault, Ilford, Essex IG6 2XG

London Bus Preservation Trust, Cobham Bus Museum, Redhill Road, Cobham, Surrey KT11 1EF

London Vintage Taxi Association, Steve Dimmock, 51 Ferndale Crescent, Cowley, Uxbridge, Berkshire UB8 2AY

Lotus Cortina Register, 'Fernleigh', Hornash Lane, Shadoxhurst, Ashford, Kent TN26 1HX

Lotus Drivers Club, Lee Barton, 15 Pleasant Way, Leamington Spa, Warwickshire CV32 5XA Tel: 01926 313514

Lotus Seven Owners Club, David Miryless, 18 St James, Beaminster, Dorset DT8 3PW

Malaysia & Singapore Vintage Car Register, 2 Asimont Lane, Singapore 1130

Manta A Series Register, Mark Kinnon, 112 Northwood Avenue, Purley, Surrey CR8 2EQ

Marcos Owners Club, 62 Culverley Road, Catford, London SE6 2LA Tel: 0181 697 2988

Marendaz Special Car Register, John Shaw, 107 Old Bath Road, Cheltenham, Gloucestershire GL53 7DA Tel: 01242 526310

Marina/Ital Drivers Club, Mr J G Lawson, 12 Nithsdale Road, Liverpool, Merseyside L15 5AX

Marlin Owners Club, Mrs J Cordrey, 14 Farthings Went, Capel St Mary, Ipswich, Suffolk IP9 2UJ

Maserati Club, Michael Miles, The Paddock, Old Salisbury Road, Abbotts Ann, Andover, Hampshire SP11 7N Tel: 01264 710312

Masters Club, Barry Knight, 2 Ranmore Avenue, East Croydon, Surrey CR0 5QA

Matra Enthusiasts Club, MEC, 19 Abbotsbury, Orton Goldhay, Peterborough, Cambridgeshire PE2 5PS Tel: 01733 234555

Mercedes-Benz Club Ltd, P Bellamy, 75 Theydon Grove, Epping, Essex CM16 4PE Tel: 01992 573304

Messerschmitt Enthusiasts Club, Graham Taylor, 5 The Green, Highworth, Swindon, Wiltshire SN6 7DB Tel: 01793 764770

Messerschmitt Owners Club, Mrs Eileen Hallam, Birches, Ashmores Lane, Rusper, Sussex RH12 4PS Tel: 01293 871417

Metropolitan Owners' Club, Mr N Savage, South Cottage, School Lane, Washington, Pulborough, Sussex RH20 4AP Tel: 01903 893264

MG Car Club, PO Box 251, Abingdon, Oxon OX14 1FF Tel: 01235 555552

MG Owners Club, Octagon House, Swavesey, Cambridgeshire CB4 5QZ Tel: 01954 231125

MG 'Y' Type Register, Mr J G Lawson, 12 Nithsdale Road, Liverpool, Merseyside L15 5AX

Midget & Sprite Club, Nigel Williams, 15 Foxcote, Kingswood, Bristol, Avon BS15 2TX

Military Vehicle Trust, Nigel Godfrey, 8 Selbourne Close, Blackwater, Camberley, Surrey GU17 0HF

Mini Cooper Club, Joyce Holman, 1 Weavers Cottages, Church Hill, West Hoathly, Sussex RH19 4PW

Mini Cooper Register, Mr R Barfoot, 'Merlin', 28 London Road, Hitchin, Hertfordshire SG4 9EW Tel: 01462 453398

Mini Marcos Owners Club, Roger Garland, 28 Meadow Road, Worcester, Hereford & Worcester WR3 7PP Tel: 01905 58533

Mini Moke Club, Paul Beard, 13 Ashdene Close, Hartlebury, Hereford & Worcester DY11 7TN

Mini Owners Club, 15 Birchwood Road, Lichfield, Staffordshire WS14 9UN

MK I Consul, Zephyr and Zodiac Club, 180 Gypsy Road, Welling, Kent DA16 1JQ Tel: 0181 301 3709

Mk I Cortina Owners Club, R J Raisey,
51 Studley Rise, Trowbridge, Wiltshire BA14 0PD
Mk II Consul, Zephyr and Zodiac Club,
170 Conisborough Crescent, Catford, London SE6 2SH
Model A Ford Club of Great Britain,
Mr S J Shepherd, 32 Portland Street, Clifton, Bristol,
Avon BS8 4JB Tel: 0117 973 9355
Morgan Sports Car Club Ltd, Mrs Christine Healey
(Registrar), 41 Cordwell Close, Castle Donington, Derby,
Derbyshire DE74 2JL
Morgan Three-Wheeler Club Ltd, K Robinson,
Correction Farm, Middlewood Road, Poynton, Stockport,
Cheshire SK12 1TX
Morris 12 Club, D Hedge, Crossways, Potton Road,
Hilton, Huntingdon, Cambridgeshire PE18 9NG
Morris Cowley and Oxford Club, Derek Andrews,
202 Chantry Gardens, Southwick, Trowbridge,
Wiltshire BA14 9QX
Morris Marina Owners Club, Nigel Butler, Llys-Aled,
63 Junction Road, Stourbridge, West Midlands DY8 4YJ
Morris Minor Owners Club, Jane White,
127–129 Green Lane, Derby, Derbyshire DE1 1RZ
Morris Register, Arthur Peeling, 171 Levita House,
Chalton Street, London NW1 1HR
Moss Owners Club, David Pegler, Pinewood,
Weston Lane, Bath, Avon BA1 4AG Tel: 01225 331509
North East Club for Pre-War Austins,
Tom Gatenby, 9 Townsend Crescent, Morpeth,
Northumberland NE61 2XW
Nova Owners Club, Ray Nicholls, 19 Bute Avenue,
Hathershaw, Oldham, Lancashire OL8 2AQ
NSU Owners Club, Rosemarie Crowley,
58 Tadorne Road, Tadworth, Surrey KT20 5TF
Tel: 01737 812412
Octagon Car Club, 36 Queensville Avenue, Stafford,
Staffordshire ST17 4LS Tel: 01785 51014
Ogle Register, Chris Gow, 108 Potters Lane, Burgess
Hill, Sussex RH15 9JN Tel: 01444 248439
Old Bean Society, P P Cole, 165 Denbigh Drive,
Hately Heath, West Bromwich, West Midlands B71 2SP
Opel GT UK Owners Club, Martyn and Karen,
P O Box 171, Derby, Derbyshire
Opel Manta Owners Club, 14 Rockstowes Way, Bristol,
Avon BS10 6JE
Opel Vauxhall Drivers Club, The Old Mill, Dereham,
Norfolk NR20 5RT
Panther Car Club Ltd, 35 York Road, Farnborough,
Hampshire GU14 6NG Tel: 01252 540217
Pedal Car Collectors Club, c/o A P Gayler
4–4a Chapel Terrace Mews, Kemp Town, Brighton, Sussex
BN2 1HU Tel: 01273 601960
Piper (Sports and Racing Car) Club, Clive Davies,
Pipers Oak, Lopham Road, East Harling,
Norfolk NR16 2PE Tel: 01953 717813
Porsche Club Great Britain, Ayton House, West End,
Northleach, Gloucestershire GL54 3HG
Tel: 01451 60792
Post 45 Group, Mr R Cox, 6 Nile Street, Norwich,
Norfolk NR2 4JU
Post Office Vehicle Club, 7 Bignal Rand Close, Wells,
Somerset BA5 2EE
Post Vintage Humber Car Club, T Bayliss,
30 Norbury Road, Fallings Park, Wolverhampton,
West Midlands WV10 9RL
Post War Thoroughbred Car Club, 87 London Street,
Chertsey, Surrey KT16 8AN
Potteries Vintage and Classic Car Club,
B Theobald, 78 Reeves Avenue, Cross Heath, Newcastle,
Staffordshire ST5 9LA
Pre-1940 Triumph Owners Club, Jon Quiney,
2 Duncroft Close, Reigate, Surrey RH2 9DE
Pre-67 Ford Owners Club, Mrs A Miller, 100 Main
Street, Cairneyhill, Dunfermline, Scotland KY12 8QU
Pre-War Austin Seven Club Ltd, Mr J Tatum,
90 Dovedale Avenue, Long Eaton,
Nottingham NG10 3HU Tel: 0115 972 7626
Pre-50 American Auto Club, Alan Murphy,
41 Eastham Rake, Wirral, Merseyside L62 9AN
Tel: 0151 327 1392
Radford Register, Chris Gow, 108 Potters Lane,
Burgess Hill, Sussex RH15 9JN Tel: 01444 248439
Range Rover Register, Chris Tomley, Cwm/Cochen,
Bettws, Newtown, Powys, Wales SY16 3LQ
Rapier Register, D C H Williams, Smithy, Tregynon,
Newtown, Powys, Wales SY16 3EH Tel: 01686 87396
Rear Engine Renault Club, R Woodall,
346 Crewe Road, Cresty, Crewe, Cheshire CW2 5AD
Register of Unusual Micro-Cars, Jean Hammond,
School House Farm, Hawkenbury, Staplehurst,
Kent TN12 0EB

Reliant Owners Club, Graham Close, 19 Smithey Close,
High Green, Sheffield, Yorkshire S30 4FQ
Reliant Rebel Register, M Bentley, 70 Woodhall Lane,
Calverley, Pudsey, Yorkshire LS28 5NY
Tel: 01532 570512
Reliant Sabre and Scimitar Owners Club,
PO Box 67, Teddington, Middlesex TW11 8QR
Tel: 0181 977 6625
Renault Freres, J G Kemsley, Yew Tree House,
Jubliee Road, Chelsfield, Kent BR6 7QZ
Renault Owners Club, C Marsden, Chevin House, Main
Street, Burley-in-Wharfedale, Ilkley, Yorkshire LS29 7DT
Tel: 01943 862700
Riley Motor Club, J S Hall, Treelands, 127 Penn Road,
Wolverhampton, West Midlands WV3 0DU
Riley Register, J A Clarke, 56 Cheltenham Road,
Bishops Cleeve, Cheltenham, Gloucestershire GL52 4LY
Riley RM Club, Mrs Jacque Manders, Y Fachell, Ruthin
Road, Gwernymynydd, Mold, Clwyd, Wales CH7 5LQ
Ro80 Club GB, Simon Kremer, Mill Stone Cottage,
Woodside Road, Winkfield, Windsor, Berkshire SL4 2DP
Tel: 01344 890411
Rochdale Owners Club, Brian Tomlinson,
57 West Avenue, Birmingham, West Midlands B20 2LU
Rolls-Royce Enthusiasts' Club, Peter Baines, The Hunt
House, Paulerspury, Northamptonshire NN12 7NA
Rootes Easidrive Register, M Molley, 35 Glenesk Road,
London SE9 1AG
Rover P4 Drivers Guild, Colin Blowers (PC),
32 Arundel Road, Luton, Bedfordshire LU4 8DY
Rover P5 Owners Club, G Moorshead, 13 Glen Avenue,
Ashford, Middlesex TW15 2JE Tel: 01784 258166
Rover P6 Owners Club, PO Box 11, Heanor,
Derbyshire DE75 7YG
Rover Sports Register, Cliff Evans, 8 Hilary Close,
Great Boughton, Chester, Cheshire CH3 5QP
Saab Owners Club of GB Ltd, Mrs K E Piper,
16 Denewood Close, Watford, Hertfordshire WD1 3SZ
Tel: 01923 229945
Salmons Tickford Enthusiasts Club, Keith Griggs,
40 Duffins Orchard, Ottershaw, Surrey KT16 0LP
Savage Register, Trevor Smith, Hillcrest, Top Road,
Little Cawthorpe, Louth, Lincolnshire LN11 8NB
Scimitar Drivers Club, c/o Mick Frost, Pegasus,
Main Road, Woodham Ferrers, Essex CM3 8RN
Tel: 01245 320734
Scootacar Register, Stephen Boyd, Pamanste,
18 Holman Close, Aylsham, Norwich, Norfolk NR11 6DD
Tel: 01263 733861
Simca Owners Register, David Chapman,
18 Cavendish Gardens, Redhill, Surrey RH1 4AQ
Singer OC, Martyn Wray, 11 Ermine Rise,
Great Casterton, Stamford, Lincolnshire PE9 4AJ
Tel: 01780 62740
Skoda Owners Club of Great Britain, Ray White,
78 Montague Road, Leytonstone, London E11 3EN
Solent Austin Seven Club Ltd, F Claxton,
185 Warsash Road, Warsash, Hampshire SO31 9JE
South Devon Commercial Vehicle Club, Bob Gale,
Avonwick Station, Diptford, Totnes, Devon TQ9 7LU
Tel: 01364 73130
South Hants Model Auto Club, C Derbyshire,
21 Aintree Road, Calmore, Southampton,
Hampshire SO40 2TL
South Wales Austin Seven Club, Mr and Mrs J Neill,
302 Peniel Green Road, Peniel Green, Swansea,
Wales SA7 9BW
Spartan Owners Club, Steve Andrews,
28 Ashford Drive, Ravenhead, Nottinghamshire NG15 9DE
Tel: 01623 793742
Sporting Escort Owners Club, 26 Huntingdon
Crescent, Off Madresfield Drive, Halesowen,
West Midlands B63 3DJ
Stag Owners Club, Mr H Vesey, 53 Cyprus Road,
Faversham, Kent ME13 8HD Tel: 01795 534376
Standard Motor Club, Tony Pingriff, 57 Main Road,
Meriden, Coventry, Warwickshire CV7 7LP
Tel: 01675 22181
Star, Starling, Stuart and Briton Register,
D E A Evans, New Wood Lodge, 2A Hyperion Rd,
Stourton, Stourbridge, West Midlands DY7 6SB
Sunbeam Alpine Owners Club, Pauline Leese,
53 Wood Street, Mow Cop, Stoke-on-Trent,
Staffordshire ST7 3PF Tel: 01782 519865
Sunbeam Rapier Owners Club, Peter Meech,
12 Greenacres, Downton, Salisbury, Wiltshire SP5 3NG
Tel: 01725 21140
Sunbeam Talbot Alpine Register, Derek Cook,
Membership Secretary, 47 Crescent Wood Road,
Sydenham, London SE26 6SA

Sunbeam Talbot Darracq Register, R Lawson, West Emlett Cottage, Black Dog, Crediton, Devon EX17 4QB
Sunbeam Tiger Owners Club, Brian Postle, Beechwood, 8 Villa Real Estate, Consett, Co Durham DH8 6BJ Tel: 01207 508296
Swift Club and Swift Register, John Harrison, 70 Eastwick Drive, Bookham, Leatherhead, Surrey KT23 3NX Tel: 01372 52120
Tame Valley Vintage and Classic Car Club, Mrs S Ogden, 13 Valley New Road, Royton, Oldham, Lancashire OL2 6BP
Tornado Register, Dave Malins, 48 St Monica's Avenue, Luton, Bedfordshire LU3 1PN Tel: 01582 37641
Toyota Enthusiasts Club, c/o Secretary/Treasurer, Billy Wells, 28 Park Road, Feltham, Middlesex TW13 6PW Tel: 0181 898 0740
TR Drivers Club, Bryan Harber, 19 Irene Road, Orpington, Kent BR6 0HA Tel: 01689 73776
TR Register, 1B Hawksworth, Southmead Industrial Park, Didcot, Oxfordshire OX10 7HR Tel: 01235 818866
Traction Enthusiasts Club, Preston House Studio, Preston, Canterbury, Kent CT3 1HH
Traction Owners Club, Peter Riggs, 2 Appleby Gardens, Dunstable, Bedfordshire LU6 3DB
Trident Car Club, Ken Morgan, Rose Cottage, 45 Newtown Rd, Verwood, Dorset BH31 6EG Tel: 01202 822697
Triumph 2000/2500/2.5 Register, M Aldous, 42 Hall Orchards, Middleton, King's Lynn, Norfolk PE32 1RY Tel: 01553 841700
Triumph Dolomite Club, 39 Mill Lane, Upper Arncott, Bicester, Oxfordshire OX6 0PB Tel: 01869 242847
Triumph Mayflower Club, T Gordon, 12 Manor Close, Hoghton, Preston, Lancashire PR5 0EN
Triumph Razoredge Owners Club, Stewart Langton, 62 Seaward Avenue, Barton-on-Sea, Hampshire BH25 7HP Tel: 01425 618074
Triumph Roadster Club, Paul Hawkins, 186 Mawnay Road, Romford, Essex RM7 8BU Tel: 01708 760745
Triumph Spitfire Club, Mr Cor Gent, Anemoon 41, 7483 AC Haaksbergen, The Netherlands
Triumph Sporting Owners Club, G R King, 16 Windsor Road, Hazel Grove, Stockport, Cheshire SK7 4SW

Triumph Sports Six Club Ltd, 121B St Mary's Road, Market Harborough, Leicestershire LE16 7DT
Trojan Owners Club, D Graham, 10 St Johns, Redhill, Surrey RH1 6QF
Turner Register, Dave Scott, 21 Ellsworth Road, High Wycombe, Buckinghamshire HP11 2TU
TVR Car Club, c/o David Gerald, TVR Sports Cars, Hereford & Worcester Tel: 01386 793239
UK Buick Club, Alf Gascoine, 47 Higham Road, Woodford Green, Essex IG8 9JN Tel: 0181 505 7347
United States Army Vehicle Club, Dave Boocock, 31 Valley View Close, Bogthorn, Oakworth Rd, Keighley, Yorkshire BD22 7LZ
Vanden Plas Owners Club, Nigel Stephens, The Briars, Lawson Leas, Barrowby, Grantham, Lincolnshire NG32 1EH
Vanguard 1&2 Owners Club, R Jones, The Villa, The Down, Alviston, Avon BS12 2TQ Tel: 01454 419232
Vauxhall Cavalier Convertible Club, Ron Goddard, 47 Brooklands Close, Luton, Bedfordshire LU4 9EH
Vauxhall Owners Club, Brian J Mundell, 2 Flaxton Court, St Leonards Road, Ayr, Scotland KA7 2PP
Vauxhall PA/PB/PC/E Owners Club, G Lonsdale, 77 Pilling Lane, Preesall, Lancashire FY6 0HB Tel: 01253 810866
Vauxhall VX4/90 Drivers Club, c/o 43 Stroudwater Park, Weybridge, Surrey KT13 0DT
Vectis Historic Vehicle Club, 10 Paddock Drive, Bembridge, Isle of Wight PO35 5TL
Veteran Car Club Of Great Britain, Jessamine Court, High Street, Ashwell, Baldock, Hertfordshire SG7 5NL Tel: 01462 742818
Victor 101 FC (1964–1967), 12 Cliff Crescent, Ellerdine, Telford, Shropshire TF6 6QS
Vintage Austin Register, Frank Smith, The Briars, Four Lane Ends, Oakerthorpe, Alfreton, Derbyshire DE5 7LN Tel: 0773 831646
Vintage Sports Car Club Ltd, The Secretary, 121 Russell Road, Newbury, Berkshire RG14 5JX Tel: 01635 44411
Viva Owners Club, Adrian Miller, The Thatches, Snetterton North End, Snetterton, Norwich, Norfolk NR16 2LD
Volkswagen '50-67' Transporter Club, Peter Nicholson, 11 Lowton Road, Lytham St Annes, Lancashire FY8 3JD Tel: 01253 720023
Volkswagen Cabriolet Owners Club (GB), Emma Palfreyman, Secretary, Dishley Mill, Derby Road, Loughborough, Leicestershire LE11 0SF
Volkswagen Owners Caravan Club (GB), Mrs Shirley Oxley, 18 Willow Walk, Hockley, Essex SS5 5DQ
Volkswagen Owners Club (GB), PO Box 7, Burntwood, Walsall, West Midlands WS7 8SB
Volkswagen Split Screen Van Club, Brian Hobson, 12 Kirkfield Crescent, Thorner, Leeds, Yorkshire LS14 3EN
Volvo Enthusiasts Club, Kevin Price, 4 Goonbell, St Agnes, Cornwall TR5 0PH
Volvo Owners Club, Mrs Suzanne Groves, 90 Down Road, Merrow, Guildford, Surrey GU1 2PZ Tel: 01483 37624
Vulcan Register, D Hales, The Hedgerows, Sutton St Nicholas, Hereford & Worcester HR1 3BU Tel: 01432 880726
VW Type 3 and 4 Club, Jane Terry, Pear Tree Bungalow, Exted, Elham, Canterbury, Kent CT4 6YG
Wanderers (Pre-War Austin Sevens), D Tedham, Newhouse Farm, Baveney Wd, Cleobury, Mortimer, Kidderminster, Hereford & Worcester DY14 8JB
Wartburg Owners Club, Bernard Trevena, 55 Spiceall Estate, Compton, Guildford, Surrey GU3 1 Tel: 01483 810493
Wolseley 6/80 and Morris Oxford Club, John Billinger, 67 Fleetgate, Barton-on-Humber, Lincolnshire DN18 5QD Tel: 01652 635138
Wolseley Hornet Special Club, S Ellin, The Poppies, 9 Cole Mead, Bruton, Somerset BA10 0DL
Wolseley Register, M Stanley (Chairman), 1 Flashgate, Higher Ramsgreave Road, Ramsgreave, Nr Blackburn, Lancashire BB1 9DH
X/19 Owners Club, Sally Shearman, 86 Mill Lane, Dorridge, Solihull, West Midlands B93 8NU
XR Owners Club, Paul Townend, 50 Wood Street, Castleford, Yorkshire WF10 1LJ
XR Owners Club, 20a Swithland Lane, Rothley, Leicestershire LE7 7SE
Yorkshire Thoroughbred Car Club, Bob Whalley, 31 Greenside, Walton, Wakefield, Yorkshire WF2 6NN
Zephyr and Zodiac Mk IV Owners Club, Richard Cordle, 29 Ruskin Drive, Worcester Park, Surrey KT4 8LG Tel: 0181 330 2159

DIRECTORY OF AUCTIONEERS

United Kingdom

Academy Auctioneers & Valuers, Northcote
House, Northcote Avenue, Ealing, London W5 3UR
Tel: 0181 579 7466
ADT Auctions Ltd, Classic & Historic Automobile
Division, Blackbushe Airport, Blackwater,
Camberley, Surrey GU17 9LG
Tel: 01252 878555
Alcocks, Wyeval House, 42 Bridge Street,
Hereford, Hereford & Worcester HR4 9DG
Tel: 01432 344322
Robert Brooks (Auctioneers) Ltd, 81 Westside,
London SW4 9AY
Tel: 0171 228 8000
Central Motor Auctions Plc, Central House,
Pontefract Road, Rothwell, Leeds,
Yorkshire LS26 0JE
Tel: 01532 820707
Christie, Manson & Woods Ltd, 8 King Street,
St James's, London SW1Y 6QT
Tel: 0171 839 9060
Coys of Kensington, 2/4 Queens Gate Mews,
London SW7 5QJ
Tel: 0171 584 7444
Dickinson Davy and Markham, Wrawby Street,
Brigg, Humberside DN20 8JJ
Tel: 01652 653666
David Dockree, 224 Moss Lane, Bramhall,
Stockport, Cheshire SK7 1BD
Tel: 0161 485 1258
Dreweatt Neate Holloways, 49 Parsons Street,
Banbury, Oxon OX16 8PF
Tel: 01295 253197
Eccles Auctions, Unit 4, 25 Gwydir Street,
Cambridge CB1 2LG
Tel: 01223 561518
Evans & Partridge, Agriculture House,
High Street, Stockbridge, Hampshire SO20 6HF
Tel: 01264 810702
Greens (UK) Ltd, Hereford & Worcester WR14 2AY
Tel: 01684 575902
H & H Classic Auctions, 385 London Road,
Appleton, Nr Warrington, Cheshire WA4 5DN
Tel: 01925 860471
Kidson Trigg, Estate Office, Friars Farm,
Sevenhampton, Highworth, Swindon,
Wiltshire SN6 7PZ
Tel: 01793 861000
Lambert & Foster, 77 Commercial Road,
Paddock Wood, Kent TN12 6DR
Tel: 01892 832325
Lawrences Auctioneers, Norfolk House,
80 High Street, Bletchingley, Surrey RH1 4PA
Tel: 01883 743323
Locke & England, Black Horse Agencies,
18 Guy Street, Leamington Spa, Warwicks CV32 4RT
Tel: 01926 889100
Onslows, Metrostore, Townmead Road,
London SW6 2RZ
Tel: 0171 793 0240
Palmer Snell, 65 Cheap Street, Sherborne,
Dorset DT9 3BA
Tel: 01935 812218
J R Parkinson Son & Hamer Auctions,
The Auction Rooms, Rochdale Road (Kershaw Street),
Bury, Lancashire BL9 7HH
Tel: 0161 761 1612/761 7372
Phillips, Blenstock House, 101 New Bond Street,
London W1Y 0AS
Tel: 0171 629 6602
Rogers Jones & Co, The Saleroom, 33 Abergele
Road, Colwyn Bay, Clwyd, Wales LL29 7RU
Tel: 01492 532176

Martyn Rowe, The Truro Auction Centre,
Calenick Street, Truro, Cornwall TR1 2SG
Tel: 01892 260020
RTS Auctions Ltd, 35 Primula Drive, Eaton,
Norwich, Norfolk NR4 7LZ
Tel: 01603 505718
Sotheby's, 34-35 New Bond Street, London W1A 2AA
Tel: 0171 493 8080
Sotheby's Sussex, Summers Place,
Billingshurst, Sussex RH14 9AD
Tel: 01403 783933
G E Sworder & Sons, 14 Cambridge Road,
Stansted Mountfitchet, Essex CM24 8BZ
Tel: 01279 817778
Thimbleby & Shorland, 31 Great Knollys Street,
Reading, Berkshire RG1 7HU
Tel: 01734 508611
Walker, Barnett & Hill, 3/5 Waterloo Road
Salerooms, Clarence Street, Wolverhampton,
West Midlands WV1 4JE
Tel: 01902 773531
Welsh Bridge Salerooms, Welsh Bridge,
Shrewsbury, Shropshire SY3 8LH
Tel: 01743 231212

International

C Boisgirard, 2 Rue de Provence,
Paris, France 75009
Tel: 00 33 147708136
Carlisle Productions, The Flea Marketeers,
100 Bryn Mawr Road, Carlisle, USA, PA 17013-1588
Christie Manson & Woods International Inc,
502 Park Avenue, (including Christie's East),
New York, USA, NY 10022
Tel: 001 212 546 1000
Christie's (Monaco), SAM, Park Palace,
Monte Carlo 98000
Tel: 00 339 325 1933
Christie's Pty Ltd, 1 Darling Street, South Yarra,
Melbourne, Victoria, Australia 3141
Tel: 00 613 820 4311
Classic Automobile Auctions BV, Goethestrasse
10, 6000 Frankfurt 1, Germany
Tel: 00 49 69 28666/8
Kruse International, PO Box 190,
5400 County Road 11A, Auburn, Indiana, USA 46706
Tel: 001 219 925 5600
Paul McInnis Inc, Auction Gallery, Route 88,
356 Exeter Road, Hampton Falls,
New Hampshire USA 03844
Tel: 001 603 778 8989
Orion Auction House, Victoria Bdg
13 Bd. Princess Charlotte, Monte Carlo, Monaco
Tel: 00 3393 301669
Silver Collector Car Auctions, E204, Spokane,
Washington, USA 99207
Tel: 001 509 326 4485
Sotheby's, 1334 York Avenue, New York,
USA, NY 10021
Tel: 001 212 606 7000
Sotheby's, BP 45, Le Sporting d'Hiver,
Place du Casino, Monaco/Cedex MC 98001
Tel: 00 3393 30 88 80
Sotheby's Zurich, Bleicherweg 20, Zurich,
Switzerland CH-8022
Tel: 00 41 1 202 0011
'The Auction', 3535 Las Vegas Boulevard,
South Las Vegas, Nevada, USA 89101
Tel: 001 702 794 3174
World Classic Auction & Exposition Co,
3600 Blackhawk Plaza Circle, Danville,
California, USA 94506

DIRECTORY OF MUSEUMS

Avon
Bristol Industrial Museum, Princes Wharf,
City Docks, Bristol BS1 4RN Tel: 0117 925 1470

Bedfordshire
Shuttleworth Collection, Old Warden Aerodrome,
Nr Biggleswade SG18 9EP Tel: 01767 627288

Buckinghamshire
West Wycombe Motor Museum, Cockshoot Farm,
Chorley Road, High Wycombe,
West Wycombe HP14 3AR

Co Durham
North of England Open Air Museum, Beamish,
Stanley DH9 0RG

Cornwall
Automobilia Motor Museum, The Old Mill,
Terras Road, St Stephen, St Austell PL26 7RX

Cumbria
Cars of the Stars Motor Museum, Standish Street,
Keswick CA12 5LS Tel: 01768 73757

Lakeland Motor Museum, Holker Hall,
Cark-in-Cartmel, Nr Grange-over-Sands LA11 7SS
Tel: 01448 53314

Derbyshire
The Donnington Collection, Donnington Park,
Castle Donnington DE74 2RP Tel: 01332 810048

Devon
Totnes Motor Museum, Steamer Quay,
Totnes TT9 5AL
Tel: 01803 862777

Essex
Ford Historic Car Collection, Ford Motor Co,
Eagle Way, Brentwood CM13 3BW

Gloucestershire
The Bugatti Trust, Prescott Hill, Gotherington,
Cheltenham GL52 4RD
Tel: 01242 677201

Cotswold Motor Museum, Sherbourne Street,
Bourton-on-the-Water, Nr Cheltenham GL54 2BY
Tel: 01451 821255

Greater Manchester
Manchester Museum of Transport,
Boyle Street M8 8UW

Hampshire
Gangbridge Collection, Gangbridge House,
St Mary Bourne, Andover SP11 6EP

National Motor Museum, Brockenhurst,
Beaulieu SO42 7ZN
Tel: 01590 612123/612345

Humberside
Bradford Industrial Museum, Moorside Mills,
Moorside Road, Bradford BD2 3HP
Tel: 01274 631756

Hull Transport Museum, 36 High Street,
Hull HU1 1NQ

Museum of Army Transport, Flemingate,
Beverley HU17 0NG
Tel: 01482 860445

Peter Black Collection, Lawkholme Lane,
Keighley BD21 3BB

Sandtoft Transport Centre, Sandtoft,
Nr Doncaster DN8 5SX

Kent
Dover Transport Museum, Old Park, Whitfield,
Dover CT16 2HL

Historic Vehicles Collection of C M Booth,
Falstaff Antiques, 63-67 High Street,
Rolvenden TN17 4LP Tel: 01580 241234

The Motor Museum, Dargate,
Nr Faversham ME13 9EP

Ramsgate Motor Museum,
West Cliff Hall, Ramsgate CT11 9JX
Tel: 01843 581948

Lancashire
British Commercial Vehicles Museum,
King Street, Leyland, Preston PR5 1LE
Tel: 01772 451011

Bury Transport Museum, Castlecroft Road,
off Bolton Street, Bury

Tameside Transport Collection, Warlow Brook,
Friezland Lane, Greenfield, Oldham, OL3 7EU

London
British Motor Industry Heritage Trust,
Syon Park, Brentford

Science Museum, Exhibition Road,
South Kensington SW7 2DD
Tel: 0171 589 3456

Norfolk
Caister Castle Car Collection, Caister-on-Sea,
Nr Great Yarmouth

Nottinghamshire
Nottingham Industrial Museum,
Courtyard Buildings, Wallaton Park

Shropshire
Midland Motor Museum, Stanmore Hall,
Stourbridge Road,
Bridgnorth WV15 6DT
Tel: 01746 762992

Somerset
Haynes Sparkford Motor Museum, Sparkford,
Yeovil BA22 7LH
Tel: 01963 440804

Surrey
Brooklands Museum, The Clubhouse,
Brooklands Road,
Weybridge KT13 0QN
Tel: 01932 857381

Dunsfold Land Rover Museum,
Dunsfold GU8 4NP
Tel: 01483 200567

Sussex
Bentley Motor Museum, Bentley Wild Fowl Trust,
Harvey's Lane, Ringmer, Lewes BN8 5AF

Foulkes-Halbard of Filching, Filching Manor,
Filching, Wannock, Polegate BN26 5QA
Tel: 01323 487838

Tyne & Wear
Newburn Hall Motor Museum, 35 Townfield
Garden, Newburn NE15 8PY

Warwickshire
Heritage Motor Centre, Banbury Road,
Gaydon CV35 0YT
Tel: 01926 645040

Museum of British Road Transport,
St. Agnes Lane, Hales Street, Coventry CV1 1PN
Tel: 01203 832425

West Midlands
Birmingham Museum of Science & Industry,
136 Newhall Street, Birmingham B3 1RZ
Tel: 0121 235 1651

Black Country Museum, Tipton Road,
Dudley DY1 4SQ

Wiltshire
Science Museum, Red Barn Gate, Wroughton,
Nr Swindon SN4 9NS
Tel: 01793 814466

Yorkshire
Automobilia Transport Museum,
Huddersfield
Tel: 01484 559086

Isle of Man
Manx Motor Museum, Crosby
Tel: 01624 851236

Port Erin Motor Museum, High Street,
Port Erin
Tel: 01624 832964

Northern Ireland
Ulster Folk and Transport Museum,
Cultra Manor, Holywood, Co Down
Tel: 01232 428428

Scotland
Doune Motor Museum, Carse of Cambus, Doune,
Perthshire FK16 6HG

Grampian Transport Museum, Main Street, Alford,
Aberdeenshire AB33 8AD Tel: 019755 62292

Highland Motor Heritage, Bankford, Perthshire,

Melrose Motor Museum, Annay Road,
Melrose TD6 9LW Tel: 01896 822 2624

Moray Motor Museum, Bridge Street,
Elgin IV30 2DE Tel: 01343 544933

Museum of Transport, Kelvin Hall, 1 Bunhouse
Road, Glasgow G3 8DP Tel: 0141 357 3929

Myreton Motor Museum, Aberlady, Longniddry,
East Lothian EH32 0PZ Tel: 018757 288

Royal Museum of Scotland, Chambers Street,
Edinburgh EH1 1JF
Tel: 0131 225 7534

Wales
Conway Valley Railway Museum Ltd,
Ffordd Hen Eglwys, Betws-y-Coed,
Gwynedd LL24 0AL
Tel: 01690 710568

Jersey
Jersey Motor Museum, St Peter's Village

Eire
Kilgarven Motor Museum, Kilgarven, Co Kerry
Tel: 00 353 64 85346

National Museum of Irish Transport,
Scotts Garden, Killarney, Co Kerry

USA
Behring Automotive Museum, 3700 Blackhawk
Plaza Circle, Danville, California CA 94506
Tel: 510 736 2280

INDEX TO ADVERTISERS

BIBLIOGRAPHY

Baldwin, Nick; Georgano, G. N.; Sedgwick, Michael; and Laban, Brian; The World Guide to Automobiles, Guild Publishing, London, 1987

Collins, Paul, and Stratton, Michael; British Car Factories from 1896, Veloce Publishing PLC, 1993.

Colin Chapman Lotus Engineering, Osprey, 1993.

Georgano, G. N.; ed: Encyclopedia of Sports Cars, Bison Books, 1985.

Georgano, Nick; Military Vehicles of World War II, Osprey 1994.

Harvey, Chris; Austin Sevens, Haynes, 1988.

Hay, Michael; Bentley Factory Cars, Osprey, 1993.

Hough, Richard; A History of the World's Sports Cars, Allen & Unwin, 1961.

Isaac, Rowan; Morgan, Osprey, 1994.

McComb, F. Wilson; MG by McComb, Osprey, 1978.

Nye, Doug; Autocourse History of the Grand Prix Car 1966–1991, Hazleton Publishing, 1992.

Posthumus, Cyril, and Hodges, David; Classic Sportscars, Ivy Leaf, 1991.

Robson, Graham; Encyclopaedia of European Sports and GT Cars, Haynes, 1980.

Sieff, Theo; Mercedes Benz, Gallery Books, 1989.

Volkswagen Beetle Restoration, Osprey, 1994.

Wherret, Duncan, and Innes, Trevor; Tractor Heritage, Osprey, 1994.

Wood, Jonathan; Wheels of Misfortune, Gidgwick and Jackson, 1988

INDEX

Notes: **bold** page numbers refer to the information boxes; *italic* page numbers refer to the colour reviews.